The Rotterdam Rules and International Trade Law

This book offers an original academic study of the Rotterdam Rules. It analyses the salient articles that will have an impact on international sale contracts governed by English law, including the most popularly used international trade law instruments, terms and standard sale contracts. Looking beyond the legal relationship of carrier-shipper and carrier-receiver, this book examines the important articles of the Rotterdam Rules that affect the ability of the trading protagonists to perform their sale contract.

Dr Ioanna Magklasi is a Senior Lecturer in International Commercial and Maritime Law and the Director of the Centre for Maritime Law at London Metropolitan University. She holds a PhD in International Commercial Law, an LLM in Maritime Law from the University of Southampton, and an LLB from the National and Kapodistrian University of Athens. She is an Attorney-at-Law and a Member of the Athens Bar Association.

The Rotterdam Rules and International Trade Law

Dr Ioanna Magklasi

Routledge
Taylor & Francis Group
LONDON AND NEW YORK

First published 2018
by Routledge
2 Park Square, Milton Park, Abingdon, Oxon OX14 4RN

and by Routledge
52 Vanderbilt Avenue, New York, NY 10017, USA

First issued in paperback 2020

Routledge is an imprint of the Taylor & Francis Group, an informa business

British Library Cataloguing-in-Publication Data
A catalogue record for this book is available from the British Library

Library of Congress Cataloging-in-Publication Data
Names: Magklasi, Ioanna, author.
Title: The Rotterdam Rules and international trade law / Ioanna Magklasi.
Description: New York, NY : Routledge, 2018.
Identifiers: LCCN 2018014842 | ISBN 9781138070141 (hardback)
Subjects: LCSH: Rotterdam Rules (2008 December 11) |
Foreign trade regulation. | Export sales contracts.
Classification: LCC K1176 .M34 2018 | DDC 343.08/7–dc23
LC record available at https://lccn.loc.gov/2018014842

ISBN 13: 978-0-367-58729-1 (pbk)
ISBN 13: 978-1-138-07014-1 (hbk)

Typeset in Galliard
by Out of House Publishing

In memory of my grandmother, Yiannoula

Contents

Table of cases

(Ross) T Smyth & Co Ltd v. TD Bailey, Son & Co [1940] 3 All ER 60
AP Moller Maersk A/S v. Sonaec Villas Sen Sad Fadoul [2010] EWHC 355 Comm.
Aston Agro Industrial v. Star Grain Ltd (SDNY 2006) 06 CV 2805 (GBD) 2006 U.S.LEXIS 91636
Attorney-General of Botswana v. Aussies Diamond Products Pty Ltd [2010] WASC 141
Biddell Bros v. Clemens Horst (E) Co [1911] 1KB 934
Bourne v. Gatliffe (1841) 3 Man & G 643 and (1844) 7 Man & G 850
Bowes v. Shand (1877) 2 App Cas 455
British Shipowners' Co v. Grimond (1876) 3 Sess Cas 4th 968
Brown v. Byrne (1854) 2 E&B 703
Brown AR, McFarlane & Co v. C Shaw, Lovell & Sons (1921) 7 Ll LR 36
Brown Jenkinson v. Percy Dalton [1957] 2 QB 621
Buckman v. Levi (1813) 3 Camp 414
C-240/97 Spain v. European Commission [1999] ECR I-6571
C-277/05 Société Thermale d'Eugenie-les-Bains v. Ministere de l'Economie, des Finances et de l'Industrie [2007] ECR I-6415
C-441/07 European Commission v. Alrosa Co Ltd [2010] 5 CMLR 11
C-87/10 Electrosteel Europe SA v. Edil Centro SpA (Third Chamber) of 9 June 2011
Ceval Alimentos SA v. Agrimpex Trading Co Ltd (The Northern Progress) [1996] 2 Lloyd's Rep 319
Clemens Horst (E) Co v. Biddell Bros [1912] AC 18
Compagnie de Commerce et Commission, SARL v. Parkinson Stove Co [1953] 2 Lloyd's Rep 487
Comptoir d'Achat et de Vente du Boerenbond Belge S/A v. Luis de Ridder Limitada (The Julia) [1949] AC 293
Cowasjee v. Thomson (1845) 5 Moore PC 165
Do-Buy 925 Ltd v. National Westminster [2010] EWHC 2862
East West Corp v. DKBS 1912 [2002] 2 Lloyd's Rep 182
Edelstein v. Schuler & Co [1902] 2 KB 144

Emilien Marie, The, (1875) 44 LJ Adm 9, (1875) 32 LT 435
Encyclopaedia Britannica Inc v. Hong Kong Producer, 422 F2d 7, 11–12, 1969 AMC 1741 (2d Cir. 1969), cert. denied, 397 US 964 (1970)
Erg Petroli SpA v. Vitol SA (The "Ballenita" and "BP energy") [1992] 2 Lloyd's Rep 455
ERG Raffinerie Mediterranee v. Chevron USA Inc (The Luxmar) [2007] 1 CLC 807
Establishment For Agricultural Product Trading v. Wesermunde, 83 F.2d 1576, 1580, 1988 AMC 2328 (11th Cir. 1988)
Exxon Corp v. Central Gulf Lines Inc 500 US 603, 612, 111 s Ct 2071, 114 L Ed 2d 649 (1991)
Exxonmobil Sales and Supply Corp v. Texaco Ltd (The "Helene Knutsen") [2003] EWHC 1964 (Comm)
Fal Oil Co Ltd; Credit Agricole Indosuez (Suisse) SA v. Petronas Trading Corporation Sdn Bhd (The Devon) [2004] EWCA Civ 822
Finska Cellulosaforeningen (Finnish Cellulose Union) v. Westfield Paper Co Ltd (1940) 68 Ll Rep 75
Foster v. Driscoll [1929] 1 KB 470
Gatoil International Inc v. Tradax Petroleum Ltd (The Rio Sun) [1985] 1 Lloyd's Rep 350
General Trading Co and Van Stolck's Commissiehandel, Re (1911) 16 Com Cas 95
Glencore International AG v. MSC Mediterranean Shipping Co SA [2017] EWCA Civ 365; [2017] 2 Lloyd's Rep 186
Goodwin v. Robarts (1875) LR 10 Ex. 337
Gordon Russell (UK) v. Warwick [2006] EWCA Civ 1851
Grange v. Taylor (1904) 9 Com Cas 223
Grill v. General Iron Screw Collier Co, 1 CP 600 (1866), affirmed in 3 CP 476 (Exch. Ch. 1868)
Hansson v. Hamel & Horley Ltd [1922] 2 AC 36
Hines Exports Pty Ltd v. Mediterranean Shipping Co SA [2001] SASC 311
Holland Colombo Trading Society Ltd v. Segu Mohammed Khaja Alawadeen and Others [1954] 2 Lloyd's Rep 45
Homburg Houtimport BV v. Agrosin Private Ltd (The Starsin) [2003] UKHL 12, [2003] WLR 711
Hood v. Anchor Line (Henderson Bros) Ltd [1918] AC 837
Holt & Holt Ltd v. Union Castle Steamship Co Ltd [1901] SC 38
Interfoto Picture Library Ltd v. Stiletto Visual Programmes Ltd [1989] QB 433
J Spurling v. Bradshaw [1956] 1 WLR 461
Kum v. Wah Tat Bank Ltd [1971] 1 Lloyd's Rep 439
Kwei Tek Chao and Others v. British Traders and Shippers Ltd [1954] 2 QB 459
Leopold Walford (London) Ltd v. Les Affréteurs Réunis Société Anonyme [1918] 2 KB 498
Les Affréteurs Réunis Société Anonyme Appellants v. Leopold Walford (London) Ltd Respondents [1919] AC 801

Liverpool & GW Steam Co v. Phoenix Ins Co, 129 US 397, 437–463 (1889)
Manatee Touring Co v. Ocean Bulk Maritime SA [1999] 2 All ER (Comm) 306
Manbre Saccharine Co v. Corn Products Co [1919] 1 KB 198
Manchester, Sheffield and Lincolnshire Ry v. Brown (1883) 8 App. Cas. 703
McCutcheon v. David Macbrayne Ltd [1964] 1 WLR 125
McWilliam (JI) Co Inc v. Mediterranean Shipping Co (The Rafaela S) [2005] 2 AC 423
Merchants Re Walkers, Winser & Hamm and Shaw, Son & Co Re [1904] 2 KB 152
Mitsubishi Corporation v. Eastwind Transport Ltd and Others (The Irbenskiy Proliv) [2005] 1 Lloyd's Rep 383
Motis Exports Ltd v. Dampskibsselskabet AF 1912 A/S (No. 1) [2000] CLC 515
Naviera Mogor SA v. SOC Metallurgique de Normandie [1988] 1 Lloyd's Rep 414
Nippon Yusen Kaisha v. Ramjiban Serowgee [1938] AC 429
Noble Resources Ltd v. Cavalier Shipping Corporation (The Atlas) [1996] 1 Lloyd's Rep 642
Norfolk Southern Railway Co v. Kirby 543 US 14, 125 SCt 385, 160 L Ed 2d 283 (2004)
Northern Progress, The, Ceval Alimentos SA v. Agrimpex Trading Co Ltd [1996] CLC 1529
NV Arnold Otto Meyer v. Aune [1939] 3 All ER 168
One World (GB) Ltd v. Elite Mobile Ltd [2012] EWHC 3706
Owners of Cargo Lately Laden on Board the David Agmashenebeli v. Owners of the David Agmashenebeli, The David Agmashenebeli [2003] 1 CLC 714
Owners of Cargo Lately Laden on Board the Ship or Vessel "Starsin" and Others (Original Respondents and Cross-appellants) v. Owners and/or Demise Charterers of the Ship or Vessel "Starsin" (The Starsin) [2004] 1 AC 715
Pagnan SpA v. Feed Products Ltd [1987] 2 Lloyd's Rep 601
Pagnan v. Granaria BV [1986] 2 Lloyd's Rep 547
Palgrave, Brown & Son Ltd v. SS Turid (Owners) [1922] 1 AC 397
Parker v. South Eastern Railway Co (1877) 2 CPD 416
Petrocochino v. Bott (1874) LR 9 CP 355
Photo Production Ltd v. Securicor Transport Ltd [1980] AC 827
Plainmar Ltd v. Waters Trading Co Ltd (1945) 72 CLR 305
Port Sudan Cotton v. Govindswamy [1977] 1 Lloyd's Rep 166
Postlethwaite v. Freeland (1880) 5 App Cas 599
Printing & Numerical Registering Co v. Sampson (1875) LR 19 Eq 462
Procter & Gamble Philippine Manufacturing Corp v. Kurt A Becher GmH & Co KG [1988] 2 Lloyd's Rep 21
Profindo Pte Ltd v. Abani Trading Pte Ltd [2013] SGHC 10 (District Court Appeal No. 5 of 2012)
Pyrene Co Ltd v. Scindia Navigation Co Ltd [1954] 2 QB 402
Regazzoni v. KC Sethia (1944) Ltd [1958] AC 301

Resources Ltd v. Cavalier Shipping Corporation (The Atlas), [1996] 1 Lloyd's Rep 642
Richardson, Spence & Co v. Rowntree [1894] AC 217
Richco International Ltd v. Alfred C Toepfer International GmbH (The Bonde) [1991] 1 Lloyd's Rep 136
Ropner v. Stoate Hosegood & Co (1905) 10 Com Cas 73
Royal Exchange v. Dixon (1887) 12 App Cas 11
Salt v. Marquis of Northampton [1892] AC 1
Samsung Corp v. Devon Industries Sdn Bhd [1996] 1 SLR 469
Scottish and Newcastle International Ltd v. Othon Galanos Ltd [2006] EWCA Civ 1750
Shepherd Homes Ltd v. Encia Remediation Ltd [2007] EWHC 70 (TCC) [2007] Build. LR 135
Soproma SpA v. Marine and Animal By-Products Corp [1966] 1 Lloyd's Rep 367
Sucre Export SA v. Northern River Shipping Ltd (The Sormovskiy 3068) [1994] CLC 433
Sun Oil Co v. M/T Carlisle, 771 F. 2d 805, 809–810, 1986 AMC 305 (3d Cir. 1985)
Sze Hai Tong Bank Ltd v. Rambler Cycle Co Ltd [1959] AC 576
Thomas Young & Sons v. Hobson & Partners [1949] 65 TLR 365
The Asiatic Prince (1901) 108 Fed Rep 287
The Delaware, 161 US 459, 471–474 (1896)
The Emilien Marie (1875) 44 LJ Adm 9
The Heidberg [1994] 2 Lloyd's Rep 287
The Jaederen [1892] P 351
The Jordan II, [2004] UKHL 49
Thornton v. Shoelane Parking Ltd [1971] 2 QB163
Transfield Shipping Inc v. Mercator Shipping Inc (The Achilleas) [2008] UKHL 48
Trasimex Holdings SA v. Addax BV (The Red Sea) [1999] 1 Lloyd's Rep 29
Tregelles v. Sewell (1862) 7 H & N 574, 582, 1508 ER 600
Tsakiroglou & Co v. Noblee Thorl GmbH [1962] AC 93
TW Ranson Ltd v. Manufacture d'Engrais et de Produits Industriels Antwerp (1922)
Vimar Seguros y Reaseguros, SA v. M/V Sky Reefer (94–623), 515 US 528 (1995)
Wah Tat Bank Ltd and Overseas Chinese Banking Corp Ltd v. Chan Cheng Kum and Hua Siang Steamship Co (Singapore) Ltd (Third Parties) [1967] 2 Lloyd's Rep 437
Welex AG v. Rosa Maritime Ltd (The Epsilon Rosa) [2003] 2 Lloyd's Law Rep 509
Wimble, Sons, & Co Ltd v. Rosenberg & Sons [1913] 3 KB 743

Table of legislation, conventions, standard contracts and terms

Table of International Conventions, Model Laws and other Rules

International Convention for the Unification of Certain Rules of Law relating to Bills of Lading, 1924 (the "Hague Rules")
International Convention for the Unification of Certain Rules of Law relating to Bills of Lading, 1924 (Hague Rules), as amended by the Visby and SDR protocols 1968 and 1979 (the "Hague-Visby Rules")
United Nations Convention on the Carriage of Goods by Sea, 1978 (the "Hamburg Rules")
United Nations Convention on Contracts for the International Carriage of Goods Wholly or Partly by Sea (New York, 2008) (the "Rotterdam Rules")
United Nations Convention on Contracts for the International Sale of Goods (Vienna, 1980) (CISG)

UNCITRAL and international rules on electronic commerce/ bills of lading

CMI Rules for Electronic Bills of Lading 1990
UNCITRAL Model Law on Electronic Commerce with Guide to Enactment 1996
UNCITRAL Model Law on Electronic Transferable Records 2017 (MLETR)

National legislation

UK

Carriage of Goods by Sea Act 1992 (COGSA 1992)
Carriage of Goods by Sea Act 1971 (COGSA 1971)
Factors Act 1889
Sale of Goods Act 1979 (SOGA)

US

Harter Act 1893

Ocean Shipping Reform Act 1998 (OSRA)
Uniform Commercial Code (UCC)
US Shipping Act 1984

Australia/New Zealand

Australian Sea-Carriage of Goods Act 1904
Shipping and Seaman Amendment Act 1911

EU legislation

Council Directive 2010/45/EU of 13 July 2010 amending Directive 2006/112/EC

ICC Rules/standard contracts/rulebooks

ICC Rules

eUCP V1.1 Supplement to UCP 600
Incoterms® rules 2000
Incoterms® rules 2010
Uniform Customs and Practice for Documentary Credits, 2007 Revision, International Chamber of Commerce (ICC) Publication No. 600 Paris. 2007, ISBN: 978-9-28-421257-6.

Standard contracts

FOSFA 53
FOSFA 54
GAFTA 100
GENCOA 2004
INTERCOA 1980
P&O Nedlloyd Bill of Lading
SERVICECON
VOLCOA

General terms and conditions of trade organisations

Shell, General terms and conditions for sales and purchases of crude oil (1980)
Total, General terms and conditions for cfr/cif/delivered ex ship sales of crude oil (2007)

Rulebooks of electronic registry systems

Bolero Rulebook
essDOCS-Databridge™

Introduction

About the Rotterdam Rules

The UN Convention on Contracts for the International Carriage of Goods Wholly or Partly by Sea, 2008,[1] widely known as the Rotterdam Rules (RR), has been open for signature since September 2009 in Rotterdam.[2]

The RR were promulgated[3] to achieve uniformity and modernisation in international maritime trade.[4] On the one hand, uniformity was intended, as there

1 The draft version of the RR was approved in July 2008 at the 41st session of the United Nations Commission on International Trade Law (UNCITRAL). The RR were adopted by the United Nations General Assembly on 11 December 2008 (63rd Session of the United Nations General Assembly) and were opened for signature on 23 September 2009 in Rotterdam. The text of the RR has been corrected for errors in Articles 1(6)(a) and 19(1)(b) of the authentic text, effective 25 January 2013. So far, Spain, Togo, Congo and Cameroon are the only countries that have ratified the RR. For information on the text, preparatory works and status of the RR see www.uncitral.org/uncitral/uncitral_texts/transport_goods/2008rotterdam_rules.html.

2 The RR were named after Rotterdam, as they opened for signature here on 23 September 2009. See Jason Chuah, *Law of International Trade: Cross-border Commercial Transactions* (5th edn, Sweet & Maxwell 2013), paras 8–103. For an approval of the title of the Convention based on the importance of the port see Nick Gaskell, 'Book Review, Sturley M, Fujita, van der Ziel, The Rotterdam Rules, The UN Convention on Contracts for the International Carriage of Goods Wholly or Partly by sea' (2013) 27 *A&NZ Mar LJ* 42.

3 For a critical assessment of intentions and results respectively brought about before and after the adoption of the RR, see Douglas G Schmitt, 'Will Rotterdam succeed? Testing the waters at CMI Buenos Aires' at www.ahbl.ca/wp-content/uploads/2012/05/Will_Rotterdam_Succeed-Testing_the_Waters_at_CMI_Buenos_Aires-Douglas_Schmitt-May2011.pdf. See also Alcántara, Hunt, Johansson, Oland, Psyden, Ramberg, Schmitt, Tetley, Vidal, '*Particular concerns with regard to the Rotterdam Rules*' at www.comitemaritime.org/Uploads/Rotterdam%20Rules/Particular%20concerns%20-%20Rotterdam%20Rules.pdf, which embarks on a critical appraisal of controversial aspects of the RR.

4 As the RR govern the carriage of goods wholly or partly by sea, one understands that they govern not only maritime but also multimodal carriage. This is why the RR are often called a "maritime plus" or "wet multimodal" convention. See preamble to the RR at www.uncitral.org/pdf/english/texts/transport/rotterdam_rules/09-85608_Ebook.pdf. For the objectives behind drafting the RR, see Francesco Berlingieri, 'Revisiting the Rotterdam Rules' [2010] *LMCLQ* 583; Gertjan van der Ziel, 'Delivery of the goods, rights of the controlling party and transfer of rights' (2008) 14 *JIML* 597, pp. 598–599.

are currently three major international maritime conventions in force, namely the Hague Rules,[5] the Hague-Visby Rules (HVR)[6] and the Hamburg Rules[7]. On the other hand, modernisation was essential so that the RR could be in line with the new situation emerging out of the containerisation[8] of goods, the increasing use of multimodal carriage and the surge of e-commerce.[9] Laudably, not only do the RR aim to strike a fairer balance[10] between the competing interests of carriers and cargo owners, but they also aspire to better allocate the risks[11] between the foregoing protagonists.

This book for the first time delineates the potential impact of the RR on international trade law, and more concretely on its international sale contract law component. This is because although hard to conceive and identify, when thinking purely in carriage of goods legal terms, we do not fully perceive the wider international trade law sphere in its entirety. This not only exists but also depends to a great extent on the legal requirements for the carriage of these goods. The RR

5 International Convention for the Unification of Certain Rules of Law relating to Bills of Lading, 1924 (the Hague Rules).

6 International Convention for the Unification of Certain Rules of Law relating to Bills of Lading, 1924 (Hague Rules), as amended by the Visby and SDR protocols 1968 and 1979 (the Hague-Visby Rules).

7 United Nations Convention on the Carriage of Goods by Sea, 1978 (the Hamburg Rules).

8 On the surge of the use of containers see UNCTAD Secretariat, '*Multimodal transport: The feasibility of an international instrument*', UNCTAD/SDTE/TLB/2003/1 (2003) para 6; Mary Brooks, 'Will the Rotterdam Rules be accepted? A liner cargo interest perspective' (2012) 35(2) *Dalhousie Law Journal* 267, p. 269 at maryrbrooks.ca/wp-content/uploads/2013/06/Brooks_Mackey-Vol-35-No-2.pdf.

9 Under the pillar of modernisation one would cluster the scope of application which has expanded from door-to-door and the evolutionary provisions on electronic contracting; see Kate Lannan, '*Navigating the UN Convention on Contracts for the International Carriage of Goods Wholly or Partly by Sea*' at www.unece.org/fileadmin/DAM/trans/wp24/wp24-presentations/documents/pres10-05.pdf.

10 The preamble to the RR clearly states "Noting that shippers and carriers do not have the benefit of a binding and balanced universal regime to support the operation of contracts of carriage involving various modes of transport" at www.uncitral.org/pdf/english/texts/transport/rotterdam_rules/09-85608_Ebook.pdf; Proshanto K Mukherjee and Abhinayan Basu Bal, 'A legal and economic analysis of the volume contract concept under the Rotterdam Rules: Selected issues in perspective' (2009) 40(4) *Journal of Maritime Law and Commerce* 579 at www.rotterdamrules2009.com/cms/uploads/Def.%20tekst%20Abhinayan%20Basu%20Bal%20-%20Volume%20Contract%20Final.pdf, pp. 5, 23, 24; Si Yuzhuo and Zhang Jinlei, '*An analysis and assessment on the Rotterdam Rules in China's marine industry*' at www.comitemaritime.org/Uploads/Rotterdam%20Rules/Paper%20of%20Prof.%20Si%20Yuzhuo%20and%20Dr.%20Zhang%20Jinlei.pdf. One such way of re-balancing interests has occurred through revisiting burden of proof provisions. Generally on the allocation of the burden of proof under the RR, see for example Regina Asariotis, 'Burden of proof and allocation of liability for loss due to a combination of causes under the new Rotterdam Rules' (2008) 14(6) *JIML* 537; Regina Asariotis, 'Loss due to a combination of causes: burden of proof and commercial risk allocation' in DR Thomas (ed), *A New Convention for the Carriage of Goods by Sea – The Rotterdam Rules: An Analysis of the UN Convention on Contracts for the International Carriage of Goods Wholly or Partly by Sea* (Lawtext Publishing Ltd 2009) 138.

11 Kofi Mbiah, 'Updating the rules on international carriage of goods by sea: The Rotterdam Rules', *CMI Yearbook* 2013, 310.

are a source of such requirements. Looking beyond the relationship of carrier-shipper[12] and carrier-receiver,[13] this book selectively analyses the articles of the RR that affect the ability of the trading protagonists to perform their sale contract when the RR apply to the overseas transit of the goods. Consequently, the individual relationships of the carrier vis-à-vis the shipper, documentary shipper, consignee and holder of a transport document/record are only analysed when they have further consequences on the trade law realm.

To date there has been no spherical study of how the RR could affect traders' rights and obligations under their sale contracts. This book identifies the major issues and advises on the solutions. Most notably, in this book, we suggest the legal way forward for the trade protagonists, with or without the RR.

The purview of the international trade law impact of the Rotterdam Rules

International trade law under the application of the RR has been chosen as the area of study, because the shipping of goods undeniably represents the backbone of international trade.[14] The contractual or international regulations of carriage of goods by sea, of which the RR aspire to constitute a modern milestone, serve to facilitate and foster international trade.[15]

This book endeavours to illustrate the potential impact of the RR on international sale contracts on English terms, and also where standard trade terms, such as the Incoterms® rules 2000 and Incoterms® rules 2010,[16] and the Uniform Customs and Practice for Documentary Credits (UCP) 600,[17] are voluntarily incorporated into the contract. The above elements, namely English law, Incoterms® and the UCP 600, form part of the study presented in this book, because they represent classic sources of terms incorporated in an international sale contract.[18]

12 In this context, we will specifically look at articles about the shipper and the documentary shipper under the terminology of the RR.

13 We will look at the position of the consignee or holder of the bill of the negotiable transport document under the terminology of the RR.

14 For the undisputed closeness of international trade transactions to the RR, see Alexander von Ziegler, 'The Rotterdam Rules and the underlying sales contract', *CMI Yearbook* 2013, 273, 275 stating "The trade transactions are the 'raison d'être' of the shipping industry. This seems to be so self-evident that one tends to forget the starting point. But it is at the same time the starting point for any definition of the scope and the nature of an international legislation covering contracts for the carriage of goods by sea".

15 See preamble to the RR; see also Filippo Lorenzon, 'International Trade and shipping documents', in Y Baatz et al, *Maritime Law* (2nd edn, Sweet & Maxwell 2011), p. 98.

16 The Incoterms® rules 2010 were released in mid-September 2010, and came into effect on 1 January 2011. They are internationally recognised standard terms and are used worldwide in international and domestic contracts for the sale of goods. See more at www.iccwbo.org/products-and-services/trade-facilitation/Incoterms®-2010/.

17 Uniform Customs and Practice for Documentary Credits, 2007 Revision, International Chamber of Commerce (ICC) Publication No. 600 Paris. 2007, ISBN: 978-9-28-421257-6.

18 Charles Debattista, 'Legislative techniques in international trade: Madness or method?' [2002] *JBL* 626.

The sale contract is the centrepiece of international trade.[19] This book looks at the articles of the RR that will affect the legal position of the seller and buyer vis-à-vis one another, when a sale contract on shipment terms is concluded. Since the RR primarily regulate the legal relationships of parties to carriage contracts,[20] meaning rights and obligations between shipper and carrier,[21] it is not pellucid which provisions of the RR could affect international trade law. There are key concepts which immediately set the context of this book; the provisions on transport documents,[22] delivery of the goods,[23] e-commerce[24] and volume contracts[25] can affect the ability of the seller/shipper[26] to procure a 'protective' contract of carriage to the buyer,[27] and respectively, an appropriate[28] transport document. We will also examine whether a certain provision/novelty of the RR included in the text to tackle a given commercial problem may nevertheless trigger other uncertainties. Optimal ways of addressing the latter ones will be presented. The topics aforementioned are linked in pragmatic and doctrinal terms; that is to say that the complexities caused from them are underpinned by a common clash of legal principles and approaches towards harmonisation of carriage and trade laws respectively.

The author's underlying research has identified provisions of the RR and associated trade law issues that have so far been unexplored. This book examines

19 See Chuah, *Law of International Trade: Cross-border Commercial Transactions*, para 8-103.

20 Article 5(1) of the RR states: "Subject to article 6, this Convention applies to contracts of carriage […]".

21 See Tomotaka Fujita, '*Shipper's obligations and liabilities under the Rotterdam Rules*' at www.gcoe.j.u-tokyo.ac.jp/pdf/GCOESOFTLAW-2010–3.pdf; S Baughen, 'Obligations Owed by the Shipper to the Carrier', in DR Thomas (ed), *A New Convention for the Carriage of Goods by Sea: The Rotterdam Rules: An Analysis of the UN Convention on Contracts for the International Carriage of Goods Wholly or Partly by Sea*.

22 Richard Williams, 'Transport documentation under the new convention' (2008) 14 *JIML* 566; Malcolm Clarke, 'Transport documents: Their transferability as documents of title; electronic documents' [2002] *LMCLQ* 356; Johan Schelin, 'Documents' (2004) *Transportrecht* 294.

23 A Diamond, 'The next sea carriage convention?' [2008] *LMCLQ* 135; van der Ziel, 'Delivery of the goods, rights of the controlling party and transfer of rights'; Regina Asariotis, 'What future for the bill of lading as a document of title?' (2008) 14(2) *JIML* 75; Regina Asariotis, 'Main obligations and liabilities of the shipper under the UNCITRAL Draft Instrument' (2004) *Transportrecht* 284.

24 Miriam Goldby, 'Electronic alternatives to transport documents and the new convention: A framework for future development?' (2008) 14 *JIML* 586. On earlier drafts of the convention see G van der Ziel, 'The legal underpinning of e-commerce in maritime transport by the UNCITRAL Draft Instrument on the Carriage of Goods by Sea' (2003) 9 *JIML* 461.

25 Mukherjee and Bal, 'A legal and economic analysis of the volume contract concept under the Rotterdam Rules: Selected issues in perspective'; Abhinayan Basu Bal, 'The impact of the volume contract concept on the global community of shippers: The Rotterdam Rules in perspective' (2010) 16 *JIML* 352.

26 When a CIF sale contract has been concluded.

27 On this duty under English law, see section 32(2) of the SOGA; also Filippo Lorenzon, 'When is a CIF seller's carriage contract unreasonable? Section 32(2) of the Sale of Goods Act 1979' (2007) 13(4) *JIML* 241.

28 The adjective "appropriate" primarily means a transport document which affords protective rights to the cargo owner against the carrier.

trade law complexities and analyses these issues in detail. For example, we include a discussion of the role of custom, usage and practice and the implications they may cause to traders when there is an agreement which contradicts the custom; usage and practice and the implications they may cause to traders when there is an agreement which contradicts the custom; an examination of the provisions of the RR on electronic commerce taking into consideration all parties of the trade chain; an assessment of their compatibility with the available frameworks which already exist; and a challenging analysis of the impact of volume contracts on third parties. In the latter context, we have gone beyond a mere observation of the difficulties and visualised the possibilities and duties in terms of notifying on derogations from the RR and drawing the third party's consent on them. Such issues represent the foremost concerns that states, policy makers and the shipping community have and which explain why they may be reluctant towards the adoption of the RR. These are research areas that we have identified, delved into and explored, presenting the ambiguities of interpretation. Most importantly, we will suggest ways to safeguard against an application that would prove controversial in a commercial contractual context or that would seem to defeat the drafting ambitions and objectives underpinning the RR.

This book has the articles of the RR with an international trade law importance at its epicentre. We will study in detail the entitlement to a transport document and will focus on documents or records that were not regulated before. Secondly, we will investigate how certain carriage contracts, namely volume contracts, could affect the traders' performance of their international sale contracts.

The purpose is to assess the RR, as the seismograph of the international carriage and trade law tensions, in order to examine whether the RR as a carriage piece of codification facilitate international trade or not.

The RR are anyway tested by the shipping and trade community in terms of whether they provide a good alternative to their carriage predecessors. To date, the RR have received four ratifications; this process may seem slow, but it is moving. The RR constitute an innovative international convention in many ways; they cover concepts such as e-commerce and right of control, and offer the possibility of contractual freedom, going far beyond both the HVR and the Hamburg Rules. In these respects they reflect and cater for certain modern trade law trends. They are therefore a step forward in many ways, compared to the previous international carriage of goods by sea conventions. Even states that are not considering the ratification of the RR are now mindful of provisions accommodating these trends in their national codes.[29] The same can be said about the industry. For instance, the need for paperless transactions has led to the creation of two major electronic registries, namely Bolero (the Bill of Lading Electronic Registry Organisation) and essDOCS, and relevant European Union Directives.

29 See the example of Germany's Act on the Reform of Maritime Trade Law 2013, which is much affected by concepts appearing in the RR, in Jason Chuah, 'The new German Act on the reform of Maritime Trade Law' (2013) 19(1) *JIML* 5, p. 6.

In respect of freedom of contract, the Baltic and International Maritime Council (BIMCO) has launched a standard volume contract,[30] and has also expressed concern that we analyse the position of small and medium cargo interests, as it has formulated committees with representations by them for the drafting of SERVICECON.[31] Additionally, BIMCO has devised a clause aimed to facilitate e-commerce; therefore, our comments on the best way to legislate on electronic paperless transactions taking into consideration the appropriate participation of trading parties is a contribution which is of current and future importance, and is equally useful to the legislators and the shipping and trade industry.

The significance of this legal study

Our findings are of essential value for the legislative way forward (after or without the RR). To the extent that the innovations of the RR represent an operational solution to problems of modern trade, but are occasionally ineffective because of the specific wording of articles or the lack of thoroughness of their provisions, we show through case scenarios what future normative texts should comprise. It becomes therefore immediately ascertainable what the wording of certain provisions should be, and this is the example that can be followed by a piece of international codification of maritime trade, if it comes after the RR have failed to be ratified. Alternatively, this example may be followed by any national legislation that wishes to update its carriage and maritime trade legislation with new, clear and unambiguous provisions. This book delineates any international trade law controversies or other misgivings by the RR, providing the platform for forward and more effective legal regulation.

Our recommendations are both legislative and contractual, thus they are opening the way to future legislative/regulatory evolution (i.e. beyond the RR and not necessarily with them), which will be equally beneficial to the trade industry and to policy makers. It has to be re-emphasised at this stage that the RR serve as a platform encapsulating the most recent developments on international carriage of goods and trade. The fact that our illustrations come from real practice examples shows that the book takes on board modern issues of seaborne trade and checks them through the provisions of the RR, but the ultimate suggestions address the commercial repercussions from a holistic international trade law mindset. The problems that the RR reserve for international sale contracts become the protagonists of this book, exactly as it is in real commercial legal practice, and the suggestions we provide are significant, regardless of whether the RR will ever come into force. We advise on issues of shipping and trade law which are debatable but also current, and cannot only be found in the RR. The RR, through the modern commercial trends they accommodate, give food for discussion.

30 'BIMCO: Documentary Committee meets in Dubai' at www.bimco.org/News/2014/05/09_Documentary_Committee_meets_in_Dubai.aspx?RenderSearch=true.

31 Ibid.

Structure of the chapters

The book starts with the identification and analysis of the legal provisions and innovations of the RR that can have an impact on international trade law. Therefore these articles are presented first, because they afford trading parties (shippers, documentary shippers, consignees, holders and third parties as per the terminology of the RR) firstly with contracting options which were unavailable in the predecessors of the RR, and secondly with provisions which are more comprehensive than those of the previous conventions.

Chapter 1 sets out the theoretical principles underpinning the surge of international codification attempts for maritime carriage liabilities and rights, and separates them from the principles behind the laws of international sales. This is to justify why a welcome solution afforded by the RR from a carriage perspective may be of uncertain outcome in the trade law sphere, as the underpinnings[32] of these two areas of law occasionally differ.

Chapter 2 has the objective to set the scene by introducing terms, parties and concepts which do not appear in the predecessors of the RR. It also highlights how certain innovations may give rise to certain commercial side effects.

Chapter 3 studies the interrelations of the RR with other standard trade terms. Because of the indisputable importance of documents in international trade, it has been extremely important to study the entitlement to a transport document and factors that affect the choice of a transport document. The synergies of the RR with other standard trade terms will be analysed back to back, in order to identify possible conflicts or discrepancies which may affect the performance of traders' obligations under their sale contracts and letters of credit.

In this chapter, it will be observed that a freedom afforded by one article, for example Article 35 of the RR, shifted attention to the articles of the RR on electronic transport records. Consequently, the study next had to gear towards the prerequisites for issuing, transferring and replacing records with documents and vice versa, according to the needs of the on-buyer. This is discussed in Chapter 4.

Chapter 4 examines the articles of the RR on electronic commerce. This is an important chapter driven by two major motivations: first, the need to confirm whether the wish of the commercial world to trade in paperless forms, which has been a major trend governing the surge of the RR, has actually been facilitated; and secondly, to check the success of the provisions of the RR on e-commerce, especially considering that the RR is the result of the shift in scope of the mission of Working Group III of UNCITRAL.[33] Although initially the UNCITRAL Working Group on Electronic Commerce aimed to create a uniform international framework for the creation of electronic substitutes to bills of lading, the gaps

32 We are here referring to theoretical and contextual idiosyncrasies of international commercial laws. These cover sources of laws, standard terms and model contracts of wide use, and ways of harmonisation and synthesis of delegations that are called to unify international commercial laws.

33 van der Ziel, 'Delivery of the goods, rights of the controlling party and transfer of rights', p. 598.

and legal national disharmonies encountered later, showed the urgent need for a harmonisation of the law relating to the contracts of international maritime carriage.[34] Therefore, Chapter 4 illustrates whether the provisions of the RR on e-commerce can operate, and whether such an operation is in line with the progress of English law in this field on the one hand, and with the private initiatives of electronic systems available to the shipping industry on the other. This search will assist with the English legal approach that has to be taken so that the RR can have a positive effect on electronic trade.

Chapter 5 offers a critical analysis of the most controversial concept of the RR, namely volume contracts, by examining the conditions for derogating from the RR. Particular attention is paid to the position of third parties, discussing what the formal steps should be, so that volume contracts can have a predictable effect on them. Ambiguities of the relevant articles of the RR as to time, form, way of notification and drawing consent to the derogations will also be discussed in this chapter.

Chapter 6 corroborates the major observations made throughout our analysis in the book identifies the rationale of the trade law imbroglios or uncertainties spotted and justifies the suggestions to rectify the drawbacks noted along the journey of this book.

In the conclusion, we epitomise the suggestions, thinking of the day after tomorrow, with or without the RR but with a reflective and considerate legal mindset for a more efficient international trade wholly or partly by sea.

To summarise, the two major poles of this book are first, the examination of the novel provisions of the RR introduced to better serve the evolution of modern international trade; and second, because the said provisions will have important international trade law repercussions, an analysis of the contractual or regulatory possibilities that the trade protagonists can utilise to rectify them will be presented.

In Chapter 6, we shed light on the philosophy of international carriage conventions on the one hand, and on the intricacies underpinning international trade and its process of standardisation – leading to important clauses and contracts – on the other. This will help us understand why the way in which the RR address certain issues may give rise to other trade implications. The justification is that trade and carriage legal drafting patterns and philosophies are permeated by different principles. Ultimately, this analysis will substantiate the appropriateness of the solutions which we put forward for a more "commercially effective" international trade law that prioritises unhindered commerce.

34 Ibid.

1 The Rotterdam Rules and international trade law

Background and characteristics

1.1 Introduction to international trade law

By "international trade law", we refer to the law of international commercial sales;[1] depending on the place of performance of the contract[2] there are sales on shipment terms (primarily CIF and FOB),[3] on E (ex works) terms[4] and D (delivery) terms.[5]

International trade is primarily maritime and is framed by a variety of contracts such as charterparties, bills of lading and contracts for the finance of sales, such as letters of credit. The multi-contractual and multipartite sea adventure needs to be enveloped with contractual, national and international frameworks so as to make overseas trade efficient, flexible and as predictable as possible.

There is an unquestionable contextual proximity of the sale contract to the contract of carriage for the transport on the one hand, and to the letter of credit for the financing of the sale on the other.[6] The interfaces of a carriage contract with these contracts have also been recognised by the drafters of the RR.[7]

1 See extensively A Lista, *International Commercial Sales: The Sale of Goods on Shipment Terms* (Informa 2017).

2 Filippo Lorenzon, *Sassoon on CIF and FOB Contracts* (6th edn, Sweet & Maxwell 2017), para 1.007.

3 There is a debate on whether sales on shipment terms are only sales on c-terms (supported by Michael Bridge in *The International Sale of Goods* (3rd edn, OUP 2013), or also sales on F-terms (FOB, FAS etc.), supported by Lorenzon, *Sassoon on CIF and FOB Contracts*, para 1.007. In the latter publication, sales on shipment terms include CIF, FOB and C&F terms. Throughout this book, sales on shipment terms are taken to include both CIF (Cost, Insurance and Freight) and FOB (Free on Board) sales, because by effectively putting the goods on board and procuring the shipping documents requested under the sale contract, the seller is performing both his physical and documentary duties under the sale contract.

4 EXW, Incoterms® 2010.

5 The existing D-terms in Incoterms® 2010 are DAT (Delivery at Terminal), DAP (Delivery at Place) and DDP (Delivered Duty Paid).

6 For the proximity and interaction of carriage and sale contract terms see generally Bridge, *The International Sale of Goods*, para 1.01; Jan Ramberg, 'Synchronisation of contracts of sale, carriage, insurance, and financing in international trade' in P Šarčević (ed), *International Contracts and Conflicts of Laws: A Collection of Essays* (1990).

7 González JM Alcántara, 'The Rotterdam Rules: Prelude or premonition?'(2010) 2(1) *Cuadernos de Derecho Transnacional* 25, p. 27 at e-revistas.uc3m.es/index.php/CDT/article/viewFile/95/93; Francesco Berlingieri, 'Report of the Chairman of the ISC on uniformity of the Law of carriage of goods by Sea' (1996); von Ziegler, 'The Rotterdam Rules and the underlying sales contract', p. 277.

Therefore, it is necessary to illustrate the two pillars of principles that are being entrenched in this book's quest on the impact of the RR on international trade. These are first, the principles underlying the predecessors of the RR, and intricate underpinnings behind the RR in particular; and second, the fundamentals of international trade law.

1.1.1 Principles of carriage of goods by sea conventions prior to the Rotterdam Rules

The RR is the most recent effort for a uniform and updated international carriage of goods (wholly or partly) by sea regime. Maritime carriage started being regulated[8] at treaty level in the first place, because the global policy makers identified the need to protect cargo interests from the carriers' tendency to abuse their strong bargaining power.[9] However, this commercial finding has changed over the years. Hence, the need for the RR has emanated from the outdating[10] of a series of previous conventions, namely the Hague Rules, the HVR and the Hamburg Rules, and the need for a modern, pragmatic instrument. Therefore, the principles behind the creation of the previous conventions generally remain relevant, subject to certain exceptions.[11] Below, we retrace the surge of the first convention in carriage of goods by sea in order to better understand the evolutionary progress towards the RR.

1.1.2 Principles behind the Hague Rules

In the late 19th century, British courts were giving effect to broad liability exemption clauses, leaving carriers liable for virtually nothing, their own negligence included.[12] On the other hand, courts in the United States (US) had a

8 The RR, as the latest international codifying attempt in maritime liability conventions in particular, is held to be a "maritime plus" or "wet multimodal" convention: see Meltem Deniz Güner-Özbek, 'Extended scope of the Rotterdam Rules: Maritime Plus and conflict of the extension with the extensions of other transport law conventions' in Meltem Deniz Güner-Özbek (ed), *The United Nations Convention on Contracts for the International Carriage of Goods Wholly or Partly by Sea: An Appraisal of the Rotterdam Rules* (Springer 2011), p. 107; Ellen Eftestöl-Wilhelmsson, 'The Rotterdam Rules in a European multimodal context' (2010) 16 *JIML* 274; Theodora Nikaki, 'Conflicting laws in "wet" multimodal carriage of goods: The UNCITRAL Draft Convention on the Carriage of Goods [Wholly or Partly] [by Sea]' (2006) 37 *Journal of Maritime Law & Commerce* 521, pp. 522–523.

9 Andrew Tettenborn, 'Freedom of contract and the Rotterdam Rules: Framework for negotiation or one size fits all?' in DR Thomas (ed), *The Carriage of Goods by Sea Under The Rotterdam Rules* (Lloyd's List 2010), para 4.1. Before the Harter Act, it was common for courts to deny effect to sea-carriers' exculpatory clauses on the grounds of their being one-sided and abusive. See for example *Liverpool & GW Steam Co v. Phoenix Ins Co*, 129 US 397, 437–463 (1889) and *The Delaware*, 161 US 459, 471–474 (1896); MA Clarke, *Aspects of the Hague Rules* (Martinus Nijhoff 1976), pp. 1–7; Gilmore and Black, *The Law of Admiralty*, (2nd edn Foundation Press 1975), sections 3-22 to 3-24.

10 Theodora Nikaki and Bariş Soyer, 'A new international regime for carriage of goods by sea: Contemporary, certain, inclusive, and efficient, or just another one for the shelves?' [2012] 30(2) *J Berkeley Int'l Law* 303, 304.

11 See for instance volume contracts.

12 MF Sturley, 'The history of COGSA and the Hague Rules' (1991) 22(1) *Journal of Maritime Law and Commerce* 1, p. 5. After the judgment in *Grill v. General Iron Screw Collier Co*, 1 CP 600

more cautious approach towards freedom of contract clauses.[13] Similarly, Japan's Commercial Code took a restrictive approach against the carrier's exemption of liability.[14] Consequently, the global disharmony in international risk allocation in sea transit gave rise to international unification efforts.

However, even before the decision for a need of an international legislative solution, there were some important national initiatives to even out the contractual privileges of carriers over cargo interests. The Harter Act,[15] for instance, was US legislation applicable to domestic and foreign trade,[16] enacted to protect traders against extensive exemption liability clauses of the carrier and the trend of forum shopping.[17] Australia,[18] New Zealand[19] and Canada[20] legislated similarly.

Nevertheless, these national legislative initiatives were not entirely satisfactory, as they only applied to domestic and outbound bills of lading.[21] US and Australian traders receiving defective goods remained unprotected.[22] It was asserted[23] that the difference between domestic legislations and an international convention would be the following: although the statutes were characterised by the aim to prevent carriers from contracting out of their obligations, the new unifying

(1866), affirmed in 3 CP 476 (Exch. Ch. 1868) carriers tended to extensively include clauses for exempting their own negligence.

13 See MF Sturley, 'The history of COGSA and the Hague Rules' (1991) 22(1) *Journal of Maritime Law and Commerce* 1, pp. 5–6 and case examples discussed therein. Sturley has submitted the following case examples: *Establishment For Agricultural Product Trading v. Wesermunde,* 83 F.2d 1576, 1580, 1988 AMC 2328 (11th Cir. 1988), cert. denied, 488 US 916 (1988); *Encyclopaedia Britannica Inc v. Hong Kong Producer*, 422 F.2d 7, 11–12, 1969 AMC 1741(2d Cir. 1969), cert. denied, 397 US 964 (1970). Later, in *Sun Oil Co v. M/T Carlisle*, 771 F. 2d 805, 809–810, 1986 AMC 305 (3d Cir. 1985), the customary trade allowance that permitted carriers to deliver only 99.5% of the cargo without discharging the onus laid upon them by COGSA was held to be plainly inconsistent with the US COGSA. The customary trade allowance placing the burden to prove that some specific cause, e.g. carrier's negligence, caused the loss, was not given effect, as contrary to the US COGSA. See also *Sun Oil Co of Pennsylvania and Sun International Ltd v. M/T Carlisle In Rem and Ore Sea Transport SA of Panama and Tradax Gestion SA (The Carlisle)* – United States Court of Appeals for the Third Circuit (Hunter and Sloviter, Circuit Judges and Cohen, District Judge) (4 September 1985) Lloyd's Maritime Law Newsletter, issue 155.

14 Sturley, 'The history of COGSA and the Hague Rules', p. 5. See the distinction between the liberal approach taken by the British courts towards broad exemption of liability and the stricter approach of US courts.

15 Signed on 13 February 1893; 27 Stat. 445 (1893); 24 Cong. Rec. 1603 (1893); Act 46 App. USC 190–195 at www.admiraltylawguide.com/codes.html.

16 Sturley, 'The history of COGSA and the Hague Rules', p. 14.

17 Ibid, pp. 12–13.

18 The Australian Sea-Carriage of Goods Act 1904 was much modelled on the Harter Act, having as its main targets the seaworthiness obligation, which was absolute, and the prohibition of these choice of law clauses that purported to displace Australian law or undermine the jurisdiction of the Australian courts. See also, Sturley, 'The history of COGSA and the Hague Rules', p. 15.

19 Shipping and Seaman Amendment Act, 1911. See 156 NZ Parl Deb 715 (1911).

20 See Sturley, 'The history of COGSA and the Hague Rules', p. 56.

21 Ibid, p. 18.

22 Ibid.

23 Ibid, p. 20.

attempt would give rise to a code which would establish rights and immunities along with responsibilities and liabilities on both carriers and cargo interests.[24]

The objectives behind the Hague Rules were twofold:[25] first, to flexibly allocate risks between carriers and cargo interests; and second, to refrain the carriers from abusing their superior bargaining position, through provisions affording protection to their counterparties.[26] Similar principles, but also varied drafting intentions led to the launch of the subsequent conventions, namely the HVR and the Hamburg Rules.

These conventions were intended to exist independently from domestic legislations, whereas today it is perhaps unavoidable that national or regional legislations would have to coexist with the RR, and this is an element of modernisation in the RR that did not exist in their predecessors. It is for the sake of this desired harmony and openness to future evolution, legislation and regulation that the RR do not provide exhaustive regulation in some areas and this is the modernisation element which underpins the RR.

Next, we delve into the intricate factors behind the emergence of the RR.

1.1.3 Principles behind the Rotterdam Rules

Since 1920, when the Hague Rules were adopted, until the 1990s, when deliberations on a modern successor for "maritime plus" carriage emerged, the needs and practices of worldwide trade had changed. It can be argued that the international texts which came after the Hague Rules were liability schemes for the loss of or damage to the goods, and not deterrents against the carrier's potential for abuse. There was also a general aim to establish a regime striking the proper balance between carriers and cargo interests,[27] which was not fulfilled. The reason for this was that courts adjudicated by trying to be consistent with several aspects of their national laws rather than with the expected "transnational" aim to resolve problems of interpretation with a view to properly balancing the rights of carriers and cargo interests in an internationally uniform way.[28]

24 Sturley, 'The history of COGSA and the Hague Rules', pp. 6–8 and Nikaki and Soyer, 'A new international regime for carriage of goods by sea: Contemporary, certain, inclusive, and efficient, or just another one for the shelves?', p. 303; see also Sir Guenter Treitel and Francis MB Reynolds (eds), *Carver on Bills of Lading* (3rd edn, Sweet & Maxwell 2011), para 9-062; Sir Guenter Treitel and Francis MB Reynolds (eds), *Carver on Bills of Lading* (4th edn, Sweet & Maxwell 2017), para 10-001.

25 Nikaki and Soyer, 'A new international regime for carriage of goods by sea: Contemporary, certain, inclusive, and efficient, or just another one for the shelves?', p. 303.

26 Ibid.

27 Sturley, 'The history of COGSA and the Hague Rules', pp. 6–8.

28 Generally, MF Sturley, 'International uniform laws in national courts: The influence of domestic law in conflicts of interpretation' (1987) 27 *Va J Int'l L* 729; Sturley, 'The history of COGSA and the Hague Rules', p. 57.

The laudable aim behind the RR was to update the law on maritime – and ideally multimodal – carriage and to fill the gaps of existing conventions in carriage of goods by sea, while achieving a broad consensus. Ultimately, the RR aspired to give robust solutions to the practical needs of modern commerce.[29] Trade in the days before the deliberations for the RR was highly characterised by the surge of containerisation[30] and the rising trend of paperless contracting.[31] The scope of liability of the carrier under the HVR had also become outdated, since carriers started receiving and delivering goods beyond the "tackle to tackle" spectrum, for example to and from the trader's warehouse.[32] The need for uniformity is clear in the preamble to the RR:

> Noting that shippers and carriers do not have the benefit of a binding and balanced universal regime to support the operation of contracts of carriage involving various modes of transport.[33]

Also derived from the preamble are the other underpinnings of the RR:[34] promotion of legal certainty; encouragement of trade development for all parties and enhancement of efficiency; and certainty and commercial predictability in the international carriage of goods.[35] As we shall see, these are also the motivations of harmonisation undertaken by UNCITRAL.[36]

29 MF Sturley, 'General Principles of Transport Law and the Rotterdam Rules' in Güner-Özbek (ed), *The United Nations Convention on Contracts for the International Carriage of Goods Wholly or Partly by Sea: An Appraisal of the Rotterdam Rules*, p. 63.

30 Nikaki and Soyer, 'A new international regime for carriage of goods by sea: Contemporary, certain, inclusive, and efficient, or just another one for the shelves?', p. 320.

31 MF Sturley, 'The UNCITRAL carriage of goods: Changes to existing law', *CMI Yearbook* 2007–2008, 254, pp. 256, 262.

32 Francesco Berlingieri, '*Multimodal aspects of the Rotterdam Rules*' at www.rotterdamrules2009.com/cms/uploads/Def.%20tekst%20F.%20Berlingieri%2013%20OKT29.pdf; Diego Esteban Chami, '*The obligations of the carrier*' at www.rotterdamrules2009.com/cms/uploads/Def.%20tekst%20Diego%20Chami%20-%20Obligations%20of%20the%20Carrier.pdf.

33 Preamble to the convention at www.uncitral.org/pdf/english/texts/transport/rotterdam_rules/09-85608_Ebook.pdf.

34 It is stated in the preamble: "Believing that the adoption of uniform rules to govern international contracts of carriage wholly or partly by sea will promote legal certainty, improve the efficiency of international carriage of goods and facilitate new access opportunities for previously remote parties and markets, thus playing a fundamental role in promoting trade and economic development, both domestically and internationally". Also Nikaki and Soyer, 'A new international regime for carriage of goods by sea: Contemporary, certain, inclusive, and efficient, or just another one for the shelves?', p. 307.

35 "The container is in the base of the project: it is not about an adaptation of the text (of the Rotterdam rules) to the container but rather it is a text thought out and designed for the container": R Illescas, 'Project of UN Convention over the contract of international carriage of goods wholly or partly by sea' (2008) 210 *El Derecho de los Negocios*, Madrid, (translation).

36 See further down in this chapter.

The philosophy of the RR has been characterised as pragmatic.[37] This is suggested by a close attention to their preparation and goals.[38] In the impetus for this new convention there were seats for everyone at the table of the negotiations: governments, expert industry representatives, big trading associations, non-governmental organisations, and national and international representations.

Pragmatism[39] was achieved in ensuring the broadest possible international uniformity and opening for participation in the deliberations.[40]

The RR are also modern and pragmatic in acknowledging new types of transport documents (especially negotiable), mirroring their diversity and frequency in modern practices and trade.[41]

Attention now shifts to the diversity of trade and carriage law sources.

1.2 International trade law: characteristics and variety of legal sources

1.2.1 Legal sources of international trade law

1.2.1.1 The role of English law

The majority of international commercial sales are sale contracts of commodities.[42] It is therein *locus classicus* that English is the governing law of the contract,[43] without the country of shipment or destination being necessarily the UK, and regardless of whether payment is to be made outside the UK or in a currency other than the English pound.[44] This preference is a tribute to the trusted expertise of English judges, and to the contribution of English common and statutory law to commercial and maritime matters.

Renowned commodity organisations use English law in their contracts.[45] The standard contracts of the Grain And Feed Trade Association (GAFTA) for instance, stipulate that English law is their applicable law.

37 Sturley, 'Transport law for the twenty-first century: An introduction to the preparation, philosophy, and potential impact of the Rotterdam Rules' in DR Thomas (ed), *A New Convention for the Carriage of Goods by Sea – The Rotterdam Rules: An Analysis of the UN Convention on Contracts for the International Carriage of Goods Wholly or Partly by Sea*, p. 24.

38 Ibid.

39 About the practical underpinning in the making of the RR see also Mbiah, 'Updating the rules on international carriage of goods by sea: The Rotterdam Rules'.

40 See M Sturley, 'What has become of the Rotterdam Rules' (2016) 83(4) *Journal of Transportation Law, Logistics and Policy* 275, p. 277.

41 See Article 47(2) of the RR.

42 Lorenzon, *Sassoon on CIF and FOB Contracts*, para 1.001.

43 Bridge, *The International Sale of Goods*, para 1.39; Lorenzon, 'When is a CIF seller's carriage contract unreasonable? Section 32(2) of the Sale of Goods Act 1979', p. 242; M Bridge, 'Uniformity and diversity in international sale contracts' (2003) 15(1) *Pace International Law Review* 55, p. 57.

44 Bridge, *The International Sale of Goods*, para 1.39.

45 Ibid.

1.2.1.2 Carriage of goods by sea statutes and conventions

If English law has been chosen as the law applicable to the carriage and sale contracts, national carriage statutes such as the Carriage of Goods by Sea Act 1992 (COGSA 1992) and 1971 (COGSA 1971) may need to be studied in a sale dispute. The same applies to carriage conventions that have taken the force of law in a certain jurisdiction.[46] Resort to carriage statutes and conventions is frequent, whenever an answer to a question regarding a right or obligation cannot be found in a statute. If the RR are ratified by the UK, they will be embedded into the English legislation, replacing the HVR.[47]

1.2.1.3 Sets of standard trade terms

If a certain trade law question cannot be addressed by trade statutes and case law or carriage statutes, conventions and case law, then study of other sale terms voluntarily incorporated may provide the answer. Two of the most popular sets are the Incoterms® and the UCP 600 drafted by the International Chamber of Commerce (ICC). Incoterms® were published for the first time by the ICC in 1936.[48] Incoterms® provide a set of official rules for the interpretation of trade terms used in international trade.[49] They are drafted and revised by experts from several nationalities chosen for their outstanding contribution to international commercial law and to the ICC over the years.[50] They are written in a very simple language for lay people lacking the specific knowledge of lawyers.[51] Incoterms® are legal, but non-binding, instruments, widely used by practitioners and voluntarily incorporated into contracts.[52] Their importance has been acknowledged by the European Court of Justice (ECJ).[53] Designed for use with the contract of sale, Incoterms® have been drafted to minimise misinterpretations and disputes between buyers and sellers. They are

46 Debattista, 'Legislative techniques in international trade: Madness or method?', p. 627.

47 See Article 89 of the RR, which states that a country that ratifies, approves or accedes to the RR and is a party to the Hague, the HVR or the Hamburg Rules, shall at the same time denounce the Convention or protocols thereto to which it is a party.

48 Bridge, *The International Sale of Goods*, para 10.62.

49 For a considerable analysis of the distinctive characteristics of major ways of arranging payment for sale of goods overseas see Miriam Goldby, *Electronic Documents in Maritime Trade: Law and Practice* (OUP 2013), paras 3.09–3.17.

50 'History of the Incoterms®: From 1936 to today: the Incoterms® rules' at www.iccwbo.org/products-and-services/trade-facilitation/Incoterms-2010/history-of-the-Incoterms-rules/.

51 Bridge, *The International Sale of Goods*, para 1.19.

52 Laurence Ravillon, 'Chronicle of informal sources on Business Law' [2012] 5 *IBLJ* 519, 542.

53 *European Court of Justice (Case C-87/10) (Third Chamber) of 9 June 2011, Electrosteel Europe SA v. Edil Centro SpA*; 'Supply of goods in a distance selling contract: the Judicial competence and the role of the Incoterms' at www.picozzimorigi.cn/main/reports.php?id=82; Melis Ozdel, 'Multimodal transport documents in international sale of goods' (2012) 23(7) *International Company and Commercial Law Review* 238.

very rare in sale contracts of dry commodities,[54] but more frequent in oil-purchase contracts.[55]

1.2.2 Reading terms and conventions with the right lenses

The relevance of the ICC publications and their underlying principles will become obvious in Chapter 2. Since these terms are business-oriented, they are more pragmatic. The ICC Commission on Commercial Law and Practice (CLP), which revises the Incoterms® on the one hand, and UNCITRAL on the other hand, work in completely adverse ways: whereas CLP starts from the individual experts coming from companies, then works actively with intergovernmental organisations and only ultimately does it collaborate with national organisations for the production of effective regulatory systems,[56] UNCITRAL[57] and the mechanisms behind the creation of international conventions, have a governmental rather than an industry starting point.[58] International conventions, the RR included, are driven by harmonisation,[59]whereas the rules created by private sources, such as the ICC, are aimed to bring predictability in practice.[60]

UNCITRAL has the following aims:[61] harmonisation, in order to minimise disparity of laws and other obstacles among jurisdictions;[62] specialisation, in order to meet current needs of international transactions and disputes;[63] modernisation, in order to take on board changes in values, technology and commercial practices;[64] codification for the elimination of obstacles paving the way for methods of communication, commerce and finance;[65] and the overall attainment of legal certainty and confidence of traders on the provisions.

54 Bridge, *The International Sale of Goods*, para 1.19.

55 Ibid, para 1.19, fn 61 therein; Shell, General terms and conditions for sales and purchases of crude oil (1980), cl. 27. Also Total, General terms and conditions for cfr/cif/delivered ex ship sales of crude oil (2007), section 1; *Erg Petroli SpA v. Vitol SA (The Ballenita and BP energy)* [1992] 2 Lloyd's Rep 455; *ERG Raffinerie Mediterranee v. Chevron USA Inc (The Luxmar)* [2007] 1 CLC 807.

56 'What do we do?: Commission on Commercial Law and Practice' at www.iccwbo.org/about-icc/policy-commissions/commercial-law-and-practice/what-do-we-do-/.

57 On the roles of UNCITRAL see in general G Herrmann, 'The role of UNCITRAL', in I Fletcher, L Mistelis and M Cremona (eds), *Foundations and Perspectives of International Trade Law* (Sweet & Maxwell 2001).

58 Debattista, 'Legislative techniques in international trade: Madness or method?', p. 637. This however does not mean that the UNCITRAL and ICC have a competitive relation. Quite the opposite, there is cooperation, as shown by the recent endorsement of Incoterms® 2010 by UNCITRAL. See Report of the Commission on the work of its 45th session (Doc A/67/17), 2012, paras 141–144.

59 Debattista, 'Legislative techniques in international trade: Madness or method?', p. 636.

60 Ibid.

61 As listed by Herrmann, 'The role of UNCITRAL'.

62 Ibid, paras 2-010 to 2-012.

63 Ibid, paras 2-013 to 2-014.

64 Ibid, paras 2-015 to 2-016.

65 Ibid, paras 2-017 to 2-020. This is the so-called "preventive unification".

1.2.3 Fusion of legal sources

International conventions on the one hand, and standard terms and contracts on the other, may prove to be of controversial application. This is because they are drawn up by rival market sectors[66] and in a "sector-specific"[67] manner. Carriage representatives support carriage interests whereas trade private bodies strive for more commercial rather than detailed shipping solutions. One should also be expecting synergies between all these sources, based on the fact that conventions have their own intricacies. Self-regulatory terms and conventions are drafted under different legislative techniques.[68]

The characteristics of the majority of international sale laws are presented in the next section, in order to complement the picture of their underpinnings.

1.3 Idiosyncrasies of international sale contracts

Import and export sales of commodities are documentary sales,[69] typically executed through two separate and independent ways of performance: physical and documentary. CIF and FOB contracts are the most well-known types of these sales,[70] also popularly called sales on shipment terms, and are distinguished from sales on delivery or arrival terms because in the former the seller is performing his obligations under the sale contract at the port of loading, i.e. on shipment.[71] CIF sales are the most original example of shipment sales.[72] A CIF seller is under the obligation to ship goods to a named destination and to procure insurance on the terms usual in the trade while the goods are in transit.[73] CIF contracts started evolving in the end of the 19th century.[74] The seller is contractually promising to put the goods on board in conformity with the contract of sale and to tender the appropriate documents to the buyer.[75] Actual delivery of the goods is not an obligation of the CIF seller.[76]

66 Debattista, 'Legislative techniques in international trade: Madness or method?', p. 632.

67 Ibid, p. 634.

68 Ibid, p. 635.

69 Bridge, *The International Sale of Goods*, p. 58.

70 Some commentators consider CIF sales as the only pure documentary sale, as opposed to FOB ones, as the documentary tender does not replace the duty to physically place the goods on board a ship: see Goldby, *Electronic Documents in Maritime Trade: Law and Practice*, para 3.04. FAS and CIP also belong in this category. These sales are called sales on shipment terms and are distinguished from sales on delivery or arrival terms because the seller is performing at the loadport, i.e. on shipment. Lorenzon, *Sassoon on CIF and FOB Contracts*, para 1.003.

71 Charles Debattista, *Bills of Lading in Export Trade* (3rd edn, Tottel Publishing 2009), p. 2.

72 Bridge, *The International Sale of Goods*, para 4.01.

73 Ibid.

74 Paul Todd, *Bills of Lading and Bankers' Documentary Credits* (4th edn, Informa 2007), para 1.6; Debattista, *Bills of Lading in Export Trade*, p. 2. For a historical perspective of the main types of sales on shipment terms see DM Sassoon, 'The origin of FOB and CIF terms and the factors influencing their choice' (1967) *JBL* 32; DM Sassoon, 'Application of FOB and CIF sales in common law countries' (1981) 1 *European Transport Law* 50.

75 Debattista, *Bills of Lading in Export Trade*, p. 5; Indira Carr, *International Trade Law* (4th edn, Routledge-Cavendish 2010), p. 7.

76 *Scottish and Newcastle International Ltd v. Othon Galanos Ltd* [2006] EWCA Civ 1750 at [43] and [55], [2006] 2 CLC 1015.

Instead, shipment of the goods, formation of an insurance policy and tender of it along with the shipping documents, serve as a substitute for the physical delivery of the goods to the buyer under a conventional contract of sale.[77] Hence international commercial sales are often interchangeably called documentary sales.[78]

Payment may be satisfied through cash against documents or via a letter of credit.[79] From a pragmatic perspective, it has been observed that string sales[80] constitute another common characteristic of international commercial sales. The market volatility[81] places important influence on the trading of documents and products; occasionally, there are sales effected in a speculative way for making profit, which requires quick decision making based on a check of the documents tendered. These will be analysed forthwith.

Another significant characteristic of international commercial sales is that the two types of obligations, physical and documentary, are independent. This further means that there are two ways of performance of the sale contract, and thus, two grounds of rejection.[82]

Below, we give indications of how trade and carriage laws interrelate, through the example of concepts which may be common, but acquire different importance

77 See Bridge, *The International Sale of Goods*, para 4.02 citing the following case law examples: *Tregelles v. Sewell* (1862) 7 H & N 574, 582, 158 ER 600 (Martin B), where the insurance policy was held to be a substitute for the goods; *Clemens Horst (E) Co v. Biddell Bros* [1912] AC 18, HL, where the bill of lading was considered a substitute for the goods; *Biddell Bros v. Clemens Horst (E) Co* [1911] 1 KB 934, 956, CA, where the bill of lading represented the goods; *Attorney-General of Botswana v. Aussies Diamond Products Pty Ltd* [2010] WASC 141 at 219; *Hines Exports Pty Ltd v. Mediterranean Shipping Co SA* [2001] SASC 311 at [26]. Also, in *Manbre Saccharine Co v. Corn Products Co* [1919] 1 KB 198, McCardie J at p. 203 stated "For in reality, as I have said, the obligation of the vendor is to deliver documents rather than goods – to transfer symbols rather than the physical property represented thereby. If the vendor fulfils his contract by shipping the appropriate goods in the appropriate manner under a proper contract of carriage, and if he also obtains the proper documents for tender to the purchaser, I am unable to see how the rights or duties of either party are affected by the loss of ship or goods, or by knowledge of such loss by the vendor, prior to actual tender of the documents".

78 Koji Takahashi, 'Right to terminate (avoid) international sales of commodities' (2003) *JBL* 102, p. 126. See also A Odeke, 'The nature of a CIF contract – Is it a sale of documents or a sale of goods?' [1993] *Journal of Contract Law* 158.

79 There are three major ways of payment in international commercial sales: the open account, the documentary collection/cash against documents and the letter of credit; see Goldby, *Electronic Documents in Maritime Trade: Law and Practice*, paras 3.09–3.17.

80 Bridge, *The International Sale of Goods*, paras 1.44, 4.05 and 4.06.

81 Lorenzon, *Sassoon on CIF and FOB Contracts*, para 1-002.

82 Carole Murray, David Holloway and Daren Timson Hunt, *Schmitthoff's Export Trade: The Law and Practice of International Trade* (12th edn, Sweet & Maxwell 2012), para 2.026. On the independent rights of rejection see *Kwei Tek Chao and Others v. British Traders and Shippers Ltd* [1954] 2 QB 459 at 481; See also *Procter & Gamble Philippine Manufacturing Corp v. Kurt A Becher GmH & Co KG* [1988] 2 Lloyd's Rep 21, 26; *Trasimex Holdings SA v. Addax BV (The Red Sea)* [1999] 1 Lloyd's Rep 29.

in the carriage and trade law realms in order to strengthen the view that the RR will have an impact on international trade law.

1.4 Interfaces between trade and carriage

Maritime transport operates for the transmission of goods purchased between domestic and international traders, and is therefore to a great extent performed across international borders. The cargo transported is therefore the link that bonds the carriage contract with the contract of sale. Arguably, it has been acknowledged by the draftsmen of the RR that carriage reflects on several fields of trade, especially in the sale contract and letter of credit realms.[83] Therefore, carriage and trade contracts have interfaces which occasionally trouble courts, as they try to separate them and identify the proper remedies under the proper contract. Studying this illustrates the controversial, for trade purposes, impact of certain provisions of the RR on rights or documents. We may notice a conflict or ambiguity in the way a sale right or obligation can be performed under the hypothetical application of the said provisions of the RR.[84] The underlying cause of this problem is the difficulty in transposing concepts from carriage to sale contracts.

Laytime and demurrage clauses are representative examples of the intensive interfaces between carriage and trade laws. These clauses usually stem from carriage contracts, but it is not rare to also find them in sale contracts.[85] Two points need to be clarified here. First, as stated several times before, carriage contracts are entered into to enable the performance of sale of goods transactions.[86] Second, charterparty laytime and demurrage clauses are inserted into contracts to compensate the carrier for any delay in the loading and discharge of the cargo, which, depending on the type of sale contract and the circumstances, may be caused by the seller or buyer. To the extent that a delay and consequently demurrage is caused by the charterer's counterparty to the sale contract, the charterer is interested in passing that cost on to his sale counterparty.[87]

Nevertheless, a demurrage clause in a sale contract, specifying the time within which the loading or discharge should be completed, exists independently and stands to specify the relevant duties of seller and buyer vis-à-vis one another.[88]

83 von Ziegler, 'Rotterdam Rules and the underlying sales contract', p. 277.

84 See especially Articles 8, 9, 10, 35, 47(2) and 80 of the RR as well as the concept of the right of control when examined from a trade perspective.

85 Jason Chuah, 'Laytime and demurrage clauses in contracts of sale – A survey of the New York Society of Maritime Arbitrators' awards (1978–2008) and English case law' in DR Thomas (ed), *The Evolving Law and Practice of Charterparties* (Informa 2009), para 9.1.

86 Charles Debattista, 'Laytime and demurrage clauses in contracts of sale – Links and connections' [2003] LMCLQ 508.

87 Ibid, p. 509. According to Charles Debattista, "The purpose of an L&D (laytime and demurrage) clause in the sale contract is to pass on to the counterparty to the sale contract the cost of demurrage paid to the shipowner by the charterer but caused by delay by the charterer's counterparty under the sale contract."

88 Ibid, p. 510.

The way these clauses should be construed, namely whether they should be interpreted in light of their particular commercial and not carriage context when found in sale contracts, is of considerable value[89] and has been judicially debated. The question for the courts has been to ascertain whether the demurrage clauses have been used as a device for bringing carriage provisions and charterparty underpinnings into a sale contract, where demurrage provisions would function as indemnity clauses,[90] or whether the sale and carriage contracts should be treated as separate and independent.[91] In *Fal Oil v. Petronas*,[92] the sale contract was concluded prior to the charterparty (which was on standard *Asbatankvoy*), and in fact, the laytime provisions in the sale and carriage contracts did not match each other.[93] Coming back to our question, the Court of Appeal judgment took the latter view, holding that the contracts were concluded independently from each other, considering the circumstances (of time and lack of foreseeability of what the charterparty would stipulate).[94] Another factor that weighed in this judgment was the likelihood that the laytime and demurrage clauses could vary among the four different charterparties.[95]

It has been argued that an independent construction of laytime and demurrage clauses of a sale contract is more in line with the priniciple of commercial certainty.[96]

In *The Bonde*,[97] an FOB contract contained a demurrage clause ("demurrage to be for sellers' account at charter-party rate") and it was followed by a provision of carrying charges, if the vessel filed after the shipment period. The buyers argued that demurrage clauses carried a wider function in the sale contract, which extends to ensuring delivery of the goods at the required time and place for the price.[98] Therefore, they contended that demurrage clauses do not merely relate to the classic carriage consequence of detention of the ship because of exceeding laytime.[99] Potter J held that:

89 Ibid.

90 Question posed and answered by Chuah, 'Laytime and demurrage clauses in contracts of sale – A survey of the New York Society of Maritime Arbitrators' awards (1978–2008) and English case law', para 9.2.

91 Chuah, 'Laytime and demurrage clauses in contracts of sale – A survey of the New York Society of Maritime Arbitrators' awards (1978–2008) and English case law', para 9.7.

92 *Fal Oil Co Ltd; Credit Agricole Indosuez (Suisse) SA v. Petronas Trading Corporation Sdn Bhd (The Devon)* [2004] EWCA Civ 822.

93 Chuah, 'Laytime and demurrage clauses in contracts of sale – A survey of the New York Society of Maritime Arbitrators' awards (1978–2008) and English case law', paras 9.4–9.6.

94 See also John Schoefield, *Laytime and Demurrage* (6th edn, Informa 2011), paras 6.284–6.286.

95 [2004] EWCA Civ 822, at [44]. See also Chuah, 'Laytime and demurrage clauses in contracts of sale – A survey of the New York Society of Maritime Arbitrators' awards (1978–2008) and English case law', para 9.7.

96 Chuah, 'Laytime and demurrage clauses in contracts of sale – A survey of the New York Society of Maritime Arbitrators' awards (1978–2008) and English case law', paras 9.13–9.15.

97 *Richco International Ltd v. Alfred C Toepfer International GmbH (The Bonde)* [1991] 1 Lloyd's Rep 136.

98 Ibid, 142.

99 Ibid.

> the sellers were right in their submissions that the purpose for the importation from the charter-party of a loading rate clause was to provide the mechanism for effecting the reimbursement of demurrage as between buyer and seller and the purpose for inserting the laytime provisions was because it was anticipated that the buyer would charter a vessel and would have to agree with the owner of the vessel on the time for loading.[100]

This judgment has been criticised from the point of view that laytime should be interpreted in light of the sale contractual nexus that binds seller and buyer.[101] In the opinion of Professor Chuah, in *The Devon (Fal Oil)*, Buxton LJ, who gave the dissenting judgment, reasoned by defining commercial sense in a wide way.[102] That presumably was that demurrage clauses are inserted into sale contracts in order to provide back to back coverage for the party liable for demurrage under the charterparty. This wider picture does not take into consideration the practicalities of the particular industry or trade.[103]

The dichotomy of whether laytime and demurrage clauses in a sale contract should be treated as free-standing, thus dealt with individually in their sale realm, or as indemnification clauses, thus tightly linked to the relevant charterparty stipulations, obtains different dimensions also from a jurisdictional point of view. For instance, in the US, whether the issue will be treated as a maritime or commercial dispute will determine the jurisdiction of the proper courts.[104] There is case law that has been concerned with whether the dispute should fall under federal or local state jurisdiction.[105]

The example of treatment of demurrage and laytime clauses was conferred as an illustration here, because it is another crucial interface where the same clauses are occasionally treated differently, either as back to back indemnity clauses, or as free-standing independent terms pertaining to the specific sale contractual matrix without necessary references to the charterparty contract. As we shall see as this book unravels, new concepts or provisions of the RR inserted therein from a carriage viewpoint, will reflect on trade, perhaps giving rise to confusions. These "crossovers" are namely the transport documents, their divisions and especially the fact that it is now possible to deal with a transport document not requiring surrender. The aforementioned dubious approach towards laytime and demurrage clauses in sale and charterparty contracts should make the trading

100 Ibid.

101 Debattista, 'Laytime and demurrage clauses in contracts of sale – Links and connections', p. 523.

102 Chuah, 'Laytime and demurrage clauses in contracts of sale – A survey of the New York Society of Maritime Arbitrators' awards (1978–2008) and English case law', paras 9.27, 9.28.

103 Ibid, para 9.27; ibid, para 9.26 for analysis of Jason Chuah on the intricacies of the oil trade.

104 Ibid, paras 9.35–9.36.

105 See for instance *Aston Agro Industrial v. Star Grain Ltd* (SDNY 2006) 06 CV 2805 (GBD) 2006 U.S.LEXIS 91636; *Norfolk Southern Railway Co v. Kirby* 543 US 14, 125 SCt 385, 160 L Ed 2d 283 (2004); *Exxon Corp v. Central Gulf Lines Inc* 500 US 603, 612, 111 s Ct 2071, 114 L Ed 2d 649 (1991).

community suspicious of probable debates in trade aspects (parties, roles, rights and documents) governed in their carriage dimension in the RR. We will not refer to the concept of demurrage any further, as freight issues per se are not covered by the RR.[106] However, the illustration of the puzzling construction of laytime and demurrage provisions is perhaps the classic "crossover" of carriage and trade, as also shown by recent case law. Similar problems may be seen also under the operation of the RR in trade.[107]

If one supposes that the above issues of jurisdictional distinction of carriage and trade matters in the US may be relevant also under the application of the RR, it could be concluded that they could cause disharmony; thus, they are of valid concern. The classic link connecting transportation and trade is the transport document.[108] For example, let us imagine the following scenario: a transport document is issued by the carrier to the seller and then transferred to the buyer. Undesirably to the buyer, this document is considered a bad tender, because it is electronic (or the opposite),[109] or non-negotiable (or the opposite), by virtue of custom.[110] It is disputed between the carrier and the cargo interests whether this document was the one that the shipper was entitled to under Article 35 of the RR on the one hand, and whether this is the document that the seller is obliged to tender under the provisions of the sale contract on the other. This could equally be considered as a carriage and a trade dispute, or, to put it more accurately, a dispute with trade and carriage interfaces. Assuming that this dispute would fall under US jurisdiction, the trading parties and the carrier could face jurisdictional problems, as sale matters are conferred before state courts, whereas carriage disputes fall under admiralty jurisdiction and could be taken before the federal courts.

Which document constitutes a good tender under a sale contract or a subsequent sale contract in string sales is of critical importance throughout this book. This is perhaps the most important indication of how difficult it is to have a carriage concept operating in the same way in the trade law realm. In a scenario of string sales, as with demurrage and laytime clauses,[111] it is important to look at the position of the first seller (who is also the shipper) and his possibility to enforce sale rights in relation to the documents and goods and rights of control and delivery against the carrier, without disregarding, at the same time, the position of the potential on-buyers who inherit that contract of carriage. Investigating how the RR reflect on trade, and de-tangling these carriage and trade interactions, is a complex mission. Thus, we will bring to the surface complexities that the trading

106 Freight is mentioned in Articles 1(24), 42 and 60 of the RR

107 *Profindo Pte Ltd v. Abani Trading Pte Ltd* [2013] SGHC 10 (District Court Appeal No. 5 of 2012).

108 von Ziegler, 'Rotterdam Rules and the underlying sales contract', p. 276.

109 See specific discussion on e-commerce in Chapter 4 of the book.

110 For the relationship between custom and agreement when it comes to the choice of the negotiable character of the document, see Chapter 3 of this book.

111 Chuah, 'Laytime and demurrage clauses in contracts of sale – A survey of the New York Society of Maritime Arbitrators' awards (1978–2008) and English case law', para 9.61.

parties are unaware of for two reasons: firstly, the RR regulate matters on which previous conventions were silent; and secondly, no one has yet moved to the effort to interpret the RR from a trade law perspective, as the carriage interpretation is already significantly puzzling in certain articles.

Another sale concept which may constitute a "crossover" under certain circumstances with the RR is that of stoppage in transit. Additionally, delivery of the goods is a function with great carriage and trade importance, and in that respect, the sometimes inadequate, from the receiver's perspective, check duties of the carrier have been criticised. Additionally, a thorough discussion has been devoted to the impact of Article 47(2) of the RR on the negotiability of bills, and the problem of wrongful delivery. In that respect, the particular practical needs of certain areas of trade had to be accommodated by the RR, but a general application of the article, for instance in trades where reliance on the negotiable transport document is sacrosanct, reveals a potential controversial application of the RR.

Eventually it will be shown from the provisions of the RR discussed in the book, that certain provisions enable carriage to perform smoothly at times, usually by giving the carrier the relevant rights. To the extent that these rights are performed with an impact on the cargo interest, especially the one who has not negotiated the carriage contract, one understands that the interfaces of transport and commerce deriving from the core interest in the goods themselves (documents representing them, rights as to form/negotiability of the documents, instructions, right of control, stoppage in transit) are by definition uneven.

In essence, in the pursuit to identify the difficulty of transplanting carriage concepts into trade, one would see that, depending on the RR and the thoroughness of drafting of the carriage and sale contracts, the RR may offer flexibility to the detriment of legal certainty (see, for instance, volume contracts) or, on the other hand, be too specific, thus leaving no margin for the desired trade flexibility (see, for instance, the analysis of non-negotiable electronic records). The RR, in broad lines, show what the shipper and carrier *may* agree, but in an international trade law dispute, we care about what the seller/shipper *should* tender to the buyer. There is a notional gap between these two underpinnings, that affects the contract of carriage that the trader inherits by his sale counterparty, and which similarly determines whether he can perform his duties towards his own buyer.

It is now time to see how the carriage and trade spheres overlap under the application of the RR. This is important in order to justify the assertion that the RR will have an impact on trade. It was mentioned previously that the Hague Rules tried to yield a fair risk allocation liability regime. This risk concerns the contingency of loss, damage, short-delivery or delay in the goods delivered. This is not only a carriage risk, but it also bears significance for international trade law.

In order to understand it, let us imagine a CIF contract scenario. The carriage contract to be arranged by the seller and, more precisely, the terms on the carrier's liability contracted for thereunder directly affect the position of the buyer. If a buyer undertakes greater liabilities under the contract of carriage, this usually means that the buyer stands in a more secure legal position in this contract of carriage.

Here is the reason. This carriage contract being subject to an international maritime convention (for instance, the HVR or the RR) becomes relevant to the buyer from the moment he claims delivery of the goods. If a bill of lading has been issued, then this will represent for the CIF buyer the evidence of the contract of carriage determining what remedies he can have against his carrier. Therefore, a fair allocation of risks between the carrier and cargo interests is an issue of common importance for trade and carriage.[112] It has to be re-emphasised here that another common thread behind trade and carriage is the transport document and its functions.

The RR seek predictability of liability for a network of parties with a primary focus on shippers, the carriers. The RR devote an important part of their provisions to transport documents. They also apply to contracts of carriage, and, if a transport document is issued, they also apply to transport documents.

For international sale contracts on the other hand, a transport document (bill of lading or sea waybill) is essential in order to assess compliance of the seller with the sale contract. However, for international trade law purposes getting the right transport document is much more important. For payment to take place in international commercial sales, the seller has to tender the appropriate documents to the buyer.[113] Therefore, it is of the utmost importance that the seller/deliverer of the goods obtains the transport document to be tendered to the buyer, so that he can show performance of the sale contract. This way, the transport document serves as evidence of the contract of carriage concluded by the seller/deliverer.[114]

The RR are applicable to contracts of carriage and not to transport documents, which means that, under their scope, a transport document does not, in principle, have to be issued.[115] Conflictingly, in international trade, the existence of the transport documents is pre-eminent for documentary performance, and thus for the overall compliance with the sale contract. However, the above remark does not negate the fact that both trade and carriage laws and rules have an interest for certainty and predictability.[116] This is particularly relevant in the context of sales down a string.

We will now discuss how the RR, which is a carriage convention, affect the certainty and predictability that underpin cross-border commerce.

In the trade of commodities, there is an interest in the goods themselves, but many traders are more interested in reselling them and making profit from the resale.[117] For bulk commodities, there will be multiple back to back sale contracts

112 See Debattista, *Bills of Lading in Export Trade*, pp. 84–85.

113 By virtue of article A3 of the Incoterms® and the case law above.

114 Or, of the contract of carriage procured by the first seller, if sales down a string are contemplated. This is reflected in the wording of *Comptoir d'Achat et de Vente du Boerenbond Belge S/A v. Luis de Ridder Limitada (The Julia)* [1949] AC 293: "on or as from shipment".

115 Bridge, *The International Sale of Goods*, para 3.21. For the relationship between the contract of carriage with a subsequently issued bill of lading, see *Pyrene Co Ltd v. Scindia Navigation Co Ltd* [1954] 2 QB 402, 419 per Devlin J.

116 Takahashi, 'Right to terminate (avoid) international sales of commodities', p. 104.

117 Ibid.

for the purchase of a quantity of goods shipped once.[118] Thus, if the market is plummeting, it is in the buyer's interest to terminate the contract. Bridge[119] states that unless the sale contract specifies otherwise, a bill of lading will have to be tendered.[120] However, if by virtue of the RR a non-negotiable transport document is issued,[121] this will be a "bad" tender, under a sale contract, if a sub-sale is contemplated. Bridge also fits transport documents, other than the bill of lading, under the expression "usual transport document" in article A8 of the CIF Incoterms® 2010.[122] The buyer's practical need for a document of title is greater if payment will take place via a letter of credit; in this case, a seller might have to pledge the bill prior to documentary tender or he may get it from the bank on trust receipt terms so that he can successfully claim delivery of the cargo from the carrier.[123]

Especially if the buyer does not possess the goods, it can be said that the documents tendered may endow him with rights of rejection of documents. A documentary defect or delivery of a non-negotiable document instead of a negotiable one are grounds triggering the right of the buyer to terminate the sale contract. This calls for the examination of whether the RR through their articles allow the seller *qua* shipper/documentary shipper to request the type of transport document requested by the sale contract, discussed in Chapter 2.

Section 32(2) of the Sale of Goods Act 1979 (SOGA) also becomes relevant in the context of CIF sales. Is the transport document tendered arming the buyer with the necessary rights against a carrier? This is important, since the risk of deterioration, damage and delay of goods passes from the seller to the buyer at the moment of shipment.[124] This is particularly relevant when a volume contract departs from the RR. This is discussed in Chapter 5.

All the aforementioned grounds demonstrate the conceptual common spine of the legal issues of maritime trade, in that an international carriage convention, is usually significant for rights under sale contracts, especially as far as documents/records are concerned. Whether a document/record is a good tender is a question to be cross-examined under international trade and carriage conventions, legislation and self-regulatory terms.

This analysis proves that to the extent that the RR regulate rights under a carriage contract through documents issued, they are of great international trade law importance. The conditions under which types of documents/records are

118 Bridge, *The International Sale of Goods*, para 4.06.

119 Ibid, para 4.68.

120 Ibid.

121 *McWilliam (JI) Co Inc v. Mediterranean Shipping Co (The Rafaela S)* [2005] 2 AC 423 at [46], per Lord Steyn.

122 See Bridge, *The International Sale of Goods*, para 4.68 and fn 241 therein.

123 Ibid, para 4.73.

124 Under English law, passage of risk in sales on shipment terms passes on or as from shipment: *Comptoir d'Achat et de Vente du Boerenbond Belge SA v. Luis de Ridder Limitada (The Julia)* [1949] AC 293; *Manbre Saccharine Co Ltd v. Corn Products Co Ltd* [1919] 1 KB 198. See also Incoterms® 2010, CIF and FOB, article A3.

issued under the RR have a varied effect on the need of trade for legal certainty, flexibility and predictability. The degree of these tenets determines whether sales down a string can be facilitated or even performed.

1.5 Conclusion

International trade and carriage laws attribute significance to the same characteristics, but occasionally prioritise them differently. Their underpinnings have been respectively presented so that one understands their difference, and consequently their contrast. Whenever unwelcome trade repercussions are identified, these will only be resolved if the principles of international commercial law gain preponderance over those of carriage. We will demonstrate in what circumstances additional terms[125] and careful contract drafting may be needed in a sale contract where shipment of the goods will be subject to a carriage contract to which the RR apply; and we will delineate what this wording should safeguard against.

In Chapter 2, the key provisos and terminology for the trade protagonists introduced by the RR will be presented. This will offer the background for understanding how, surprisingly, provisions inserted by the RR to rectify problems of trade[126] may prove unsatisfactory in other respects when goods are sold down a string. An awareness of international trade legal issues will be followed by contractual and regulatory solutions.

125 In an attempt to resolve ambiguities stemming from the RR, we will make suggestions for additional trade terms, either individually negotiated by the parties (contractual), or drafted by bodies such as the ICC, or last national legislation, where the particular example of the UK will be of reference.

126 Such examples are the articles of the RR on the documentary shipper and the right of control.

2 Novelties of the Rotterdam Rules

Do they facilitate international trade?

2.1 Introduction

In this chapter, the central provisions of the RR which are novel and at the same time critical for international trade law will be presented. These are significant, either because they initiate new entities that did not exist in previous international carriage conventions, or because they change the law, as framed by these conventions and English law.[1] Some of these provisions are presented because they create grey areas as to rights which need to be clarified when looking at them alone;[2] they also have to be studied alongside other standard terms of international trade law which also apply in the shipping contracts[3] or because they conflict with other terms of international trade law.[4] This chapter will analyse specific provisions of the RR which may have a positive or negative impact on international trade law. We will discuss the need for flexibility or legal certainty in the following areas: in getting the transport document so that the seller complies with the sale contract; in controlling the goods to protect the real cargo owner's interests; and in ensuring delivery of the goods to the proper receiver.

1 Although the UK is not a signatory to the RR, the impact of the RR on English law was considered of high importance due to the leading role of English law (especially of the Carriage of Goods by Sea Act 1992 and the Sale of Goods Act 1979) in shipping and overseas commercial contracts. The scope of this book is centred around the impact of the RR on international sale contracts concluded on English law terms, which may also incorporate transnational legal instruments (namely the Incoterms® and the UCP 600). Although these contracts are of an international character, as the buyer and seller will be located in different countries, English law will to a great extent be the law of reference. It is usually the parties' choice to have English law as the law applicable to their contract, in the use of their individually negotiated and standard terms. This choice is instructed by the effectiveness of English law in commercial matters and the expertise of English courts in commercial and maritime disputes.

2 Generally harmonisation may not have a uniformly successful or crystal clear effect. See Chuah, *Law of International Trade: Cross-border Commercial transactions*, para 1-032 and Munday, 'The uniform interpretation of international conventions' [1978] *ICLQ* 450.

3 By shipping contracts we broadly refer to the carriage contract and the sale contract for the goods carried by sea.

4 Harmonisation may not be entirely successful over all the desirable issues: see Chuah, *Law of International Trade: Cross-border Commercial Transactions*, para 1-032; also Munday, 'The uniform interpretation of International Conventions'. Also Charles Debattista, 'Carriage conventions and their interpretation in English Courts' [1997] *JBL* 130.

2.2 The terminology of the Rotterdam Rules

The RR are innovative in the sense that they apply to contracts of carriage with an international sea leg and not merely to bills of lading, as is the case with the HVR.[5] The concept of the documentary shipper has been introduced to support the commercial interest of the FOB seller in getting the transport document from the carrier.[6] Additionally, the term "bill of lading" has disappeared, and instead there are transport records, which are negotiable and non-negotiable. Documents are further divided into documents requiring and not requiring surrender.[7] Next to the documents, there is the term electronic transport record, inaugurating electronic commerce provisions in the RR.

Next, the roles of shipper and documentary shipper are examined. These will prepare for the scenarios to follow, which will come to show how the RR, instead of facilitating trade, may increase uncertainty to the trade protagonists.

2.3 Shipper and documentary shipper in FOB sales

Article 1(8) of the RR reads as follows: "shipper means a person that enters into a contract of carriage with a carrier". Since the FOB buyer is the person entering into a contract of carriage with the carrier,[8] he[9] qualifies as a shipper under the RR. Under this capacity, even if one looks at the HVR,[10] the FOB buyer/shipper is primarily the person authorised to request issuance of the bill of lading to himself under the carriage contract. However, the seller needs the bill of lading in the first place to prove shipment of the goods. To allow for this contingency, the RR initiated the entity of the "documentary shipper".[11] This is defined as "a person, other than the shipper, that accepts to be named as 'shipper' in the transport document or electronic transport record".[12]

Although, prima facie, one would assume that an FOB seller is always a documentary shipper from the inclusion of his name in the shipper's box, this would be frivolous. An FOB seller does not automatically qualify as a documentary shipper; in practice he may deny becoming a documentary shipper so that he avoids liabilities.[13] As we shall see further down, a transport document may not be

5 Article 6 of the RR; Mbiah, 'Updating the rules on international carriage of goods by sea: The Rotterdam Rules', p. 314.

6 See Yuzhuo and Zhang, 'An Analysis and Assessment on the Rotterdam Rules in China's Marine Industry', p. 7.

7 This further division stems indirectly from the entirety of provisions of the RR, especially Article 47(2), which regulates delivery without surrender of the document/record.

8 FOB, articles A3 and B3 of the Incoterms®, publication No. 715 E.

9 For simplicity purposes we use the pronoun "he" to replace the words buyer, seller, shipper, documentary shipper, carrier, holder and consignee.

10 HVR article III r.3.

11 Gertjan van der Ziel, 'The issue of transport documents and the documentary shipper under the Rotterdam Rules' available online.

12 Article 1(9) of the RR.

13 As per Article 33 of the RR.

issued. In essence, no conclusive answer as to the time the documentary shipper comes into existence can be voiced, before looking at Article 35 of the RR. This states that the documentary shipper may request a transport document/record with the consent of the shipper.[14]

However, as we shall see, the "device" of the documentary shipper is not a panacea for FOB sellers, as it is an option (depending on the shipper's decision) and not an obligation. The problematic position of an FOB seller who is not named as documentary shipper on the transport document is discussed forthwith.

2.4 The right of the FOB seller to request the transport document and the right to delivery

Here, our objective is to investigate the difficult position of an FOB seller who is not named as a documentary shipper under his sale contract. The purpose is to elaborate on how an FOB seller not having the transport document can protect his payment or property rights,[15] when the RR apply, but also in order to investigate whether and how the RR allow him to perform his sale contract obligations.

An FOB sale is different from a CIF contract as the buyer is the party arranging for the sea transportation.[16] Accordingly, the seller is not a party to the contract of carriage, so he cannot qualify as the shipper, as defined in Article 1(8) of the RR.[17] As he is not the shipper, he cannot ask for the issuance of the transport document.[18] Having loaded the goods, he will then find himself in possession of the mate's receipt, usually signed by the master or an agent. Sometimes the contract of carriage might also provide (as many charterparties do) that the bill of lading may be obtained in exchange for the mate's receipt.[19] If the seller obtains the bill of lading (or negotiable transport document) and is named on it as (documentary) shipper, he can then obtain the capacity of the documentary shipper, as defined in Article 1(9) of the RR.

The FOB seller will be qualified as such, where the shipper has accepted that the former is so named in the transport document, thus acquiring the rights

14 Subject to the agreement and the custom.

15 On these see extensively Richard Zwitser, 'Cash against mate's receipt under the Rotterdam Rules' (2010) 16(5) *JIML* 380, p. 396.

16 FOB, A3, B3, ICC Publication No. 715E. Under English law see Chuah, *Law of International Trade: Cross-border Commercial Transactions*, paras 2-029 to 2-032; *Cowasjee v. Thomson* (1845) 5 Moore PC 165; *Pyrene Co Ltd v. Scindia Navigation Co Ltd* [1954] 2 QB 402; *Wimble, Sons & Co Ltd v. Rosenberg & Sons* [1913] 3 KB743. See generally, Jason Chuah, 'The FOB seller as shipper' (2007) SL Rev 50(Spr), 54.

17 The FOB seller would qualify as a shipper, had the Hamburg Rules been applicable. Under article 1.3 of the Hamburg Rules, "shipper means any person by whom or in whose name or on whose behalf a contract of carriage of goods by sea has been concluded with a carrier, or any person by whom or in whose name or on whose behalf the goods are actually delivered to the carrier in relation to the contract of carriage by sea".

18 Article 35 of the RR.

19 See Zwitser, 'Cash against mate's receipt under the Rotterdam Rules', p. 381.

and obligations of the shipper.[20] If this happens, then as Article 35 of the RR stipulates, the FOB seller is entitled to request the transport document at the shipper's option. The unpleasant repercussions for an FOB seller who would like to be but in fact is not mentioned as a shipper on the transport document will be further elaborated on.

2.4.1 Trade difficulties when holding a document which is not a transport document under the Rotterdam Rules

The relevance of the above analysis becomes obvious from the following example given by Zwitser:

> It is assumed that an FOB seller ships the goods in good order and condition. The transport document is directly issued to the buyer/shipper, and the latter fails to pay the seller for the goods.[21]

As Zwitser has rightly pointed out, three possibilities need to be investigated:[22] firstly, whether or not the unpaid seller can ask for the transport document, so that he exercises control over the goods until payment is obtained; secondly, whether he can claim the goods; and thirdly, whether he can at least instruct the carrier not to deliver the goods to the buyer until payment is received, depending on whether the document is negotiable or non-negotiable.

As discussed above, had the transport document named the seller as documentary shipper, then the seller would be perfectly entitled to request that it is issued to him; that way he would have the document as a protection until he receives payment.

However, as there is no obligation for the seller to be named as the documentary shipper in a transport document, the FOB seller can only secure his position by inserting a relevant provision in the contract of sale. As an FOB sale is usually concluded prior to the shipment of the goods, it may provide for all the obligations of the parties. This being the case, it is permissible that the sale agreement illustrates how the carriage contract should be drafted. The role of the documentary shipper introduced by Articles 1(9) and 35 of the RR would arguably allow an exception to the privity of contract doctrine,[23] as indeed the seller

20 Articles 1(9), 33 and 35 of the RR.

21 On the above see Zwitser, 'Cash against mate's receipt under the Rotterdam Rules', p. 396. The same steps need to be followed when it is impossible to request a transport document and instead only a mate's receipt is issued.

22 These concerns were expressed in Zwitser, 'Cash against mate's receipt under the Rotterdam Rules', p. 396.

23 See The Law Commission, 'privity of contract: contracts for the benefit of third parties', Item 1 of the Sixth Programme of Law Reform: The Law of Contract, at lawcommission.justice.gov.uk/docs/lc242_privity_of_contract_for_the_benefit_of_third_parties.pdf. The doctrine is explained to mean "a contract does not confer rights on someone who is not a party to the contract".

becomes, with the consent of the buyer, a party to the contract of carriage from the perspective of the RR.

Continuing with the hypothetical scenario of Zwitser, assuming that the seller is not mentioned as a documentary shipper, the next question of interest for international trade law is this: in a case where a buyer has further sold the goods but the first seller remains unpaid, can the unpaid seller ask for the delivery of the goods at the port of destination, bypassing the last buyer?[24] Article 47(1) of the RR is critical:

> When a negotiable transport document or negotiable transport record has been issued: (a) the holder of the negotiable transport document or negotiable transport electronic record is entitled to claim delivery of the goods from the carrier after they have arrived at the place of destination [...].

With regards to who is to claim delivery of the goods, the wording of the RR is sufficiently clear. If the document is negotiable, no party other than the holder of the transport document, i.e. the buyer, has the right to claim delivery. Therefore the real owner of the cargo (the FOB seller) remains unprotected.

The last resort of the seller in this problematic situation would be a right to give instructions to the carrier to deliver to the mate's receipt holder instead of the bill of lading holder. Do the RR give such a possibility? If on the one hand, the document is negotiable not requiring surrender, Article 47(2)(a)(ii) of the RR would designate that if the carrier is not convinced that the holder is entitled to delivery, he would seek instructions from the shipper and documentary shipper, and the FOB seller is neither of them. If the document is non-negotiable, Article 45(c)(ii) of the RR is applicable, and the outcome is the same. This states that in the absence of the name and address of the consignee, it is the controlling party who can advise the carrier of such a name and address.

Accordingly, if the transport document in the above hypothetical scenario does not contain the name and address of the consignee, which very frequently happens it is the controlling party who should give these instructions.[25] The definition of the controlling party in Article 1(13) refers the reader to Article 51 of the RR. The first paragraph of this article sets the default position.

To conclude, it seems that the RR do not provide a solution to the complexities which arise from the mate's receipt being the only document an unpaid FOB seller possesses; it is apparent that this does not qualify as a transport document as it is merely a receipt for shipment and does not evidence the contract of carriage.[26] The root of the problem in that case is that the RR do not automatically consider

24 Zwitser, 'Cash against mate's receipt under the Rotterdam Rules', p. 396.

25 Article 45(b) of the RR states: "If the name and address of the consignee are not referred to in the contract particulars, the controlling party shall prior to or upon the arrival of the goods at the place of destination advise the carrier of such name and address".

26 In A/CN.9/645, para 114, it is stated that a mere receipt would not constitute a transport document for the purposes of the Convention. See also Treitel and Reynolds (eds), *Carver on Bills of Lading* (3rd edn), para 8-099, fn 551 therein, and Treitel and Reynolds (eds), *Carver on Bills of*

the consignor/FOB seller as a documentary shipper. On a secondary level, one could also attribute this commercial uncertainty to the fact that the RR have a scope that looks beyond negotiable documents, but this does not extend beyond sea waybills.

The situation remains as it was under the HVR. However, we suggest that the legal position of the FOB seller/mate's receipt holder against the non-contractual buyer's actions, when the goods have been sold on to another buyer, should be secured otherwise.

One solution would be the insertion of a provision into the contract of sale requiring that the seller is mentioned as the documentary shipper on the transport document. Alternatively the parties can agree to trade over a mate's receipt instead of a negotiable transport document.[27] Nevertheless, it is doubtful whether this will be welcomed by the trade community, as it is risky to trade over a document which does not give title to sue.[28]

If no step is taken in that direction by the parties, it will then be the decision of the courts to resolve the inequitableness that arises in the above situation. This means that the unpaid FOB mate's receipt holder should be considered as a party to the contract of carriage. This could be achieved if the courts adopt a reasoning similar to the one taken in *Pyrene v. Scindia*.[29] This case concerned a sale on FOB terms. While a fire tender was being lifted and before passing the ship's rail, it was dropped and damaged. As Devlin J held, it should be implied that since loading is part of carriage, despite the bill of lading not being issued, the intention of the original parties to the contract should have been that the seller is also a party to the carriage contract.[30]

The unfairness noted for the unpaid documentary shipper/mate's receipt holder stems from the importance attached by the RR to transport documents, divided into negotiable and non-negotiable, thus embracing the current trade division of bills of lading, straight bills of lading and sea waybills. The importance of transport documents will be more visible in Chapter 3.

Lading (4th edn), para 8-019 to 8-023. The mate's receipt is not a transport document or electronic transport record, because it does not evidence or contain a contract of carriage; *Nippon Yusen Kaisha v. Ramjiban Serowgee* [1938] AC 429. Exceptionally, in the case *Wah Tat Bank Ltd and Overseas Chinese Banking Corp Ltd v. Chan Cheng Kum and Hua Siang Steamship Co (Singapore) Ltd (Third Parties)* [1967] 2 Lloyd's Rep 437, the Federal Court of Malaysia was convinced that by virtue of a custom in the local trade the mate's receipt was treated as a document of title.

27 See Zwitser, 'Cash against mate's receipt under the Rotterdam Rules', p. 381.

28 Under English law, the mate's receipt is not mentioned in section 1(4) of the Factors Act 1889, which lists examples of documents of title; Debattista, 'Legislative techniques in international trade: Madness or method?', p. 629.

29 *Pyrene Co Ltd v. Scindia Navigation Co Ltd* [1954] 2 QB 402.

30 Ibid, p. 426. It was stated: "In brief, I think the inference irresistible that it was the intention of all three parties that the seller should participate in the contract of affreightment so far as it affected him".

For now, after considering the obstacles that ensue in this FOB sale scenario, the text of the RR seems to follow a much more literal classification of documents, in which the mate's receipt is not being acknowledged as a transport document, failing to evidence the contract of carriage.

Now the analysis will shift to more complex issues. As expected, the relevant articles of the RR which are of key importance from a trade viewpoint are the ones that deal with delivery under negotiable and non-negotiable documents, rights of control and ways of transferring rights. Articles from Chapter 9 of the RR on delivery, Chapter 10 on rights of the controlling party, and Chapter 11 on transfer of rights will be particularly relevant for trade purposes. As we shall see, despite the intention to facilitate trade behind these provisos,[31] the synergies arising from the potential application of the RR and the SOGA in English law will be cumbersome.

More precisely, attention will now be paid to the role of the "controlling party". The rights of the controlling party deserve specific consideration for trade law purposes as this person will occasionally be *inter alia* the seller *qua* shipper, or the buyer *qua* shipper, or the consignee-buyer depending on who has the right of control. Investigation of the right of control is also a necessary sequence from the complexity noted in the FOB scenario above, so that we see what the seller can do if he remains unpaid for other reasons (e.g. due to the insolvency of the buyer).

2.5 Control of the goods under the SOGA and the Rotterdam Rules

Provisions on the right of control have been inserted in the RR to assist trading parties who would like to enforce their rights under their sale contracts by controlling the goods and instructing the carrier.[32] They were aimed at facilitating cooperation between the carrier and trade protagonists, which is why they also systematically fall under the scope of this chapter. On the acknowledgement of trade practicalities,[33] the drafting intention behind the RR in this specific respect was to insert a regulation analogous to the seller's right to control[34] the goods in transit, often referred to as the "right of stoppage in transit" under the SOGA.[35] The United Nations Convention on Contracts for the International Sale of Goods (CISG) also regulates stoppage in Article 71(2).[36]

31 Anders Møllmann, 'Right of control and transfer of rights' at curis.ku.dk/ws/files/22386264/Right_of_control_and_transfer_of_rights.doc.

32 See von Ziegler, 'Rotterdam Rules and the underlying sales contract', pp. 284, 285.

33 See Møllmann, 'Right of control and transfer of rights'.

34 On the nature of the right of control see generally Treitel and Reynolds (eds), *Carver on Bills of Lading* (4th edn), paras 1.032, 1.040.

35 Regulated by section 44 of the SOGA; Debattista, *Bills of Lading in Export Trade*, paras 2.50–2.56.

36 Article 71 of CISG reads: (1) A party may suspend the performance of his obligations if, after the conclusion of the contract, it becomes apparent that the other party will not perform a substantial part of his obligations as a result of: (a) a serious deficiency in his ability to perform or in his creditworthiness; or (b) his conduct in preparing to perform or in performing the contract. (2) If the seller has already dispatched the goods before the grounds described in the preceding paragraph

However, it is more accurate to say that the provisions of the RR on the right of control show an awareness of the trade dimensions and implications of the control of and interests in the goods carried, when for instance certain communication needs to take place between carrier and shipper or consignee.[37] This should not be taken to mean that the RR are exactly mirroring sale concepts, although this was the intention behind their addition;[38] in fact, the function of the right of control may clash with the exercise of the right of stoppage in transit. This will be unravelled in the following lines.

Article 51(1) of the RR lays down who the controlling party is in different circumstances:[39]

> Except in the cases referred to in paragraphs 2, 3 and 4 of this article:
>
> (a) The shipper is the controlling party unless the shipper, when the contract of carriage is concluded, designates the consignee, the documentary shipper or another person as the controlling party;
> (b) The controlling party is entitled to transfer the right of control to another person. The transfer becomes effective with respect to the carrier upon its notification of the transfer by the transferor, and the transferee becomes the controlling party; and
> (c) The controlling party shall properly identify itself when it exercises the right of control.

When a negotiable transport document is issued, the controlling party is the holder,[40] and when a non-negotiable document that requires surrender is issued, the shipper is at first the controlling party.

The controlling party is a new entity introduced by the RR and defined as the party who is entitled to exercise the right of control pursuant to Article 51 of the RR.[41] The right of control, defined in Article 1(12) of the RR, is the exclusive right to unilaterally give the carrier instructions regarding the goods while

become evident, he may prevent the handing over of the goods to the buyer even though the buyer holds a document which entitles him to obtain them. The present paragraph relates only to the rights in the goods as between the buyer and the seller. (3) A party suspending performance, whether before or after dispatch of the goods, must immediately give notice of the suspension to the other party and must continue with performance if the other party provides adequate assurance of his performance.

37 On the fine lines and interfaces between ownership, possession and control of the goods see MF Sturley, T Fujita and G van der Ziel, *The Rotterdam Rules* (Sweet & Maxwell 2010), paras 9.001 to 9.007.

38 On the drafting intentions behind the right of control with a view of matching trade concepts, see von Ziegler, 'The Rotterdam Rules and the underlying sales contract', p. 284.

39 Article 51(1) of the RR.

40 Article 51(3) of the RR.

41 See definition in Article 1(13) of the RR: "'Controlling party' means the person that pursuant to article 51 is entitled to exercise the right of control."

they are under the carrier's responsibility. Knowing who the controlling party is each time a relative right is exercised is very important for trade law purposes. According to Article 50(1) of the RR, the controlling party has the right to give or modify instructions in respect of the goods;[42] the right to obtain delivery of the goods at a specific port of call;[43] and the right to replace the consignee by any other person, including the controlling party.[44]

As it has been highlighted, the controlling party may not necessarily be the shipper.[45] Article 51 of the RR further lays down who may be the controlling party in different circumstances. If a negotiable document has been issued, the controlling party will be the holder of all three originals.[46] Therefore, if the right of control has been transferred, the carrier is under a duty to comply only with the instructions of the holder of the negotiable document, (and not with those of the shipper), as Article 50(1) of the RR designates. In the sale contract context, this is important when the shipper does not possess the transport document, although he needs it for payment, as illustrated in the previous section.

Attention now has to shift to the analysis of the compatibility of the right of control initiated by the RR with the right to stop the goods in transit in the SOGA.[47]

This study is of obvious international trade law significance, as it looks at the right to redirect delivery of the goods in order to protect the payment rights of the rightful seller.

Section 44 of the SOGA provides that when the buyer of goods becomes insolvent, the unpaid seller who has parted with the possession of the goods has the right of stopping them in transit, that is to say, he may resume possession of the goods as long as they are in course of transit and may retain them until payment or tender of the price.[48] Evidently, the right of stoppage is a property right, the transfer of which is subject to national laws.[49] Although, the RR govern issues stemming from the contract of carriage only and leave property rights aside, their provisions might in practice create confusion or conflict with the right of stoppage in transit under the SOGA.

The following scenario from Carver is illustrative:[50]

42 Article 50(1)(a) of the RR.

43 Article 50(1)(b) of the RR.

44 Article 50(1)(c) of the RR.

45 Treitel and Reynolds (eds), *Carver on Bills of Lading* (4th edn), paras 1.033–1.035.

46 Article 51(3)(a) of the RR.

47 On this issue, see also Treitel and Reynolds (eds), *Carver on Bills of Lading* (4th edn), para 1.038.

48 Debattista, *Bills of Lading in Export Trade*, para 2.55. These requirements need to run concurrently.

49 The SOGA applies to domestic sales, but also to international ones when the contract specifically requires that it be governed by English law. However, it has to be emphasised that the right of stoppage cannot be claimed when the transport document has been transferred to a third party and accepted in good faith and for value: Treitel and Reynolds (eds), *Carver on Bills of Lading* (4th edn), para 6.047, by virtue of section 10 of the Factors Act 1889 and section 47(2) of the SOGA.

50 This case scenario is from Treitel and Reynolds (eds) *Carver on Bills of Lading* (4th edn), para 1-038.

> Seller A ships the goods and gets a transport document to be transferred to B. A is not the controlling party, either because the transport document was transferred to B, or because the contract of carriage initially designated another person, in this case B, as the controlling party. B then sells the goods to C and instructs the carrier to deliver to C.

As per Carver, we suppose that B is the controlling party and that while the goods are in transit, B becomes insolvent. A, as the seller of B, wants the goods redirected to himself (A), as entitled under section 46(4) of the SOGA.[51] The critical question that emerges is this. If both the RR and the SOGA apply, shall the carrier follow the instructions of A for delivery to himself, or of B for delivery to C? Evidently, a conflict arises between section 46(4) of the SOGA and Article 51(2) of the RR.[52]

This kind of consideration somewhat arose, rather as *obiter*, in *AP Moller Maersk A/S v. Sonaec Villas Sen Sad Fadoul*,[53] where a straight bill of lading had been issued with the buyer being the named consignee under an FOB sale contract.

From the perspective of Article 50(1)(a) of the RR, the carrier is in no breach if he abides by the instructions of B, as this is the controlling party. On the other hand, the property rights of the unpaid seller remain unprotected. Prima facie, this conflict of the SOGA with the RR is justified[54] by the different relationships that the two instruments protect, namely property rights in the sale contractual sphere under the SOGA and control in transit in a purely carriage context under the RR. Nevertheless the exercise of the control and stoppage rights through the instructions given to the carrier will trigger legal uncertainty. This may lead to litigation; therefore, this ambiguity needs to be resolved.

We believe that it will be up to the UK legislation, either to harmonise or put a hierarchy between the sections of the SOGA and the RR (if ratified and enacted); otherwise one right will seem to interfere with and even actually work to the detriment of the other.

Alternatively, it can be argued that the sale contract can prevent such a contingency, if it is concluded before the contract of carriage. The sale contract may, for instance, stipulate that a negotiable bill of lading should be issued[55] and made

51 Article 46(4) of the SOGA reads: "When notice of stoppage in transit is given by the seller to the carrier or other bailee or custodier in possession of the goods, he must re-deliver the goods to, or according to the directions of, the seller; and the expenses of the re-delivery must be borne by the seller".

52 Article 51(2)(a) of the RR reads: "When a non-negotiable transport document has been issued that indicates that it shall be surrendered in order to obtain delivery of the goods: (a) The shipper is the controlling party and may transfer the right of control to the consignee named in the transport document by transferring the 35 document to that person without endorsement. If more than one original of the document was issued, all originals shall be transferred in order to effect a transfer of the right of control".

53 [2010] EWHC 355 Comm.

54 Treitel and Reynolds (eds) *Carver on Bills of Lading* (4th edn), para 1-038.

55 See also Articles 35 and 47 of the RR.

out to the order of the seller. In this case, the seller may, by withholding the bill of lading, pass title to the goods only after payment is made.[56]

It has been submitted that the carrier in that case has to give precedence to the RR, as this is the regime applicable to carriage relations and also because he is not privy to the underlying sale contract.[57] However, if such a case goes to litigation, it would really be interesting to see how the courts would protect the unpaid seller's property rights. Therefore, it is apparent that the right of control may conflict with the right of stoppage in transit of the SOGA and have a detrimental effect on international trade, especially in the lack of thorough contract drafting. In this scenario, we would see the operation of a concept provided for by the text of the RR in order to facilitate trade, namely the right of control, causing ambiguity or uncertainty and not facilitation of trade, despite the latter being the original drafting intention during the preparatory works, as explained earlier. Although there may seem to be a conflict, the right of control relates to the contract of carriage and does not have the same scope as the right of stoppage in transit. Clarifying the commercial expectations, however, is sacrosanct, especially because the concept of the right of control can be misinterpreted. Although, the rights may be of a different nature, their exercise can create confusion and conflict in respect of the instructions given to the carrier in the exercise of these rights. Regardless of whether we see this as a conflict of rights or a conflict of instructions, it is an issue that can ignite great uncertainty in the shipping and trade practice.

At this point, having enshrined the complexities arising from the right of control, the analysis will be centred on the controversial regulation[58]of aspects of the final stage of the carriage contract, which is delivery of the goods by the carrier to the appropriate consignee under the RR. Delivery to the entitled receiver is sacrosanct for the interests of a buyer who has paid for the goods, but also for the seller if payment is agreed to take place wholly or partly on delivery.

2.6 Delivery of the goods under the Rotterdam Rules: some reflections

2.6.1 Articles 45(a) and 46(a) of the Rotterdam Rules: delivery against non-negotiable documents

Article 45(a) of the RR regulates delivery when non-negotiable transport documents are issued.[59] It reads as follows:

> When neither a negotiable transport document nor a negotiable electronic transport record has been issued:
>
> (a) The carrier shall deliver the goods to the consignee at the time and location referred to in article 43. The carrier may refuse delivery if the

56 *(Ross) T Smyth & Co Ltd v. TD Bailey, Son & Co* [1940] 3 All ER 60; Debattista, *Bills of Lading in Export Trade*, para 5.18.

57 See Treitel and Reynolds (eds), *Carver on Bills of Lading* (4th edn), para 1.038.

58 Stuart Beare, 'Rotterdam Rules: Some controversies' at www.comitemaritime.org.

59 Baatz Debattista, Lorenzon, Serdy, Staniland and Tsimplis, *The Rotterdam Rules: A Practical Annotation*, para 45.02; Treitel and Reynolds (eds), *Carver on Bills of Lading* (4th edn), para 6.022.

> person claiming to be the consignee does not properly identify itself as the consignee on the request of the carrier.

In order to determine which documents are non-negotiable, Article 45 of the RR needs to be read in conjunction with Articles 1(15)[60], 1(16) and 1(19) of the RR.

Article 1(16) states:

> "Non-negotiable transport document" means a transport document that is not a negotiable transport document.

Therefore, a transport document is non-negotiable when it does not indicate that the goods have been consigned to the order of the shipper, to the order of the consignee or to the bearer.[61] Thus, a sea waybill, a straight bill of lading or a non-negotiable receipt which qualifies as a transport document could fall under this definition.[62] When the transport document is a sea waybill or a straight bill of lading, the article specifies that the carrier should deliver to the consignee.

Article 45(a) is particularly significant for international trade law, because it prescribes the steps that the carrier *may* or *should* take before releasing the goods to the alleged consignee. The use of "may" in the article plays an important role[63] and entails two considerable stipulations: first, the consignee needs to identify himself only *if the carrier asks him to*;[64] and secondly, if the carrier does ask him to identify himself and the consignee fails to do so, the carrier *may* but does not need to refuse to deliver the goods to him.

Therefore, it follows that in practice, Article 45(a) of the RR entitles the carrier to deliver the goods to a person who asks for the goods and simply *says* he is the consignee. The carrier is not under the obligation to ask for identification or to deny delivery to someone who refuses or fails to identify himself as the consignee.

Hence, Article 45(a) of the RR is crucial for the players of international trade for two reasons: first, the position of the seller is affected, as the article contains very few check requirements, thus making the risk of him not being paid more likely;[65] and second, had there been a duty to ask for identification, as opposed to a *discretion* to do so, the seller would not have been put in such a vulnerable position.

60 For Article 1(15), see previous section.

61 The rest of the paragraphs of Article 46 as well as Article 47 will be further discussed in a following section in order to see how the identification check will be performed, on what data and at what stage, in the case of an electronic transport record.

62 See Baatz et al, *The Rotterdam Rules: A Practical Annotation*, para [45-02].

63 "The carrier shall deliver the goods to the consignee at the time and location referred to in article 43. The carrier may refuse delivery if the person claiming to be the consignee does not properly identify himself as the consignee on the request of the carrier;".

64 Emphasis added by the author.

65 Point made by Charles Debattista, in his speech at the conference, Debattista, 'The Rotterdam Rules appraised', p. 4.

We submit that this article of the RR offers a great liberty to the carrier in terms of delivery and it is very surprising that the prerequisites for identification checks seem to leave the carrier not liable, irrespective of whether he delivers to the right person or not. Consequently, it is advisable that sellers avoid taking sea waybills or straight bills when they doubt the ability or certainty of the buyer to pay.

The legal dangers lurking underneath Article 45 of the RR could be avoided via a carefully drafted condition in the sale contract. This may either take the form of a duty to tender a negotiable bill of lading which requires surrender or through the prohibition that the seller tenders a non-negotiable document to the buyer.

In terms of documentary sales, banks should also consider Article 45 of the RR with caution and take their own contractual measures against possible risks of non-entitlement to payment:[66] They should ensure that it is themselves and not the buyers who are mentioned as the consignees on a sea waybill.

The lenience awarded to the carrier by Article 45(a) of the RR can prove detrimental to both the consignee and the seller *qua* shipper. We believe that this provision might cause controversies. The word "may" refutes the assurance that, in the case of sea waybills and most importantly straight bills of lading, the carrier would ensure that he delivers to the actual consignee. Under the RR, the carrier has the discretion to ask for identification and is also *entitled* to deliver even if this identification is deliberately withheld or, without fault, not given.

On the one hand, this provision constitutes an innovation of the RR since it was missing from all their predecessors. It purports to address a problem of commercial reality which was left unresolved.[67] On the other hand, the fact that the carrier is left non-liable for misdelivery, even if he delivers without asking or delivers to whom he thinks is the right person, with respect, manifests the inadequacy of this provision. We understand that the carrier is not an expert and that he does not possess the investigative skills to carry out this identification process. It is also acknowledged that time is precious and that delay under one contract of carriage might trigger the carrier's liability for breach of the subsequent fixture. Had the verb "may" been replaced by "must", no additional requirements for identification would be necessary in the sale contract. Since this is not the case, delivery to the right consignee can be secured through the following term in the sale and carriage contracts: "The carrier *shall* deliver the goods to the consignee at the time and location referred to in article 43. The carrier *must* refuse delivery if the person claiming to be the consignee does not properly identify himself as the consignee on the request of the carrier."

Nevertheless, counterarguments have been conferred which do not see any particular risk behind Article 45(a). In these views, the article, as it currently is, might not be of frequent application, in the sense that, in practice, the majority of sale contracts (especially if a letter of credit is involved) have the issuance of a negotiable transport record among their documentary requirements. Especially

66 Ibid.

67 See Debattista, *Bills of Lading in Export Trade*, pp. 38–39, for instance when the ship arrives before documents.

in CIF sales, article A8 of the Incoterms® asks the seller to provide the buyer, at his own expense and without delay, with the usual transport document for the agreed port of destination.[68]

This requirement remains the same under the Incoterms® 2010. Similarly, in FOB Incoterms® 2010, article A8 requires that "the seller must provide the buyer, at the seller's expense, with the usual proof that the goods have been delivered in accordance with A4."[69]

Interestingly, this provision of Incoterms® also entails that unless such proof is a transport document, the seller must provide assistance in obtaining a transport document for the buyer at the buyer's request, risk and expense.

Taking into consideration the frequency of international sale contracts concluded on CIF and FOB terms, it can be argued that although, Article 45 of the RR seems problematic, most frequently a bill of lading (negotiable transport document) is requested. Therefore, hopefully, the above paradox is unlikely.

2.6.2 Concluding suggestions

It is freedom of contract that can be trusted to give episodic solutions in order to counteract the RR's aforementioned misgivings. This being the situation, the solutions we suggest for traders and banks are as follows: the trading parties may exclude the issuance of a non-negotiable transport document with a specific provision in their contract of sale ensuring that delivery is made to the right person. However, if the parties wish to use the above type of documents, their sale contract should also provide for a contract of carriage that is drafted in a way that *requires* the carrier to check thoroughly the identity of the consignee. Also, letters of credit should be precisely drafted pursuant to the contract of sale, so that the bank may be safe in the knowledge that it is named as the consignee on the straight bill of lading or the sea waybill.

Again, irrespective of whether the identification check is a formal obligation derived from the RR or English common law, it is the contract of sale which can set aside the vagueness of Article 45 of the RR.

Having seen the delivery steps the carrier "may" or "has to" pursue before delivery, the attention will now rapidly shift to another category of non-negotiable documents, that is of those that need surrender, regulated by Article 46(a) of the RR.

Article 46(a) reads as follows:

> When a non-negotiable transport document has been issued that indicates that it shall be surrendered in order to obtain delivery of the goods:
>
> (a) The carrier shall deliver the goods at the time and location referred to in article 43 to the consignee upon the consignee properly identifying

68 See Incoterms® 2000, ICC Official Rules for the interpretation of trade terms, ICC, p. 70.
69 See Incoterms® 2010, ICC Official Rules for the interpretation of trade terms, ICC, p. 92.

> itself on the request of the carrier and surrender of the non-negotiable document. The carrier may refuse delivery if the person claiming to be the consignee fails to properly identify itself on the request of the carrier, and shall refuse delivery if the non-negotiable document is not surrendered [...]

The latter article keeps the wording of Article 45(a), that the carrier may refuse delivery if the person claiming to be the consignee fails to properly identify himself on the carrier's request. However, Article 46(a) differs in stating that the carrier shall refuse delivery, if the non-negotiable document is not surrendered.

Again, the carrier may ask for identification and may or may not act upon it. It has been advocated that the type of identification needed for this document is merely the surrender of the document.[70]

A lot more concerns have been expressed with regards to Article 47(2) of the RR, regarding the identification of the consignee and the liberty of non-presentation of negotiable documents.

2.6.3 Articles 47(1) and 47(2) of the Rotterdam Rules: negotiable transport documents and their peculiarities

Bills of lading are vital for sales down a string, as they are documents of title. Article 47(1) of the RR deals with delivery against a negotiable document and stipulates that the holder of such a transport document needs to surrender it and identify himself in order to obtain delivery. In contrast with the aforementioned articles of the RR, under Article 47(1) of the RR, both the surrender of the document and the identification of the alleged consignee are cumulative conditions for delivery.

Article 47 is, by definition, significant for international trade law, as sales down a string are mainly performed, with the goods being sold consecutive times while afloat. These purchases can only be performed via the endorsement of the negotiable title to the goods, namely the negotiable transport document/record, and not via the physical handing over of the goods, as they are still in transit. The importance of the negotiable documents in sales conducted overseas and the puzzling wording of Articles 47(1) and (2) of the RR to that effect merit the discussion of their potential implications in this section.

The first problematic issue regarding Article 47(1) is the meaning of *identification*.[71] It is unclear whether the holder has to prove who he is or whether he needs to prove that he is the holder.[72] Especially in the latter case, in terms of

70 See Debattista, 'The Rotterdam Rules appraised', p. 5. Also Debattista, 'UNCITRAL Colloquium on Rotterdam Rules: The Goods Carried – Who gets them and who controls them?' at www.rotterdamrules2009.com/cms/uploads/Def%20%20tekst%20Charles%20Debattista%2031%20OKT29.pdf.

71 See Baatz et al, *The Rotterdam Rules: A Practical Annotation*, para [47-08].

72 See Debattista, 'The Rotterdam Rules appraised', p. 5.

evidence it will be very difficult for the carrier to check the chain of endorsements as some may be in blank and others in full.[73]

Disagreement has been expressed with regards to the criticism[74] expressed on the identification requirement.[75] A view is taken that negotiable bills of lading have always facilitated trade and particularly "trading down the line" through consecutive endorsements. Therefore, the mere presentation of the bill of lading should be sufficient to justify lawful delivery. Extra effort for identification will assist with attacking delivery against fraudulent bills of lading. Such a case was *Motis Exports Ltd v. Dampskibsselskabet AF 1912 A/S (No.1)*,[76] where it was held that the carrier is liable if he delivers on presentation of a prima facie genuine bill of lading which is later revealed to be forged. In this case, the carrier had delivered the goods against presentation of fraudulent bills of lading, which at the time looked genuine. When sued by the cargo owners/consignees of the original bills, the carrier alleged that he was not liable, characterising delivery to the wrong person as theft, which as per a relevant clause in the carriage contract meant the carrier could not be found liable. On appeal, the court held for the cargo owners; the goods were lost because of the presentation of the forged bill. The carrier had a contractual duty to check whether the documents were original. Failing this duty, the loss suffered by the consignees was due to wrongful delivery, which did not fall underneath the alleged exemption clause.

With extra care in the drafting of the provisions of the sale contract relating to the identity of the holder of the non-negotiable document, misdelivery can be satisfactorily addressed.

However, it can be counter argued that the interpretation of "identification" might be complicated and negatively affect international trade, as identification might in some cases prove time-consuming and costly. This delay may, in a given sale contract, trigger liability of the seller for delay in delivery[77] and be remarkably detrimental in cases of perishable cargo. However, in our opinion, the requirement of identification of the holder of the transport document discourages fraud, adds greater security in transactions and prevents unnecessary litigation. It is believed that this advantage of Article 47(1) of the RR outweighs the drawback of the possible delay caused due to checking, and it is a provision that would be greatly beneficial to English law, as discussed above.

2.6.4 Article 47(2) of the Rotterdam Rules: negotiable documents not requiring surrender

The discussion will now cover another category of negotiable transport documents, regulated by Article 47(2) of the RR. This article is about negotiable

73 Ibid.

74 Ibid; also Debattista, 'UNCITRAL Colloquium on Rotterdam Rules: The Goods Carried – Who gets them and who controls them?'.

75 Ibid.

76 [2000] CLC 515.

77 For this point see Baatz et al, *The Rotterdam Rules: A Practical annotation*, para [47-09].

documents that expressly state that their presentation is not necessary for delivery of the goods.[78] Since these documents share characteristics of both negotiable and non-negotiable documents some legal scholars have called them "hybrid".[79]

The provision has been inserted in the RR to eliminate the need for a letter of indemnity when the goods arrive but the holder does not yet possess the bill of lading to claim delivery.[80] This rationale, of the unavailability or delay in transfer of the bill of lading, has also underpinned the provisions of the RR on electronic trade, discussed in a subsequent chapter. Despite the laudable objective of the article to rectify problems of trade, conflicting opinions have already been advocated with regard to the practical operation of Article 47(2) of the RR.[81]

Interestingly, Article 35 of the RR, dealing with the entitlement to a transport document, and to specific divisions of documents and records, does not specifically refer to this type of document.[82] Article 1 of the RR on definitions is equally silent. Prevention of the repercussions originating from the use of this negotiable document presupposes good knowledge of the RR, which non-sophisticated traders may not have. Whether their entitlement can be contemplated or precluded on the basis of Article 35 of the RR, will be discussed in Chapter 3.

78 See Caslav Pejović, 'Article 47(2) of the Rotterdam Rules: Solution of old problems or a new confusion?' (2012) 18 *JIML* 348.

79 This is how Charles Debattista refers to them in his speech, 'UNCITRAL Colloquium on Rotterdam Rules: The Goods Carried – Who gets them and who controls them?', para 19; for a considerable analysis see also Pejović, 'Article 47(2) of the Rotterdam Rules: Solution of old problems or a new confusion?'.

80 Gertjan van der Ziel, 'Delivery of the Goods' in Alexander von Ziegler, Johan Schelin and Stephano Zunarelli (eds), *The Rotterdam Rules 2008, Commentary to the United Nations Convention on Contracts for the International Carriage of Goods Wholly or Partly by Sea* (Kluwer Law International 2010), para 9.6.2. The unavailability of the bill of lading is extremely high in the bulk trades and especially in the oil trade. The reasons may vary: delays in the documentary process or sales to a long series of buyers.

81 For scholars in favour, see Francesco Berlingieri, 'An analysis of two recent commentaries of the Rotterdam Rules' (2012) *Il Diritto Marittimo*, 3, 39; van der Ziel, 'Delivery of the Goods', para 9.6.2. Against, see Agenda Item 6, 'R, Informal document WP.24 No. 2 (2009) at www.unece.org/fileadmin/DAM/trans/wp24/wp24-inf-docs/documents/id09-02e.pdf, para c; 'The Rotterdam Rules: An attempt to clarify certain concerns that have emerged' at www.comitemaritime.org/Uploads/Rotterdam%20Rules/5RRULES.pdf. Concerns have been voiced also by Jan Ramberg, 'UN Convention on Contracts for the International Carriage of Goods Wholly or Partly by Sea' (2009) *CMI Yearbook* 2009, 277, p. 280 at www.comitemaritime.org/Uploads/Yearbooks/YBK_2009.pdf; Asariotis, 'What future for the bill of lading as a document of title'; Pejović, 'Article 47(2) of the Rotterdam Rules: Solution of old problems or a new confusion?'.

82 Article 35 reads: Unless the shipper and the carrier have agreed not to use a transport document or an electronic transport record, or it is the custom, usage or practice of the trade not to use one, upon delivery of the goods for carriage to the carrier or performing party, the shipper or, if the shipper consents, the documentary shipper, is entitled to obtain from the carrier, at the shipper's option: (a) A non-negotiable transport document or, subject to article 8, subparagraph (a), a non-negotiable electronic transport record; or (b) An appropriate negotiable transport document or, subject to article 8, subparagraph (a), a negotiable electronic transport record, unless the shipper and the carrier have agreed not to use a negotiable transport document or negotiable electronic transport record, or it is the custom, usage or practice of the trade not to use one.

If the RR come into force, the trading community will have to draw particular attention to this "semi-negotiable" document, and international sale contracts will have to be particularly comprehensively drafted. The terms bill of lading, sea waybill and others will probably be replaced by the term "transport document" of the RR. Accordingly, the term "negotiable document" being a request under the sale contract may give rise to unexpected documentary tenders and consequences.

If a sale contract is requesting a negotiable transport document, nothing precludes that, under the RR, a negotiable document that does not require surrender may be issued.[83] If, however, the buyer is particularly interested in the "conveyancing function"[84] that a negotiable document such as the bill of lading has, he may not welcome this contingency. Arguably the terminology needs to be carefully thought out and used here. So far, in shipping documents the term "negotiable" referred to the bill of lading. Before the RR, no one would have even contemplated that there may be a document which is *negotiable, but does not need surrender*.[85]

From one point of view, it has been argued that Article 47(2) attacks the essence of the bill of lading as a document of title.[86]

Moreover, Article 47(2) of the RR may trigger grave consequences when a letter of credit is issued to finance the purchase contract: a transport document may, prima facie, be negotiable, but if presentation is not critical for delivery, this negotiable document will have a reduced value as a document of title, and therefore will be of questionable documentary security.[87]

It has been contended that confusion will also arise with regard to the person entitled to the goods.[88] If the holder does not claim delivery, or the carrier fails to localise him, the carrier may request delivery instructions from the shipper.[89]

83 On the draft version of the article, see Asariotis, 'What future for the bill of lading as a document of title?', p. 77.

84 On this function, see in detail Treitel and Reynolds (eds), *Carver on Bills of Lading* (4th edn), paras 6.080–6.087.

85 The phrase is in italics for emphasis.

86 See Alcántara et al, 'Particular Concerns with regard to the Rotterdam Rules'; A Diamond QC, 'The Rotterdam Rules' (2009) *LMCLQ* 445, p. 521; Asariotis, 'What future for the bill of lading as a document of title?'.

87 On this point, see Asariotis, 'What future for the bill of lading as a document of title?', p. 77, though the article refers to a previous draft of the Convention, where the number of the article at question was number 49.

88 Ramberg, 'UN Convention on Contracts for the International Carriage of Goods Wholly or Partly by Sea'; Asariotis, 'What future for the bill of lading as a document of title?' pp. 76–77.

89 Article 47(2)(a) reads: "If the goods are not deliverable because (i) the holder, after having received a notice of arrival, does not, at the time or within the time period referred to in article 43, claim delivery of the goods from the carrier after their arrival at the place of destination, (ii) the carrier refuses delivery because the person claiming to be a holder does not properly identify itself as one of the persons referred to in article 1, subparagraph 10(a)(i), or (iii) the carrier is, after reasonable effort, unable to locate the holder in order to request delivery instructions, the carrier may so advise the shipper and request instructions in respect of the delivery of the goods."

What if the party designated by the shipper is not entitled to the goods?[90] Arguably, increase of the risk of maritime fraud through Article 47(2) is another valid concern.[91] A shipper could collude with the first buyer to the detriment of the subsequent purchasers.[92]

Instructions for delivery to the wrong holder may also be unintentional. In this case, the shipper (S), who is also the first seller of CIF sales down a string, may not be aware of the third buyer in the chain, and thus simply designate his own buyer (B), as this will have been the trader who paid against the negotiable transport document.[93] The real holder of the document, for example (F), will have paid for the goods, without being entitled to request delivery. The only available remedy that the lawful holder would have is to sue the shipper (S) in conversion.[94]

The person that the carrier can seek instructions from may also be the documentary shipper. If an FOB scenario is contemplated for instance, the documentary shipper comes second in line for instruction purposes under Article 47(2) of the RR.[95] This documentary shipper is unrelated to the sales conducted on CIF terms by his buyer, as he must have not been involved in the arrangement of the contract of carriage at all.[96]

Therefore, the buyer/consignee/holder of the transport document may realise that the carrier has followed instructions from the shipper to deliver elsewhere, thus being more vulnerable to the contingency of misdelivery without having a right to get compensated.[97] It is, therefore, arguable that the potential implications of Article 47(2) of the RR may be negative for buyers.

What is primarily being denuded from such documents is their negotiable character, which is connected to their need for presentation so that delivery takes place.[98] When it comes to negotiable documents, transfer of rights goes together with the transfer of documents. The same concerns apply to banks paying under

90 Ramberg, 'UN Convention on Contracts for the International Carriage of Goods Wholly or Partly by Sea', p. 280.

91 See point 5.3 in 'FIATA Position on the UN Convention on Contracts for the International Carriage of Goods Wholly or Partly by Sea (the "Rotterdam Rules")', at www.comitemaritime.org/Uploads/Rotterdam%20Rules/3FIATA.pdf.

92 Pejović, 'Article 47(2) of the Rotterdam Rules: Solution of old problems or a new confusion?' (2012), p. 357.

93 Ramberg, 'UN Convention on Contracts for the International Carriage of Goods Wholly or Partly by Sea', p. 280.

94 On this point see Asariotis, 'What future for the bill of lading as a document of title?', p. 77.

95 Article 47(2) last sentence: "If, after reasonable effort, the carrier is unable to locate the shipper, the carrier may so advise the documentary shipper and request instructions in respect of the delivery of the goods;".

96 See article A3 of the Incoterms® 2010: "the seller is not obliged to book a vessel".

97 See Regina Asariotis, 'Reflections on the Rotterdam Rules' in MA Clarke (ed), *Maritime Law Evolving: Thirty Years at Southampton* (Hart Publishing 2013), pp. 151–152.

98 See Pejović, 'Article 47(2) of the Rotterdam Rules: Solution of old problems or a new confusion?', pp. 349, 355. See also Asariotis, 'What future for the bill of lading as a document of title', p. 77.

letters of credit as a negotiable document which does not require surrender and that would not provide collateral security.[99] Although no specific article exists under the UCP 600 for this category of documents, it would seem that banks would discourage acceptance of such documents, except when the buyer inserts a term to the contrary in his letter of credit.[100]

It has been submitted that the criticism of Article 47(2) of the RR is confirmed by its incompatibility with the Incoterms® requirement under article A8, that the document procured must enable the buyer to claim the goods from the carrier at the port of destination.[101] Our opinion is that this inconsistency with Incoterms® is rather indirect; if both the RR and Incoterms® apply, the document would still entitle to delivery, but this entitlement seems not to require production of the document under the RR.

On the other hand, some reassuring voices have been heard.[102] These come from academics who do not foresee anything particularly risky in the application of Article 47(2).[103]

They assert, for instance, that the acknowledgement of negotiable documents not requiring surrender adds nothing new since they were not prohibited under the HVR.[104] The reassuring voices confirm that Article 47(2) was inserted to cover for the frequent possibility of the bill of lading being unavailable when the ship is ready to unload. The practice of letters of indemnity being issued in such scenarios will be laudably discouraged, through the document of Article 47(2) of the RR.[105] It has also been contended that banks that receive such documents under letters of credit will not face a radically different risk compared to sea waybills and straight bills of lading.[106]

Additionally, it has been contended that the carrier's right to seek instructions when the holder cannot be localised is reconciled with the charterparty practice of the carrier having to act under the instructions of the charterer.[107]

Nonetheless, the difficulties that ensue when the shipper is not able or willing to provide delivery instructions have raised eyebrows. Below we examine how this legal uncertainty can be minimised.

99 See Pejović, 'Article 47(2) of the Rotterdam Rules: Solution of old problems or a new confusion?', p. 362.

100 Ibid.

101 Ibid.

102 'A response in attempt to clarify certain concerns over the Rotterdam Rules' at www.mcgill.ca/files/maritimelaw/Summationpdf.pdf, p. 6; von Ziegler, Schelin and Zunarelli (eds), *The Rotterdam Rules 2008*, para 9.6.2; van der Ziel, 'Delivery of the goods, rights of the controlling party and transfer of rights', pp. 604, 605.

103 See Debattista, 'The Rotterdam Rules appraised', p. 6.

104 Ibid.

105 See preparatory works of the RR, DOC A/63/17, para 154; van der Ziel, 'Delivery of the goods, rights of the controlling party and transfer of rights', p. 604, 605; Baatz et al, *The Rotterdam Rules: A Practical Annotation*, para 47-02.

106 See also 'The Rotterdam Rules: An attempt to clarify certain concerns that have emerged'.

107 von Ziegler, Schelin and Zunarelli (eds), *The Rotterdam Rules 2008*, p. 208.

2.6.5 Ways of making Article 47(2) of the Rotterdam Rules be of a positive impact

After the RR come into force, the above category of documents may officially operate. In our suggestion, the only protection for the buyer/holder would be to explicitly prohibit in his sale contract and the letter of credit the tender of a negotiable document which does not require surrender.

Consequently, taking into consideration the foregoing concerns, one could say that there is a case for reform of the UCP 600.[108] In the revised version of the UCP, such documents may either be clustered as a bad tender, or otherwise be accepted, perhaps with some additional security required.

2.6.6 Observations on Article 47(2) of the Rotterdam Rules

It has been submitted that the rationale behind Article 47(2) of the RR was to afford trade with legal certainty when the bill of lading is delayed and thus unavailable.[109] The practical implications to arise however make us agree more with the above security concerns in terms of the non-requirement of surrender for release of the goods. We assert that this type of transport document should be treated with great caution. It would be expected that the carrier would still be granted a letter of indemnity by the shipper or the consignee, so that he delivers without much hesitation, and therefore the practice of letters of indemnity may not decrease, despite this being originally contemplated.[110]

It seems that the RR, via Article 47(2), make a drastic alteration to the role of documents of title known to date, and thus it is highly questionable whether this provision – and consequently the RR in general – will be welcomed by the trading community.[111]

2.7 Conclusion

In this chapter we discussed some major new terms, concepts and articles which were inserted in the RR to envelop maritime trade with legal certainty and facilitation. As international harmonisation of any laws is far from perfect, there are trade implications originating from these provisions. These undermine the potential of the RR for a positive impact towards a more harmonious international trade, but also necessitate awareness and protective contract drafting of the sale contracts and letters of credit. This is merely a preview of forthcoming changes

108 See also Pejović, 'Article 47(2) of the Rotterdam Rules: Solution of old problems or a new confusion?', p. 353.

109 van der Ziel, 'Delivery of the Goods', para 9.6.2, p. 207.

110 Ibid.

111 So far, FIATA, CLECAT (The European Voice of Freight Logistics and Customs Representatives) and the ESC have reacted to the provision: see Pejović, 'Article 47(2) of the Rotterdam Rules: Solution of old problems or a new confusion?', in fns 13, 14, 15.

to be anticipated if the RR come into force. The analysis of their potential impact shows that the rationale underpinning the drafting of specific articles of the RR does not necessarily reflect ideal international trade law solutions; not without additional consideration and contractual, regulatory or legislative actions. The regulation of the right of control and the provisions of the RR applicable in occasions, where the negotiable transport document is unavailable at the time of delivery, could also create commercial paradoxes.

When the RR come into force, in the matter of stoppage in transit, our suggestion is that English law should be reformed, so that the provisions of the SOGA and the RR (after ratification) are reconciled; the aim is to avoid a clash of instructions given to the carrier by the traders. As far as the negotiable documents that do not require surrender are concerned, Article 47(2)(a) offers greater flexibility in the carriage context, but does not automatically ensure legal certainty; at least not for a trader who has not carefully considered the risks discussed above when the sale contract allows issuance of a transport document expressly stating that it does not require surrender. For this reason, it is recommended that the possibility of delivering without presentation of the negotiable document should be contracted out by traders who are not willing to undertake such risks. The UCP 600 should also be reformed accordingly, so that banks do not lose collateral security.

In Chapter 1, it has been shown that principles of trade and carriage are largely common, but sometimes divided by fine lines. The RR initiate modern, pragmatic solutions, reflecting the understanding of what is current in international trade (e.g. documents sometimes being unavailable at the time of delivery); international trade, on the other hand, is permeated by the issuance, use and reliance on documents of title, so that sales down a string can be fostered. The RR in this respect allow for more freedom than traders would even contemplate, and this flexibility seriously undermines commercial legal certainty.

Certainty can be secured through careful contract exclusion of the negotiable document not requiring surrender, or with the hope that Incoterms® will recognise it as customary in the trade and envelop it with a clear framework, which will stipulate under which circumstances trades or types of sales would be a good tender. Until this happens, it might be wise for the UCP 600 to exclude it due to the security arguments discussed above. So far, we have seen that the flexibility and pragmatism of the RR can menace the established reliance[112]on documents of title; therefore, the impact seems ambiguous and, occasionally, threatening for international trade law. This harm is not only targeted against sales down a string, but against the very essence of documentary sales. Will the same be argued when Article 35 of the RR is explored in the next chapter?

In Chapter 3, we will carry on to illustrate the potential implications between the RR and other standard trade terms. As described in Chapter 1, in order to

112 Pejović, 'Article 47(2) of the Rotterdam Rules: Solution of old problems or a new confusion?', p. 349.

determine whether a buyer can have certain documentary requests from his seller, sale terms and legislation have to be checked first. However, the seller's compliance with these requests also depends on the carriage contract and his respective rights against the carrier under the applicable mandatory national and international frameworks. This is how the RR come to interact with trade terms and contracts. The focus will now shift to the areas of overlap or clash of the RR with private sets of rules, the latter being extensively used by players of international trade. These private sets of rules include Incoterms® 2000 and 2010, and UCP 600 launched by the ICC, and the model contracts of GAFTA and FOSFA (Federation of Oils, Seeds, and Fats Associations Limited).

In Chapter 3, whether the RR can provide the legal certainty, that the document requested under a sale contract, can be ultimately issued by a carrier will be examined. This will assist in the overall pursuit to examine whether the fundamental principles and theoretical concepts of international trade law, as reflected in model terms and standard contracts, are promoted or not through the RR. Subsequently, we will be able to identify inconsistencies among the provisions of the above rules on the issuance of a certain type of document and advise on how to best promote legal certainty in trade.

3 The Rotterdam Rules and standard trade terms

3.1 Introduction[1]

In this chapter, we study the relationship between the RR and other sets of standard terms used in overseas sales such as Incoterms® 2010, UCP 600[2] and other model contracts[3] such as GAFTA 100,[4] FOSFA 53[5] and FOSFA 54.[6] The RR will provide which transport document (if any) the seller *qua* shipper/documentary shipper may get, but if this document does not satisfy the requirements of the sale contract or ultimately of the letter of credit, the seller will not get paid. The sale contract may incorporate Incoterms® and/or be based on a standard contract.

First, entitlement to transport documents under the RR will be examined. This is important so that the seller can ensure tender of documents in compliance with the sale contract. Then, the RR and Incoterms® will be studied and ambiguities or other complexities observed from the two texts will be discussed. Incoterms® are prioritised because they are often incorporated in international sale contracts. Their popularity is due to their function as "gap-fillers" in sale contracts, thus creating a safety net to refer to when the intention of the parties is not sufficiently clear.[7] CIF and FOB Incoterms® in particular are extensively incorporated into the majority of overseas purchase contracts.[8]

The analysis of areas of overlap and conflict between the RR and the UCP 600 will follow, as the latter are used in a more specific context, i.e. when payment is

1 On the issues addressed in this chapter see also Ioanna Magklasi, 'Documents' complexities under the Rotterdam Rules' (2011) *International Journal of Public Law and Policy* 1(4), pp. 434–442.

2 ICC Uniform Customs and Practice for documentary credits (UCP 600).

3 For the connection between model contracts and string sales see Bridge, *The International Sale of Goods*, paras 1.20 and 1.21.

4 GAFTA No. 100, effective 1st January 2007.

5 FOSFA 53, revised and effective from 1st October 2004.

6 Revised and effective from 1st October 2008.

7 Such as passage of risk, costs, documentary obligations. Secondly, Incoterms® present a selection of important provisions a sale contract could contain.

8 Bridge, *The International Sale of Goods*, para 1.08.

contracted to take place via a letter of credit.[9] More precisely, the RR's provisions will be examined back to back with the respective articles of the UCP 600, in order to ascertain whether their provisions regarding compliant presentation of transport documents are identical. Finally, the most popular contract formats of GAFTA and FOSFA will be scrutinised in order to assess whether their provisions on transport documents, delivery, identification of the carrier and signature differ from the relevant articles of the RR.

In this chapter, the underpinnings between self-regulated trade terms (Incoterms® and the UCP 600) and the RR will stand out.[10] In more teleological terms, this study examines how the RR connect freedom of contract to customs and usages of the trade. This is crucial so that legal certainty can be afforded to the trade players along with flexibility to get the documents they need in order to perform their international sale contracts.

Therefore the pressing questions that seek answer in this chapter are: does Article 35 of the RR facilitate documentary sales and letters of credit or not? Is the trade reliance on documents preserved?

It can be anticipated that the synergies to stem from Article 35 of the RR are due to the lack of definition of terms[11] and to the lack of a hierarchy between conflicting agreements and usages. Solutions will be provided after the shortcomings have been identified.

3.2 The Rotterdam Rules and Incoterms®

We will now examine how Incoterms® 2010 and the RR may correlate and work together. As mentioned previously, particular focus is given to Incoterms®, as they are frequently incorporated into international sales in order to help with the definition or ascertainment of some of the terms of a sale contract, especially with the allocation of costs and risks between seller and buyer.[12] Their use is preferred and acknowledged not only by practitioners, but also by courts when there is imprecise wording in a sale contract.[13] Incoterms® are also essential in maritime

9 Roberto Bergami, 'The Rotterdam Rules and bills of lading: Challenges for letter of credit transactions', Paper from Conference Proceedings, CITEM, Tabor, 7–9 December 2011, 14, p. 17 at www.academia.edu/2542584/BERGAMI_Rotterdam_Rules; R Burnett, *Law of International Business Transactions* (3rd edn, The Federation Press 2014), p. 170.

10 Debattista, 'Legislative techniques in international trade: Madness or method?', pp. 634–636.

11 The terms are the following: custom, usage and practice.

12 For the importance of Incoterms®, see Lorenzon, 'When is a CIF seller's carriage contract unreasonable? Section 32(2) of the Sale of Goods Act 1979', p. 242. Also case C-87/10 *Electrosteel Europe SA v. Edil Centro SpA (ECJ)*, para 21, available on line at curia.europa.eu/jurisp/cgi-bin/form.pl?lang=en&alljur=alljur&jurcdj=jurcdj&jurtpi=jurtpi&jurtfp=jurtfp&numaff=C-87/10&nomusuel=&docnodecision=docnodecision&allcommjo=allcommjo&affint=affint&affclose=affclose&alldocrec=alldocrec&docdecision=docdecision&docor=docor&docav=docav&docsom=docsom&docinf=docinf&alldocnorec=alldocnorec&docnoor=docnoor&docppoag=docppoag&radtypeord=on&newform=newform&docj=docj&docop=docop&docnoj=docnoj&typeord=ALL&domaine=&mots=&resmax=100&Submit=Rechercher.

13 Ibid.

commerce, since they distribute carriage and documentary obligations to sellers and buyers.[14]

Incoterms® 2010[15] present a few key changes compared to Incoterms® 2000, keeping pace with the evolution of global commerce, like the RR. First, Incoterms® 2010 acknowledge the phenomenon of sales down a string.[16] Second, they have been divided into "Rules for any mode or modes of transport" and "Rules for sea and inland waterway transport".[17] This mirrors one of the underlying aims of the RR, which was to encompass provisions not only for sea transit but also for multimodal transport.[18] Third, Incoterms® 2010 are also in the same vein as the RR, as they both provide that traders' documentary duties (and records-keeping) can be performed electronically.[19]

In the next section, we will discuss the entitlement to issue a transport document of a specific type under the scope of the RR and Incoterms® 2010.

The questions that are posed concern whether or not the provisions are sufficiently clear; we will highlight the complexities expected to emerge through the combined application of both the RR and Incoterms® in a sale (and/or carriage) contract when it comes to the document that the seller will obtain to pass it on to his buyer. This is an issue which was first opened in Chapter 2 and is fully discussed here.

Specific critical reflections will be made for the case where the sale contract is not sufficiently precise or when there is a contrary custom. In this study, it has been discovered that the request for an unusual transport document affects the common law requirement that the seller should enter into a reasonable contract of carriage when Incoterms® also apply.[20] This will be introduced in this chapter, but it will be exhaustively analysed in the chapter of volume contracts (Chapter 5), because these contracts deserve an individual analysis.

14 See Jan Ramberg, 'Incoterms® 2010 – Why and how' (presentation 22 July 2010) under the heading "The interrelation between Incoterms® and other contracts" at www.law.utoronto.ca/documents/conferences2/IACCL10-Ramberg.pdf.

15 Available from 1 January 2011.

16 'Professor Debattista on Incoterms® 2010 in the Lloyd's List', on 2nd February 2011. The distinction is evident in the wording of A3 CIF "The seller must contract or *procure a contract* for the carriage" and of A4 "The seller must deliver the goods either by placing them on board the vessel or *by procuring the goods* [...]".

17 For this remark, see 'Professor Debattista on Incoterms® 2010 in the Lloyd's List'. Also in the Editorial of (2010) 16 *JIML*, pp. 339–340. Incoterms® 2000 were classified in alphabetical order starting from the Incoterms® Ex Works (EXW), then going to the F, C and D terms respectively.

18 See MF Sturley, T Fujita and G van der Ziel, *The Rotterdam Rules* (Sweet & Maxwell, London 2010), para 1.003. Also Eftestöl-Wilhelmsson, 'The Rotterdam Rules in a European multimodal context'. This is further proven by the creation of the terms DAP (Delivery at Port) and DAT (Delivery at Terminal), which fall under the multimodal category. See Ian Vicary, 'New Incoterms® set sail' at www.lloydslistintelligence.com/llint/print-article.htm;jsessionid=C615CE19402D23B6F2814D08608AAF9F?documentId=262122&docType=. The old DAF, DES, DEQ and DDU have now been abolished.

19 "by electronic means [...] as long as the parties agree or is customary". See Incoterms® 2010 (Dutch–English version), ICC, p. 132.

20 See section 32(2) of the SOGA.

3.2.1 The entitlement to the transport document and the role of custom: some preliminary remarks

Article 35 of the RR is about the entitlement of the shipper[21] to ask for the transport document. In an attempt to accommodate international harmonisation, the scope of application of the RR is not purely documentary,[22] or trade-related.[23] This is why the RR are not document-centred. Article 35 specifies that the right to request a transport document/record is primarily reserved for the shipper (or the documentary shipper subject to the shipper's consent).[24] This article is similar to article III r. 3 of the HVR; however, it differs substantially in aspects that are crucial for international trade law.[25] The entitlement to a transport document (or a specific type of it) and its correlation with the contrary custom, usage or practice of the trade or agreement and the ability to request a non-negotiable document or an electronic record in particular,[26] constitute an innovation of the RR. A comparison with their predecessors will show that with clarity.[27]

21 If the shipper consents, the request may be initiated by the documentary shipper (Article 35 of the RR).

22 Such as the HVR.

23 For the development and philosophy behind the wider approach that the RR take compared to the Hague, HVR and the Hamburg Rules, see Michael F Sturley, 'Solving the Scope-of-application puzzle: Contracts, trades and documents in the UNCITRAL transport law project' (2005) 11 *J INT'L MAR L* 22, 39.

24 Article 35 reads as follows: "unless the shipper and the carrier have agreed not to use a transport document or an electronic transport record, or it is the custom, usage or practice of the trade not to use one, upon delivery of the goods for carriage to the carrier or performing party, the shipper or, if the shipper consents, the documentary shipper, is entitled to obtain from the carrier at the shipper's option:(a) A non-negotiable transport document or, subject to article 8, subparagraph (a), a non-negotiable electronic transport record, or (b) An appropriate negotiable transport document or, subject to article 8, subparagraph (a), a negotiable electronic transport record, unless the shipper and the carrier have agreed not to use a negotiable transport document or negotiable electronic transport record, or it is the custom, usage or practice of the trade not to use one."

25 See article III r. 3 of the HVR: "After receiving the goods into his charge the carrier or the master or agent of the carrier shall, on demand of the shipper, issue to the shipper a bill of lading [...]".

26 For a thorough analysis of custom and usage see C. Schmitthoff, 'The unification or harmonisation of law by means of standard contracts and general conditions' (1968) 17 *Int'l & Comp L Q* 551, 554; 'Custom and Trade Usage: Its application to Commercial Dealings and the Common law' (Dec 1955) *Columbia Law Review*, 555(8) 1192 at www.jstor.org/discover/10.2307/1119639?uid=3739256&uid=2&uid=4&sid=21103581046271; JH Levie, 'Trade usage and custom under the common law and the Uniform Commercial Code'(1965) 40 *NYU LRev* 1101; JD Heydon, '*How the courts develop commercial law by looking outside the trial record into the external world; usage of trade: impact on agreement*' at learntheucc.wordpress.com/2011/11/06/usage-of-trade-impact-on-agreement/.

27 See Francesco Berlingieri, "A comparative analysis of the Hague-Visby Rules, the Hamburg Rules and the Rotterdam Rules", paper delivered at the General Assembly of the International Association of Average Adjusters-AMD, Marrakesh, 5–6 November 2009, p. 25, at www.uncitral.org/pdf/english/workinggroups/wg_3/Berlingieri_paper_comparing_RR_Hamb_HVR.pdf.

Under the RR, first, there is an entitlement and not a duty to issue a document, and second, the shipper or documentary shipper may request from a range that includes documents or records, which may be negotiable or non-negotiable.

Therefore, it can be directly derived from Article 35 of the RR that unless the carrier and shipper have agreed not to use a transport document/record, or it is the custom/usage or practice of the trade not to use one, the choice of the document and its form (paper/electronic) stays with the shipper or documentary shipper, if so authorised by the shipper.[28] Although in our opinion, the mindfulness as to usages/or existing practices shows the draftsmen's great understanding of the significance of the law merchant,[29] the impact of Article 35 may be complex and uncertain.[30]

By virtue of Article 5(1),[31] the RR apply to contracts of carriage with an international sea leg and not just to documents of title, be they bills of lading or similar documents of title.[32] To understand this innovative approach, again it has to be recalled that the RR were designated as an interim step to harmonise the laws of maritime contracts of carriage so that UNCITRAL could then proceed to draft provisions of e-commerce for maritime carriage.[33] The role of the custom, practice or usage of the trade is, for the first time, acknowledged in a carriage of goods by sea convention in that context.[34]

Reasonably one would wonder about the purpose of this insertion. The answer is that the RR have a broader scope of application in order to embrace all major international peculiarities when it comes to contracts of carriage.[35] European short-haul shipments, for instance, frequently perform without the issuance of

28 See Treitel and Reynolds (eds), *Carver on Bills of Lading* (4th edn), para 6.083, 10-045.

29 International trade has very much evolved customarily. The *Lex Mercatoria* is defined as: "This part of transnational commercial law which is uncodified and consists of customary commercial law, customary rules of evidence and procedure and general principles of commercial law, including international public policy." in Roy M Goode, 'Usage and its reception in transnational commercial law' (1997) 46(1) *ICLQ* 1, p. 2; KP Berger, *The creeping codification of the lex mercatoria* (Kluwer Law International 1999), p. 40 et seq.

30 See also Treitel and Reynolds (eds), *Carver on Bills of Lading* (4th edn), para 10-045.

31 "Subject to article 6, this Convention applies to contracts of carriage in which the place of receipt and the place of delivery are in different States, and the port of loading of a sea carriage and the port of discharge of the same sea carriage are in different States, if, according to the contract of carriage, any one of the following places is located in a Contracting State: (a) The place of receipt; (b) The port of loading; (c) The place of delivery; or (d) The port of discharge."

32 As under article I(b) of the HVR.

33 See van der Ziel, 'Delivery of the goods, rights of the controlling party and transfer of rights', pp. 598, 599.

34 Goode, 'Usage and its reception in transnational commercial law', p. 2 reciting "the purpose of most conventions or contractual codifications is not to reproduce an existing set of universally adopted usages-for in truth no such universality exists – but, rather, to build on existing usage and to provide best solutions to current problems."

35 From Article 5 of the RR it becomes evident that the RR apply to contracts of carriage with an international sea leg, subject to the precise details of the convention, and not solely to bills of lading as is the case in the HVR. Therefore, the application of the RR is decoupled from documents.

bills of lading or comparable transport documents.[36] Moreover, Article 35 of the RR is purposefully so broadly drafted as to further allow the choice of electronic transport records, as long as Article 8(a) of the RR is complied with.

3.2.1.1 The role of custom and usage under the Rotterdam Rules and Incoterms® 2010

Attention should be drawn first to the possible uncertainty caused by a custom or usage of the trade. Though it has been argued that rarely would a national court ascertain that no transport document would customarily be issued,[37] the international trade players have to contemplate for the contingency of such an adverse custom. In fact, a transport document/record may not be issued.[38]

According to the article, at first instance the shipper is entitled to a transport document. This entitlement, however, is made subject to two separate conditions, which may run independently: either a contrary agreement, or a contrary custom, usage or practice of the trade.

By not requiring any formal request, the RR show that the default situation is that a transport document is expected to be issued as long as there are no opposite agreements or usages.[39] This provision is favourable to English law, as by authority,[40] in sales on shipment terms, the seller is required to tender a negotiable transport document, even when the sale contract is silent.

The wording of Article 35 shows that the choice of the type of document issued lies primarily with the agreement between shipper and carrier. However, the article makes specific reference to the contrary custom, usage or practice of the trade of the place of delivery of the goods to the carrier. From the puzzling

36 For more on the simplification of documentary procedures in the continent see Mark Yonge, US Dept of Transport, Maritime Admin, 'European Union short sea shipping' 9(2004) at advancedmaritimetechnology.aticorp.org/short-sea-shipping/create3s-european-commission-initiative-/EUSSS_04-2004.pdf. For documents being characterised as "bottlenecks" see www.shortsea.be/html_nl/publicaties/documents/Rapportv5E.pdf; also "A single transport document and uniform liability regime for intermodal transport in Europe" at www.shortsea.fr/Extrait-magazine_BIC-CONTAINERS-1-2-2012.html stating that there is actually no genuine transport document for intermodal transport, with the inland waterways consignment note being the transport document for inland waterways.
See also T Fujita, 'Transport Documents and Electronic Transport Records' in von Ziegler, Schelin and Zunarelli (eds), *The Rotterdam Rules 2008*, p. 164; G van der Ziel, 'Rights of the controlling party' in Güner-Özbek (ed), *The United Nations Convention on Contracts for the International Carriage of Goods Wholly or Partly by Sea: An Appraisal of the Rotterdam Rules*, para 10.4.

37 See Fujita, 'Transport Documents and Electronic Transport Records', p. 164. Also Bridge, *The International Sale of Goods*, para 10.63.

38 'The Rotterdam Rules: an attempt to clarify certain concerns that have emerged'; 'Reconciliation and harmonization of civil liability regimes in intermodal transport' Informal document WP.24 No. 2 (2009) at www.unece.org/fileadmin/DAM/trans/wp24/wp24-inf-docs/documents/id09-02e.pdf; 'Declaration of Montevideo' at asadip.files.wordpress.com/2010/10/rr-answer-to-montevideo-declaration-eng.pdf.

39 See Baatz et al, *The Rotterdam Rules: A Practical Annotation*, p. 100.

40 See *Soproma SpA v. Marine and Animal By-Products Corp* [1966] 1 Lloyd's Rep 367.

wording of the article the following scenarios will arise depending on what the contract of sale, the contract of carriage, which is concluded in execution of the former, and the specific customs of the place specify.

Firstly, if the contract of sale asks for a transport document, or if the contract of carriage is drafted accordingly, and the custom of the trade does not prohibit its issuance, then there is no conflict and the transport document may in principle be issued.[41]

Secondly, if the contract of sale asks for a transport document or the contract of carriage is silent with regard to it and the custom is that the carrier is under a duty to issue one, then, it follows that the shipper is entitled to ask for the transport document, under the RR.[42]

Thirdly, if the agreement of the parties or the custom/usage/practice of trade is that a negotiable document cannot be issued, then the shipper or documentary shipper may request a non-negotiable transport document and vice versa.[43]

It is even more challenging to determine first whether the terms "usage", "trade", and "practice" are used interchangeably and what will happen in the case when the agreement of the parties to issue a transport document or a particular type (i.e. negotiable or non-negotiable) contradicts the custom. The answer seems uncertain. This will be the subject of analysis in the following paragraphs.

Primarily, we study the role of custom and usage under the RR, but many of the remarks to be made also relate to the role of the "usual" transport document and to what is considered "customary" with reference to Incoterms®, and this will be highlighted where applicable.

Indeed, many of the observations made also relate to the role of the usual transport document according to what is considered customary with reference to Incoterms®. This will become obvious forthwith. Now we will present scenarios, considering both Article 35 of the RR and article A8 of the CIP (Carriage and Insurance Paid To) and CPT (Carriage Paid To) Incoterms® Rules 2010, which reads: "If customary or at the buyer's request, the seller must provide the buyer with the usual transport document."

This wording leads us to the following conclusions as to the document to be issued if the RR apply.

Firstly, if it is the custom that the seller should provide the usual or a specific transport document, then, in the absence of agreement to the contrary, the seller may, in principle, perform his documentary obligation towards the seller under both Incoterms® and the RR.

Secondly, assuming there is no specific agreement, if the custom does not require or, worse, if it prohibits the issuance of a transport document, then, again,

41 See also Sturley, Fujita and van der Ziel, *The Rotterdam Rules*, para 7.016.

42 Ibid, paras 7.015, 7.016, p. 209.

43 Ibid, para 7.016.

the application of both Article 35 of the RR and article A8 of the CIP Incoterms® indicates that the carrier is under no obligation to issue one.[44]

It is observed from the above that the document, when finally issued, is subject to two independent conditions: the agreement of the parties and the contrary custom, usage and practice. There remains a question as to what will happen if these two conditions contradict each other, but more analysis should be conducted before the answer is provided. Now, we will study the definition of custom, usage and practice.

3.2.1.2 Definition of custom, usage and practice

The RR do not provide any definition of custom, usage or practice either in Article 35 or in Article 1. Would it be proper then to interpret that the custom is different from the usage and practice of the trade or are they all the same?[45] Next we will see the approach of English law on these matters.

The starting point[46] for the definition of terms "usage", "practice" and "custom" under English law is the case *Royal Exchange v. Dixon.*[47] This case concerned the carriage of 125 bales of cotton on deck. The ship grounded and some of the bales were damaged. The owners of the vessels trading between those particular ports were in the habit of stowing goods on deck in violation of their contract with the shipper. The shipowners would accept full responsibility for the consequences. The bills for the 100 bales contained the words "under deck", whereas the ones for the remaining 25 did not. The shipowners alleged

44 Ibid.

45 See Lorenzon in Baatz et al, *The Rotterdam Rules: A Practical Annotation*, para 35-02. The relevance of usages and customs of various ports has been discussed in *Sucre Export SA v. Northern River Shipping Ltd (The Sormovskiy 3068)* [1994] CLC 433. See also *Bourne v. Gatliffe* (1841) 3 Man & G 643 and (1844) 7 Man & G 850; *Petrocochino v. Bott* (1874) LR 9 CP 355; *The Emilien Marie* (1875) 44 LJ Adm 9; *British Shipowners' Co v. Grimond* (1876) 3 Sess Cas 4th 968, *Postlethwaite v. Freeland* (1880) 5 App Cas 599; *The Jaederen* [1892] P 351; *Holt & Holt Ltd v. Union Castle Steamship Co Ltd* [1901] SC 38 (a South African case); *The Asiatic Prince* (1901) 108 F 287 (a decision of US Federal Court of Appeals, Second Circuit); *Grange v. Taylor* (1904) 9 Com Cas 223; *Ropner v. Stoate Hosegood & Co* (1905) 10 Com Cas 73; and *The Vladimir Vaslyayev*, a decision of the Supreme Court of Cyprus. In the *Sucre Export SA v. Northern River Shipping Ltd (The Sormovskiy 3068)* [1994] CLC 433 it was held that there is breach of contract if the defendants deliver without presentation of the bill of lading, unless there is either a rule of law or a custom in the strict sense in Vyborg that the master must deliver the cargo to the CSP, as the agent of the plaintiffs, without insisting upon the production of an original bill of lading ([1994] CLC 433, at 444).

46 See Lorenzon in Baatz et al, *The Rotterdam Rules: A Practical Annotation*, para [35-04] suggesting that the case is applicable for the definitions of usage, practice and custom, as well as for what needs to prove existence of each of them. For a similar discussion see also Williams, 'Transport documentation under the new convention', p. 569.

47 (1887) 12 App Cas 11 (HL). See Lorenzon in Baatz et al, *The Rotterdam Rules: A Practical Annotation*, para 35-04; and Williams, 'Transport documentation under the new convention', p. 569.

that, by virtue of the custom of the port of New Orleans and the custom *of the trade*,[48] in which the vessel was engaged, the defendants were entitled to carry a deck cargo and to stow the cotton on deck.[49] The terminology used along the way is not very consistent. At first instance, Cave J held that owners of vessels trading between New Orleans and Liverpool were *in the habit* of stowing on deck, in violation of their contract with the shipper accepting full responsibility for the consequences.[50] Further down, it was stated that "it is the practice or custom to carry on deck, which the plaintiffs must be taken to have known and assented to".[51]

The most enlightening part of the judgment comes from the dicta of Lord Watson: "The appellants did not maintain that they had established a proper mercantile custom, which, if not excluded by the terms of the bills of lading, would become an implied term of the contracts thereby constituted."[52]

Two conclusions can be derived from the above dicta. First, that under English law, a mercantile custom *stricto sensu* is different from a practice/usage, such as the one alleged, in the geographic voyages from New Orleans to Liverpool. Second, if the custom is not excluded by the contract, in this case by the bill of lading, the custom will become an implied term of the contract, which *a contrario* means that the custom can be excluded by agreement. With regards to the conduct required to signify such consent to a modification of the agreement by virtue of a custom, it is not clear from the judgment whether that should entail a positive reaction or mere silence. Because carriage on deck was received as a practice and not a custom, the learned judge held that the lack of objection, "their non-interference", did not amount to a modification of the contract, despite their awareness of the practice. That is to say that in the lack of a specific reaction, the practice was not in a position to modify the agreement of the bills of lading.

By reference to the actual holding, it was upheld that the shipowners were liable for breach of contract.

In an attempt to visualise the outcome of the case, had Article 35 of the RR been applicable, it could have been concluded that the existence of custom would become part of the agreement and would modify it, if not expressly excluded.[53] Under English law, practice and usage seem to have a lesser regulatory value compared to custom.

48 The expression "practice" of the port and of the trade reminds us of the division acknowledged by Goode, 'Usage and its reception in transnational commercial law', p. 11 stating that a trade usage may be geographical (by reference to a particular port, town or region,), political, economical, legal, or commercial, by reference to a particular trade (e.g. commodities) or market. So far, in the case discussed, the practice/usage seems to be rather geographical.

49 (1887) 12 App Cas 11, at p. 12.

50 Ibid.

51 Ibid, p. 13.

52 Ibid, p. 18.

53 Ibid, p. 18 "had established a proper mercantile custom, which, if not excluded by the terms of the bills of lading, would become an implied term of the contracts thereby constituted."

3.2.1.3 Custom and usage in academic theory and more recent case law

It has been suggested that the position of an international convention towards usage may vary:[54] A convention may constitute evidence of a usage, or operate simultaneously with the usage, or, lastly, set the usage aside. A convention may also create or evidence new usage, or, in the case it is not adopted, portray low significance as evidence of this usage.[55]

At first glance, it can be argued that the RR seem to run concurrently with any existing usage when it comes to not issuing a transport document, as it does not reverse it or negate it. The same can be advocated with regards to the attitude of the RR towards freedom of contract, when choosing not to issue a type of document or any document at all. The question which arises is whether the terms custom, usage or practice of the trade are used interchangeably,[56] or whether they are defined differently.[57] It also has to be noted that, although the RR are a carriage convention, they are very much in line with the main principles of international trade law.

In academic theory, it is acknowledged that the terms "usage", "custom" and "practice" usually lead to confusion.[58] In the opinion of Goode, although occasionally the terms "usage" and "custom" are held to be used interchangeably in modern times,[59] slight distinctions could be found in the past. For instance, it has been submitted that usage was sometimes used to signify a pattern or behaviour, or a pattern of behaviour which has elevated to the extent of a norm.[60] Another distinction was made on the basis that a custom was the practice of a particular locality, whereas usage was the practice of a trade or vocation.[61] Others supported that usage is a pattern or behaviour, whereas custom was the application of the usage from a sense of obligation. In the context of transnational commercial law,[62] which can be defined as the amalgam of rules which are anational and have their force by virtue of their international usage and fashion by the merchant community, the term "usage" is more common.[63]

54 See Goode ,'Usage and its reception in transnational commercial law', p. 18.
55 Ibid, p. 19.
56 Contrast this with the US definition of usage, which is not determined by case law, but codified. See Article 1-205(2) of the UCC: "A usage of trade is any practice or method of dealing having such regularity of observance in a place, vocation or trade as to justify an expectation that it will be observed with respect to the transaction in question."
57 The preparatory works are not enlightening in that respect.
58 See Goode, 'Usage and its reception in transnational commercial law', fn 20 therein.
59 Ibid, see fn 6 being made subject to fn 20 in Goode 'Usage and its reception in transnational commercial law'. For an interchangeable use of the terms custom, practices of the merchants and trade usages see JD Heydon, '*How the courts develop commercial law by looking outside the trial record into the external world*', pp. 46, 47, where he stated that it is an objective of commercial law that it is identical or comes as close as possible to practices of commercial men (p. 46).
60 Goode, 'Usage and its reception in transnational commercial law', fn 20 therein.
61 Ibid.
62 Ibid, p. 1.
63 See Goode, 'Usage and its reception in transnational commercial law', fn 20 therein.

3.2.1.4 Can the agreement exclude the custom/usage/practice under English law, the Rotterdam Rules and Incoterms® 2010?

With regards to the ambiguity as to the hierarchy between custom and a contrary agreement, the important insufficiency of Article 35 of the RR is that it does not make any reference to the situation where there is an agreement between shipper and carrier to issue a transport document, but there is a custom to the contrary.[64]

As far as custom is concerned, there is international diversity regarding its position in the law. In most civil law countries, it is acknowledged as a source of law, i.e. of rights and obligations, but there are still some countries where it stands solely as a source of interpretation of the law. The resolution of this ambiguity may be crucial in order to ascertain whether an agreement of the parties to issue a transport document may prevail over a contrary custom. This is equally relevant to Incoterms®, as article A8 of the CPT and CIP Incoterms® refers to "customary" and *inter alia* states that "the seller must provide the buyer with the usual transport document". The questions that arise are firstly, if it is customary to issue a usual transport document, can the buyer ask for an unusual one? Secondly, if it is not customary to issue one type of transport document, can the buyer ask for a transport document at all? These questions will be answered forthwith.

Under English law, the principal source of the parties' obligations is the contract itself.[65] Accordingly, when concluding their contract, the parties will specify the rights and obligations and how the contract should be performed through individually negotiated or standard terms. If the rights and obligations are consistent and crystallised,[66] reference to codified law may be unnecessary. However, it is possible that uncertainties or gaps appear, in which case recourse may also be sought from written law and unwritten customs or usages of merchants. Thus, the custom or usage plays an ancillary role to the contract; it determines the content of indefinite terms, or helps define them in light of it. The court may seek evidence of a trade custom or usage in order to imply a term into the contract or in an attempt to interpret it.[67] However, this is done only insofar as the custom or usage is not inconsistent with the express or implied terms of the contract[68]or its nature.[69]

Having seen what happens in case of inconsistencies or conflicts between customs and agreements, the critical question which has to be answered now is

64 As long as the usage and custom are not inconsistent with the agreement, mercantile contracts are to be construed according to the usage and custom of merchants *Re Walkers, Winser & Hamm and Shaw, Son & Co* [1904] 2 KB 152.

65 See LS Sealy and RJA Hooley, *Commercial Law, Text, Cases and Materials* (5th edn, Oxford University Press, 2017), pp. 20, 21 and Roy Goode (ed by E McKendrick), *Goode on Commercial Law* (5th edn, Penguin Books 2016), p. 11.

66 For the importance of having a crystallised custom see Bridge, *The International Sale of Goods*, paras 10.63 and 10.64.

67 Sealy and Hooley, *Commercial Law, Text, Cases and Materials*, p. 24.

68 Ibid, p. 23. See the case *Kum v. Wah Tat Bank Ltd* [1971] 1 Lloyd's Rep. 439.

69 Sealey and Hooley, *Commercial Law, Text, Cases and Materials*, p. 23.

whether an agreement can definitively exclude the custom, and if so, how and when the RR apply. This question has great international trade law significance for various reasons. First, its answer will show the possible uncertainties lurking for trade parties if their agreement is not sufficiently specific in stipulating if a document/record is required and, if so, in what form. This will then suggest the contractual steps traders need to take when entering into their sale and carriage contracts to safeguard against these possibilities. Second, the hierarchy between custom and agreement, before and – hypothetically – after the RR, is also significant in order to illustrate whether the RR may change the current status, and most importantly, in order to reveal the potential of contractual freedom available under the RR, especially compared to English law as it stands.

It is asserted that, under English law, the law merchant is not an "all-encompassing opinio juris", but is composed of trade usages and customs practised from time to time.[70] These usages and customs can be excluded by agreements.[71] A term cannot be implied by virtue of custom if it contradicts the express terms of a contract.[72] In the case *Leopold Walford (London) Ltd v. Les Affréteurs Réunis Société Anonyme*,[73] it was held that a custom only binds parties in the absence of special agreement inconsistent with it. Scrutton LJ stated "if the custom exists as pleaded, it can be excluded by agreement between the parties."[74] The most important dicta are the following:

> It would be absolutely fatal to all commercial business in the city of London if parties who have signed documents can afterwards say that by virtue of a custom that which they have signed is not binding upon them. If this decision upsets the practice in the city of London, let business men read the contracts they sign and alter the form of the commission clause if they want it to conform to the custom. So long as they sign documents they must expect the Courts to pay more attention to what they have signed than to a custom which conflicts with their written contract.[75]

Overall, there seems to be a disagreement between the current position of English law in terms of the conflict of customs and agreements and an academic opinion[76]

70 M Bridge, *The Sale of Goods* (OUP 1997), p. 9; *Goodwin v. Robarts* (1875) LR 10 Ex. 337; *Edelstein v. Schuler & Co* [1902] 2 KB 144. Also in Bridge, *The International Sale of Goods*, para 1.19.

71 Bridge, *The Sale of Goods*, p. 9; *Palgrave, Brown & Son Ltd v. SS Turid (Owners)* [1922] 1 AC 397; *Brown v. Byrne* (1854) 2 E&B 703. Also in Bridge, *The International Sale of Goods*, para 1.19.

72 E Baskind, G Osborne and L Roach, *Commercial Law* (2nd edn, OUP 2016), p. 13.

73 *Leopold Walford (London) Ltd v. Les Affréteurs Réunis Société Anonyme* [1918] 2 KB 498, 503. See also the House of Lords judgment, *Les Affréteurs Réunis Société Anonyme Appellants v. Leopold Walford (London) Ltd Respondents* [1919] AC 801, at p. 809, per Lord Birkenhead LC and the holding of Lord Atkinson at p. 813: "I cannot conceive that there should be in any line of business a custom which would provide that no matter what written agreement was to be entered into, the custom is not to be excluded, but is to prevail over the terms of the written document".

74 [1918] 2 KB 498, p. 507.

75 Ibid, at p. 508. See also, the House of Lords judgment [1919] AC 801, 813.

76 See Lorenzon in Baatz et al, *The Rotterdam Rules: A Practical Annotation*, para 35-02.

on the interpretation of Article 35 of the RR. It has been suggested that in case of conflict between a custom and the agreement, the former should prevail.[77]

With all due respect, our opinion in this book is that there is nothing explicit in the wording of Article 35 to suggest any predominance of the contrary custom over an agreement. In any case this is what can be argued now; since the RR do not yet have the force of law, as the minimum number of ratifications has not yet been met, any predictions are tentative.

For international trade law purposes, it is of paramount importance to ensure that the seller obtains the transport document in order to be paid. Therefore, our suggestion is that the parties should make sure not only that their agreement is clear in specifying that, for instance, a negotiable transport document is needed (and in light of Article 47(2) of the RR whether a document not requiring surrender would be an acceptable tender), but also in stipulating that the agreement should prevail over the contrary custom of the particular trade. In other words, the custom, usage or practice should be expressly excluded in the carriage contract (and ideally also in the sale contract).[78] Of course, this further means that the shipper has to become aware of the practices, usages of the trade, market and port of shipment, as his lack of knowledge may not be excused and consequently it may not suffice to displace the usage/practice/custom.[79]

3.2.1.5 *Concluding remarks*

It is true that the functions of bills of lading and similar documents are to a great extent formed by practice and usage or case law.[80] National laws may prescribe different rights and obligations between shipper, consignee and the bill of lading holder.[81] This welcome consideration as to what is usual or common in the trade also appears in both Incoterms® 2000 and 2010.[82]

Reference to custom is made in article A8 of the CIP Incoterms® Rules 2000, which states that, if customary, the seller must provide the buyer with the usual transport document.[83] The 2010 version is slightly different. It adds another alternative to what is customary so that, ultimately, the seller is under an obligation to

77 Ibid.

78 *Exxonmobil Sales and Supply Corp v. Texaco Ltd (The "Helene Knutsen")* [2003] EWHC 1964 (Comm).

79 See for instance Article 9(2) of the CISG: "The parties are considered, unless otherwise agreed, to have impliedly made applicable to their contract or its formation a usage of which the parties knew *or ought to have known and which in international trade is widely known to, and regularly observed by, parties to the contracts of the type involved in the particular trade concerned.*" (emphasis added by the author).

80 See van der Ziel, 'Delivery of the goods, rights of the controlling party and transfer of rights', p. 598.

81 Ibid.

82 See article A8 of the CIF/CFR Incoterms®.

83 "If customary [...], the seller must provide buyer with the usual transport document [...]"

provide the buyer with a transport document, if it is customary *or at the buyer's request.*[84]

At this point two important observations can be made. The RR, in Article 35, initiate two negative conditions, each one of which may on its own grounds hinder entitlement of the shipper to obtain the document. On the other hand, CIP Incoterms® 2010[85] is phrased differently: article A8 provides two elements,[86] which alternatively *establish the obligation.* Thus, the RR refer to an *entitlement* whereas Incoterms® depict the prerequisites for a *duty.* Both paragraphs are written in a way that does not specify whether and how the entitlement or the obligations are modified if the custom and the buyer's request, in the relevant agreement, contradict each other. It is critically important to know this in order to be in a position to ascertain whether an agreement may prevail over a custom after the enactment of the RR, and accordingly to predict what traders may encounter in their efforts to comply with the contract of sale. Secondly, article A8 of both the CIP[87] and CPT Incoterms® needs to be studied carefully in contrast with the respective paragraph of the CIF Incoterms® as they seem to bear further complexities. An interesting excerpt from article A8 follows:

> *If customary or at the buyer's request*, the seller must provide the buyer, at the seller's expense, *with the usual transport documents(s) for the transport contracted* in accordance with A3.[88]

It has become clear that the first issue arising is this: What is customary and what can the buyer request? This will be discussed, in the context of both Incoterms® and the RR, checking them back to back.

The second issue deserving consideration is the second half of the first sentence of article A8, as cited above. It is therein stated that the seller has to tender the usual transport document for the type of transport in that particular case, if it is customary or if the buyer requests it. The first question triggered out of this is about the definition of the "usual" transport document – how can it be defined? Does it mean usual in the particular trade or port, or usual in the specific parties' transactions?

Furthermore, does article A8 of the Incoterms® allow one to infer that the buyer is allowed to request a transport document other than the customary one? Are the two components of the sentence independent, or does the one complement the other? In principle, it follows on from article A8 that the buyer may ask

84 Article A8 of the CIP Incoterms® 2010 reads: "If customary or at the buyer's request, the seller must provide the buyer [...] with the usual transport document".

85 Same applies to CPT.

86 "If customary or at the buyer's request [...]".

87 The seller must provide the buyer at the seller's expense, if customary, with the usual transport document or documents (for example a negotiable bill of lading, a non-negotiable sea waybill, an inland waterway document, an air waybill, a railway consignment note, a road consignment note, or a multimodal transport document) for the transport contracted in accordance with A3.

88 Article A8 of the CIP/CPT Incoterms® 2010 version (emphasis added).

for the usual document.[89] But what if the buyer requires an alternative one? This will be discussed thoroughly in the following.

In general, CIF Incoterms® are referring to a transport document which is "usual". Nevertheless, with the emergence of the RR, there are differences of which traders should be aware. Although article A8 of the CIF Incoterms® administers the duty of procuring a "usual transport document", the RR go beyond that, by further taking into consideration the agreement of the parties and the negotiability of the document. As already said above, this is done without a clear hierarchy among them.

Even though the 2010 CIP and CPT version is more aligned with the RR (and richer), by contemplating the (buyer's) request and what is customary, the requirement for a usual transport document constitutes a considerable restriction. In that respect, Incoterms® seem to be of a narrower scope in comparison with the RR. One should not forget at this stage that there will often be cases where something is requested or is customarily expected by parties operating in two different contractual realms: for example where the contract of carriage is governed by the RR, whilst the sale contract incorporates the Incoterms, these need to be aligned. The trader vested as shipper/documentary shipper is the one who brings these two spheres together, ensuring that what is contractually expected under a sale contract can be requested and issued under a carriage contract. Understanding that a usage/practice/custom, as used under Incoterms® refers to trade and relationships between buyers/sellers whereas the RR specifically look at the relationship of carrier and shipper/or documentary shipper shows how complex and multipartite a maritime trade transaction is.

Overall, it can be concluded that Incoterms® 2010 have two categories of provisions in relation to the RR. Some of their provisions vary from the respective ones of the RR, which are more specific; others may, occasionally, be outside the spectrum of the RR. Ultimately, whether these two sets of rules will eventually be in absolute accordance will be a matter of fact, or worse, of luck. Irrespective of the fact that the shipping practice is in general terms homogeneously repetitive, it may at times also bear surprises, especially in the context of a new Convention (the RR), which may apply to a range of different nations with individual customs.

This remark brings us back to the initial problem of whether the RR, in an attempt to bring uniformity but also flexibility, open the great door to unknown customs. If the parties' agreement is not solid enough to show awareness of

89 It has been suggested by Bridge, *The International Sale of Goods*, that the "usual" in Incoterms® denotes a bill of lading. See Bridge, *The International Sale of Goods*, para 4.68 and fn 241 therein. However, one should not be absolute as ICC also recognised the surge of non-negotiable documents in modern trade. Jan Ramberg, 'INCOTERMS® 2000 – The necessary link between contracts of sale and contracts of carriage', (2008) 58(1–2) *Zbornik PFZ* 35–46. In p. 38 he states: 'Thus, the seller could fulfill his obligation to tender the documents not only by using of the Bill of Lading but also by using other customarily used transport documents, such as a sea waybill. Consequently, the Free Carrier clause had to reflect this change of practice by referring to 'the usual document or other evidence of the delivery of the goods'. Also Jan Ramberg, *Guide to Incoterms®* (1980 edn), p. 31.

adverse customs/usages/practices and clear hierarchy clauses, carriage and trade disputes will be frequent.

3.2.1.6 Observations

The current position under English law seems to be that, if the parties use express clauses in their carriage contract regarding the type of transport document that needs to be issued, the contract will supersede any contrary custom. However, the seemingly dissenting academic view cited above[90] poses an extra drafting task on trade players. They have to be clear on whether and what transport document they want to receive under the sale and carriage contracts, and additionally, insert terms clarifying that the existing contrary customs should be excluded by virtue of the agreement(s). This extra drafting caution is another fundamental change that the RR will introduce into trade. Hence, until case law clarifies the ambiguities, traders need to insert clear, specific and unambiguous clauses in both the carriage and sale contracts.

On the other hand, as mentioned above, if the contract is silent and shipment is from a place where the custom does not require a particular type of transport document or a transport document to be issued at all, then the shipper will not be entitled to request one. This justifies why the parties need to be aware of the usages or practices of a particular type of trade or place. Accordingly the parties should state as precisely as possible in their contract whether they intend to be bound by this custom, as the position is unclear in such a situation. Additionally, in occasions where article A8 of CIF Incoterms® applies, where the term "customary" or "usual" is used, it should either be displaced in the sale contract, or be followed by a term stipulating that the agreement excluding custom goes beyond the Incoterms®.

3.2.2 What could go wrong

Although, in our opinion it has been illustrated that, after interpreting Article 35 of the RR in light of English law, the agreement will prevail over a conflicting custom, legal uncertainty remains for other legal systems. As we have seen, Article 35 of the RR does not make specific distinction between adverse agreements and customs. Therefore, there may be different legal conceptions with regard to the role of the custom or distinctions between custom and trade usages;[91] they may either be considered as a source of law serving for interpretation,[92] or be of a normative or contractual character[93] and constitute an independent source of rights

90 Expressed in Baatz et al, *The Rotterdam Rules: A Practical Annotation*, para 35-02.

91 C Schmitthoff, 'International trade usages' (1987) *Institute of International Business Law and Practice*, ICC, pp. 25–26.

92 As is the position under English law. See Bridge, *The Sale of Goods*, p. 9.

93 Schmitthoff, 'International trade usages', pp. 25–26.

and obligations that cannot be contracted out. Practices on the other hand might not have an independent binding force.

More illustratively, if the law of the place of shipment does not allow contractual freedom to create the obligation for the issuance of a transport document because there is custom/usage of trade to the contrary, the transport document cannot be issued.

This ambiguity originates from the wording of Article 35 of the RR (and the lack of definition of trade, usage and custom by the RR) and is of high commercial and legal importance. It is first and foremost traders and carriers who should be concerned about it as this article regulates the entitlement to a transport document. Therefore, it stands as the key article for documentary performance under the sale contract. The tender of the appropriate transport document triggers three things: firstly, delivery of the goods is sought usually with the release of the document; secondly, if the tender is contractual, payment is due, and when payment is effected via a letter of credit, the document goes through the banks' check; finally, if goods are to be traded down the line, title to the goods from the seller can be transferred to the buyer by obtaining a negotiable transport document (and preferably, for security purposes, by obtaining one that requires surrender).[94]

We are aware that one might argue that it is perhaps difficult or impossible to find a jurisdiction forbidding the issuance of a negotiable or non-negotiable transport document, as per the customary law or usage or practice of trade of the place of shipment. However, it is the wording of Article 35, "or it is the custom, usage or practice of trade not to use one (transport document or electronic transport record)", which infers that there might be such a contingency, therefore all the possibilities should be investigated. This is also unequivocally stated in one of the first commentaries on the RR.[95] The RR are not yet in force, so, even if this is not yet the case with the existing signatories, nothing prevents us from thinking that there might be countries signing/ratifying the RR in the future who have such contrary shipping customs, practices and usages.

Now that the above clarification has been presented, we will illustrate the unpleasant legal surprises that traders may encounter due to a contrary custom or usage or practice of trade. Case scenarios where Incoterms® may apply will be presented.

If the sale contract is governed by English law without the incorporation of any Incoterms® and is silent on the issue of what transport document should be tendered, then case law[96] demands the issuance of a negotiable transport document. According to Article 35 of the RR, if there is a custom or usage not to issue a transport document of any type in particular, no transport document will be issued.[97]

94 Parties should ensure that they contract out of Article 47(2) of the RR, as discussed in the previous chapter.

95 See also von Ziegler, Schelin and Zunarelli (eds), *The Rotterdam Rules 2008*, p. 163.

96 See the *Soproma SpA v. Marine and Animal By-Products Corp* [1966] 1 Lloyd's Rep 367.

97 See von Ziegler, Schelin and Zunarelli (eds), *The Rotterdam Rules 2008*, p. 163.

The above concerns are very significant for international trade law, as the seller *qua* shipper will be in breach of the sale contract if it is governed by English law. The problem remains if the purchase contract incorporates CIF Incoterms®, as under article A8 the seller "must, at its own expense, provide the buyer without delay with the usual transport document [...]".[98]

For this reason, it is recommended that before the sale and the carriage contracts are entered into, the seller or the buyer, depending on who is going to be the shipper, will have to find out whether they can arrange for an appropriate contract of carriage and transport document. If they discover that there is custom or usage not requiring the issuance of a transport document at a specific port/trade, the responsible party for carriage might have to ship elsewhere. As a consequence, complications might arise, as discussed in the next section.

If sales are concluded on FOB terms, things become even more difficult with regard to documentary credits, as the transport document needs to be presented to the bank so that the seller can receive payment. Let us suppose that the seller was expecting to receive the customary documents. Thus, it may be that the FOB seller is only entitled to the mate's receipt, for instance, and not a transport document, or, in some cases, no document at all. In this case, the buyer and consequently the bank would have been better secured by getting a bill of lading, which is, however, unavailable due to Article 35 of the RR.

Therefore, although theoretically it is a great freedom and factor of flexibility that no particular document is required, unless requested, trading without the bill of lading attacks the flow of international trade and imposes obstacles on the payment mechanism. If a particular FOB buyer wants to sell goods to another buyer on CIF terms, a mate's receipt will be of very little value. As discussed in Chapter 2, the mate's receipt is not a transport document under the RR.

We suggest this solution to get out of the above dead end: the contract of sale will have to provide for cash against documents.[99] In such a case, however, it is difficult to see how the goods in question might be sold down a string (most likely in CIF terms). Especially if traders are based in several countries and they need the bank's assistance to finance the sale contract, the letter of credit is their best solution. This complexity is remarkably detrimental to international trade, hindering its very essence; thus sales down a string cannot be performed smoothly or at all.

Another significant question to ask is does the CIF shipper need to be aware of customs that juxtapose the stipulations of the sale contract? This is an issue that has attracted much academic debate and the legal position on this may vary among different jurisdictions.[100] Secondly, can the CIF seller/shipper be held

98 Article A8 CIF Incoterms® 2000, ICC, p. 70 and Incoterms® 2010, ICC, p. 238 (of the Dutch–English edition), respectively.

99 Some argue that this will be impracticable due to anti-money laundering regulations, but Michael Bridge takes a different view in his book, *The International Sale of Goods*, para 6.21. Letters of credit are frequent in the oil trade, whereas, in the trade of dry commodities imported from America to Europe, cash against documents is prevalent.

100 See Schmitthoff, 'International trade usages', pp. 16–17.

liable if he has not informed the other parties so that they can make different arrangements? It could be argued that if the carrier is aware of the contrary custom, he will never agree to issue a transport document that is not customarily issued. However, although the above scenario is prima facie extreme, it is likely to occur, especially after the sale contract has been concluded and the goods are on board. If the buyer, in a CIF case, is waiting for the transport document to be issued, but receives notification by the shipper that one cannot be issued, he will be faced with difficult commercial and legal decisions that have to be made promptly.

The lack of information with respect to the unexpected practice, or the difficulty caused in trying to identify whether the agreement or the usage will prevail, might trigger a delay in the shipment and performance of the contract of sale. This delay will then cost money, time and efficiency, especially if this buyer has entered into a subsequent sale contract; if Buyer 2 expects a specific transport document, Buyer 1 will face important commercial pressure. The seller may eventually fail to ship within the shipment period, giving the buyer the right to terminate the sale contract.[101] Consequently, there are two possibilities here: either the seller will have to find another carrier and ship elsewhere; or it might be in the buyer's interest to enter into a sale contract with another trader at another port. This, in turn might lead to a loss of profit and time or to the marginalisation of traders from specific countries where the trade customs are "strict".

Alternatively, transhipment of the goods is another solution, so that the transport document is issued at a subsequent port. Thus, the sale contract will be performed in the first place by a shipment evidenced in another shipping document, perhaps falling outside the definition of the transport document, such as the mate's receipt. However, as the desired transport document will then be issued by a subsequent carrier, the sale contract requirement can be ultimately satisfied. For this solution to be practical, the shipper has to act promptly so as to ship within the shipment period of the sale contract.

Therefore, here again is the need for express requirements and hierarchy clauses in the sale contract. More specifically, the parties have to clarify whether and what type of document is needed first, and whether there is an existing custom or usage to the contrary which is excluded in favour of the agreement. Evidently, buyers in the middle of the trade chain have to be more cautious. They always have to ensure that the first and subsequent sale contracts are concluded back to back, so that they can coordinate their sellers/shippers accordingly. In the terminology of Incoterms®, the document will be "procured".[102]

Under the Incoterms®, the mate's receipt is not a transport document, but it can, for example, be considered a valid tender, in an FOB contract as proof of delivery. However, the Incoterms® also specify that "The seller must provide

101 Time is of the essence in a sale contract. See *Bowes v. Shand* (1877) 2 App Cas 455 (HL); Takahashi, 'Right to terminate (avoid) international sales of commodities'.

102 Article A8 of the CIF Incoterms®.

the buyer, at the seller's expense, with the usual proof that the goods have been delivered in accordance with A4. The seller must provide assistance to the buyer, at the buyer's request, risk and expense, in obtaining a transport document." A concern arising from the Incoterms® is that there is no definition of the "usual" transport document for a particular mode of transport, especially in the context of Incoterms® used for multimodal transportation.[103] This is important, as several types of documents may be used for maritime transportation, depending on the trade. A negotiable transport document was traditionally an established practice which enabled transfer of the title of the goods, and could satisfy the "usual" requirements.[104] This was also suitable for the purpose of consecutive sales, since the prospective buyers would not be in possession of the goods. However, it is submitted that as time has progressed, the change of trade practices and modes of transport have also brought a cumulative change in the norms.[105]

For instance, it is now common to see types of documents being used in maritime transport, which previously were only typical to other types of transport.[106] At the same time, in maritime carriage,[107] non-negotiable bills of lading have been in use, particularly when traders have established prior business together.[108] Nevertheless, the question remains: what document would fall under the scope "usual" transport document[109] which would customarily be issued in an era of massive containerisation and frequent changes to practices? This will be discussed in the following section.

3.2.2.1 Consolidated suggestions with regard to the "custom" and "usual" interpretational concerns under the Rotterdam Rules and Incoterms®

As it has already been observed, the RR and Incoterms® 2010 can cause confusion due to terms such as "custom", "usual", "usage" and "trade practice". Both of them fail to state what "usual" and "custom" mean, but they also leave many occasions unregulated. For instance, article A8 of the CPT Incoterms® does not indicate whether the buyer may request a transport document which is not usual. Perhaps this should not be of concern, as Incoterms® are not mandatorily incorporated into sale contracts. This means that there can be other supplementary terms purposefully inserted to define their content or restrict their application to a specific case. Disputes may also arise in cases where there is a misunderstanding as to what is usual in a particular trade or port of shipment or place of delivery, in multimodal transport cases; for example, what will happen when the buyer has requested a transport document which is not usual, and the

103 See Jan Ramberg, *ICC Guide to Incoterms®*, ICC, under A8.

104 Ibid, p. 115.

105 Ibid.

106 Report by the UNCTAD Secretriat, '*The use of transport documents in international trade*' at unctad.org/en/docs/sdtetlb20033_en.pdf for statistics regarding multimodal documents.

107 Ibid.

108 Ibid.

109 As per the Incoterms® terminology.

seller has failed to obtain the specific one requested, but has tendered the usual one, for reasons amounting to local custom? Is he in breach of the sale contract, when CIP/CPT Incoterms® are incorporated therein? In our opinion, the plausible view could be that tender of a usual document would be compliant with CIP/CPT sales. If, on the other hand, the contract of sale is silent, only the usual document is a compliant tender under CIF terms. A parallel look at article A10 is always advisable, as in complex cases, a solution might be suggested by the seller proving how necessary the document he is requesting is.[110]

We need to be aware of the following variations as well: what is customary in one area of trade may be an electronic document, but what is customary, for example at a certain port of Malaysia, may be a mate's receipt. Would the English buyer, the Malaysian captain and the local seller understand the same by "usual document" or "usual document of title"? Can these understandings and commercial expectations be reconciled or avoided at contractual level? The trade conundrum that parties need to be more aware of under the RR and the Incoterms®, is the diversity of usages of trade depending on the type of goods, but parties also need to be aware of the local (port) usages of different countries of shipment and the legal recognition of these customs and the legal characterisation of what is issued under the different jurisdictions (of shipment, delivery of the goods and the chosen English forum and jurisdiction).

The "usual" requirement of Incoterms® refers to the transport document and not to the carriage contract as such. It is also uncertain whether by virtue of Article 47(2) of the RR, a negotiable document which does not require surrender could be considered usual or customary within Incoterms®. In the next section, we delve into other categories of shipping documents, which are of varied recognition among different jurisdictions.

3.3 Reflections on the role of custom and the applicable law when considering other types of shipping documents with reference to the Rotterdam Rules

The RR adopt a flexible definition of negotiable transport documents, combining the role of uniform and national law.[111] The purpose in the following discussion is firstly, to investigate whether the RR, through the definition of negotiable documents and the application of Article 35 of the RR, open the gates for the recognition and legitimate request of documents other than the popular bill of lading. Secondly, we investigate whether customary shipping documents, other than the bill of lading or the sea waybill, will be considered compliant tenders under a sale contract when the RR will also apply. The reason for this search is that these documents may be particularly popular in certain trades or ports but may not be recognised or enforced under certain jurisdictions.

110 Advice provided at the seminar 'Incoterms® 2010 Rules and trade practice', 14 November 2011, LSLC.

111 Sturley, Fujita and van der Ziel, *The Rotterdam Rules*, para 7.011.

Our point here is that a document may, by virtue of a custom, be considered negotiable in a certain trade or jurisdiction, but there are two additional questions that have to be answered when looking at the coverage of the document by the RR and its compliance with the sale contract. First, does the document issued pass the threshold of Article 35; and second, does it qualify as a negotiable document under the RR? Additionally, does the document issued constitute a good tender under the sale contract? Here, focus will be placed on switch bills of lading and mate's receipts. Our purpose in this section is to demonstrate that some documents may only ostensibly seem to be negotiable, but they may ultimately not constitute transport documents recognised by the RR. This is what happens with documents that are documents of title by custom but do not evidence the contract of carriage.

On the other hand, there may be documents or non-transport documents that are validly issued because the custom or usage enables their issuance, but these documents may not constitute a good tender under English law if the latter governs an international sale contract. A particular research into switch bills of lading and mate's receipts is useful at this stage.

The practice of switching bills of lading is not uncommon,[112] especially in Asia.[113] Switch bills are essentially replacement bills issued upon the request of the holder of the original set of bills. A replacement bill may be necessary in order to change the name of the original shipper[114] and instead designate a subsequent seller as shipper, as usually happens in string sales. Frequently, switch bills are requested in order to amend the actual port of discharge or loading as it may have subsequently changed,[115] or in an attempt to conceal it in order to avoid unfavourable Customs' duties.[116] The particular problem associated with the use of switch bills is the danger of the original and replacement bills coexisting when the original bills have not been returned to the carrier. Most importantly, there is a fear that bills will be switched in an attempt to circumvent mandatory legislation. From the existing case law, it seems that different countries have a different approach towards the practice of recognising and enforcing switch bills.

In the Singapore High Court case *Samsung Corp v. Devon Industries*,[117] the FOB buyer colluded with the carrier's agent for the issuance of 18 replacement bills showing the former as shipper, without having paid the seller or having surrendered the original bills of lading to the carrier. Selvam J appeared supportive of the use of switch bills, to the extent that the original set is duly endorsed to the buyers and then returned to the shipowners or their agents.[118]

112 Toh Kian Sing, 'Of straight and switch bills of lading' [1996] *LMCLQ* 416.

113 S Girvin, *Carriage of Goods by Sea* (2nd edn, OUP 2011), para 11.11.

114 Ibid, para 11.12.

115 Or in order to divide quantities of cargo: *Voyage Charters*, para 18.82

116 On this particular reason see Kian Sing, 'Of straight and switch bills of lading', pp. 419, 420.

117 [1995] SGHC 246; [1995] 3 SLR (3) 603. Mentioned by Kian Sing, 'Of straight and switch bills of lading', p. 418 and Girvin, *Carriage of Goods by Sea*, para 11.12.

118 See Kian Sing, 'Of straight and switch bills of lading', p. 419.

Concerns over the use of switch bills are justified when it is suspected that fraud lurks behind their issuance.[119] Inducing the issuance of replacement bills to breach the law[120] may prove to be in conflict with English public policy thus rendering the carriage contract evidenced by such switch bills unenforceable.[121]

It has been argued[122] that, according to *Soproma SpA Marine & Animal By-Products Corp*,[123] tender of a switch bill of lading would be satisfactorily accepted as a negotiable document of title. The critical question to ask at this stage is whether a switch bill of lading would match the definition of negotiable transport document under Article 1(15) of the RR.

According to Article 1(15) of the RR, negotiable transport document means:

> a transport document that indicates, by wording such as "to order" or "negotiable" or other appropriate wording recognized *as having the same effect by the law applicable to the document*,[124] that the goods have been consigned to the order of the shipper [...].

Considering also the wording of Article 35 of the RR, we will see that it suggests that the custom may determine the issuance of a (negotiable or non-negotiable) transport document, but there may be cases in which a negotiable document is a bad tender under the sale contract for several reasons. For instance, if a scenario such as that of *NV Arnold Otto Meyer v. Aune*[125] occurs in practice, a switch bill would prima facie be tendered because, for example, ocean bills in exchange of coastal bills comply with a recognised custom in the Philippines. The question that has to be asked is how would that be interpreted by an English court faced with a dispute arising out of an international carriage or sale contract governed by English law. The answer, in that particular respect, would be that, from a carriage perspective, the carrier has the right to issue switch bills of lading because that is the custom of the port (namely the Philippines in our hypothetical example) as per Article 35 of the RR, but for trade law purposes, the document also has to comply with the requirement of English law, in that the bill of lading tendered to the buyer should not only be negotiable, but also cover the goods from the port of dispatch to the port of destination,[126] which did not happen here. The following dictum of Branson J is very illustrative:[127]

119 *Noble Resources Ltd v. Cavalier Shipping Corporation (The Atlas)* [1996] 1 Lloyd's Rep 642, 644 where Longmore J underlined that the issuance of switch bills raises "obvious opportunities for fraud".

120 Kian Sing, 'Of straight and switch bills of lading', p. 419.

121 Ibid, pp. 419–420, who cited the cases *Foster v. Driscoll* [1929] 1 KB 470 and *Regazzoni v. KC Sethia (1944) Ltd* [1958] AC 301.

122 Ibid.

123 [1966] 1 Lloyd's Rep 367.

124 Emphasis added by the author.

125 [1939] 3 All ER 168.

126 *Hansson v. Hamel & Horley Ltd* [1922] 2 AC 36; *NV Arnold Otto Meyer v. Aune* [1939] 3 All ER 168.

127 [1939] 3 All ER 168, 172,173.

> If, in any particular trade, there is a custom that bills of lading should have other characteristics in addition to, or in substitution for those generally required by the custom of merchants, then, *in that trade*, bills of lading, to be a good tender, *need only conform to that custom.*[128]

The following conclusions follow from our analysis. From a pure carriage perspective, more documents, especially switch bills, may pass the test of Article 1(15) of the RR with regards to their negotiable character, as they have been characterised as "full-fledged documents of title".[129] However, attention to the detail needs to be paid here in order to determine how difficult it is to have them issued in the first place, as far as the RR are concerned. Article 35 determines which document the shipper and documentary shipper can request from the carrier.

Assuming that the party seeking the switch of the bills is the buyer, consignee or holder, this means that what can be requested has to be assessed by reference to the provisions of the RR on right of control. Thus, the holder would, most likely, be the controlling party if a negotiable document is issued and it will be an issue of interpretation to see whether a change of the name of the consignee or shipper is allowed. According to Article 50(1)(c) of the RR, the controlling party has the right to replace the consignee by any other person. However, with regards to changing the name of the shipper, the answer does not seem to be straightforward. It can be argued that Article 54 of the RR could be relevant, as the new requirements of the "switch bill" could be construed to fall under "variations to the contract of carriage other than those referred to in article 50, subparagraphs 1(b) and (c)".[130] What needs to be emphasised is that any remarks made at this stage are tentative, as, so far, commentators have not related the issuance of the switch bills to any international convention of this type. Therefore, we have to remember that, as the RR stipulate the right of control, the right of the controlling party, in Article 54 of the RR, is subject to the agreement of carrier and the controlling party.

The problem remains as to whether, from a trade law perspective this time, tender of the switch bill constitutes a breach of the sale contract. The requirement for continuous documentary cover under English law may treat the tender of a replacement bill as a breach of the sale contract. Secondly, and most importantly, the issue remains as to the possible varied perception of these tenders, from the trade and carriage law perspective, taking into consideration the jurisdiction, the customs of the trade of that jurisdiction and the possible conflict with a certain jurisdiction's public policy when fraud lurks underneath. From that viewpoint, whether a switch bill of lading can be issued under the RR is uncertain, but it is important.

However, what happens at the stage where rights are claimed under a switch bill is of primordial significance. Generally, a switch bill of lading, or an

128 Emphasis added by the author.

129 Kian Sing, 'Of straight and switch bill of lading', pp. 421–422.

130 Article 54(1) of the RR.

accompanying letter of indemnity, may be considered illegal or unenforceable by a national court.[131] English courts take a reluctant approach towards switch bills. On the other hand, courts in the South East Asia do not share the same approach. This is illustrated by the following dictum of Selvam J in *Samsung Corp v. Devon Industries*:[132]

> The practice of cutting and releasing 'global bills of lading' is perfectly in order provided the [original] bills of lading issued to the real shippers [...] have been received lawfully by the [buyers] duly indorsed and surrendered to the ship owners or their agents. In other words, ship owners may issue "global bills of lading" in exchange for the first set of bills of lading issued to the shippers.

It is also critical to make some clarifications here with regards to the mate's receipt. A question that may be interesting for trade is whether under the RR a mate's receipt can by virtue of custom be considered a negotiable transport document, which was also of importance in *Kum v. Wah Tat Bank*.[133]

It has to be clarified here that the RR do not provide any definition for documents of title. Their closest reference to them is the term "negotiable transport documents/records". These are defined in Article 1(15) of the RR as seen above.

In the preparatory works, it was clarified that:[134]

> In any event, it was also pointed out that the scope of the reference to applicable law was limited to the question of which expressions might legally be equivalents of words such as "to order" or "negotiable".

This means for example, that if under a certain law applicable to the transport document, a wording such as "to the consignee or his assigns" is an alternative way of stipulating "to the order of the consignee", then this document would be considered negotiable under the RR.[135] It has to be emphasised therefore that the role of the applicable law under Article 1(15) of the RR relates to the wording of the document, and this is what matters for the assessment of its negotiable character. It has to be added at this stage that the document should also not contain a phrase rendering it non-negotiable. This takes us to a case where the customary use of a mate's receipt as a document of title and the wording in particular were at stake.

131 *Brown Jenkinson v. Percy Dalton* [1957] 2 QB 621.
132 This abstract is cited in Kian Sing, 'Of straight and switch bill of lading', p. 419.
133 [1971] 1 Lloyd's Rep 439 PC.
134 UNCITRAL, Report of Working Group III (Transport Law) on the work of its twenty-first session (Vienna, 14–25 January 2008), A/CN.9/645, para 120.
135 See Sturley, Fujita and van der Ziel, *The Rotterdam Rules*, Illustration 7-1.

A mate's receipt is usually issued before the bill of lading, which is then obtained in exchange of the former.[136] The Federal Court of Malaysia found that it was customary to treat mate's receipts as documents of title in the Singapore-Sarawak trade.[137] However, by virtue of the wording of the particular receipts issued (named "non-negotiable") the Privy Council held that this was not the case, as the custom was inconsistent with the words "non-negotiable".[138] The custom and the wording of a document become important under Article 1(15) of the RR. However, the case would have been decided in the same way under the application of the RR, as, despite the custom, the wording in that case, under the applicable law, would determine that the document was non-negotiable. It is plausible to think that the outcome could be different had the restrictive wording not been there. In essence, no recourse is needed here to the wording of Article 1(15) of the RR: mate's receipts do not seem to be covered by the RR because they merely operate as receipts and do not evidence the contract of carriage, meaning that they cannot be considered as transport documents at all.[139] It is this consideration that disqualifies them.

However, the above case is thought-provoking, inviting us to consider whether the custom could indeed broaden the possible "legitimate" tenders of documents under Article 35 of the RR, assuming that the wording of the document did not cause obstacles. The RR seem more open in this regard, but there will be additional checks along the way in light of the definitions of the RR, the applicable law, the place of the issuance, the jurisdiction of the courts seized and the terms of the sale contract (Incoterms® if applicable etc.).

In the following section the discrepancies between the RR and the UCP 600 are revealed.

3.4 The Rotterdam Rules and the UCP 600

As stated above, the RR and their impact on international trade law cannot be read in an isolated way. They need to be studied in conjunction with the other sets of rules that govern an international transaction, such as the UCP 600. Both sets of rules are analysed in order to assess when tender of the transport document complies with both rules, so that the seller gets paid.

Presentation of a transport document compliant with the UCP 600 is critical, as it signifies that the seller is entitled to receive payment. For this to happen, the beneficiary (seller) needs to be aware of all the requirements both under the RR and the UCP 600. Possible points of controversy between these sets of rules will hereby be investigated. The reader should remember that the RR do not directly apply to letters of credit. If and what transport document will be issued depends

136 *Nippon Yusen Kaisha v. Ramjiban Serowgee* [1938] AC 429.

137 *Wah Tat Bank Ltd and Overseas Chinese Banking Corp Ltd v. Chan Cheng Kum and Hua Siang Steamship Co (Singapore) Ltd (Third Parties)* [1967] 2 Lloyd's Rep 437; Lorenzon, *Sassoon on CIF and FOB Contracts*, p. 160.

138 *Kum v. Wah Tat Bank Ltd* [1971] 1 Lloyd's Rep 439 PC.

139 Article 1(14) of the RR.

on the RR and the agreement of the parties, as discussed at the beginning of the chapter. However, from a holistic international trade law perspective, the transport document also has to meet the threshold of the UCP 600, otherwise it will be rejected by banks.

As soon as the individual provisions of the letter of credit are agreed, they should be strictly complied with[140] otherwise the beneficiary-seller is condemned to remaining unpaid. Articles 19–26 of the UCP 600 will be discussed, along with the relevant articles of the RR. Article 20 of the UCP 600 will be compared to Article 36 and 39 of the RR to determine whether the two sets of rules contain identical provisions for the identification and signature of the carrier. Finally, the RR and the UCP 600 provisions on the "shipped on board" or "ready for shipment" bill of lading (transport document) will be studied, along with the requirements on the name of the vessel in order to discover possible discrepancies.

The first remark that can be made after reading both the RR and the UCP 600 is that there are different types of classification of transport documents. The RR have one basic distinction between negotiable and non-negotiable documents, while the UCP 600 further breaks them down into specific documents such as bills of lading, charterparty bills of lading, non-negotiable sea waybills etc. Therefore the terminology used is slightly different between the two sets of rules.

For instance, Article 27 of the UCP 600, although entitled "clean transport document" also applies to documents under Articles 19–26 of the UCP 600, even though they are not entitled "transport documents". The problem is that there is an additional burden on traders and banks' checkers who have to take into consideration both sets of requirements (the RR and the UCP 600) and their classifications. First, a seller needs to check whether the carriage contract complies with the requirements of the RR when they apply; and second, there needs to be a double-check to ensure that the same document can be approved by the bank for payment. One could argue with regards to this that it should not be seen as a problem as all the respective articles for the different types of documents start with the phrase: "A x-document, however named [...]".

This can give rise to complications where the transport documents are wrongly titled: for example, when a document is titled as a non-negotiable document, or where their type is mistakenly judged because of their title. It is essential that the document itself is scrutinised[141] to determine what type of document it is. A banks' checker looks at the documents on their face, and it is uncertain how deeply they might search to find the type of the document. Our opinion is that the phrase "A x-document, however named [...]", indeed renders the situation

140 M Barnett and M Isaacs, 'International trade finance – Letters of credit, UCP 600 and examination of documents' (2007) 22 (12) *Journal of International Banking Law and Regulation* 660; Jason Chuah, 'UCP 600 new challenges and issues' (2007) 13(2) *JIML* 73; M Hwaidi, 'The story of the English strict compliance principle in letters of credit and its consistency with the UCP' (2014) *JIBLR* 71.

141 Even this control cannot always be exhaustive, see for instance Article 22(b) of UCP 600.

even more complicated as it is evident that the title of the document gives no clue as to its type.

Overall, our point is that the phrase "however named" is positive, in providing flexibility in terms of documents that serve the same functions but have different provisional titles. At the same time, this may lead to ambiguity, since the RR use the "transport document" terminology in a different, specific context.[142] Ideally, the UCP 600 could adopt the division and document names of the RR, after the RR come into force. This will enable a better alignment and reconciled application of both frameworks for a positive impact on both the trade and carriage realms. Until the sets of rules and relevant documents are redrafted with the purpose that they all match each other in their definitions, academics, legal practitioners and not least traders need to be aware of the differences that exist between the two regimes with regards to the same issues. Now we look at specific provisions of the RR and the UCP 600 in order to decipher issues of possible incompatibility and their importance in international trade law.

3.4.1 Identification of the carrier

Article 36 of the RR is a significant article for international trade. Article 36(2)(b) of the RR specifies that the contract particulars of the transport document should contain the name and address of the carrier. The latter requirement has constituted another innovation of the RR in relation to the previous carriage regimes.[143] On the other hand, the respective Articles 19–23 of the UCP 600 request only the inclusion of the name of the carrier.[144] The question triggered is this: If the document shows only the name and not the address of the carrier, what is the legal consequence? Article 39(1) of the RR[145] provides the answer:

> The absence or inaccuracy of one or more of the contract particulars referred to in article 36, paragraphs 1, 2 or 3, does not of itself affect the legal character or validity of the transport document or of the electronic transport record.

But why then does the UCP 600 ask only for the name and the RR for both name and address? The preparatory works[146] make it clear that the intention during

142 Article 1(14) of the RR states as follows: "Transport document" means a document issued under a contract of carriage by the carrier that: (a) Evidences the carrier's or a performing party's receipt of goods under a contract of carriage; and (b) Evidences or contains a contract of carriage.

143 See Baatz et al, *The Rotterdam Rules: A Practical Annotation*, para [36-07].

144 Articles 19–23 of the UCP 600, para a(i).

145 Article 37(2) of the RR provides directions as to who will be deemed to be the carrier if no person is identified as such in the contract particulars.

146 UNCITRAL Doc A/CN.9/526, para 32 Report of Working Group III (Transport Law) on the work of its eleventh session (New York, 24 March to 4 April 2003).

the deliberations was that the provisions of the RR on the contract particulars[147] could match with the requirements of the (then) UCP 500. In the meantime, the UCP have been updated. The requirement of the UCP 500 for "name and address" has been reduced to a requirement for the "address" of the carrier only in the UCP 600.[148] Although, the need to amend the respective article of the RR was pointed out and accepted in the deliberations,[149] the article was not amended.[150] Perhaps this was due to the discussion dealing with suggestions by delegations of the developing countries to impose additional compulsory information on the particulars of the transport document such as the ports of loading and destination and the address of the consignee.[151] If, according to Article 39(1) of the RR, a lack of a requirement of Article 36 of the RR, such as the address, can always be disregarded without making the transport document invalid, this may only cause additional obstacles to the trader who may be vainly pushing his carrier to comply with this formality.

Awareness of this discrepancy between the UCP 600 and the RR is however important. A trader (shipper/documentary shipper) might insist on the inclusion of the address, from fear that otherwise the transport document will not comply with Article 36 of the RR. If the shipper (or documentary shipper) insists on this requirement, the carrier may refuse, and this may result in delay of issuance of the transport document. The advice to traders is that the transport document does not need to evidence the address. The document, if generally compliant with the UCP 600, will make it through the banks' documentary check as an acceptable tender.

In the following section we examine the signature requirement contained in both the RR and the UCP 600.

3.4.2 *Signature*

Signature of the transport document is another crucial issue that should be regarded with caution. Article 38(1) of the RR specifies that "the document shall be signed by the carrier or a person acting on their behalf". This obligation is not described further. For instance, agency issues are not regulated and it has been held that they should be left to the applicable law.[152]

147 The contract particulars are defined in Article 1(23) of the RR as: "any information relating to the contract of carriage or to the goods (including terms, notations, signatures and endorsements) that is in a transport document or an electronic transport record".

148 Doc A/CN.9/621, para 276. The draftsmen agreed that the requirements relating to the identity of the carrier had to become aligned with UCP 600. There was no need to request the address too.

149 Doc A/CN.9/621, para 277. It was stated that "The Working Group agreed to review paragraph 2(a) (of draft article 37) to ensure its consistency with UCP 600".

150 Doc A/CN.9/645, para 131.

151 A/CN.9/SR.871. Summary record of the 871st meeting.

152 See Sturley, Fujita and van der Ziel, *The Rotterdam Rules*, para 7.058. Especially on the considerations what the RR should provide for the electronic signature and what should be left for national

The UCP 600, on the other hand, have more comprehensive signature requirements. For instance, Article 20 of the UCP 600 stipulates that the document must be signed by the carrier or ***a named agent*** and not merely a ***person acting on its behalf***. It further provides that any signature by the carrier, master or agent must be identified as that of the carrier, master or agent, and that any signature by an agent must indicate whether the agent has signed for or on behalf of the carrier, master or agent.

Thus, if the transport document contains "X as agents", this will not constitute a compliant tender under UCP 600 as it does not make clear whether there is authorisation for the signature. Similarly, it has been pointed out that the indication "X as agents only" does not satisfy the banks' requirements concerning letters of credit as it is not clear on behalf of whom the agent signs.[153] Additionally, it has been suggested that, if a P&O Nedlloyd Bill of Lading, which indicates the full address of P&O's head office on the reverse, is issued stating the address of the head office on the reverse and signed with the statements "X & Co as agents only" or "X as agent of the carrier", it would be a bad tender under the UCP 600.[154]

To conclude, the RR contain less requirements on signature compared to the UCP 600. Consequently, a bill of lading (or negotiable transport document) for instance, may be in compliance with the RR but not with the UCP 600. This means that the carrier may have complied with his obligations towards the shipper under the RR, but the seller will be deprived of payment under the letter of credit. Hence, there is an element of disharmony there that can have an international trade law impact.

Accordingly, traders should take the provisions of the UCP 600 under consideration to ensure that their more thorough requirements are met when there is a letter of credit involved in overseas sales. This is particularly important for sellers as beneficiaries under letters of credit. The same caution towards the UCP 600 requirements has to be met especially in strings of sales, regardless of whether the first sale is a cash against documents transaction. The trader who buys against documents (on FOB or CIF terms) but sells further on and has agreed to get paid under a letter of credit, has to be particularly meticulous in the requirements to be fulfilled with regards to the transport document that has to be received by his seller. This transport document will then be procured down a string, and if non-compliant, it will not satisfy the documentary credit's check.

The following section deals with provisions on "received for shipment" or "on board" documents and the requirements on the name of the vessel specification under the two sets of rules.

law, see A/CN.9/576, Report of Working Group III (Transport Law) on the work of its fifteenth session (New York, 18–28 April 2005), paras 201–203.

153 For the two cases above, see Filippo Lorenzon, 'Transport documents through the bankers' sieve: Rotterdam Rules v UCP 600', Conference paper at the 3rd Arab Conference for Commercial and Maritime Law (ACCCML 09), Alexandria, Egypt, 18–19 April 2009, p. 3.

154 Ibid, citing ICC Doc. 470/TA.678rev (UCP600).

3.4.3 Shipped on board bill of lading: the name of the vessel

Article 20(a)(ii) of the UCP 600 states that a bill of lading, however named, must appear to indicate that the goods have been *shipped on board a named vessel* at the port of loading. A shipped on board bill of lading with the name of the vessel is thus clearly required under the letter of credit. On the other hand, the respective article of the RR, Article 36(3)(b), specifies that: "The contract particulars, in the transport document [...] shall further include (b) The name of the ship, if specified in the contract of carriage."

As far as information regarding shipment is concerned, Article 36(2)(c) of the RR stipulates that:

> The contract particulars in the transport document [...] shall include the date on which the carrier or a performing party received the goods, or on which the goods were loaded on board the ship, or on which the transport document was issued.

Although the need for the name of the vessel was of particular interest to some states,[155] eventually it was clarified that perhaps the name of the vessel is not known at the beginning of the voyage. It might also be time-consuming to get it, and in any case it could be added in a prior agreement.[156]

From the above, it is evident that the UCP 600 are stricter in their requirements as they ask concretely for a shipped on board bill of lading that names the carrying vessel. This means that traders have to be able to comply with the stricter provisions of the UCP 600 to secure payment. Accordingly, this means that sellers *qua* shippers/documentary shippers should be afforded the possibility, by virtue of their sale contract, to exercise pressure on the carrier to comply with the more stringent provisions of the RR.

Difficulties may arise when a sale contract does not state its requirements regarding the ship's name on the transport document and the UCP 600 apply.[157] Therefore, at any time when documents such as the contract of carriage or bill of lading do not stipulate the name of the vessel, complexities may occur.

In this case, although there would not be a breach under the RR, the transport document would not amount to a valid tender under the UCP 600.[158] It is

155 For instance Senegal. See UNCITRAL Doc A/CN.9/SR.871, Summary Record of the 871st meeting, Finalization and approval of a draft convention on contracts for the international carriage of goods wholly or partly by sea (continued) (A/CN.9/642, A/CN.9/645 and A/CN.9/658 and Add.1–13), para 37. Also for Egypt, ibid, para 17.

156 Ibid, para 15.

157 Articles 19–23 state: (a) ii. "indicate that the goods have been shipped on board a named vessel at the port of loading stated in the credit" for shipped bills. And (b) "If the bill of lading contains the indication "intended vessel" or similar qualification in relation to the name of the vessel, an on board notation indicating the date of shipment and the name of the actual vessel is required."

158 See Lorenzon, 'Transport documents through the bankers' sieve: Rotterdam Rules v UCP 600', p. 3.

also our view that there is disparity between the two sets of rules (the UCP 600 and the RR) which would be detrimental to the seller if he has agreed on a documentary sale.[159]

Below we have come up with scenarios to better corroborate the view and advise on the solution of the above repercussion. Let us start with sales on "straight" FOB terms.[160] In this type of contract of sale, it is the buyer's duty to procure the contract of carriage. Thus, the buyer is the shipper and the seller does not exercise any control over the conclusion of the contract of carriage. The seller needs to be sure that he can satisfy the documentary requirements of the UCP 600.

As stated before, one of the requirements is that the goods have to be shipped on board a named vessel. The seller then needs to provide the bank with a transport document, where the carrier is under a duty to specify this. This obligation of the carrier has to have been provided for by the buyer in his carriage contract. However, even the buyer has to be under a legal duty to that effect.

This can be secured by the diligent drafting of the sale contract. If the sale is concluded before the contract of carriage is drafted, then the former should require that the carriage contract imposes the duty and, accordingly, that the bill of lading specifically names the carrying vessel. However, this is possible only if the sale contract is concluded before the carriage contract.

If the carriage contract is subsequent to the sale contract, then there are two possible scenarios: if it is a CIF sale, the seller should request that the name of the ship is known and declared on the transport document, since he will conclude the contract of carriage; if, however, the sale is on FOB terms, whether the name of the ship will be in the contract of carriage is up to the buyer to decide. Since the purpose of the contract of carriage is to facilitate the performance of the sale contract, it is expected that the buyer who has opened the letter of credit will ensure that the name of the ship is included in the carriage contract. However, the possibility, that he may not have done this remains high, and the incapacity of the FOB seller to contractually compel his buyer to declare the name of the vessel in the carriage contract means that, unfortunately, the former might find himself exposed to the risk of not complying with the letter of credit.

In the next sections, we will investigate whether the RR and templates of sale contracts of big trading associations are aligned. This analysis is indispensable in order to ascertain to what extent certain terms contained therein have to change to match the RR and the needs of modern trade. The selection of these contracts has been mandated by their popularity in modern international trade.

159 Ibid.

160 For the definition of straight FOB contracts, see Debattista, *Bills of lading in Export Trade*, para 1.18.

3.5 Compliance of the Rotterdam Rules with templates of sale contracts

3.5.1 GAFTA No. 100

GAFTA No. 100[161] specifically asks for a negotiable and transferrable bill of lading, which can similarly be issued under the RR.[162] Provision number 6 of the contract asks for a "shipped on board" bill of lading, which again is within the framework of Article 36(2)(c) of the RR. Also, GAFTA No. 100, Article 12(3) of the RR and the UCP 600 Articles 19–23(c) cover transhipment.

Concerns are raised, as clauses 12(c), (d) and (e) of GAFTA No. 100 provide for alternative documents such as an indemnity or guarantee to be presented when the transport documents are not available for presentation when requested by the buyers. These would trigger breaches of Articles 47(1)(a) and 47(1)(b) of the RR, as the latter prohibits the carrier from delivering the goods if the requirements of the former are not satisfied.

Therefore a breach of Article 47(1) of the RR may only be avoided if the transport document itself "expressly states that the goods may be delivered without the surrender of the transport document or the electronic transport record", as per Article 47(2) of the RR. However, GAFTA No. 100 does not include such a specific requirement for the transport document to be issued; of course, the parties are free to include such a clause.

At the same time, if clauses 12(c), (d) and (e) of GAFTA No. 100 are also contained in a contract of carriage, they may constitute breach of Article 79(1)(a) or (b) of the RR since delivery, in exchange of the shipping documents, is one of the major carrier's obligations; letters of guarantee, as discussed in Chapter 1, will not be an excuse under the RR.

Clauses 12(c) and (d) of GAFTA No. 100 provide situations for which negotiable documents not requiring surrender were created by the RR. Now, as discussed above, transport documents which do not require surrender are clearly within the scope of the RR.[163] We believe that the practice of guarantees and indemnities should be treated with caution, as the lack of security when delivering without presentation cannot always be counterweighed by a letter of guarantee. This practice may promote speed in transactions, but it does not always lead to proper delivery of the goods, if fraud is involved. Therefore, perhaps a clause that would provide for electronic records or negotiable documents not requiring surrender, as allowed by the RR, would be a useful inclusion in a future update.

161 Effective 1 March 2016. Interestingly, Incoterms® are excluded by the contract. However, since the contract is entitled TALE QUALE CIF terms, and as confirmed by the wording of clause 2 "sellers shall have the option of shipping", it can be considered a hybrid CIF contract.

162 As per Articles 1(14) and 1(15) of the RR, the transport document may be negotiable or non-negotiable.

163 See Article 47(2) of the RR.

The subsequent sections will now address a similar analysis of two popular FOSFA contracts.

3.5.2 FOSFA 53 and FOSFA 54

Another sale contract that has been studied is FOSFA 53,[164] where Incoterms® are not excluded.[165] Clause 14 is study-worthy, as it allows payment if a clean bill of lading or a clean mate's receipt is issued (lines 106, 107). The "clean" requirement is something expected for sales of goods overseas, although it is additional to the RR. The fact that in this contract payment is also triggered in exchange for a mate's receipt, means it is commercially flexible. The seller is not the shipper, according to the RR, so he is not in a position to exchange the mate's receipt for the bill of lading.[166] All the seller needs in order to obtain payment is the mate's receipt (which he would receive when he loads the goods), although the RR do not acknowledge it as a transport document. On the other hand, the buyer will not have any issues claiming delivery of the goods from the carrier, or selling them on, as he is a party to the contract of carriage and can obtain a bill of lading (now called negotiable transport document) in exchange for the mate's receipt.

Another standard contract that deserves consideration is FOSFA 54. A significant clause of FOSFA 54, in terms of its compliance or conflict with the RR, is the one which gives buyers the right to declare the port of destination. Under Articles 1(13) and 51 of the RR, this will be allowed only before the transport document is signed, the reason being that instructions or directions to the carrier are allowed only by the shipper or documentary shipper after the signature of the transport document. Thus, when the clause applies to changes of destination after the ship sails, these will have to be directed to the carrier only via the seller *qua* shipper or documentary shipper, which is what clause 3 suggests.

Furthermore, under both FOSFA 53 and the RR we see the obligation for a transferrable or negotiable bill. The bill needs to be a shipped one ("on board"), which is also an option under the RR. However, the major point of discrepancy between the RR and FOSFA 54, is that under the former, the buyer cannot take delivery without showing the negotiable bills of lading or simply by furnishing the carrier with a letter of guarantee. This may only be resolved if the transport documents expressly state that they do not require surrender, so that there is no breach of Article 47(1) of the RR, effectively triggering the application of Article 47(2).

3.6 Conclusion

To conclude, the above sets of private sales and documentary credits terms were studied because their cumulative application with the RR is expected to be a

164 Revised and effective from 1st October 2004.
165 Unlike GAFTA 100, where they are excluded.
166 This eliminates the issue discussed in Chapter 2.

commercial and legal reality that may give rise to several complexities. As it was already discussed through specific scenarios, ambiguity will ensue with regards to the entitlement to a usual transport document when both the RR and Incoterms® apply in a given sale (and carriage) contract when the relevant obligation is vaguely or not at all stipulated. Moreover, problems can occur as an unusual transport document may be issued under an unreasonable contract of carriage. The links of these "unusual" elements with a possible breach of the RR, Incoterms® and the SOGA will be examined fully in Chapter 5, on volume contracts.

Moreover, the UCP 600 had to be compared with the RR in order to raise awareness of what is compulsory under the different texts, and highlight which omission of information cannot be alleviated, preventing the seller from complying with the letter of credit. Finally, FOSFA and GAFTA contracts have been analysed from a critical point of view to see whether carrier and shipper have the same rights and duties as under the RR or not. Some useful conclusions were made upon the varied way in which the RR and the contracts acknowledge the function of the mate's receipt and regulate delivery aspects when the bill of lading is unavailable. Finally, we investigated the compliance of less conventional documents such as "switch bills" with the RR and relevant English case law on international commercial sales.

The principles considered in this chapter have been on the one hand the consideration for uniformity and the modernisation aspect lying in the new neutral terminology of the RR (terms such as bills of lading, sea waybills have vanished), and on the other hand, the consideration that different trades may be characterised by specific types of documents. So that the will of the parties, as expressed in the sale contract, does not surrender in favour of a contrary custom, it should explicitly exclude it. Otherwise, implied agreements or vague requirements of negotiable documents might not suffice to trigger entitlement to bills of lading. This again infects the documentary requirements for bills of lading in sales of commodities, and can prove an obstacle in string sales. Payment under a letter of credit may fail if a negotiable document not requiring surrender is unexpectedly issued and legitimately not received.

The principles that clash were the attempt for uniformity of the RR, and thus all sources of obligation, namely custom and agreement, were acknowledged. Flexibility was also pervading Article 47 of the RR, when the possibility of a transferrable transport document not requiring surrender was described. Both uniformity and flexibility of carriage fetter the need of trade for predictability and certainty. Additionally, one should not forget the other major underpinning, obvious in FOSFA and GAFTA contracts: sales down a string operate through endorsements and surrender of documents of title. These are the considerations that made us prioritise the underpinnings of trade first, in order to rectify the problems likely to occur from the operation of the specific articles of the RR.

It has overall been pointed out that Article 35 of the RR restricts legal certainty. In this chapter the legal controversies stemming from the application of the RR are justified due to the fact that the RR and standard contracts follow a different way of harmonisation. Starting with the RR, it seems that they follow an inconsistent approach of codification. They add factors to the entitlement to the document other than the agreement without defining these terms, but most importantly without putting a hierarchy between them. One could say that in that respect, they follow a broad way of codification. On the other hand, while recognising new documents, or the chance that no document is issued, they leave documents aside, so in that respect they are more specific in codifying. The Incoterms® are also abstract in the way of standardising factors entitling to documents, but the default position is that a transport document should be obtained, unlike under the RR. At the same time, the coverage of popular transport documents is broader under the Incoterms® as opposed to the RR, which makes necessary the familiarity of the commercial parties with their different scopes and definitions under the two frameworks.

It is reasonable that the Incoterms® are more generic because they usually serve as a source of incorporation, which can be enriched by more specific terms in a sale contract. In the event however that a vaguely drafted sale contract does not have provisions on contingencies of contrary customs and the RR apply, the trade protagonists may not obtain the transport document they want. In that respect, CISG is clearer in that it specifies when parties may be bound by practices of the trade.[167] The codification of Article 35 of the RR seems incomplete and may threaten legal certainty and smooth performance of sale contracts. Only the drafting of the sale contract and the insertion of clauses excluding any applicable different customs in the demonstrable lines we have drawn can minimise this danger.

At the same time, Article 35 of the RR opens the possibility to trade electronically, if there is a relevant agreement or custom. Therefore, Article 35 will allow issuance of electronic records instead of paper transport documents in areas of trade where they are customarily issued.[168] This opportunity introduces us to the articles of the RR on e-commerce, namely Articles 8–10.

As the RR have epitomised yearly negotiations in pursuit of a carriage convention that accommodates electronic contracts of carriage, the following analysis sheds light on the impact of the RR on electronic commerce.

167 See CISG, Articles 9(1) and 9(2).

168 Dan Dicker: '*How electronic trading changed (ruined) crude oil prices*' at www.futuresmag.com/2013/10/01/dan-dicker-how-electronic-trading-changed-ruined-c; also 'Today's number: Trading crude oil electronically' openmarkets.cmegroup.com/6799.

4 The impact of the Rotterdam Rules on electronic commerce

4.1 Setting the scene: electronic transport records under the Rotterdam Rules[1]

A major innovation of the RR compared to their predecessors has been the acknowledgement of electronic transport records.[2] The exponential use of electronic commercial documents has been occurring over the last years.[3] The need for the timely transfer of the bill of lading to the overseas buyer has led to a surge in the use of electronic bills of lading.[4] In practice, it is not unusual to see cargo arriving at the port of destination before the shipping documents.[5] There is already English case law concerning the electronic release of cargo.[6] However, the use of electronic bills preceded the existence of any specific rules,[7] and for many years there has been no specific framework to envelope the function of e-commerce, especially in terms of bills of lading.[8] It is trite law that the bill of

1 On the issues deciphered in this chapter see also Ioanna Magklasi, 'Electronic transport records: Assessing the contribution of the Rotterdam Rules to e-commerce' (2013) 29(2) *Computer Law and Security Review*, 120–126.

2 Faye Wang, *Law of Electronic Commercial Transactions: Contemporary Issues in the EU, US and China* (Routledge 2010), pp. 21–22; M Goldby, 'The performance of the bill of lading's functions under UNCITRAL's draft convention on the carriage of goods: Unequivocal legal recognition of electronic equivalents' (2007) 13 *JIML* 160, 161; Johan de Haan, 'A test case for the Rotterdam Rules' (2011) *Maritime Risk International* 25(7) 20.

3 Manuel Alba, 'Electronic commerce provisions in the UNCITRAL Convention on Contracts for the International Carriage of Goods Wholly or Partly by Sea' (2009) 44 *Texas International Law Journal* 387, 388.

4 This has been more obvious in the oil trade. See van der Ziel, 'Delivery of the Goods', para 9.6.2.

5 Ibid. Also Chapter 2, for the same reasons leading to the drafting of Article 47(2) RR.

6 *Glencore International AG v. MSC Mediterranean Shipping Co SA* [2017] EWCA Civ 365; [2017] 2 Lloyd's Rep 186.

7 See Russell Hurling, 'Legal Mechanisms of the ESS Databridge Services and Users Agreement' in London Shipping Law Centre, "Electronic transport records – How secure are they in shipping transactions?", February 2011, para 1, materials of the Forum organised by the London Shipping Law Centre on 23 February 2011 (LSLC 2011). More on the positive steps that have to be taken see Alexander Goulandris, 'Electronic bills of lading have come of age' (2011) 25(3) *MRI*.

8 With the exception of the Electronic Communications Act 2000 in relation to electronic signatures.

lading has a historic role in maritime trade.[9] It is the document which serves as a receipt of the goods shipped, as an evidence of the contract of carriage and as a document of title.[10] However, there are reasons necessitating the evolution of maritime practices by decoupling rights deriving from the document, and allowing this function to perform in the electronic environment.

The main reason behind the need of electronic alternatives[11] has been the time difference between the arrival of the goods and the arrival of the documents, with goods sometimes arriving before the documents, thus troubling collection of the goods by the consignee/holder.[12] If one adds, that the documents may travel to several intermediate buyers and that individual trades have particular needs,[13] it becomes obvious why the use of paper bills of lading is being challenged.[14] However, the commercial world still is not entirely convinced that a framework can offer the spearheaded advantages of speed, security and elimination of fraud in the use of electronic records.[15]

The first organised efforts for the creation of an electronic liability regime were undertaken by the Comite Maritime International (CMI), launching the CMI Rules for Electronic Bills of Lading[16] and then with the UNCITRAL Model Law on Electronic Commerce with Guide to Enactment 1996. The most well-known

9 M Goldby, 'Legislating to facilitate the use of electronic transferable records: A case study. Reforming the law to facilitate the use of electronic bills of lading in the United Kingdom', paper prepared for the UNCITRAL Colloquium on Electronic Commerce New York 14th to 16th February 2011, at www.uncitral.org/pdf/english/colloquia/EC/Legislating_to_facilitate_the_use_of_electronic_transferable_records_-_a_case_study_.pdf. de Haan, 'A test case for the Rotterdam Rules', p. 21, where it is stated that traces of the bill of lading appear in *Ordonnance de Philippe II*, the *Ordonannace d'Anvers* and the *Ordonnance d'Amsterdam*.

10 See the respective chapters of Treitel and Reynolds (eds), *Carver on Bills of Lading* (4th edn).

11 Berlingieri, 'A comparative analysis of the Hague-Visby Rules, the Hamburg Rules and the Rotterdam Rules', p. 57.

12 See Goldby, 'Legislating to facilitate the use of electronic transferable records', pp. 1–2.

13 See N Gaskell, Y Baatz and R Asariotis (eds), *Bills of Lading: Law and Contracts* (LLP 2000), para 1.54: "Oil cargoes may commonly be sold 20 times on the spot market during a voyage from the Persian Gulf to Europe and many problems have occurred when the bills of lading are still stuck in the banking system while the vessel has arrived at the discharge port".

14 See Goldby, 'Legislating to facilitate the use of electronic transferable records', p. 2. Also Paul Todd, 'Dematerialisation of shipping documents' in C Reed, I Walden and L Edgar (eds), *Cross-Border Electronic Banking: Challenges and Opportunities* (Informa 2000), p. 67: "for many cargoes, and in particular the carriage of bulk oil, the paper bill of lading [is] simply no longer serving its original function".

15 As far as prevention of fraud is concerned, see Clarke, 'Transport documents: Their transferability as documents of title; electronic documents'. Also RB Kelly, 'The CMI charts a course on the sea of electronic data interchange: Rules for Electronic Bills of Lading' [1991–1992] *Tulane Maritime Law Journal* 349; P Mallon, 'The Legal Implications of Electronic Commerce in International Trade' (1997) 8 *Computers and Law* 24; R Merges and G Reynolds, 'Towards a computerized system for negotiating ocean bills of lading' (1986) 6 *Journal of Law and Commerce* 36; Todd, 2000; AN Yiannopoulos, General Report to the XIVth International Congress of Comparative Law, Chapter 1 in AN Yiannopoulos (ed) *Ocean Bills of Lading: Traditional Forms, Substitutes, and EDI Systems* (Kluwer Law International 1995), pp. 17–19.

16 Comité Maritime International, Rules for Electronic Bills of Lading (1990).

private initiatives are those of Bolero[17] and CargoDocs.[18] Both sets of rules introduce the concept of paperless transmission of trade data via computer systems for the formation or in performance of a contract, under the term "Electronic Data Interchange" (EDI).[19] More recently, we have had BIMCO introducing a standard e-bill of lading clause in charterparties,[20] and the UNCITRAL Model Law on Electronic Transferrable Records 2017 (MLETR).

Moreover, Article 8(1) of the United Nations Convention on the Use of Electronic Communications in International Contracts 2005 provides that "a communication or a contract shall not be denied validity or enforceability on the sole ground that it is in the form of an electronic communication".

In the European context, Article 9(1) of the Directive 2000/31/EC, provides that "Member states shall ensure that their legal system allows contracts to be concluded by electronic means". Member states shall in particular ensure that the legal requirements applicable to the contractual process neither create obstacles for the use of electronic contracts nor result in such contracts being deprived of legal effectiveness and validity on account of their having been made by electronic means. More recently, member states of the EU had to adopt the Council Directive 2010/45/UE,[21] which establishes equal treatment between paper and electronic invoices, until December 31, 2012.[22]

In this chapter, the ways in which the RR purport to facilitate the issuance and transfer of electronic transport records will be introduced. The first purpose is to assess whether provisions of the RR operate in international trade as it stands; secondly whether they provide an effective mechanism for electronic cargo documentation, and in which ways. The deficiencies in drafting will be discussed in depth and supplementary or alternative drafting will be suggested. Finally, it is of interest to see how the RR are similar to or discrepant from known EDI systems trusted in practice; Bolero and CargoDocs constitute successful examples of third party electronic service providers; Bolero's rules and operation will be studied as an example in conjunction with the RR.

The overall purpose of this chapter is to delineate the impact of the RR in procuring carriage contracts electronically; where the impact seems to be unsatisfactory, more efficient and trustworthy ways of completing the RR with additional regulation will be suggested to make them a more effective springboard for paperless trade.

17 Bolero. See www.bolero.net/

18 essDOCS-Databridge™, atwww.essdocs.com/edocs/cargodocs/;www.essdocs.com/resources/ebls/

19 See UNCITRAL Model Law on Electronic Commerce with Guide to Enactment, Article 2(b), at www.uncitral.org/pdf/english/texts/electcom/05-89450_Ebook.pdf.

20 www.ukpandi.com/fileadmin/uploads/uk-pi/Documents/2017/Legal_Briefing_e_bill_of_Lading_WEB.pdf

21 Council Directive 2010/45/EU of 13 July 2010 amending Directive 2006/112/EC on the common system of value added tax as regards the rules on invoicing.

22 See www.essdocs.com/resources/elegislation.

4.2 Initiating the provisions on paperless records and communication in the Rotterdam Rules

The need for speed, flexibility and protection against fraud in international trade has been expressed through efforts for the dematerialisation of the sale documents. Over the past two decades,[23] there has been a need for an electronic version of several types of contractual documents: the carriage of goods by sea contract, the booking note[24] and of the letter of credit application.[25]

Before we get into a deeper analysis of the RR, it is useful to start with the definitions. The cornerstone of the electronic transaction is the electronic transport record. Article 1(18)[26] of the RR stipulates the kind of information that forms part of the electronic transport record, clarifying that this information is needed as evidence for the contract of carriage by the carrier or performing party, and for the receipt of the goods under it.

The term "electronic communication" is also defined in Article 1(17) as "information generated, sent, received or stored by electronic, optical, digital or similar means with the result that the information communicated is accessible so as to be usable for subsequent reference". This provision was added to provide a minimum legal recognition to information, in case an electronic record cannot be issued.[27]

As far as the definition of the electronic transport record is concerned, it can be noted from the first reading that it contains tautologies: "information logically associated with the *electronic transport record* [...] or otherwise linked to the *electronic transport record* [...] so as to become part of the *electronic transport record*" (emphasis added). This is said because the term "transport record" is surprisingly being defined by reference to other information, and specifically, information linked or associated with the transport record.

Unfortunately such tautologies may add confusion. Since there is reference to a brand new term and concept in international carriage of goods by sea – which is

23 See Alba, 'Electronic commerce provisions in the UNCITRAL Convention on Contracts for the International Carriage of Goods Wholly or Partly by Sea', p. 388.

24 For electronic booking notes see Nicholas Gaskell, 'Bills of lading in an electronic age' [2010] *LMCLQ* 233, pp. 243–252.

25 For most of the fore written range of documents see Alba, 'Electronic commerce provisions in the UNCITRAL Convention on Contracts for the International Carriage of Goods Wholly or Partly by Sea', p. 391.

26 Article 1(18) of the Rotterdam Rules reads: "An electronic transport record means information in one or more messages issued by electronic communication under a contract of carriage by a carrier, including information logically associated with the electronic transport record by attachments or otherwise linked to the electronic transport record contemporaneously with or subsequent to its issue by the carrier, so as to become part of the electronic transport record, that (a) Evidences the carrier's or a performing party's receipt of goods under a contract of carriage; and (b) Evidences or contains a contract of carriage."

27 Where under Article 35 of the RR, one is not by agreement or custom issued. For a criticism on this distinction, as a factor that enhances complexity and international disharmony depending on whether electronic transport records are acknowledged, see de Haan, 'A test case for the Rotterdam Rules', p. 20.

the *record* – accuracy would be a condition *sine qua non*. As it will be illustrated in due course, the purpose of the RR is to initiate the electronic version of transport *documents* as an equal alternative to the paper ones. Had the RR stated "contract of carriage" instead of "electronic transport record", there would be no space for ambiguity.[28] This observation is made so that the analogy contained in Article 1(18) of the RR points to what the commercial world is already familiar with, i.e. shipping documents evidencing or containing the contract of carriage – the *transport document* in the terminology of the RR. This means that traders should link the record with information expected to appear in a contract of carriage.

In the following section we explore the preconditions of the agreement for the issuance of an electronic transport record.

4.3 Issue and transfer of an electronic transport record

Article 8 of the RR administers the equivalence of paper transport documents and electronic transport records, subject to the consent of the carrier and the shipper, as follows:

> Anything that is to be in or on a transport document under this Convention maybe recorded in an electronic transport record, provided the issuance and subsequent use of an electronic transport record is with the consent of the carrier and the shipper; and (b) The issuance, exclusive control, or transfer of an electronic transport record has the same effect as the issuance, possession, or transfer of a transport document.

As the article does not specify the form in which consent to the issuance of an electronic transport record can be made, it may be in writing, or implied.[29] Most of the charterparties and sale contracts do now provide for the contingency of electronic records,[30] and, as more and more business is conducted electronically, it is to be anticipated that complications might arise. These complications will concern the form and time in which consent is given, as Article 8 is silent in this respect. Consent can be given in any form and at any time before the issuance of the electronic transport record or after the issuance of a paper one, but always before delivery of the goods, as the transport record or document would cease to operate.

The necessary speed in procuring shipped goods in sales down a string demands quick decision making and, as a result, although the issuance of an electronic

28 This is a definition similar to "transport document", which in our view should preferably be given, instead of repeating the same phrase multiple times.

29 For the disparity among other jurisdictions 149, 150, 151 of P Jones, 'A new transport convention: a framework for e-commerce?' (2002) 9 *Electronic Communication Law Review* 145, pp. 149–151.

30 See above, the comment about BIMCO. Electronic bills of lading are also popular in the metals and iron ore trade in the Asia–South Pacific area.

transport record can be agreed at any stage, it should already be included as a crucial term in the sale and carriage contract[31] to avoid unnecessary delay.

Confusion may also arise from Articles 1(17) and 3 of the RR about *electronic communication* on the one hand and Article 8(a) of the RR about *electronic transport records* on the other.[32] Most commentators do not highlight any such confusion, but we are raising it as the RR impose different requirements for "electronic communication" and "electronic transport records", and traders need to be cautious with the wording used.

For electronic transport records, which are more specific in notion and scope than electronic communication, only the consent of the shipper and carrier is necessary.[33] On the other hand, in terms of *electronic communication for notification*, Article 3 requires the use of electronic means to be with the consent of the person by which it is communicated and of the person to which it is to be communicated. Such communication may concern parties such as the carrier, controlling party, shipper, documentary shipper and consignee.

The risk is that if the parties are not sufficiently precise, a consent designated only for the electronic communication of notices might mistakenly be considered as also applicable to the use of electronic transport records if provided by shipper and carrier.[34]

Therefore, we believe that the consent for the use of electronic means of communication should clearly demonstrate two things: firstly, the parties providing it; and, secondly, the specific purpose for which the electronic consent is given, namely that it is either for electronic communication purposes only or for the issuance of an electronic transport record. Only if this distinction is clear will parties know when they can validly trade over an electronic transport record. Otherwise, they may wrongly perceive that they have started the process for an electronic record and rely on that for electronic performance of a sale contract or payment under eUCP, and then ultimately realise that this has never been taken as a contractual binding effect from the other party (carrier/shipper).

More concretely, such misconceptions might arise due to the fact that the concept of electronic contracting is from a legal point of view relatively new and to a certain extent unexplored. Evidently, although the terms used are similar, they may lead to different legal consequences.

In the following section, we will explore the core provisions regulating the functions of an electronic transport record under the RR, starting with the transfer. Moreover, we will reveal[35] more deficiencies and suggest ways to supersede them

31 Other commentaries on the RR do not discuss the type of consent as a separate issue. However, we deal with it, as there are jurisdictions where the consent needs to be in writing to have legal effect.

32 See Alba, 'Electronic commerce provisions in the UNCITRAL Convention on Contracts for the International Carriage of Goods Wholly or Partly by Sea', p. 403.

33 Articles 1(17) and 3 of the RR.

34 Magklasi, 'Electronic transport records: Assessing the contribution of the Rotterdam Rules to e-commerce', p. 121.

35 On this see Magklasi, 'Electronic transport records: Assessing the contribution of the Rotterdam Rules to e-commerce', pp.121–126.

in order to visualise how the framework of electronic records of the RR can be more complete, consistent and operational, limiting non-performance of sale contracts and litigation to the minimum.[36]

4.4 Article 8 of the Rotterdam Rules: issues relating to the transfer of the electronic transport record

Article 8(a) of the RR states that "anything that is to be in or on a transport document under this Convention may be recorded in an electronic transport record, provided the issuance and subsequent use of an electronic transport record is with the consent of the carrier and the shipper".

It has been suggested[37] that the words "anything"[38] and "in" or "on" can also embrace electronic signatures and endorsements in addition to the usual information that a transport document may contain, such as the name of the carrier, type of goods, quantity, quality, place of shipment and destination.

The possibility of transferring title to the goods electronically (if the record is negotiable) would indeed be an essential function, and as the wording of Article 8(a) of the RR is positive, the record seems to replicate all the functions of the paper bill of lading; the electronic transport record is not merely an alternative way of displaying the key information, it also encompasses the mechanisms of circulating information and rights of control among carrier and traders.

Unfortunately, the RR mention nothing about the format or the display of the electronic transport record,[39] and consequently the commercial world might not be prepared for its possible appearance. Our concern here is as follows: the electronic version of the paper document, as illustrated by Article 1(18) of the RR, may not look like the traditional paper bill of lading or sea waybill. Usually, the paper version of a bill of lading or a sea waybill is one or more double-sided A4 documents containing all the main information. In the electronic era, the information may be fragmented (*in one or more messages*) and arrive at different times (*contemporaneously or subsequent to its issue*), partly in one email, partly elsewhere. So, unlike the transport document that is *one* paper, the electronic transport record is a *collection* of information, which may not be found simultaneously in one piece of electronic communication. This on its own requires vigilance from the parties involved, namely both carrier and trader, so that no information passes unnoticed or missed.[40] On the other hand, third party registries may collate the information on certain platforms or formats to imitate the paper function.

36 Ibid.

37 See Baatz et al, *The Rotterdam Rules: A Practical Annotation*, para [8-04], and Sturley, Fujita and van der Ziel, *The Rotterdam Rules*, para 3.028. This however does not apply to non-negotiable transport records as they cannot be transferred.

38 Sturley, Fujita and van der Ziel, *The Rotterdam Rules*, para 3.028. The word "anything" can embrace all kinds of information.

39 See Gaskell, 'Bills of lading in an electronic age', pp. 272–273.

40 Magklasi, 'Electronic transport records: Assessing the contribution of the Rotterdam Rules to e-commerce', p. 122.

Thus, in practical terms, although the commercial world might visualise the electronic transport record as a "printable electronic transport document",[41] this might not be the case. It may be that all the information is gathered together in one electronic message, but the potential holder may also have to browse, access and gather the information that "logically associates or otherwise links to"[42] the (electronic version of) a transport document. In other words, the electronic transport record may be a compilation of electronic communication included in several electronic messages. If more attention is paid to the words used in Article 1(18) of the RR, it will be noticed that on the one hand there is a paper document, and on the other hand an electronic transport *record* not an *electronic document.*

It has rightly been clarified that: "The fact that UNCITRAL created a new term also illustrates its recognition that an electronic transport record is *not* a document, but that the record under the equalisation method should *function* like a document."[43] This is an example of the RR making a step, not a radical one however, towards the recognition of electronic documents. This is the reason why existing examples of frameworks of private systems for the issuance of electronic documents will be studied in the course of this chapter. The aim is to provide an apt illustration of what needs to be regulated, so that the RR in conjunction with other combined efforts (national and private) can produce a positive effect on electronic maritime trade.

Article 8(a) of the RR allows the issuance and subsequent use of the transport record but only if the carrier and shipper have agreed to them. We think that the request for an agreement between the carrier and the shipper is reasonable, as this document or record encompasses all the reasons which may hold the carrier liable for any defect of the goods or delay in their arrival. The carrier is the person who signs the documents and undertakes the responsibility for carriage; accordingly, this document or record should be approved by him so that he delivers the goods to the appropriate holder/consignee. If the electronic issuance presupposes systems that the carrier does not possess or that he has not subscribed to, or, if for any reason, he cannot conclude carriage contracts electronically, then the carrier will not want to be contractually bound to issue an electronic transport record. All that the parties need to do is to provide their consent, regardless of whether a prior transport document exists or not.

Things can become more complicated with regards to whether and how frequently the electronic transport record may be subsequently used. Firstly, the wording of Article 8(a) of the RR does not clarify whether consent given for the first use is also valid for any subsequent use of the record or whether every individual usage needs a new specific consent from the shipper and carrier.[44]

41 CargoDocs issue electronic bills which are the exact electronic replica of an A4 paper bill of lading.

42 See Article 1(18) of the RR using the verbs in quotations.

43 Sturley, Fujita and van der Ziel, *The Rotterdam Rules*, p. 49, fn 15 therein (emphasis added).

44 For the same question see Baatz et al, *The Rotterdam Rules: A Practical Annotation*, para [8-06].

Moreover, the article does not distinguish whether or not this applies to negotiable or non-negotiable records. Hence, the question that arises is whether a negotiable record can truly be a freely negotiable record.

Issuance and use of the documents, although tightly linked, can work separately. If there is agreement on the issuance, this does not mean that there is going to be a transfer of the record. If the carrier precludes the record from being used "subsequently", but the goods are intended to be sold more than once, then quite rightly this is not what comes to mind when thinking about a negotiable record. Similarly, if the parties agree that the record will only be used once, the record qualifies as "non-negotiable". The draftsmen thought it evident that Article 8 of the RR is about negotiable records, but someone not familiar with the provisions of the RR could not assume this.[45]

The paradoxes discussed above can only be rectified through a restrictive interpretation of Article 8(b) of the RR.

Firstly, the words "exclusive control, transfer" should be interpreted so as to refer only to negotiable transport records.[46] Secondly, in order to preserve the transferability of a negotiable record, a teleological interpretation should be adopted, extending the initial consent of shipper and carrier to the subsequent use of the record so that it suffices for *every* potential transfer.[47] Otherwise, the need for individual consent would somehow engender the ability of the holder/controlling party to also agree on issuance and transfer, which cannot be implied by Article 8 of the RR.[48] This would trigger delays and unnecessarily block the flow of string sales.

It is our opinion that the scope of application of Article 8(a) is vague, not only with respect to the extent of use of the electronic transport record, but also with respect to the parties who are required as per the article to consent to such issuance and use. The parties not expressly included and the complexities that may emerge because of the restrictive wording of the article will be discussed in the following section.

We submit that the noted international trade law synergies can be attributed to the drafting underpinnings of the RR – harmonisation and not exhaustive codification – and the trade's need for predictability. The RR evidence abstract and minimal codification, particularly in the e-commerce sphere, as they would like to promote technological neutrality. This vagueness however can link to uncertainty rather than to the desired trade facilitation. The ambiguities of the RR can be rectified through contractual clauses specifying that once the use of the record is authorised, it should be unlimited.

45 See Sturley, Fujita and van der Ziel, *The Rotterdam Rules*, p. 55 and fn 53 therein.

46 This is usually referred to as the singularity approach.

47 Magklasi, 'Electronic transport records: Assessing the contribution of the Rotterdam Rules to e-commerce', p. 122.

48 The significance of this remark will be illustrated below when we talk about replacement.

4.5 Complications: why does the documentary shipper not have a role in electronic records?

Article 8(a) of the RR does not refer to the documentary shipper. In an international trade context, the FOB seller becomes the documentary shipper with the condition that he is also mentioned as shipper on the transport document or record. This party, as underlined in previous chapters, plays an important role as he is usually the seller in sale contracts concluded on FOB terms. Therefore, the omission of the documentary shipper from the list of parties who can agree to the issuance of an electronic transport record might have trade law complications.[49] The documentary shipper assumes the rights and liabilities of the shipper and can be contacted by the carrier for instructions,[50] but eventually, he may still not be authorised by the shipper to take the transport record (under Article 35 of the RR). Thus, the RR seem to empower the FOB buyer with privileges, leaving the seller *qua* documentary shipper at an inferior position.[51] This derives mainly from Article 33(1) of the RR, which states:

> a documentary shipper is subject to the obligations and liabilities imposed on the shipper pursuant to this chapter and pursuant to Article 55 of the RR, and is entitled to the shipper's rights and defences provided by this chapter and by chapter 13.

One could argue that, if we recall Article 35 of the RR, we may understand the omission. Although, as per Article 35, the documentary shipper, at the shipper's option, is entitled to a negotiable or non-negotiable transport document or record, as long as there is no agreement or contract to the contrary, the documentary shipper plays no role in the choice of the type of document/record (negotiable or non-negotiable) that will be issued.[52] He is merely entitled to the document if he has this authorisation from the shipper. Whether a party will have a role as a documentary shipper depends on the shipper. Therefore, it could be argued that it is quite reasonable that the choice of issuance of an electronic transport record is limited between shipper and carrier.

At the same time, Article 35 of the RR might be read differently. The documentary shipper is entitled to the document, (as long as the shipper consents); as this is one of the fundamental rights afforded by the RR, why should he

49 Magklasi, 'Electronic transport records: Assessing the contribution of the Rotterdam Rules to e-commerce', p. 122.

50 See Article 33 of the RR.

51 Goldby, *Electronic Documents in Maritime Trade: Law and Practice*), para 6.98. Goldby thinks that the omission of the entity of the seller from Article 35 of the RR can prove detrimental to the expansion of electronic bills.

52 The article states: "Unless the shipper and the carrier have agreed not to use a transport document [...]".

be deprived of having a say as to the issuance (and transfer) of an electronic record? Does this omission not reveal a paradox? In essence, if a documentary shipper cannot decide on the issuance of an electronic transport record, even his role under Article 35 is inferior to the shipper's, as the documentary shipper/ FOB seller, ultimately, can only request what the shipper authorises.[53] The legal implications emerging from this unfairness are illustrated in the following scenario.

An overseas sale is concluded on FOB terms[54] and the goods are to be carried by sea. The RR apply to the contract of carriage. The sale contract is silent with regards to whether the transport document is going to be in paper or electronic form, negotiable or non-negotiable. If the carrier convinces the shipper that it is quicker or safer to have the bill of lading in an electronic format and freely transferrable, but the seller/documentary shipper disagrees, the latter cannot object to the issuance of an electronic record under the RR. This may have greater consequences for the seller, if UCP (and not eUCP) apply to the letter of credit, which as per the sale contract stipulate payment against a bill of lading. The only way he could have to protect his position, would be by having a relevant provision in the contract of sale exactly prescribing what the document should be like and how it would be issued, or requiring that his consent should also be requested where an electronic transport record is under negotiation between shipper and carrier.[55] Our example further highlights that the involvement of the documentary shipper/seller in letter of credit transactions is appropriate, as it ensures that the seller is in control of the type of record on which payment depends. It also allows a reconciled perpetual drafting of corollary contracts in the international maritime trade chain.

The above suggestion could have been a subsection of Article 8(a) of the RR, stating that where one party has the role of a documentary shipper in the contract, his consent should be necessary for the issuance and subsequent use of the electronic transport record. If this was the case, there would be no surprises for the shipper-buyer, carrier and documentary shipper *qua* seller. This means that the seller would be in a position to furnish the confirming bank with the record, if this is what the letter of credit required. The issuance of the electronic transport record would be completely consensual and the flow of the record would not create complications when the goods are further sold down a string.

However, the documentary shipper is not the only party omitted by Article 8(a) of the RR. The same is observed for the consignee/holder.[56] The commercial

53 Magklasi, 'Electronic transport records: Assessing the contribution of the Rotterdam Rules to e-commerce', pp. 122, 123.

54 In this type of contract, it is the buyer's duty to conclude the contract of carriage.

55 Magklasi, 'Electronic transport records: Assessing the contribution of the Rotterdam Rules to e-commerce', p. 123.

56 As we shall see, when a negotiable document/record is issued, Article 10 of the RR gives the holder the right of replacement.

importance of provisions on the holder and the extent to which the RR provide this will be elaborated on in the following section.

4.6 The position of the consignee/potential holder of the goods under Article 8(a) of the Rotterdam Rules

It is our view that Article 8(a) should not have left the consignee's/holder's consent out of its scope.[57] The justification of this argument is, to a great extent, in the same line as that of the previous section, but it is understood that it may not be very obvious. This is a recommendation that we make thinking outside the narrow context of a carriage contract, considering the wider international trade law perspective. In the contract of sale, the consensus of both traders is needed over the type (electronic or paper) of transport document or record as it is the cornerstone of the shipping documents in their transaction. Accordingly, if the consignee-buyer requests an electronic transport record under article A8 of the CIF Incoterms® 2000/2010, the seller has to comply with this requirement of the sale and the contract of carriage will be drafted accordingly. In pursuance of the former, the shipper and carrier will have to agree that an electronic record will be issued, and particularly a negotiable one.

However, in sales down a string, traders do not always have the luxury of the sale contract being concluded before the carriage contract. It is also possible that in the same string of consecutive sales, the same traders want to (or have to) trade with their potential buyers on different terms. Things could potentially prove problematic when a case scenario like the following arises.[58]

The shipper *qua* seller (S) and a trader (B) enter into a CIF sale contract. As per the sale and carriage contract, it is expressly written or implied that the transport document will be issued in paper form. The transport document is issued to the order of the consignee (B) or his assigns. After the goods have been shipped, and while they are still afloat, the buyer (B) wants to sell the cargo to (F). (F) is a big trading company which conducts business globally only on the basis of electronic transport records, to correspond to the need for speed and preference of its clients. Thus, it is against its practice and interests to accept a paper transport document. Neither (B) nor (F) are shippers under the contract of carriage. Can they enforce their wish to issue an electronic transport record, either against the shipper or the carrier?

As S is not a party to the second contract of sale, he is not obliged to agree to the procurement of an electronic record. The contract of carriage is still operative as the goods have not been delivered and only the carrier and the consignee (B) are the common parties to this carriage operation. Hence, the question posed above will, at first and on the basis of Article 8 of the RR alone, be answered negatively. Article 8(a) does not give the holder the power to ask for an electronic record.

57 Magklasi, 'Electronic transport records: Assessing the contribution of the Rotterdam Rules to e-commerce', p. 123.
58 Ibid.

However, the above situation is resolved through Article 10(1)(b) (and the opposite is allowed via Article 10(2)) of the RR. Article 10 refers to replacement[59] of a negotiable transport document by a record and *vice versa*.

Replacement is a mechanism devised to offer flexibility when goods are sold down a string, and to ensure that all the different legal regimes and their approach towards the recognition of paper and electronic transport documents are satisfied.[60] Replacement is now covered also by the Model Law on Electronic Transferable Records (MLETR).[61] This means that practically the holder and carrier can agree to replace the electronic version with a paper one, and vice versa, in circumstances such as the following: if the shipper or subsequent holder (known or any potential holder in a negotiable transport document endorsed in blank) does not have the infrastructure to issue or transfer an electronic transport record; or if in a certain jurisdiction electronic transport records are not acknowledged as equal to paper documents of title. Replacement could also be practicable in the case where only a record or paper is specifically required to establish a right of the seller, for instance to request payment under the letter of credit.

The holder of the negotiable transport document, (F) in our case scenario, can agree with the carrier that an electronic transport record will be issued, replacing the paper transport document. Article 10(1) of the RR specifies that:

> 1. If a negotiable transport document has been issued and the carrier and the holder agree to replace that document by a negotiable electronic transport record:
>
> (a) The holder shall surrender the negotiable transport document, or all of them if more than one has been issued, to the carrier;
> (b) The carrier shall issue to the holder a negotiable electronic transport record that includes a statement that it replaces the negotiable transport document; and
> (c) The negotiable transport document ceases thereafter to have any effect or validity.

The purpose of our scenario was to reveal the practical significance of Article 10 of the RR and its link with Article 8.

Would the answer be different if (B) wanted a non-negotiable transport record instead?[62]

4.7 The functional equivalence vacuum revealed by Article 10 of the Rotterdam Rules

Before we answer this question, it is appropriate to state the purpose behind it. The primary objective is to examine whether the framework of the RR is perfectly

59 Generally on replacement see Hakan Karan, 'Transport documents in the light of the Rotterdam Rules', in Güner-Özbek (ed), *The United Nations Convention on Contracts for the International Carriage of Goods Wholly or Partly by Sea: An Appraisal of the Rotterdam Rules*, para 9.5.

60 von Ziegler, 'The Rotterdam Rules and the underlying sales contract', p. 278.

61 Articles 17 and 18 of the MLETR.

62 Magklasi, 'Electronic transport records: Assessing the contribution of the Rotterdam Rules to e-commerce', pp. 123, 124.

consistent with regards to the principle of functional equivalence when both negotiable and non-negotiable documents/records are concerned. Functional equivalence forms part of the overall principle of trade facilitation that underpins the RR. It is worth investigating whether the RR cover certain case scenarios which may occur in current international trade transactions.

To answer the question, Article 10 of the RR, which deals with the replacement of a document with a record, is our only reference. Careful reading shows that this provision along with Article 9 of the RR does not alternatively refer to every type of document or record; only the negotiable ones are regulated. Thus, it seems that the question is answered in the negative, as the RR only allow for the replacement of a *negotiable* document with a similarly negotiable transport record.

For an explanation of this omission, the preparatory works roughly indicate that although some delegates wished for non-negotiable documents/records to be covered too, it was decided that there was no need to include them in Article 10, as non-negotiable bills had a limited use.[63] This stemmed from consideration of market factors.[64] The main reasons given were that this type of document does not provide adequate security, it cannot be transferred to anyone other than the named consignee, and the banks are reluctant to accept it because it is of insufficient collateral security for financing the sale.[65] However, we maintain the opinion that non-negotiable records should have been covered so that the RR are internally consistent. In the Guide to the Incoterms®[66], the surge in the use of non-negotiable documents is also highlighted. Besides, the data in the 2003 United Nations Conference on Trade and Development (UNCTAD) Report may be out of date, as the dynamics of shipping have changed in the years since those deliberations. The RR proclaimed to bring uniformity, and the functional equivalence is a specific face of it, and recognised by the Convention.

Although "unpopular", non-negotiable documents and records constitute a separate category acknowledged by the RR in the definitions.[67] Consequently, it is expected that this category of records could be further regulated, also in the replacement aspect. Moreover, this would increase the choices of the parties and advance the popularity of the RR, since they would not seem to favour a particular type of document and thus would not counter contractual freedom. If our point on this was implemented, it would be one of the very few occasions where a convention would manage to broaden as opposed to limit the parties' choices, despite its comprehensive codification. This aim of amplifying the ways of contracting would be well-received by international trade law, since its major

63 See Sturley, Fujita and van der Ziel, *The Rotterdam Rules*, para 3.034, under the explanation for excluding non-negotiable records from Article 9; it is thereby stated that the general provisions of the RR were adequate, due to the restricted function of the non-negotiable document, namely as receipt of the goods and evidence of the contract of carriage.

64 Report by the UNCTAD Secretariat, '*The use of transport documents in international trade*', paras 72–74.

65 Ibid, Table 5.

66 ICC Guide to Incoterms® 2010, p. 72.

67 See Article 1(20) for non-negotiable transport records. However, this is not the only example of the role of non-negotiable records being disregarded. Article 8(a) administers the transfer of the record without distinguishing, although by definition this scenario does not apply to non-negotiable records.

tenet is freedom of contract. Consequently, if a non-negotiable electronic record is recognised by the RR in its use, why should it not also be replaceable? Besides, the total lack of reference to non-negotiable records would seem to question why this chapter of the RR was not ultimately named "negotiable electronic records".

The practical significance of this question is even more apparent when payment is agreed to be effected via a letter of credit under an FOB sale contract; the letter of credit is made before the carriage contract, and it is explicitly made subject to the UCP 600. In a hypothetical scenario, the buyer *qua* shipper, knowing that trading in electronic sea waybills is the new commercial trend and knowing that the carrier has an established registry for issuing electronic sea waybills, agrees to the issuance of one. However, the seller is uncertain of whether the paper equivalent of the non-negotiable record is necessary. This is a typical situation, when the parties want to comply with the letter of credit. As shown by the terminology of the UCP 600, banks deal with documents. Although there is no definition of the document in the UCP, it can *a contrario* be concluded that by the existence of the "Supplement for Electronic Presentation eUCP Version 1.1",[68] when the word "document" is used in the general UCP context, only a document in a traditional paper form is denoted.[69]

Electronic documents are left to be covered by the eUCP Supplement in specific eUCP articles.[70] Technically, replacement would not be necessary if the eUCP could automatically apply. Interestingly, according to article e2(a) of the eUCP: "a credit subject to eUCP is also subject to the UCP without express incorporation of the UCP". It seems that the opposite is not allowed. According to article e1(b) of the eUCP: "The eUCP shall apply as a supplement to the UCP *where the credit indicates that it is subject to eUCP*" (emphasis added).

Returning to the FOB example under discussion, where only UCP 600 and not eUCP apply, the bank will want to examine the paper version of the electronic transport record. Since the example is about a non-negotiable electronic transport record, its paper equivalent is a sea waybill.[71] Accordingly, the bank will request the paper version of the sea waybill, and will examine compliance of the

68 Hereafter, any article of the eUCP cited without any other reference is considered to be an article of eUCP V1.1 Supplement to UCP 600.

69 Magklasi, 'Electronic transport records: Assessing the contribution of the Rotterdam Rules to e-commerce', p. 124.

70 These are the following articles: 1) Article e-1(a): The supplement to the Uniform Customs and Practice for Documentary Credits for Electronic Presentation ("eUCP") supplements for Uniform Customs and Practice for Documentary Credits (2007 Revision, ICC Publication No. 600) ("UCP") in order to accommodate presentation of electronic records alone or in combination with paper documents. 2) Article e2(c): If an eUCP credit allows the beneficiary to choose between presentation of paper documents or electronic records and it chooses to present only paper documents, the UCP alone shall apply to that presentation. If only paper documents are permitted under an eUCP credit, the UCP alone shall apply. 3) Article e3(a)(ii): document shall include an electronic record. 4) Article e3(iv): paper document means a document in a traditional paper form.

71 See Baatz et al, *The Rotterdam Rules: A Practical Annotation*, para [45-01], comments under Article 45(Delivery when no negotiable transport document or negotiable electronic transport record is issued), where it is submitted that the article applies straight bills of lading or sea waybills.

document with the credit as per Article 21 of the UCP 600. This article is applicable by definition as it is entitled "Non-negotiable sea waybill".[72]

The only solution[73] available to the FOB seller/documentary shipper would be to request his buyer, the applicant of the documentary credit, to amend the letter of credit, stating that "by an amendment, this letter of credit is made subject to the eUCP".[74]

As to whether the answer would be different if the buyer wanted a negotiable transport record instead, the answer is likely to be the same as above, as there is no direct article on this in the RR. In theory, both requests of the consignee can be satisfied insofar as the carrier agrees. The latter is the person that issues the document, but it seems that there is no explicit legal obligation imposed on the carrier in this respect under the RR.

This is relevant in the context of market prices rising, as the buyer under the first sale of the cargo may be interested in selling it further. Therefore, he wants to replace his non-negotiable transport record with a negotiable transport record. As discussed, this is not addressed by the RR, as replacement refers to forms of the same documents, and it only applies to negotiable documents/records. In our opinion it is a missed opportunity that would have allowed consecutive sales to multiply with flexibility and speed.[75] However, there can be contractual options to achieve this flexibility. This may be achieved through an agreement with the electronic registry system; with the emergence of third party registries, such as Bolero and essDOCS, this can be a term in the standard frameworks, if not already. Alternatively, this option could be provided for in national legislations, which should step in and encourage electronic commerce.[76]

However, from an *a contrario* interpretation of Article 8(a), it looks as though the alternative side of the phenomenon, i.e. the possibility to turn a negotiable record to a non-negotiable one, is permitted[77] by the RR.[78] Since Article 8 does not distinguish between negotiable and non-negotiable records, the mere disagreement of carrier or shipper with the subsequent use of a negotiable transport record seems to suffice to render it technically and *practically*[79] non-negotiable.[80]

72 This is the reverse example of the one in Sturley, Fujita and van der Ziel, *The Rotterdam Rules*, p. 57, fn 69 therein.

73 Magklasi, 'Electronic transport records: Assessing the contribution of the Rotterdam Rules to e-commerce', p. 124.

74 This is by virtue of article e1(c) of the eUCP. It recites as follows: This version is Version 1.1. A credit must indicate the applicable version of the eUCP. If it does not do so, it is subject to the version in effect on the date the credit is issued or, if made subject to eUCP by an amendment accepted by the beneficiary, on the date of that amendment.

75 Magklasi, 'Electronic transport records: Assessing the contribution of the Rotterdam Rules to e-commerce', pp. 121, 124.

76 Ibid, p. 123.

77 Ibid, p. 124.

78 Although it looks like this omission by the drafters is more accidental than intentional.

79 Italicised for emphasis.

80 For additional certainty, if the words "to order" or "negotiable" appear on the document, they should be deleted from an *a contrario* interpretation of Article 1(19) this time. This additional step is justified by the reading of the definitions for negotiable documents/records, the usage of the

4.8 Documents and records: mutually exclusive or coexistent?

The RR are thought to be capable of promoting the popularity of electronic transport records, as an equal alternative of paper documents, mainly through Article 8(a).[81] It is submitted here that from Article 10 of the RR derives the presumption that the paper document and electronic record do not coexist;[82] when a transport document replaces an electronic transport record (and vice versa), the former ceases to operate[83] – it cannot be used again. Thus, the question that springs to mind is whether this means that the electronic record ceases to exist even for reference purposes or for the contingency of discrepancies or typos and for other possible claims by the consignee, so that one can argue that the paper document is not the exact original replica of the electronic record and vice versa.

Article 10 of the RR is not precise on this issue. We assume that it is permissible[84] since it is not explicitly prohibited; besides, our inference would make commercial sense.[85] Cross-checks between the electronic record and the transport document should be allowed when it is suspected that the data after the replacement are not exactly the same as these of the original document/record.

The possibility of referring back to the previous format of the contract of carriage (document or record) – for the purposes of reissuance or replacement – can also prove useful in another context. If there has been a loss of the transport document, the buyer would be prevented from claiming delivery of the goods. Delivery without presentation is a classic scenario frequent in shipping litigation. It is also the main rationale behind the practice of letters of indemnity.[86]

However, in the context of this example, we only deal with the position of a consignee who is in good faith and has indeed lost possession of the transport document. We are limiting the scope of the scenario because otherwise the provision suggested would permit itself to be abused by any "alleged" holder of records/documents, who in essence may have no title or contractual right to

document is not a criterion on its own to classify it as such. The only criteria for understanding the type of the document are the words: "to order" or "negotiable" and/or the applicable law to the record.

81 Without overseeing the criticism made above.

82 As per Article 10(2)(c): "The electronic transport record ceases thereafter to have any effect or validity."

83 Ibid.

84 However, for additional certainty, a relevant section at the end of Article 10 of the RR would be enlightening.

85 Magklasi, 'Electronic transport records: Assessing the contribution of the Rotterdam Rules to e-commerce', p. 125.

86 As discussed, attacking the practice of letters of indemnity is one of the purposes behind Article 47(2) of the RR and the drafting purpose of the chapter of the RR on electronic commerce.

the goods but purports to deceive the carrier into releasing possession of the goods. The provision should only stand for the protection of the real holder, who, due to unforeseen circumstances, cannot prove his entitlement. Otherwise, the provision would juxtapose legal certainty, whereas our aim is to enhance it. Consequently, this is why occurrence of loss should be further qualified. It is suggested that only exceptional circumstances pertaining to *force majeure* (in the example of US legislation) and theft should permit replacement of the original.[87] Since the buyer is unable to claim delivery without the originally issued record or the document, the reissuance of the transport document or the replacement of the missing document with an electronic transport record is most likely going to be requested.

Below we will investigate how contract drafting can complement Article 10 of the RR if situations like the above arise.

Article 10 of the RR states that the document or record needs to be submitted in exchange/substitution of the record for replacement to occur; something which is impossible here. Unfortunately, there is no other article in the RR suggesting a solution, so ultimately the right to a second chance has to be stipulated elsewhere to protect a bona fide receiver who is fraudulently deprived of the transport document.

It is our view that to address a situation like the above, a carriage contract between the carrier and shipper could have an additional provision entitled "exceptional cases", with two subsections: one for replacement without use of the original, and the other for reissuing. However, these provisions should be thoroughly drafted, and if possible, exhaustively mention the exceptional circumstances for their application, e.g. "The article should be applicable only in cases of theft, *force majeure* or in certain (defined) circumstances."[88]

Our insistence on this precise wording and guidance as to the restrictive interpretation of the provision is for the protection of the buyer's commercial interests. The provision should be explicit and exhaustive, thus perhaps discouraging the carelessness of holders; only exceptional circumstances will be covered. Proving the absence of fraud is key in this context, and if the carrier (or the court) is convinced by the evidence, the carrier may *reissue* a transport document or *replace* the lost document with an electronic transport record. Of course, if reissuance or replacement occurs, it should have the effect that the previously issued document or record stands void. The clause should be explicit in this regard, and also

87 A similar clause, as far as documents of title are concerned, appears in the UCC, applying in the US, section 7-502(b)(2) stating: "Subject to Section 7-503, title and rights acquired by negotiation are not defeated by any stoppage of the goods represented by the document of title or by surrender of the goods by the bailee and are not impaired even if: [...] (2) any *person has been deprived of possession of a negotiable tangible document by misrepresentation, fraud, accident, mistake, duress, loss, theft, or conversion*" (emphasis added). In our opinion, the same protection of the cases in italics, should be afforded to sea waybills after the RR come into force, or it could be included in the COGSA, when amended.

88 An *ejusdem generis* construction to be applied.

specify that reissuance or replacement due to loss is only allowed once, in order to prevent abuse of the provision.[89]

We have devised this solution, because by virtue of Article 45(b) of the RR; if the goods are undelivered to the consignee, for the reasons stated in the article, the carrier may seek instructions for delivery by the shipper or documentary shipper. If the seller has any of these roles, depending on whether this is a CIF or FOB contract, and assuming he has been paid, he may act fraudulently to have the goods delivered to a person other than the consignee. If the seller and buyer are the shipper and documentary shipper respectively, and they give conflicting instructions, unusual delay may also arise. Therefore, our suggestion for a contractual provision, inserted in the sale and carriage contract, will secure the consignee who is unable to identify himself at the port of discharge. If this provision is also inserted into the sale contract, it will ensure which person has to be approached for instructions, and thus, the seller and buyer will have to unanimously designate the buyer in that case.[90]

Reissuance will provide the legal basis for preventing goods from falling in the wrong hands, thus attacking misdeliveries. In other words it would, in actuality, suggest a way of attacking fraud, which was among the objectives of the RR. It would also explicitly give guidance as to what a carrier should do when the holder cannot identify himself as the party entitled to the goods. So far, where there is incapacity of the holder to identify himself, it is the decision of the carrier to seek other evidence or request instructions from the shipper as to whether to deliver to the consignee. The parties might even have to wait for a court order providing guidance so as to know whether to deliver or not. This legislative lacuna can be effectively superseded by the adoption of our suggestion. Ultimately, the benefit of this insertion will be threefold.[91]

First, replacement will not be a privilege of negotiable documents/records, thus the use of non-negotiable documents/records will not be discouraged. Second, replacement as promulgated will allow for the parties to accommodate their commercial needs, as electronic or paper versions of the contract may be equally necessary under different contracts (e.g. the electronic *record* may be necessary for the carriage contract, whereas the straight bill of lading is suitable for compliance with the letter of credit). Third, the consignee who cannot prove his entitlement through the transport document will not have to depend on the honesty of his own seller, especially since the latter will have received payment.

To the extent that carriers are willing to reissue transport documents in specific circumstances, the insertion of this contractual provision in the sale and carriage

89 This, however, does not seem to apply in replacement under Article 10 of the RR, as it now stands.

90 The provisions of the RR on right of control cannot assist in this scenario, because, so that the right of control can be exercised, the controlling party has to have all originals of the transport document/record (Article 51(2)(b) of the RR).

91 Magklasi, 'Electronic transport records: Assessing the contribution of the Rotterdam Rules to e-commerce', p. 125.

contracts will credit legal and commercial practice with greater legal certainty, which may potentially be an exemplary way for setting letters of indemnity aside.

The deficiencies of the RR in the regulation of electronic contracting will now be examined in more detail. These deficiencies will show the way that the national frameworks or individual (sale and carriage) agreements should take to secure proper performance of international sale contracts, avoiding certain repercussions.

4.9 Assessment of omissions of the provisions of the Rotterdam Rules on e-commerce

4.9.1 The constrictive scope of Article 8 of the Rotterdam Rules leads to fusion of contracts

As discussed above, a major commercial concern is that only the carrier's and shipper's consent is required for the issuance and use of electronic transport records.[92] The documentary shipper is omitted as he cannot have the transport record without the authorisation of the shipper/seller.[93] However, it has to be re-emphasised that the documentary shipper may hold an important role in the trade realm, as it happens in the context of an FOB sale where he is the seller. Since the importance of electronic transport records is evident not only in the carriage realm but also in the context of international trade law, the documentary shipper *qua* seller's rights also have to be adequately secured while the carriage contract is performed.

This becomes more comprehensible if the following is considered: in theory, the consent of the documentary shipper is not needed because the shipper is the party to enter into such a contract of carriage in order to satisfy the prerequisites of the previously concluded sale contract. In practice, however, complications can arise and problems such as delays and other circumstances often occur, which may induce the shipper to collude with the carrier to conceal them (through forgery of the record). Secondly, it should not be disregarded that even though there may be a genuine intention of the shipper to comply with the stipulations of the sale contract when entering into the carriage contract, there may be aspects/ specifications of the sale contract as to the contract of carriage which are reflected differently in the latter. In addition to that, discrepancies should be expected if we recall that the parties' negotiation of the carriage and sale contracts involves different parties. Accordingly, the argument that the FOB seller's consent as to the form will always be provided in advance in the sale contract, and therefore he should not have a say when the carriage contract is entered into, can be refuted.[94] It is possible that the sale contract is silent in terms of form, in which case, the documentary seller/shipper can only be faced with a surprise.

92 Article 8 of the RR.

93 Article 35 of the RR.

94 Only to the extent that privity of contract is not infringed.

Instead of having additional provisions in different contracts on the same matter, it would have been more efficient, if the RR had provided for all the parties in the sale contract (i.e. seller and buyer) to consent to the issuance of the electronic transport records – and, if necessary, differentiate the circumstances. This equally applies to the consignee/holder, who should be aware of his rights and obligations and the ways in which he can have access to the electronic system, i.e. he should know how to perform the obligation to surrender and his right to claim delivery of the goods.

Otherwise, it should be up to the third party registries to provide for the role of sellers and buyers who do not have the status of the shipper, if the carriage contract does not involve provisions for their rights when an electronic transport record is issued. And registries do so.[95]

Although Article 9 of the RR is a welcome provision, there is still a need to outline the procedure which guarantees the desired security in the transaction and exclusive control over the electronic transport record.[96]

From the trade law viewpoint, what is still to be addressed in the sense that the articles of the RR do not provide for it, is what happens when there is a diversity of provisions from different contracts that do not match one another. On the one hand, there will be the provisions of the sale contract whereby seller and buyer will have to protect their *electronic interests* vis-à-vis one another. On the other hand, the same will be purported for the interests of carrier and shipper in the contract particulars of the carriage agreement. Nevertheless, the position of the consignee (thus of the CIF buyer vis-à-vis the carrier) and of the documentary shipper-FOB seller against shipper and carrier will unlikely be contemplated in any agreement; it will merely be coincidental[97] to see that either the sale contract or the carriage contract or both somehow provide for the legal position of the aforementioned parties in paperless transactions.

It is equally possible to find that no contractual framework secures the parties' interests in a homogeneous way. This is evident in the following scenario: a sale contract is concluded on FOB terms and the seller is required to tender either a transport document or an electronic transport record. The buyer *qua* shipper enters into a contract of carriage where the carrier will issue an electronic transport record. However, the carrier's framework/registry[98] does not recognise any role for the documentary shipper. Thus, the carrier and shipper-buyer decide to accede to the framework of a third party service provider.[99] This framework is proved to have terms which are different from the definitions of the RR. For

95 See Bolero and CargoDocs.

96 Our criticism is also shared by Treitel and Reynolds (eds), *Carver on Bills of Lading* (4th edn), para 8-101.

97 Or usually requested by the specific framework of the private electronic registry.

98 By this, we mean the set of rules of his own system for electronic records.

99 Such examples are Bolero and CargoDocs.

example, there may be no definition for the documentary shipper,[100] or the controlling party in the registry's framework; or there may be a vague definition of the shipper, such as "The shipper is the user that enters into the contract of carriage with the carrier or the user that puts the goods on board a vessel". In this case, the capacities of shipper and documentary shipper are confused, and thus, it is difficult to distinguish where the rights of the seller start and stop. This would be necessary so that, from the point of transfer of the right of control, the buyer is able to know when and how he can exercise control over the goods electronically. Registries claim that they have the infrastructure to enable this, but this usually follows the doctrine of novation and not specifically the series of steps pertaining to right of control and rules of transfer of the RR. When the RR obtain the force of law, these procedures would need to additionally comply with the RR. Lastly, there may be a complete omission of definition for the documentary shipper in the registry's framework.

Another problematic example where the framework of a third party registry may prove to vary from the terminology of the RR is where the transport document is more vaguely defined, as in Bolero Rulebook Article 56, Transport Document: Any Document originated by a Carrier which is either a Sea Waybill or a Ship's Delivery Order.

This reflects as follows in the slightly varied example that we have devised.

There is again an FOB sale contract which requires a negotiable transport document, or an electronic transport record, in the definition of the RR. The shipper enters into such a contract of carriage, but the carrier does not have the infrastructure for issuing electronic transport records, or his system does not have a framework with rules on the rights of the documentary shipper. Thus carrier and shipper (i.e. the FOB buyer) decide to cooperate with a third party service provider to issue an electronic transport record. If this is defined as the transport document in Bolero above, an electronic ship's delivery order would suffice under the contract that the carrier and shipper have with the registry. The seller is the documentary shipper and therefore is not in a position to negotiate the terms and conditions of the third party registry. The buyer would be in breach of the sale contract as the electronic contract finally issued would not be the bill of lading that the seller wanted. This is regardless of the fact that the agreement he entered into seemed to allow for the issuance of an electronic transport record. If the consent of the documentary shipper was included in Article 8(a) of the RR, and if he could also appear as the holder,[101] the seller of our discussion would

100 As in the Bolero Rulebook. The Rulebook is defined as a common user agreement entered into between all the parties using the Bolero System at bolero-1.hs-sites.com/download-bolero-rulebook?__hstc=14749097.9c97b32a11d0b53201df95dc8a3c8d16.1391018257678.1391018257678.1391018257678.1&__hssc=14749097.1.1391018257678&__hsfp=2911068739.

101 Bolero Rulebook section 1.1. (33): Holder: A User who is or becomes Designated to the role of Holder. "Holdership" is the status of being a Holder. A User may be the Holder of a Bolero Bill

have the opportunity to prevent the buyer from entering into this "inappropriate" contract with the third party registry, or at least he could have suggested redrafting of the controversial terms.

Any agreement which is concluded in pursuance of the contract of sale will have to match the requirements of the latter.

This is why we strongly believe that the variety of the agreements, however specific they may be, can cause confusion. The parties will have to enter into an agreement with a third party service provider, which will also have its own standard terms and conditions. Accordingly, the need for individual changes and adaptations will not be an easy task for traders, carriers or electronic registries. Even when a deficiency is noted, if it is not observed by a party to the contract of carriage, for example by the FOB buyer, it will have the unavoidable effect that the misperformance of the sale contract cannot be prevented.

There is no contractual right of the seller/documentary shipper to prevent the carrier and shipper from entering into a problematic agreement with a third party registry or to have a say on the issuance of a transport record, unless that party obtains a role provided for by the rules of the electronic service provider. However, it seems uncertain how a person who is the holder of the record under the RR can enforce rights pertaining to his holdership, if he has not signed an agreement (with the carrier/shipper) and with the registry. This probably explains why registries require the subscription of both holders and carriers to their system.

There are, however, additional concerns: who will have to surrender and accede to whose rules? How easy is it for a carrier or trader who has built an established practice of trading over electronic transport records of an X system, to change to Y system?[102] In that case, one of the parties has to compromise and follow the system/registry of the carrier or of the other trader. The negotiating and market power of the strongest parties, in terms of market power, will probably force the other party to subscribe to the system of the electronic provider of the former.

This is why we assert that it would be better to have a body of law or an agreement epitomising all parties' roles and obligations. The use of the word "roles" is not random. Firstly, it is used because this is necessary in order to interpret how the given capacities of the parties under the RR as shipper and consignee/holder reflect in the international trade realm, where the parties are entering into a contract as "seller" and "buyer". Secondly, the word is used to remind us that the systems of third party providers, such as Bolero, work in a way that also attributes roles to the parties entering into their agreements. Sometimes new terms appear thereunder such as "consignee holder".[103]

of Lading without occupying another Role, or Holdership may be joined to another role as in the case of a Holder-to-order, Bearer Holder, Pledgee Holder, or Consignee Holder.

102 For instance, if a carrier and the seller customarily cooperate with Bolero, but a chain of buyers use the service of CargoDocs.

103 Bolero Rulebook, Rule 1.1.(22).

Since the RR do not prescribe a decisive role for all the trade protagonists, it is left to the sale contract to specifically address their role so that they can fall under the terms of the framework of the registry.

Having illustrated the deficiency of Article 8(a) of the RR and its possible legal consequences, our analysis will now move to a study of the procedures under Article 9 in order to complete the overview of Chapter 3 of the RR. Compliance of the RR with other sets of rules, with the view to provisions on electronic documents, will subsequently follow.

4.9.2 Assessment of Article 9 of the Rotterdam Rules: are the procedures listed effective?

Article 9 of the RR, in very general terms, outlines some procedures that should govern the use of negotiable transport records. We use the word "some" because the cases covered under Articles 9(1)(a), (b) and (c), namely the method of the issuance and transfer of the record, the security that the record retains its integrity and the manner in which the holder will identify himself, are not sufficiently precise.[104]

A sound observation stemming from Article 9 of the RR, is that it recommends three elements: first, procedures of issuance and transfer have to be structured through a given method[105] and ensure the integrity of the record;[106] second, there must be certainty as to how the holder demonstrates that he is the holder;[107] and third, there must be certainty as to how delivery to the holder proves to have taken place.[108] Nevertheless, how can anyone, and particularly potential holders in string sales, be aware that Article 9 has been complied with, when there is no standard provided for these procedures?[109] It is our opinion that this lack of a minimum standard is bound to produce not only uncertainty, as in theory even one rule, no matter how abstract, can satisfy the need that the previous tenets are satisfied, but also disharmony, as the different possible registry systems may differ in their strictness. This will have an impact on trade, as eventually some systems may be favoured over others. This is also a factor that allows third party registries to work autonomously, aside of the RR or the Carriage of Goods by Sea Act (COGSA) 1992. We favour party autonomy, but we need to be aware that disputes on misdelivery, title to sue, replacement and switch bills tend to revolve around carriage statutes and/or conventions, which means that if ratified, the RR and their respective provisions on electronic records will be of relevance. The idea that this book aims to convey in this chapter is that instead of realising it at the

104 See Article 9(1) paras (a), (b) and (c) of the RR respectively.
105 Article 9(1)(a) of the RR.
106 Article 9(1)(b) of the RR.
107 Article 9(1)(c) of the RR.
108 Article 9(1)(d) of the RR.
109 For similar criticisms of uncertainty see de Haan, 'A test case for the Rotterdam Rules'. Contrast this with the thoroughness of the MLETR, which talks about standards in Article 12.

dispute level, it is best to ensure that all agreements, those of third party registries included, should be aware of and make amendments to reflect alignment with the RR.

The list of requirements of Article 9 of the RR is too abstract. Thus, it fails to justify the belief shared by some legal scholars that the RR have successfully provided a mechanism to deal with electronic commerce. Our view has been reflected in the recent MLETR, which has been created to enhance legislation on electronic records and makes reference to the RR in the Explanatory Note. There are several more aspects that need to be contracted on with specific guidance from the RR. If not contracted for, there will be parties, such as the documentary shipper, left unprotected, and space will be available for disparities among sale contracts, carriage contracts and agreements with third party registries. This will unavoidably happen since sale and carriage contracts can be controversially or insufficiently drafted unless they are issued by big trading and shipping associations, which run deeper checks. However, even in these contracts there may be divergent terminologies.

On the other hand, the rulebooks of third party registries are very thorough and detailed, and wherever there are contractual gaps, these may be filled in accordance with parameters that often the trading parties and carriers may not have predicted.

These details, which do not appear in the RR, can be contractually added, using as examples the rules of Bolero and essDOCS-Databridge™. For instance, the RR do not set out the powers that each party may have in connection to the electronic record (other than in the vague lines of Article 8)[110] and do not explain how discrepancies between a record and its paper equivalent can be resolved.[111]

It is submitted that the insufficiency of the RR deriving from Article 9 is not the failure to set forth the concrete technical means which will allow the procedures to work in practice, it is instead the failure to set the standards through which the aspects of the tenets of Article 9(1) will be assured.[112] Lack of standards means that there is no measure to check which registries or procedures comply with the RR. It also alludes to the conclusion that the framework of the RR is not robust. One might regard this suggestion as exaggerative, questioning why the solution to the deficiency should be "exhaustive codification". However, an indicative list of requirements for what the agreements and systems for electronic transport records should encompass would be a substantial guideline and point of reference. This has been taken into account by the MLETR. Anyway, the RR have proven to be more comprehensive, in other aspects. Once more, the complexities noted here reveal the uncoordinated scope of codification of the RR, as concluded also in the previous chapters.

An area which has not been regulated before by an international convention on carriage of goods would be expected to go beyond Model Laws and set

110 Bolero regulates that in Rule 3.8.

111 Bolero regulates that in Rule 3.7.3.

112 This has been remedied by Article 12 of the MLETR.

certain standards. The argument that very detailed procedures would narrow the applicability of Article 9 and thus be detrimental to the timelessness of the RR is persuasive; but our view is that the desired detail would affect the contractual standards framing the issuance and transfer of electronic records, and not the technological ones.

In the following section the elements that Articles 8 and 9 of the RR lack will be examined and suggestions of contract drafting or extra legislation will be provided. These are considered necessary to render paperless maritime trade trustworthy and demonstrably effective, after or without the application of the RR.

4.9.3 Deficiencies of Article 9 of the Rotterdam Rules

Our arguments do not contradict the idea that the RR should allow for future technological evolution. One could argue that some of the following points are taken on board by popular existing frameworks and thus there is no need for them to be specifically addressed by the RR. With respect, our counterargument is that, despite the established registries, commercial parties are still reluctant to trade electronically. The following remarks that we make are specific characteristics that parties should pay attention to when trading over electronic records. These can either be considered as implied characteristics of Article 9, (perhaps in the light of the MLETR which is more thorough in this regard) or as provisions that the individual contracts should be explicit on.

4.9.3.1 Scope

The first area that may receive criticism is the scope of application of Article 9 of the RR. It is very unwelcome to read that the security warranties, outlined in Article 9 of the RR, only apply to negotiable transport records. Reasonably, the need for protection is higher for negotiable documents since the holder may be unknown – not prescribed by name – and the record may be transferred numerous times down a string.

It has been argued that Article 9 only applies to negotiable records and not to non-negotiable ones because there is no electronic equivalent of a non-negotiable record that requires surrender.[113] This disregards the fact that although Article 45 of the RR is entitled "Delivery when no negotiable transport document or negotiable electronic transport record is issued", it applies to non-negotiable documents and non-negotiable records, even though the word "non-negotiable records" does not appear in the *chapeau* of the article. It has been clearly stated by commentators of the RR that this article covers a straight bill of lading or sea waybill (or equivalent electronic record).[114]

The paradox is that although non-negotiable records are acknowledged as a division of records where the RR apply, and defined in Article 1(20) of the

113 See Gaskell, 'Bills of lading in an electronic age', fn 243 therein.
114 See Baatz et al, *The Rotterdam Rules: A Practical Annotation*, para [45-02].

RR, the main articles dealing with electronic transport records in general, (i.e. Articles 8, 9 and 10) seem to only refer to negotiable records. In our view, this undermines the whole purpose of having electronic equivalents of non-negotiable documents and makes one think that the functional equivalence between paper and electronic contracts established in Article 8 of the RR is only partial.

4.9.3.2 Identification

By omitting reference to non-negotiable records, there is already much flexibility granted to electronic registry systems for loosening the network protection to these records,[115] thus increasing the possibility of fraud occurrence. Besides, the electronic infrastructure will have to ensure certain security levels for negotiable records. Accordingly, the same could easily be applicable to every type of transport record. Our suggestion aims to provide full equivalence and a harmonised security framework for all transport records regardless of their negotiable character. Otherwise the limited scope of Article 9 would open itself to abuse since the parties may be tempted to trade on non-negotiable records just to avoid the burden of the safety net imposed on the use of negotiable records. If, however, complementary national legislation follows, such phenomena will be precluded. The MELTR has been completed in 2017 with some more detail in certain directions. These are notably in the spirit of our recommendations for the provisions of the RR on electronic records. However, as it has been clarified in the Explanatory Note,[116] electronic transport records falling under the scope of application of the RR could be excluded from the scope of application of the MLETR. Nevertheless, we will occasionally reflect on or bring forward provisions of the MLETR, as it is contemporary Model Law in order to make important remarks about the RR. This also corroborates the importance of the underlying research for this book which precedes the MLETR.

The next area that needs further regulation is "identification". The RR require that the carrier, the shipper and holder of a transport document should be identified in the contract particulars.[117] Nevertheless, they should have specifically prescribed for procedures capable of showing who the holder or the controlling party is each time he exercises a relative right when electronic records are used.[118] This is needed due the broad scope of the RR definitions for these parties.

Article 51 of the RR is also crucial in electronic trading as it sets forth the requirements for the identification of the controlling party and regulates the transfer of the right of control.[119] According to Article 51, the shipper who is

115 As Article 9 of the RR will not apply to them.

116 Para 29.

117 See Articles 37, 31(1) and 1(10) of the RR respectively.

118 See Gaskell, 'Bills of lading in an electronic age', p. 280.

119 The entire purpose behind articles on right of control was to ensure the concept of exclusive control for negotiable electronic records.

initially the controlling party may, after the conclusion of the contract, vest this role to the documentary shipper or the consignee. This transfer of the right of control is valid for the carrier only after he has received the relevant notification. Thus, it is our opinion that Article 9 of the RR should require that the electronic registry system used by the parties is able to evidence the notification to the carrier on the electronic contract particulars only after this occurs electronically, should the potential actions regarding the right of control be available. Instead, this specification may be provided for contractually and enhance legal certainty. In other words, if the notice of transfer of the right of control is not electronically tendered and registered, the electronic registry should "lock", block or invalidate any exercise of the right of control by the new party.

Moreover, in our opinion, the controlling party should identify itself by name and also role each time it exercises the right of control, i.e. whether it is the shipper, documentary shipper or consignee. This is advised for additional clarity and for further control of actions under both the contract of carriage and the sale contract. It is important to check under which role an action was made, as apart from the role of the controlling party the person retains their role as shipper, documentary shipper and consignee. More concretely, this would allow parties to check which of the rights and obligations that were performed under a carriage contract are in compliance with what was prescribed in the sale contract. A more comprehensive provision to that effect can be found in Article 11 of the MLETR, where a reliable method is prescribed to establish exclusive control of the record, and the identification of the person in control.

Another ambiguity of the RR concerns the "access" to the electronic information. The RR do not specify when and how the documentary shipper will have access to the electronic information and give deadlines, the expiry of which will prevent the shipper or documentary shipper from inserting extra or amending the initial electronic contract particulars. Any change of data regarding the goods, the ship and the key parties crucial for a contract of carriage should be visible to the appropriate parties. At the same time, a provision allowing the consignee to trace and read the record and preventing the shipper and the documentary shipper from having any effect on the content of the record after the goods have been shipped and the transport record has been electronically signed, would also enhance legal certainty.

This is significant for passage of risk purposes when the sale at issue is a sale on arrival terms. In this type of sale contract the seller performs his duty to deliver through the actual arrival of the goods at the agreed port of destination and not just by delivery at the load port, as is the case with shipment sales. This means that the risk lies with the seller until the ship arrives at its destination. In these circumstances, it is critical that control of the goods in transit is available for the seller *qua* documentary shipper if the buyer has entered into the contract of carriage with the carrier.

Again, the MLETR is more inclusive of this, by indicating that a specific respect in which a reliable method should be used is the ability to prevent unauthorised access to and use of the system (Article 12(a)(iii)).

4.9.3.3 Singularity

The parties' agreements on e-contracting should contain procedures (e.g. the obligation of conditions to be met, passwords) to define the role of the parties and the conditions under which each record is surrendered and exhausted, where the electronic transport record will be issued in sets.

A more thorough provision could have been inserted in the RR whereby the users would agree that electronic communications would be treated as valid, and that no user could deny that a message originated from them if it contains their electronic signature.[120] The benefit of this is that it will strengthen the legal certainty of the parties relying on the electronic messages. It would also ensure that the parties have given adequate consideration to the terms and conditions of all their contracts regarding provisions of electronic contracting and therefore that they have not signed blindly; in the MLETR this is ensured through Articles 10(1)(a) and 10(2). Bolero satisfies the above through its principle of repudiation,[121] which aims to make the parties fully aware and thus fully responsible for the agreements that they sign.

This principle which serves to coordinate all the users in the trade chain (carriers, importers, exporters, banks, forwarders and other intermediaries) is missing from the RR. This is because the RR is a carriage of goods convention, and it hesitates to impose on parties, beyond the definitions of shipper, carrier and holder, the obligation to enter into a multilateral agreement. Therefore, a fortiori, the RR avoid involving other parties such as banks, as this is a step further, more pertinent to the sale and not the carriage transaction. Laudably, private registries, on their own initiatives invite and therefore bind all of these parties through a multilateral agreement.[122]

4.9.3.4 Reliability of the system of a third party registry

It is remarkable that the RR are missing provisions on the reliability of the potential electronic registry system. When third party providers are responsible for the issuance and use of electronic transport records, the RR should contain a provision enabling anyone among carrier, shipper, documentary shipper and consignee to check whether the system provided by the third party complies with the RR, before signing the relative agreement.[123] This control is needed so that the parties

120 This has been secured by Bolero. See www.bolero.net/platform/rulebook?__hstc=233546881.acfb1eff276b11c3d11785ea68b548b8.1390838640826.1390838640826.1391064342817.2&__hssc=233546881.6.1391064342817&__hsfp=64566324.

121 This principle is found in Bolero. For the necessity of this principle, see Jones, 'A new transport convention: A framework for e-commerce?', p. 159.

122 CargoDocs and Bolero www.bolero.net/platform/rulebook?__hstc=233546881.acfb1eff276b11c3d11785ea68b548b8.1390838640826.1390838640826.1391064342817.2&__hssc=233546881.6.1391064342817&__hsfp=64566324.

123 See also Jones, 'A new transport convention: A framework for e-commerce?', p. 160.

cannot subsequently question the reliability of the system chosen on the basis of known flaws (purposefully not addressed) previously noted.

An assurance that the third party provider meets the standards of the RR and of other sets of rules (eUCP, EU Directives etc.) that regulate paperless contracting can be guaranteed by an organisation which will supervise compliance of individual private frameworks with the international conventions. To date, the registries themselves herald their compliance with these rules,[124] and contain clauses on applicable law and jurisdiction.

Our points are in fact administered by the MLETR which now indicatively – and not exhaustively – suggests that a method can be as reliable as appropriate for the fulfilment of the function for which the method is being used, in the light of all relevant circumstances, which may include: any operational rules relevant to the assessment of reliability;[125] the regularity and extent of audit by an independent body;[126] the existence of a declaration by a supervisory body, an accredited body or voluntary scheme regarding the reliability of the system;[127] and any applicable industry standard.[128] These are some of the sub-sections of Article 12(a) of the MLETR.

4.9.3.5 Format of the electronic record

The RR do not specify a required format for the information. They do not illustrate how the contract particulars will be organised, what is expected after issuance and how the record can be traced. The RR should at least invite the parties to specify a format in which the electronic record is going to be presented;[129]in other words, it should specify that the record must be easily or somehow recognisable.[130] The general expression "information associated or linked"[131] of the definition of the transport record should be ascertainable through perceivable criteria. An indicative example of a format, such as "email with attachment of the terms and conditions of carriage or a web-link referring to them", would be a welcome provision contained in the RR, since it would facilitate the filtering of which

124 essDOCS allows the electronic presentation of documents to multi-banks under the eUCP, covers compliance documents such as Safety Data Sheets (SDS) required under REACH, GHS or similar legislation at www.essdocs.com/about-us/about-ess. Similarly, Bolero, complies with eUCP for Letters of Credit and supports the full range of presentation options from paper, to mixed (paper/electronic) and to fully electronic at www.bolero.net/products-overview?id=11.

125 MLETR, Article 12(a)(i).

126 MLETR, Article 12(a)(v).

127 MLETR, Article 12(a)(vi).

128 MLETR, Article 12(a)(vii).

129 Bolero does that, see Jones, 'A new transport convention: A framework for e-commerce?', p. 162. So does the essDOCS-Databridge™, providing a replica bill of lading; see also Gaskell, 'Bills of lading in an electronic age', pp. 272, 273.

130 Gaskell states *inter alia* for the electronic record: "but for it to be used it must be visible in some recognisable way": Gaskell, 'Bills of lading in an electronic age', p. 272.

131 The MLETR, in Article 2 also defines an electronic record in a similar way: "information generated, communicated, received or stored by electronic means, including where appropriate, all information logically associated with or otherwise linked together so as to become part of the record, whether generated contemporaneously or not."

emails contain necessary information for the contract of carriage.[132] Moreover, our suggestion is in line with article e4 of eUCP, which initially requires the credit to specify the formats in which electronic records are to be presented.[133]

This is needed for two reasons: the first reason is the existing variety of private third party providers and the disparity of formats they provide, with the result of complicating the assessment of compliance with the RR. Secondly, a *main format/scheme* should be suggested by the Convention in order to contribute to the security and flexibility needed in international trade. This will also contribute to systematising which information would be part of the contract particulars and the transport record. Thus, no information which should be in the transport record will be missed, and any faults that happen to be contained will be easily detected. An indicative way of doing this would be via filling the relevant gaps in an online platform with the information of contract particulars that would appear on emails (free-format text) or attachments.[134] The latter method recalls the classic boxes that have to be completed in a paper bill of lading.

A suggested (but not exclusive) acceptable format[135] has the incomparable advantage of an easy detection of possible discrepancies between the record and the contract of sale by the first and future buyers. The advantages of a required format also prove useful at the time of replacement of the record by a transport document. Finally, it needs to be highlighted that the format will constitute the basis for other useful functions of electronic carriage and trade: for instance, a given format would allow the electronic signature to appear in an identifiable context.[136]

Article 9 does not show which requirements should be satisfied and through which methods,[137] such as for making it obvious on the record who the holder is, or for ascertaining who should be held liable for the loss of the integrity of the document in breach of Article 9(1)(b) of the RR. Additionally, there should be precise rules about how the records are supposed to be exhausted upon delivery. More particularly, the RR should specify how the concept of surrender of the negotiable transport record applies to electronic records, at least on an indicative basis.

A way of proving title could be if the potential holder owns a unique password or token which can be inserted in a device in the possession of the carrier when the goods are at their final destination. The other alternatives are that the holder inserts the password into the electronic registry system that is in use and then prints out a verification enabling him to claim delivery from the carrier. However,

132 For these suggestions see also Gaskell, 'Bills of lading in an electronic age', p. 272.

133 The article of *e*UCP does not prescribe a legal consequence in the case of breach as the second tenet of the article allows the electronic record to appear in any format if it has no specific format.

134 Bolero offers both possibilities.

135 Or suggestions as to criteria pertaining to a format.

136 See Gaskell, 'Bills of lading in an electronic age', p. 277. His argument is in the same line as ours, as he suggests that a facsimile signature could presumably appear in the end of a pdf file of an on-screen bill.

137 See also Gaskell, 'Bills of lading in an electronic age', p. 275.

this would mean that in essence there cannot be an absolutely paperless contract of carriage, since, in the end, there would always be some reference to the paper document.

It is also observed that the RR do not state any sanctions, remedies or other legal consequences for breach of any of the obligations contained under Articles 8, 9 and 10, which, if existed, would denote a firm and consistent framework. But, this is the correlate problem of not having a standard, non-compliance with which would trigger the above. Again the MLETR now suggests in Article 12 that a supervisory body can safeguard or designate the level of reliability of the method.

Electronic signatures[138] are also relevant in this study. The RR are very abstract as far as requirements for electronic signatures are concerned, leaving their regulation to national law. It is positive that many leading trading nations have adopted legislation which recognises that electronic signatures are valid and enforceable. But, the question remains: when can a transport record be considered invalid?

4.9.3.6 Signatures

Article 38(2) of the RR contains the requirements for electronic signatures when electronic transport records are used. The first is that an electronic transport record shall include the signature of the carrier or a person acting on their behalf. Secondly, this electronic signature has to identify the signatory in relation to the electronic transport record and indicate the carrier's authorisation of the electronic transport record.

The criticism that has been made to the above is that the RR do not provide guidance as to the way in which the electronic signature can be related to the record.[139] Also, how the authorisation of the carrier for the issuance of an electronic transport record can be shown is not specified.[140] Moreover, Article 9 was the appropriate section to illustrate how the requirements of Articles 38(2) and 38(3) of the RR on electronic signatures could be met, but as said above, it is abstract.

The electronic signature is not defined under the RR and the reliability of the method for this signature seems also to be purposefully left to the applicable national law.[141] The view that prevailed on this matter during the deliberation for the Convention was that a given definition might prove outdated if more advanced technology emerged.[142] However, we do not share this view as then

138 At EU level, since 1 July 2016, the Regulation (EU) N°910/2014 on electronic identification and trust services for electronic transactions in the internal market (better known as the eIDAS Regulation) came into full effect and the eSignature Directive of 1999 was repealed.

139 See Gaskell, 'Bills of lading in an electronic age', 277.

140 Ibid, where he suggests that the wording of the UCP 600 "for and on behalf of the carrier" can be added. It should be recalled that the mismatches between the requirements of the UCP 600 and the RR were discussed in a previous chapter of this book.

141 See Sturley, Fujita and van der Ziel, *The Rotterdam Rules*, para 7.059.

142 See 15th Session Report, para 203.

more complex questions are triggered, such as which law shall apply? Even within the 15th session of the Working Group, there have been different opinions on this matter, as then arguably choice of law issues arise. Secondly, if it is suggested that national law applies, there might be nations that do not have provisions for the validity of electronic signatures. The legal problems which might occur vary from a vacuum of law to conflicts of laws[143] and they could have been rectified by the adoption of a "functional" definition. This is why leaving the reliability and validity methods of an electronic signature to the applicable law can be problematic and misleading.[144]

In our opinion, as national laws across different continents may vary, an international harmonised regulation should be set forth. This intended harmony was partly achieved by other rules, such as international Model Law conventions, namely the UNCITRAL Model Law on Electronic Commerce 1996 Article 7(1)(b),[145] or the UN Convention on the Use of Electronic Communications in International Contracts 2005 Article 9(3)(b).[146] Therefore, our argument is that due to the guiding mission of Model Laws, which serve as interpretation tools, the respective additions should necessarily be impliedly incorporated into agreements should any ambiguities or insufficiency of laws arise. Alternatively, as suggested several times above, national legislation shall be enriched in this direction in order to give specific content to the ambiguous provisions.

Since the RR do not mention how the signature should appear on an electronic transport record,[147]a solution similar to what the essDOCS Draft E-bill provides could be acceptable: that a facsimile signature is visible at the end of the formatted electronic record, for example at the end of a pdf document,[148] and this can be contracted for in the parties' multipartite agreement.

In light of the desired principles of uniformity and functional equivalence, the RR fail to state that the transfer of an electronic transport record in accordance

143 See 15th Session Report, para 204.

144 See 15th Session Report, para 203.

145 Article 7 reads: Signature (1) Where the law requires a signature of a person, that requirement is met in relation to a data message if:(a) a method is used to identify that person and to indicate that person's approval of the information contained in the data message; and (b) that method is as reliable as was appropriate for the purpose for which the data message was generated or communicated, in the light of all the circumstances, including any relevant agreement.(2) Paragraph (1) applies whether the requirement therein is in the form of an obligation or whether the law simply provides consequences for the absence of a signature. (3) The provisions of this article do not apply to the following: […].

146 Article 9(3) reads: Where the law requires that a communication or a contract should be signed by a party, or provides consequences for the absence of a signature, that requirement is met in relation to an electronic communication if: (a) A method is used to identify the party and to indicate that party's intention in respect of the information contained in the electronic communication; And (b) The method used is either: (i) As reliable as appropriate for the purpose for which the electronic communication was generated or communicated, in the light of all the circumstances, including any relevant agreement; or (ii) Proven in fact to have fulfilled the functions described in subparagraph (a) above, by itself or together with further *evidence*.

147 Gaskell, 'Bills of lading in an electronic age', pp. 276–278.

148 See more on this in Gaskell, 'Bills of lading in an electronic age', pp. 262, 272.

with the procedures of Article 9 is considered valid, binding and acceptable as it would be with documents. This is instead advocated by the MLETR.[149] Even where physical endorsement and delivery of a document of title are required for the transfer of the ownership of goods, this on its own shall not suffice for the recognition of electronic transport records. This can instead be implemented in the parties' agreement and is in line with the response to the observation/finding of the UNCTAD Secretariat in its Report of 2001 that existence of "jurisdictions in which physical endorsement and delivery of a document of title are necessary for the transfer of the ownership of goods" will obstruct the use of electronic bills of lading.[150]

4.9.3.7 Time

Furthermore, a provision should be inserted in individual contracts, or desirably be provided for by national legislation, that will specifically request from the procedural rules of electronic records' transmission to comprise of provisions about the time of sending and receipt,[151] and how the parties should deal with wrongly delivered messages. Again, the MLETR is more specific in this regard.

The RR lack any provisions with regard to time of dispatch and receipt of the electronic documents: there is the "reception rule", also adopted by CISG, that the contract is concluded when the message enters the computer system of the offeror. However, this relates to the conclusion of contracts, which the RR do not govern. We suggest that the parties should contractually stipulate which date is going to be the date of the record: should it be the date it leaves the computer of the sender, the date it enters the system of the offeree, or the time it is read? Which is the time that matters for contractual purposes? Is it the procedural time on the email, or the time in the content of the email, such as time of shipment?

This ambiguity may have legal consequences as time is of the essence in overseas sales. The date of shipment on the bill of lading gives the buyer the right to terminate the sale contract if the date is not contractual. Time of arrival of the documents themselves might also be an issue where the buyer has an interest in the bill of lading itself. If the market is falling, a prompt identification of a contractual deficiency will entitle him to terminate the sale contract. As it has been argued in previous chapters, this is the main reason that explains the use of letters of indemnity given by sellers or buyers to the carrier when delivery is claimed at a time where presentation is impossible.[152]

149 Article 19.

150 The reference to the report can be found in Clarke, above, p. 361, as taken from Yiannopoulos in Yiannopoulos (ed), *Ocean Bills of Lading: Traditional Forms, Substitutes and EDI Systems*, para 6.2: part of a general report on the basis of national reports compiled before that. See also the MLETR.

151 Such as Article 15 of the UNCITRAL Model Law on Electronic Commerce.

152 See FOSFA No. 54, lines 122–124 (delivery against guarantee).

Therefore, it will be in the interest of all parties to have some assurance that this obligation is upon all the parties of the agreement: the shipper, the carrier and the consignee. Finally, remedies for breach may also be provided through contracts, national or international legislation.

Another valid suggestion would be the legal description of an example of an e-commerce platform/registry enabling both tracking and tracing of the carriage process.[153] The purpose behind our suggestion is in line with the neutrality principle, that the RR should not promote one issuer of private and public keys, i.e. a particular third party registry.[154] Various third party service providers with their own rules are already in practice. Had the RR contained provisions requiring the independent companies to ensure that their definitions, terms, conditions and procedures absolutely reflect those of the RR when these would be compulsorily applicable to avoid misinterpretations, compliance of the registries with the RR, uniformity of interpretation and neutrality without fettering competition among them would have been attained. Since this is not the case, this check is the joint responsibility of carrier, shipper and consignee/receiver before the signing of the subscription agreement, to the effect that the parties cannot deny the validity of the transactions on the basis that the third party provider does provide for the concepts of the RR.

For instance, Rule 1.1(56) of the "transport document" in the Bolero Rulebook[155] that "any document originated by a carrier which is either a sea waybill or a ship's delivery order" aims to distinguish all these documents from the Bolero Bill of Lading (BBL).[156] Ideally, this can be replaced by the definition 1(14) of the RR, when they apply to the carriage contract.[157]

4.9.3.8 Applicable law

Choosing the applicable law and jurisdiction to govern issuance and use of electronic records is also crucial and deserves an explicit agreement by the parties. Especially carriers and traders should know the jurisdiction and the law under which they can sue for damages and losses against third party registries, due to faults of the latter. For instance, this applies to the scenario where the electronic transport record proves faulty or fraudulent due to the safety incompetence of the system of the third party registry. As the majority of electronic third party

153 See IM Technologies Ltd, Executive Summary and Final Report of 'The economic impact of carrier liability on intermodal freight transport', London 10.1.2001, p. 43 for use and information of the European Commission.

154 See Erik Røsæg, 'New procedures for bills of lading in the Rotterdam Rules' (2011) 17 *JIML* 181, p. 193.

155 Available online at www.boleroassociation.org/downloads/rulebook1.pdf.

156 This is because Bolero is focusing on transfer of bills of lading.

157 See Article 1(14) of the RR: "'Transport document' means a document issued under a contract of carriage by the carrier that:(a) Evidences the carrier's or a performing party's receipt of goods under a contract of carriage; and (b) Evidences or contains a contract of carriage."

registries working in shipping and trade have their own rulebook, they usually have standard exemption or limitation of liability clauses in their favour, which may leave uninformed cargo interests unprotected in case of serious losses.[158] These frameworks should probably be overlooked by a higher authority, in the spirit that the MLETR now suggests.[159]

Article 9 of the RR could prima facie prescribe the procedures for the integrity of the record and thus set forth some guarantees/standards (like the MLETR)[160] that the individual registries should meet above and which the registries cannot contract, would be a notable insertion. Otherwise, this can only be left to the respective national legislations.[161]

Parties are advised to pay particular attention when specifying jurisdiction and choice of law separately for documents and records, and where this is meant to be the same it should be explicit in the relevant agreement. This is relevant irrespective of whether a transport document or an electronic transport record is issued in the first place. This suggested clarity is essential for documents because Article 10 of the RR is not explicit on the issue; namely it does not state whether after replacement, the choice of law agreement on the replaced document or record is the same as that of the record or document that replaces it. The choice of law clauses applicable to the agreement of the third party registry may be different from the general choice of law for claims under the contract of carriage between the carrier and the shipper.[162] There may be conflicts of law issues in case the carriage and sale contracts and the agreement for the issuance and use of electronic transport records do not include express choice of law clauses, as there will usually be a separate choice of law provision in the rulebook of the registry. Thus, it is for the parties to ensure that the choice of law and jurisdiction for disputes under the electronic transport records between carrier, shipper, documentary shipper and consignee against the third party registry or any other provider appears in the electronic transport record.[163] If the choice of law for disputes attributed to the fault of the registry is left to national laws, repercussions may arise, as "electronic legislation" along nations is not uniformly advanced or comprehensive.[164]

158 See Røsæg, 'New procedures for bills of lading in the Rotterdam Rules', para 2.4, p. 193.

159 MLETR, Article 12(a)(vi).

160 See the tenets of Article 12 of the MLETR. On the MLETR see R Harrington, 'News from the United Nations Commission on International Trade Law (UNCITRAL): The work of the fiftieth commission session' (2017) 22(4) *Uniform Law Review* 996.

161 However, it would be preferable for this initiative to be put forward by the RR, as national legislations may or may not take the steps to comply with this need and in the best case, they may do it at a low speed. This again would cause disharmony, which is not wanted.

162 See the Bolero Rulebook, for instance, in Rule 2.5, subsections 3 and 4.

163 It should at this point be highlighted that this agreement about jurisdiction should be as precise as possible, so that the parties bound by it are not confused with the general agreement for the forum of the disputes under the contract of carriage. The parties are free to opt-in the article for jurisdiction, which is Article 74 of the RR.

164 See Røsæg, 'New procedures for bills of lading', p. 194.

The overall purpose of our suggestion about the resolution of disputes when a third party registry is involved, is for the parties to make sure that these issues are dealt with once and for all, and that there are not fragmented provisions conflicting with each other in various – usually standard – contracts causing unnecessary confusion and claims submitted before incompetent courts.

Having identified the issues not covered by the RR themselves, in the subsequent section the compatibility of existing tools of paperless contracting with the RR will be studied. This shall deal with the UNCITRAL Model Law on Electronic Commerce, which paved the way for electronic contracts on the one hand, and the renowned Bolero on the other. Finally, the eUCP will be discussed to verify why the alleged deficiencies throughout this analysis are valid.

4.10 Relationship of the Rotterdam Rules with the UNCITRAL Model Law on Electronic Commerce, the MLETR and Bolero

The UNCITRAL Model Law on Electronic Commerce[165] with Guide to Enactment 1996 with additional Article 5 bis as adopted in 1998 has been an important step of harmonisation of non-paper based methods.

As stated among its objectives,[166] the Model Law can serve as a tool of interpretation where there are legal obstacles in the use of electronic commerce. In the meantime, with technology advancing quickly, private entities have developed their own registry systems and rules in order to serve the performance of electronic contracts, some of them with specialisations in international carriage contracts. As noted above, the MLETR was adopted in 2017, affording electronic transferable records, nations, academics and policy makers with a more up-to-date safeguard of the directions in which electronic transferable records can be transferred across borders. It also comes to assist with the implementation of the RR, as it is stated in the Explanatory Note that:[167]

> "In 2011, when the Commission decided to undertake work in the field of electronic transferable records, support was expressed for that work in light of benefits that the formulation of uniform legal standards in that field could bring to the promotion of electronic communications in international trade generally as well as to the implementation of the Rotterdam Rules and to other areas of transport business specifically. UNCITRAL decided to prepare a model law to enable the use of electronic transferable records on the basis of their functional equivalence with transferable documents or instruments, building upon the fundamental principles underlying existing UNCITRAL texts in the area of electronic commerce, namely non-discrimination against

165 UNCITRAL Model Law on Electronic Commerce with Guide to Enactment 1996 with additional Article 5 *bis* as adopted in 1998. Hereafter 'Model Law'.

166 See full text at www.uncitral.org/pdf/english/texts/electcom/05-89450_Ebook.pdf, under objectives, para 5, p. 17.

167 This is para 7 of the Explanatory Note of the MLETR.

the use of electronic communications, functional equivalence and technological neutrality."

Although, controversially, the Explanatory Note denotes that the RR could be exempted[168] as a subject matter from the scope of application of the MLETR, the specific reference to its supportive function towards the RR and the steps that the the MLETR takes forward compared to the RR, are exactly in line with our views on the possible criticisms to the RR and make the MLETR of great value.

Our aim in the following paragraphs is to study the Model Law and the framework of a popular private third party provider, namely Bolero,[169] and to investigate their differences from the RR. Once the RR are enacted with the force of law, they will coexist in international commercial practice. Thus our purpose is to use the above systems as indicative tools of electronic trade legislation, regulation and self-regulation, with the objective of comparing their provisions with the RR to explore whether the latter are more effective. In this context, we will suggest possible redrafting of some clauses of Bolero to make them more operational in paperless contracting.

4.10.1 The UNCITRAL Model Law on Electronic Commerce and the MLETR

As dictated by its name and clarified in its objectives,[170] the purpose behind the UNCITRAL Model Law on Electronic Commerce is to assemble principles and suggest rules with the intention of helping national legislators sidestep legal obstacles in regulating electronic commerce. Simultaneously it aims to function as an example for the update of legislation.

This Model Law is one of the first legal texts to administer the "functional equivalency approach"[171] suggesting the alternative possibility to trade over "documents", which though not in paper, encompass information legible by all:[172] this information is reproducible, it can remain unaltered over time[173] and the originator can be located (by means of a signature). This approach is also reflected in Article 8(a) of the RR.

The Model Law contains a separate chapter devoted to rules applying to carriage of goods. Article 16(a) of the Model Law corresponds to Article 36(1) of the RR, and Article 16(1)(b) (about instructions) corresponds to Articles 46 and

168 Para 29 of the Explanatory Note.

169 See above Jones, 'A new transport convention: A framework for e-commerce?', p. 155. However, clarification available at the essDOCS website (www.essdocs.com)'; and other authors will be cited where appropriate.

170 Guide to Enactment.

171 Article 5 of the Model Law: "Information shall not be denied legal effect, validity or enforceability solely on the grounds that it is in the form of a data message".

172 Guide to enactment, para 16.

173 Guide to Enactment, para 16.

47 (about delivery) of the RR, with the difference that the elements of Articles 16.1(a)(ii) and (iv) of the Model Law do not have to be contained in the contract particulars under the RR. Furthermore, Article 17 of the Model Law, which is entitled "Transport documents", is similar to the Incoterms®, as it uses a definition which is broader than that of the RR. Thus, under the Model Law, the term "transport document" does not only cover bills of lading, but also other documents.[174]

As with the RR, actions relating to a contract of carriage can be contained in one or more data messages under the Model Law, recalling the correspondence – but not equation – established by the RR between document and record. Articles 17(3) and 17(4) deal with the reliability of the electronic procedures in a vague way, like Article 9 of the RR, and this confirms that there is no conflict between the RR and the Model Law. However, the recent MLETR, which is subsequent even to the RR, talks about a "reliable method" with greater precision and attains flexibility and neutrality of technology.[175] The Model Law is reasonably drafted in a more general way in order to encompass more specific national laws, but one would expect more from the RR. In the case of a series of conventions which deal more or less with the same issue, arguably one would expect the more recent to be more specific and up-to-date than the older one.

Additionally, Article 17(5) of the Model Law corresponds to Article 10 of the RR about replacement, with the difference that the former seems to apply to every type of transport document, not only to negotiable ones. The Model Law only applies to the replacement of data messages by a paper document, i.e. it does not work vice versa, unlike under the RR, which are more flexible.

As it has been discussed above, under the RR it is not explicit whether it is perfectly possible to have an electronic procedure from the issuance of the record until delivery of the goods. The question thus arising is whether this is shown from the Model Law. In other words, are documents and records not only equivalent, but also independent?

The purpose of Article 17(5) of the Model Law is to eliminate the risk of information regarding the allocation of rights and obligations being found on duplicate transport documents, and arguably, the Model Law does not have to provide a specific solution for every deficiency; the latter is left to national laws or more specific pieces of codification and standard contracts. By the same token, the MLETR fortifies the recognition of transferable records, and provides more specific legislative provisions in the direction of replacement and standards, etc. that arguably a modern international transport convention like the RR, which is promulgated to finally embrace modern changes in maritime trade, should have provided for.

174 See para 122 of the Guidelines to enactment of the Model Law, page 63: "However given the broad scope of application of article 17, which covers not only bills of lading, but also a variety of other transport documents".

175 See Article 12 of the MLETR.

To conclude, in our opinion it is very positive for the Model Law to be drafted in a way that makes it of assistance without any clashes with the RR, but at the same time, it is disappointing to see that a carriage of goods convention, such as the RR, is drafted with a vagueness pertaining to Model Laws, especially because it was subsequent to the Model Law. The deficiencies of the RR in this regard have been accounted for and also constitute a drive for the interpretation in light of the MLETR and supplementary contract drafting, regulation and legislation in the above discussed directions.

4.10.2 Synergies between Bolero and the Rotterdam Rules

In this section, the Bolero provisions that would have to be amended if both Bolero and the RR applied to a carriage contract will be discussed for streamlining purposes. The Bolero Rulebook[176] contains detailed definitions, terminology and procedures for the issuance and use of the electronic transport documents in such a way that it constitutes perhaps a good example to complement the provisions of the RR. For Bolero to apply, the parties (the shipper/seller, carrier and the consignee) need to enter into a subscription contract with it: this wider cooperation of commercial parties is something the RR fail to mirror, as discussed under the previous headings.

Bolero offers a trustworthy way of guaranteeing that only the holder has exclusive control over the record.[177] The way identification is checked is unclear, without this meaning that it is practically difficult.[178] The operational system of Bolero allows for potential holders to be added, as well as pledgees.[179] Replacement is also allowed, and laudably, the Rulebook provides that in case of conflict between the paper and electronic version of the bill of lading, the latter will prevail.[180] This supports our foregoing submission that reference to the document before replacement would in certain situations be vital.[181] This provision is not binding on third party endorsees, apparently because they will not be registered users of the Bolero system.[182]

As far as terminology is concerned, to avoid confusion with the RR, the term "message" and the definitions of "electronic communication" and "electronic

176 Analytically on Bolero see Goldby, *Electronic Documents in Maritime Trade: Law and Practice* paras 11.20–11.25; E Laryea, *Paperless Trade, Opportunities, Challenges and Solutions* (The Global Trade and Finance Series, Kluwer Law International 2002), pp. 83–5; Todd, 'Dematerialisation of shipping documents'; Robert Caplehorn, 'The Bolero System', in Reed, Walden and Edgar (eds), *Cross-Border Electronic Banking: Challenges and Opportunities.*

177 Goldby, *Electronic Documents in Maritime Trade: Law and Practice*, para 11.24.

178 S Heard, 'E-bills: Will they deliver? (2000) Oct LEGAmedia, as cited in Goldby, *Electronic Documents in Maritime Trade: Law and Practice*, p. 299, fn. 58 therein.

179 Rule 1.1. (42).

180 Rule 3.7.3.

181 See above in this chapter.

182 See Goldby, *Electronic Documents in Maritime Trade: Law and Practice*, para 11.23, fn. 58 therein.

transport record" should be copied from the RR to avoid discrepancies between the two sets of rules.

In addition, when the RR apply, the Bolero Rulebook should have provisions in accordance with the division in the RR of negotiable and non-negotiable documents or clarify that the terms transferable and negotiable are used interchangeably. In terms of authority this is already the case. According to *Kum v. Wah Tat Bank*,[183] Lord Devlin stated that "it is well settled that, (negotiable) when used in relation to a bill of lading, means simply transferred".[184] However, for the sake of clarity, it should be specified.

Moreover, the Bolero provision of novation (provision 3.5 of Part 3) might need redrafting under the influence of the RR; novation is a concept of Bolero whereby a contractual relationship is found between carrier and holder/consignee which replaces the contract between shipper and carrier each time the record is being transferred; the latter vanishes with few exceptions. Similarly, clause 3.a of the Bolero Rulebook will have to be redrafted, as under Article 79 of the RR it will not be possible for the shipper to deny his liabilities below the minimum standard established by the RR. The shipper, carrier and consignee should be in a constant contractual relationship, as is the case under the RR. It is interesting to note that although both the MLETR and the RR promote functional equivalence, Bolero seems to suggest the following intricate detail: clause 3.7.3 recites that in case of discrepancy between a BBL which is then replaced by a paper bill, the former should prevail.

Moreover, provision 2.3.3 under the title "Compliance with Regulations" should be redrafted so as to comply with the RR. In order to tally with Article 10 of the RR, Rule 3.7 of Part 3 could also be renamed from "Switch to paper" to "Replacement". It is noteworthy that Bolero only allows switch from electronic form to paper, whereas the RR also allow the opposite. Therefore, the Rulebook should be redrafted accordingly, simply to denote explicitly that the trade protagonists can decide to enter Bolero eventually, after a paper bill of lading has been in place.

Rule 2.5.2 "Applicable law"[185] should be drafted as follows: "This Rulebook is governed by and shall be in accordance with English law and (x) national law". In the following heading, we compare the eUCP with provisions of the RR on electronic transport records.

4.10.3 eUCP versus the Rotterdam Rules

The purpose of this section is to discuss how the provisions of the RR are similar to the terminology and structure of the eUCP. Thus, in certain provisions, eUCP

183 [1971] 1 Lloyd's Rep 439 (PC), 446.

184 Ibid, 446.

185 Rule 2.5.2. reads: "Applicable Law. This Rulebook is governed by and shall be interpreted in accordance with English Law".

could be followed as an example. This is of vital importance so that the sellers can comply with an electronic letter of credit.

The first positive remark which can be made is that under both eUCP and the RR, the electronic replica of a paper document,[186] as this is defined under each set of rules respectively, is a *record*.[187] The definition of an electronic record is provided by article e3(b)(1)of the eUCP:

> An electronic record means data created, generated, sent, communicated, received or stored by electronic means, that is capable of being authenticated as the apparent identity of a sender and the apparent source of the data contained in it, and as to whether it has remained complete and unaltered, and is capable of being examined for compliance with the terms and conditions of the eUCP credit.

This definition is, in general terms, very similar to the definition contained in Article 1(18) of the RR and to that of the MLETR.[188] However, the deficiency of the RR to provide a format for the electronic transport record is not something that the eUCP can be accused of. Article e4 specifies that an eUCP credit must specify the formats in which electronic records are to be presented. If the format of the electronic record is not so specified, the record may be presented in any format.[189]

Evidently, the obligation concerning the specification of the format is not absolute; however, it is positive in that the article arguably initiates an inquiry that the format of the credit is specified.[190] The RR do not reflect that, but it is advisable that parties provide for a format.

Another step the eUCP have taken, which the RR have not, is that they provide for the date of issuance of an electronic record in article e9. This states that "unless an electronic record contains a specific date of issuance, the date on which it appears to have been sent by the issuer is deemed to be the date of issuance. The date of receipt will be deemed to be the date it was sent if no other date is apparent".

This provision is significant if one takes into consideration that the UCP and eUCP are standard terms in the trade and that, for checking compliance with

186 We need to take into consideration that under the RR the crucial terms are transport documents and electronic transport records and that in the UCP's context, the documents are those listed under Articles 19–25 and 28.

187 See article e1a: "The supplement [...] eUCP supplements the Uniform Customs and Practice for Documentary Credits 2007 Revision ICC Publication No. 600) ("UCP") in order to accommodate presentation of electronic documents alone or in combination with paper documents".

188 Article 2 reads: "'Electronic record' means information generated, communicated, received or stored by electronic means, including, where appropriate, all information logically associated with or otherwise linked together so as to become part of the record, whether generated contemporaneously or not".

189 Article e4 of the eUCP.

190 Similarly, the electronic bill of lading of the essDOCS is identical to the paper one, which can be used instead.

them, banks may receive many shipping documents (bills of lading, sea waybills, commercial invoices). A contract of carriage is the core subject of the RR and a fortiori provisions about the date and format of the transport record would be needed. Article e10 complements article e9 by suggesting what the date of shipment will be, if the electronic record evidencing transport does not indicate a date of shipment or dispatch.

In conclusion, it has to be noted that the eUCP, which is a fundamental set of rules for electronic banking and trade, contains 12 articles, four of which concern requirements which create certainty around the definition, format and date of issuance of an electronic record. The RR being a carriage of goods convention containing 96 articles in total and three in the specific electronic records context could a fortiori have devoted one or two provisions for additional clarity on these matters. However, eUCP are complex too, since electronic documents can be sent directly by third parties, but there the beneficiary has to deposit a "notice of completeness" at the end.[191]

Next, we will show the way English law can update its legislation in line with the RR avoiding the ambiguities noted earlier in the chapter.

4.11 The way forward: how English law should be updated

The articles of the RR on electronic records in principle operate, but not without the assistance of further actions. The RR are said to be drafted more loosely on purpose, so that they allow technological legislative initiatives to evolve.[192] This means national legislations may be the key so that electronic trade can be said to have a framework. Our opinion is that, since the RR have been drafted and are open to ratification, it would be preferable to suggest the above recommendations as examples that the national legislations on e-commerce which will follow should embrace. The focus in the following will be on how English law can be updated so as to pave the way for electronic contracting. The recommended update of UK legislation has to take place regardless of whether the RR obtain the necessary number of ratifications or not, as the law in this area needs to be updated.

It has been suggested[193] that "one of the main reasons why electronic bills of lading are not used as much as desired in practice is the lack of legal regulation which causes concern to the parties regarding their legal value and effect, so that they hesitate to accept electronic bills of lading and prefer traditional

191 Roberto Bergami, 'The Rotterdam Rules and negotiable electronic transport documents in letter of credit business' 297, p. 299 at www.kmice.cms.net.my/ProcKMICe/KMICe2010/Paper/PG296_301.pdf.

192 Goldby, 'Legislating to facilitate the use of electronic transferable records', p. 5; also Goldby, *Electronic Documents in Maritime Trade: Law and Practice*, para 6.91, "it (article 9) lays down minimum requirements for procedures for the use of negotiable electronic transport records and leaves the rest to the parties."

193 Caslav Pejović, 'Main legal issues in the implementation of EDI to bills of lading' [1999] *European Transport Law* 163, pp. 164–165 as cited in Goldby, 'Legislating to facilitate the use of electronic transferable records', p. 7.

paper documents. [...] The parties in international trade might refuse to accept documents in electronic form because of doubt as to their legal value. If such a document is to enjoy the same legal status as a paper document, the law must be changed so that legal effect can be recognized not only as to paper documents, but also as to documents created and transmitted by computers." This statement could also apply with regards to sea waybills.[194]

This suggestion does not undermine party autonomy. It may be open to carriers and traders to develop a set of independent standard terms governing the use of electronic alternatives to bills of lading that may apply by contractual incorporation whenever an electronic alternative is used.[195] This approach would not be entirely independent of national substantive law. The latter would continue to determine all issues governing the contract of carriage save for any issues involving the use and effect of electronic alternatives, which would be governed by the agreed standards.

As far as legislative reforms of English law are concerned, additional provisions could be issued primarily under section 1(5) of COGSA 1992 providing for the application of the Act to electronic alternatives that satisfy the singularity requirement.[196] The steps forward already evidenced by the provisions of the RR on electronic records, however imperfect, can be optimised through attention to details, in line with our and other scholars' critical suggestions.

English law needs to be similarly updated in order to acknowledge electronic alternatives.[197] The revision suggested by Goldby is indicative:

> For the purposes of subsection (4) the term "bill of lading" shall include a negotiable electronic transport record as defined by the Regulations issued under Section 1(5) of COGSA 1992. It shall also include a non-negotiable electronic transport record that requires surrender and that satisfies the requirements of those regulations.[198]

It has also been suggested that[199] an electronic signature, as defined in section 7 of the Electronic Communications Act 2000 shall have the same effect as a manual signature, so that electronic signatures are admissible.[200] Additionally it has been suggested that section 1 of The Factors Act 1889, "bill of lading", shall include a

194 With regards to waybills see A Higgs and G Humphreys, 'Waybills: a case of common law laissez-faire in European commerce' [1992] *JBL* 453, pp. 455–456.

195 See Goldby, 'Legislating to facilitate the use of electronic transferable records', p. 15.

196 Ibid.

197 Ibid.

198 Ibid, pp. 19, 22.

199 Ibid, p. 19, citing DH Griffiths and J Harrison, 'United Kingdom', in D Campbell (ed) *E-Commerce and the Law of Digital Signatures* (OUP 2005), p. 656.

200 Goldby, 'Legislating to facilitate the use of electronic transferable records', p. 20. Section 7 of the Electronic Communications Act 2000 has nothing to say about the veracity or validity of an electronic signature. The new provision will deal with the admissibility of evidence.

negotiable electronic transport record as defined by the Regulations issued under section 1(5) of COGSA 1992".[201]

4.12 Suggested amendments to English legislation and/or contracts

The following articles of the RR, amended in accordance with our comments in this chapter, could be included in the relevant Acts of the UK legislation, particularly if the RR do not get ratified.

4.12.1 Suggested revision of Article 1(18) of the Rotterdam Rules

The suggested version of Article 1(18) would be:

> The electronic transport record is the electronic version of the transport document. It is an electronic document in pdf or other similar format which can be seen and read on a computer screen or other electronic device imitating the contents of the transport document, as well as procedures for its replacement with a paper transport document and procedure for its subsequent transfer.[202] It consists of information in one or more contracts of carriage messages issued by electronic communication under a contract of carriage by a carrier; this includes information logically associated with the contract of carriage by attachments or otherwise linked to the contract of carriage contemporaneously with or subsequent to its issuance by the carrier so as to become[203] part of the electronic transport record; that in turn evidences the carrier's or a performing party's receipt of goods under a contract of carriage and evidences or contains a contract of carriage.

The potential contribution of this provision that we have devised is that by requiring a specific format for the electronic transport record, it will make the electronic transport record more visible and tangible in the cyber world, since it will imitate all the functions of the transport record. This will reduce confusion between what should be classified as an electronic communication and an electronic transport record. The core information to be found in a transport document (and in an electronic transport record) will be easily ascertained and litigation due to confusion arising from the crucial information being spread over various emails and attachments will be decreased.

4.12.2 Suggested revisions of Article 8 of the Rotterdam Rules

The suggested version of Article 8 would be:

> Anything that is to be in or on a transport document may be recorded in an electronic transport record. The issuance of a non-negotiable transport

201 Suggested by Goldby, 'Legislating to facilitate the use of electronic transferable records', p. 22.

202 This, in essence, is the content of the full-equalisation method, which was one of the two major methods advocated in the attempt to find the ideal way in which to introduce the functional equivalent of a transport document. See Sturley, Fujita and van der Ziel, *The Rotterdam Rules*, p. 48.

203 Same as in the definition of electronic records under the MLETR.

> record is subject to the agreement of the carrier, the shipper and the documentary shipper where the latter exists. The issuance and unlimited subsequent use of a negotiable transport record must be with the consent of the carrier, the shipper and the documentary shipper where one exists.
>
> The issuance and exclusive control of a negotiable or non-negotiable transport record has the same effect as the issuance and exclusive control of a negotiable or non-negotiable transport document. The transfer of a negotiable electronic transport record has the same effect as the transfer of a negotiable transport document.

We are confident that the major benefit of this provision is that it is mindful of the documentary shipper's interests. From an international trade law perspective, this means that the provision will take the interests of the FOB seller into consideration; the latter would otherwise exercise no control over the type of contract of carriage that will be entered into. This would also help provide the documentary shipper with the full possible rights, as it is an acknowledged party by the RR, although it still has a limited role in the contract of carriage.

Our suggestion to insert the division of negotiable and non-negotiable documents, aspires to add clarification so that "transfer" cannot mistakenly be inferred to apply to non-negotiable records.

A provision should also be added about replacement, so that it expands the scope of Article 10 of the RR. The word "negotiable" should be deleted so that the article applies to both negotiable and non-negotiable transport documents, and the article should be titled "Replacement of a transport document or an electronic transport record".

This would make the provision more complete, as in our opinion, non-negotiable documents/records also need to be replaceable. Despite the possibility that when the RR were drafted the case may have been that non-negotiable documents were not as popular in use as the negotiable ones, trade customs change quickly and the purpose of the RR is to better respond to modern and upcoming commercial trends. Predictability and flexibility are advantages that would be credited to the RR if there was no discrimination in the replacement function between negotiable and non-negotiable documents. Secondly, as discussed above, this new provision will eliminate discrimination between negotiable and non-negotiable records under the RR. At the same time, the principle of functional equivalence between documents and records, initiated by Article 8(a), will prove to apply homogeneously and not partially, i.e. not only in favour of negotiable transport documents.

Furthermore, the article should contain two extra sections: "If a transport document is lost or the key to the electronic transport record is lost, and the consignee provides substantive evidence that he acts in good faith, he has exercised due care and diligence and the carrier is convinced by the above, then the carrier may reissue another transport document if the consignee requests one. The reissuance of an electronic record to replace the missing transport document can be effected, if the consignee requests one."

We suggest that this should be inserted for greater certainty: "If the transport document allegedly contains discrepancies, clerical mistakes or deficiencies, the electronic transport record shall be used as a point of reference, acting as a mirror-image, reflecting the original content."

For instance, if the record contains a typo on the quantity of the goods, or the name of the consignee, the transport document should be of assistance.

4.13 Conclusion

The challenge for the RR was the legislative intention to initiate, systematise and regulate electronic bills of lading that can be trustworthy, traceable, fast-travelling and fraud-resistant. The objective for modernisation of the international framework in order to keep up with the needs of the trade has underpinned the relevant articles of the RR. The same can be argued for flexibility, which is a shared underpinning between international trade law and the RR. Provisions on replacement of records reflect our observation, as traders may have to get a document in a form that allows performance under a subsequent sale contract or a letter of credit.

The RR themselves dedicate more provisions on negotiable records than on non-negotiable ones. However, one could extend this principle to negotiable documents not requiring surrender because in this case, the record/document is negotiable and it does not have to be presented to the carrier. Nevertheless, it is unsatisfactory to see that a document that does not have to be presented to the carrier can be replaced, whereas a non-negotiable cannot. One could argue in this respect that this is unnecessary because in principle the consignee does not change in the latter scenario. There may however be other reasons for replacement necessitating its application, as otherwise non-delivery for non-presentation might be unreasonably denied.

By promoting negotiable records over non-negotiable, the RR seem to foster strings of documentary sales. A negotiable transport document, as seen in the preceding chapters, constitutes a better security for potential buyers and banks involved in the letter of credit. The internal inconsistency though remains of selectively applying the functional equivalence doctrine only to negotiable documents. Should the reluctance of the market towards electronic sea waybills change, however, the RR will have failed to pave the way for their promotion, and this can also be seen as an obstacle against future modernisation.

To conclude, arguably the RR contain some important provisions for electronic bills of lading. They are a welcome step further, but they are not sufficient. There are deficiencies which can be rectified by inserting the contractual and legislative provisions and interpretation methods suggested above. It is only if further requirements are added to individual sale (and carriage) contracts, or to national legislation that the scope of the "electronic" provisions of the RR can aptly facilitate paperless trade.

The security guidelines offered by the RR are more generic than expected. This also explains why the MLETR had to subsequently step in. Legal uncertainty has been a main factor of distrust against paperless contracting in shipping, despite the existence of electronic registries. Perhaps one could see the generality of the RR as an encouragement of freedom of contract.

With respect, it is submitted that this is too much a burden to be left on the contractual parties. For some jurisdictions the lack of any robust international framework on e-commerce, as the case seems to be with the RR, discourages them to adopt regulations on electronic transactions. Therefore, the enforcement of the parties' contractual rights in electronic records is always subject to the national courts, and freedom of contract may not protect parties sufficiently. Hence, contract drafting, which has to come to ensure legal protection of traders' rights comes as a need, and thus, it is not so much an indication of freedom of contract. The narrow scope in the parties' participation and replacement on the one hand, and too much abstraction in the standards for electronic procedures on the other, prove that the RR may occasionally increase legal uncertainty and potentially hamper electronic trade facilitation.

This chapter highlights how the concerns of Chapters 1 to 3 (parties, entitlement to documents, delivery provisions) materialise in the electronic commercial world. Article 35 of the RR has offered this link, as electronic records are a choice introduced for the first time in the RR.

In the following chapter, the practical implications of volume contracts are analysed: these contracts represent the most hotly debated innovation of the RR, as they allow derogation from the Convention under certain circumstances. From the perspective of the legal principle of harmonisation in maritime trade, it is the first time that a piece of codification explicitly allows its contractual exclusion, when historically the predecessors to the RR have come to refrain this uncontrollable contractual freedom. This is a factor of flexibility, which is usually desirable in sales down a string, but whether this will promote trade facilitation without ambiguities or compromises to legal certainty remains to be seen.

Volume contracts are carriage contracts allowing serious derogations from the RR. This impact of volume contracts on trade when the RR do not apply to them is very likely because of the proximity of carriage and sale contracts. It is significant to investigate the type of contract of carriage a seller can arrange for his buyer when contracting under a volume contract that derogates from the RR. This is particularly essential if the latter is unsuspicious or uninformed of the derogations. Therefore becoming familiar with them is not only challenging for cargo interests, but also necessary. In Chapter 5, we assess whether there are circumstances where the RR are being unduly displaced in a way that serves a carrier's or, more rarely, a trader's legal and commercial interests in a one-sided and controversial way. At the same time we will unravel the legal controversies that derogating from the RR entails and assess the impact that this can have on international carriage and sale contracts.

5 The impact of volume contracts on the trading parties

5.1 Introduction and significance

The possibility of displacing the RR provisions via the formation of volume contracts has been a highly contentious issue, perhaps the most criticised area of the RR.[1] Volume contracts will have a serious impact on the legal position of carriers and traders because they allow the freedom of evading the mandatory liability regime of the Convention, if certain requirements are met.[2] The deregulation, i.e. the evasion of an otherwise mandatory application of the Convention inherent in the core Article 80 of the RR[3] through volume contracts, permits the partial or more extensive exclusion of the compulsory scope of the RR. This has already raised polarised opinions for and against[4] regarding their potential repercussions for modern trade law as far as unsophisticated parties are concerned, but also regarding its impact on the materialisation of the objective of international uniformity.[5] Varied voices have been expressed from academics,[6] the

1 Baatz et al, *The Rotterdam Rules: A Practical Annotation*, para 80-01.

2 Basu Bal, 'A legal and economic analysis of the volume contract concept under the Rotterdam Rules: Selected issues in perspective', *Journal of Transportation Law Logistics and Policy*, 27; Vesna Foglar, 'Volume Contracts after the Rotterdam Rules' (2010) 49(164) *Comparative Maritime Law* 221.

3 See Peter Jones, 'The UNCITRAL Convention on Carriage of Goods by Sea: Harmonization or De-harmonization' at www.forwarderlaw.com/library/view.php?article_id=602.

4 Regina Asariotis, 'UNCITRAL (Draft) Convention on Contracts for the International Carriage of Goods Wholly or Partly by Sea: Mandatory rules and freedom of contract'. in Antapassis, Athanassiou and Røsæg (eds), *Competition and Regulation in Shipping and Shipping Related Industries* (Martinus Nijhoff 2009), pp. 356–363; Asariotis, 'Reflections on the Rotterdam Rules'.

5 Also Asariotis, 'Reflections on the Rotterdam Rules', p. 155; Baatz et al, *The Rotterdam Rules: A Practical Annotation*, para 80-05.

6 Mankowski, 'The Rotterdam Rules – Scope of application and freedom of contract' (2010/12) *EJCCL* 9; Bal, 'The impact of the volume contract concept on the global community of shippers: The Rotterdam Rules in perspective'; Lars Gorton, '*Volume contracts of affreightment: some features and principles*', at www.scandinavianlaw.se/pdf/46-3.pdf; Filippo Lorenzon, 'Validity of contractual terms', in Baatz et al, *The Rotterdam Rules: A Practical Annotation*; Hannu Honka, '*Scope of application and freedom of contract*', at www.rotterdamrules2009.com/cms/uploads/Def.%20tekst%20Hannu%20Honka.pdf; Hannu Honka, 'Validity of contractual terms' in von Ziegler,

industry,[7] states[8] and other organisations.[9]

The impact of volume contracts on international trade law constitutes a predominant chapter of this book because the concept of volume contracts is particularly important to traders. If the carrier is allowed to reduce his liability, this burden will be shifted;[10] either to the shipper who is usually the CIF seller, or to third parties, who may be buyers-consignees, or to the FOB seller, who has the role of the documentary shipper, when the carriage contract is governed by the RR. What is important about these parties is that most of them will not be aware, and thus will not be able to contribute to the drafting or rejection of a volume contract which derogates before the goods are shipped. Consequently, traders will be faced with "inadvertent oversights" stemming from the carriage contract and notably the sale contract and this gives an impetus for studying how volume contracts are defined. Which contracts of carriage may qualify as such and which are the prerequisites that allow derogation from the RR?

The major concerns emerging from the framework of volume contracts are firstly, the possibility that the cargo interest may conclude a contract unaware of the full content and importance of the derogations;[11] And secondly, the foothold that the RR give to carriers to entice smaller or simply unsophisticated cargo interests to non-desirable volume contracts in exchange of smaller freight rates,

Schelin and Zunarelli (eds), *The Rotterdam Rules 2008*; Bergami, 'The Rotterdam Rules and bills of lading: Challenges for letter of credit transactions'.

7 David Maloof, '*Concerns about volume contracts*', at mlaus.org/archives/library/1904.pdf; 'The Rotterdam Rules seen by the ESC' at www.europeanshippers.eu/wp-content/uploads/2013/07/pr%C3%A9sentation-RR-pour-MTC-juin-2013.pdf; 'View of the European Shippers' Council on the Convention on Contracts for the International Carrying of Goods Wholly or Partly by Sea also known as the "Rotterdam Rules"' at www.uncitral.org/pdf/english/texts/transport/rotterdam_rules/ESC_PositionPaper_March2009.pdf. CLECAT, Position Paper on the Rotterdam Rules at www.comitemaritime.org/Uploads/Rotterdam%20Rules/4CLECAT.pdf; FIATA, Position Paper on the Rotterdam Rules at www.comitemaritime.org/Uploads/Rotterdam%20Rules/3FIATA.pdf.

8 Australia and France have expressed their fear for abuse of the ambiguous wording of Article 80 by wary, sophisticated carriers and big shippers: Transport Law: Preparation of a draft Convention on the carriage of goods wholly or partly by sea. Joint proposal by Australia and France on freedom of contract under volume contracts, A/CN.9/WG.III/WP.88 and A/CN.9/612; Oppositions have been voiced also by A/CN.9/658/Add.2 (New Zealand); A/CN.9/658/Add.11 para 22 (Germany); A/CN.9/658/Add.11 paras 19–20 (China); Anastasiya Kozubosbskaya-Pellé, 'Contractual flexibility in volume contracts: Rotterdam Rules and French law perspective' (2013) 115 *Il Diritto Marittimo* 326; 'Australian comments on the UNCITRAL draft convention on contracts for the international carriage of goods wholly or partly by sea' (2008) 22 *A&NZ Mar LJ* at 124; CLECAT, Position Paper on the Rotterdam Rules at www.uncitral.org/pdf/english/texts/transport/rotterdam_rules/CLECATpaper.pdf.

9 UNCTAD Document, '*Carrier liability and freedom of contract under the UNCITRAL draft instrument on the carriage of goods [wholly or partly] [by sea]*', UNCTAD/SDTE/TLB/2004/2 at unctad.org/en/Docs/sdtetlb20042_en.pdf; 'Adoption of a new United Nations Convention on Contracts for the International Carriage of Goods Wholly or Partly by Sea: The Rotterdam Rules', Review of Maritime Transport 2009, p. 129.

10 Bergami, 'The Rotterdam Rules and bills of lading: Challenges for letter of credit transactions', p. 16.

11 Anything can be derogated from the RR, apart from the obligations listed under Article 80(4) of the RR.

especially if more carriers adjust to similar freight and liability standards for competition reasons. The latter contingency would nullify the potential to conclude a contract which does not deviate from the RR.[12]

At a more abstract, national and international level, volume contracts have to be examined closely to the extent that they contradict with existing sets of rules (including legislations), and thus raise eyebrows as to the ratification of the Convention.[13]

The initiative and justification for the insertion of volume contracts in the RR are introduced forthwith.

5.2 Volume contracts and original parties

5.2.1 Specialised and customised agreements: tracing the origins of volume contracts

Contracts for the carriage of a specified quantity of goods in a series of shipments within a certain period of time are specifically covered to a considerable extent by an international carriage of goods convention.[14] The original parties to these contracts will have the chance of displacing the Convention's obligatory regime.[15] A similar concept was roughly outlined also in the Hamburg Rules, in Article 2(4).[16] However, in the Hamburg Rules, contracts on "series of shipments" were not given a particular name, and it was stated therein that the individual shipments will be covered by their scope.[17]

The idea of catering for a category of carriage contracts that allow for the transportation of a specified quantity of goods, in a series of shipments over a period of time originated from the intention to foster a trade relationship equally beneficial for the carrier and the cargo interest.[18] The flexibility to contract on

12 This is one of the official prerequisites of the RR under Article 80(2)(c); See Asariotis, 'UNCITRAL Draft Convention on Contracts for the International Carriage of Goods Wholly or Partly by Sea: Mandatory Rules and Freedom of Contract', pp. 358, 363; Asariotis, 'Reflections on the Rotterdam Rules', pp. 154–155.

13 Kozubovskaya-Pellé, 'Contractual flexibility in volume contracts: Rotterdam Rules and French law perspective', p. 332; also UN Doc A/CN.9/612 containing the Joint proposal by Australia and France on freedom of contract under volume contracts at www.un.org/ga/search/view_doc.asp?symbol=A/CN.9/612.

14 Asariotis, 'Reflections on the Rotterdam Rules', p. 153.

15 See Asariotis, 'UNCITRAL (Draft) Convention on Contracts for the International Carriage of Goods Wholly or Partly by Sea: Mandatory Rules and Freedom of Contract', p. 351; Asariotis, 'Reflections on the Rotterdam Rules', p. 152.

16 The article reads: "If a contract provides for future carriage of goods in a series of shipments during an agreed period, the provisions of this Convention apply to each shipment."

17 On the consideration of existence of framework contracts by the Hamburg Rules see also Kozubovskaya-Pellé, 'Contractual flexibility in volume contracts: Rotterdam Rules and French law perspective', p. 332.

18 David Wood, 'National Report: An Australian perspective on the Rotterdam Rules' (2001) 17 *JIML*, 147, at 152.

business-tailored terms and the encouragement of better negotiations would in theory be a laudable objective. Also, the advantages for carriers lie in securing booking space on their vessels and hence continuing business in the future.[19] Similarly, the security of having space booked for a certain period of time has advantages for shippers.[20]

The "ancestors" of volume contracts can be traced in the UK, French and Swedish maritime codes.[21] In the UK, they come under the name "contracts of affreightment", although what is implied by this term is not unequivocal, and it has changed over the years.[22] This term usually alludes to two concepts: firstly, it can be used as a synonym of the "contract of carriage"; or secondly, it means a specified carriage of goods over a period of time, or a service contract.[23]

The model on which the idea of freedom of contract was adjusted was that of service contracts in the US, introduced after the Ocean Shipping Reform Act 1998 (OSRA).[24] The factual underpinning of freedom of contract is based on the assertion that in some trades reportedly more than 80% of cargo is carried under such contractual schemes.[25]

Volume contracts belong to the category of framework agreements.[26] The rationale allowing contractual freedom from the mandatory coverage of the RR is the idea that the parties' (i.e. carriers and shippers) bargaining power is nowadays equal. Therefore, there is no particular need for statutory protection of a weaker party against unfair contract terms.[27] As Honka clarified in his article, there is no longer an established belief that the cargo interests are the vulnerable ones as opposed to the carrier.[28] It was also the view of certain states'

19 Ibid. Also Mukherjee and Bal, 'A legal and economic analysis of the volume contract concept under the Rotterdam Rules: Selected issues in perspective', pp. 591–96.

20 Mukherjee and Bal, 'A legal and economic analysis of the volume contract concept under the Rotterdam Rules: Selected issues in perspective', pp. 583, 586, 587, 591, 593.

21 For the Swedish provisions see Gorton, 'Volume contracts of affreightment', p. 70.

22 COA (Contract of Affreightment) at www.shipinspection.eu/index.php/home/k2-item-view/item/227-coa-contract-of-affreightment.

23 See Lorenzon, *Sassoon on CIF and FOB Contracts*, para 5-002.

24 Asariotis, 'Reflections on the Rotterdam Rules' p. 153. According to the National Industrial Transportation League (NITL), which is an organisation of companies that conduct industrial and/or commercial operations throughout the US and internationally, the OSRA is reflected by the nearly two million service contracts entered since the adoption of OSRA. It is also contended that tens of thousands of service contracts are concluded annually: 'Comments of the National Industrial Transportation League in support of the Petition P1-08' (before the Federal Maritime Commission) at www.google.co.uk/search?q=Comments++of+the+National+Industrial++Transportation+League+in+support+of+the+Petition+P1-08+(before+the+Federal+Maritime+Commission&sourceid=ie7&rls=com.microsoft:en-gb:IE-SearchBox&ie=&oe=, p. 3.

25 See 'Response to the National Industrial Transportation League to the European Shippers' Council Position Paper on the Rotterdam Rules' at www.uncitral.org/pdf/english/texts/transport/rotterdam_rules/NITL_ResponsePaper.pdf, p. 5.

26 See Hannu Honka, '*Scope of application, freedom of contract*', p. 10. The same applies to the OLSAs, which are the example on which the RR are regulated.

27 Asariotis, 'UNCITRAL Draft Convention on Contracts for the International Carriage of Goods Wholly or Partly by Sea: Mandatory rules and freedom of contract', p. 357.

28 See Honka, 'Scope of application, freedom of contract', p. 9.

representatives during the deliberations (notably from the US) that the protective legislative measures could become looser, giving priority to personalised negotiation deals.[29]

During the drafting of the RR, it was affirmed that there were types of shipping contracts, namely volume contracts, contracts of affreightment, service contracts, towage contracts and non-traditional charterparties which clearly did not fit either under a bill of lading classification or under a charterparty.[30]

Volume contracts were included in the RR, after the Working Group was convinced by the initiative of the US delegates for the inclusion of "special and customised agreements" in the Convention.[31] It was thereby[32]explained that "the parties to an OLSA [Ocean Liner Service Agreement] often enter into such contracts with the purpose of designing a customised transportation relationship based on the business needs of the parties". This should not be surprising as the concept of trading under volume contracts is not entirely new.[33] Maybe a "contract of affreightment" is unfamiliar as a type of volume contract, but it matches the core function of volume contracts, which is contracting on carrying more than one consignment in a time range. The RR have preferred the least known but existent term of "volume contract".

The US proposal for volume contracts is susceptible to various interpretations, and thus has fuelled debates and reactions from various jurisdictions, trade committees and organisations against the ratification of the RR. Many dissenting opinions have been expressed during the consultations, and as it shall be seen, Article 80 of the RR is an evidence of the apt contention of Honka that:

> The Rotterdam Rules must be understood to be a compromise. There are always some other ideas on what the best solution should have been, but to implement one's own opinions, and one's own opinions only, on the global arena with real effect and consensus is more easily said than done.[34]

5.2.2 *Definition of volume contracts under the Rotterdam Rules*

Volume contracts are defined in Article 1(2) of the RR and are regulated by Article 80, constituting the most controversial aspect of the RR. A volume contract is "a contract of carriage that provides for the carriage of a specified quantity of goods in a series of shipments during an agreed period of time. The specification of the quantity may include a minimum, a maximum or a certain range."[35]

29 Ibid.

30 Sturley, Fujita and van der Ziel, *The Rotterdam Rules*, para 13.041.

31 See preparatory works, Doc A/CN.9/WG.III/WP.34, para 27.

32 Ibid, para 24.

33 Some main standard volume contracts already in existence will be analysed later. For the difference between the European and American perception of volume contracts see Philippe Delebecque, 'L'evolution du transport maritime' (2009) *DMF* 16, p. 19.

34 See Honka, 'Scope of application, freedom of contract', p. 19.

35 See Article 1(2) of the RR.

There is disagreement as to whether special needs should attract such specific reference[36] in an international convention. There is still the fear that the exception from the mandatory scope of the RR might lead to abuse of power, especially to the detriment of small shippers.[37] This shall be discussed later, as the framework is not yet completely crystallised. The parties need to satisfy some conditions and what is problematic about them, as we shall see, is that they need proof of vague aspects; the RR mainly require proof of previous negotiations or opportunities of contracting on regular RR terms. These are theoretical concepts which cannot be proven. Besides, the party with stronger bargaining power can always present a contract with onerous, well hidden terms as a safe and attractive contractual option; thus the safeguard of negotiations may become obsolete.

In the following heading we present the format example of volume contracts, which are the OLSAs from the US jurisdiction.

5.2.3 Ocean Liner Service Agreements

The US delegates wanted the draft instrument to be mindful of accommodating provisions for the "specialised and customised agreements"[38] of ocean liner services. The intended model was the practice of OLSAs, or service contracts;[39] the US delegates specified that these contracts apply only to liner services, therefore they are not applicable to charterparties, or industrial or private carriage of bulk, tanker, neo-bulk or other non-liner services.[40] However, they could extend to the land part of a voyage.[41] The revolution was triggered by the US Shipping Act 1984,[42] which allows shippers to conclude service contracts for a certain quantity of cargo over a specified period of time. The main benefits of these contracts were that the freight rates were attractive, due to their flexibility. Moreover, service contracts could contain provisions for liquidated damages.[43]

Service contracts were defined in section 3(21) of the US Shipping Act 1984 and currently in 46 CFR (Code of Federal Regulation) 530§3(q):

36 Through Articles 1(2) and 80 of the RR.

37 See Asariotis, 'UNCITRAL Draft Convention on Contracts for the International Carriage of Goods Wholly or Partly by Sea: Mandatory Rules and freedom of contract', p. 361.

38 See preparatory works at A/CN.9/WG.III/WP.34, para 18.

39 These terms will be used interchangeably throughout the chapter.

40 See preparatory works, A/CN.9/WG.III/WP.34.

41 See Mukherjee and Bal, 'A legal and economic analysis of the volume contract concept under the Rotterdam Rules: Selected issues in perspective', 587.

42 1984 was the year when "freight deregulation" started emerging. Until then, most of the international shipping lines were organised in liner conferences. The main characteristic of liner conferences is that carriers gather under the umbrella of the conference and offer sea transport services under a common tariff. The operation of the carriers-members of the liner conferences are subject to statutory enactments, but it is optional for a carrier company to join the conference. On the other hand, the liner conferences should compulsorily be open to all shipping lines.

43 See Mukherjee and Bal, 'A legal and economic analysis of the volume contract concept under the Rotterdam Rules: Selected issues in perspective' p. 587.

> "Service contract" means a written contract, other than a bill of lading or receipt, between one or more shippers and an individual ocean common carrier or an agreement between or among ocean common carriers in which the shipper makes a commitment to provide a certain minimum quantity or portion of its cargo or freight revenue over a fixed time period, and the individual ocean common carrier or the agreement commits to a certain rate or rate schedule and a defined service level, such as, assured space, transit time, port rotation, or similar service features. The contract may also specify provisions in the event of non performance on the part of any party.

As shall be analysed in the following section, volume contracts are in accordance with the above definition of service contracts, with the difference that there is no obligation for a certain minimum of quantity specification.

5.2.4 Differences between volume and service contracts: risks lurking underneath

Surprisingly, the RR do not sufficiently specify the quantity, or the minimum/maximum series of shipments, or the period of time that determine when a contract of carriage is a volume contract.[44] This lack of stipulation of quantity has been severely criticised for allowing great freedom to the parties, especially in comparison to OLSAs. The word "range" is also very ambiguous. The logic behind this omission of a restraint on quantity was considered by the Working Group to better suit the commercial practice of volume contracts.[45] A minimum quantity would be too restrictive; on the other hand, an "estimated quantity" would suffice, whereas total absence of the quantity requirement would not denote "volume contracts". This type of contract has rightly been illustrated by some commentators as a "package deal".[46]

In our opinion, the leading criterion in ascertaining whether a contract entered into is a volume contract is the intention of the parties. If the purpose is to contract on the basis of a package deal, i.e. for a series of shipments within a given amount of time, then this is presumably a volume contract. If the goods were originally shipped as one consignment, but due to other constraints, such as high freight rates in the market that can only be circumvented by contracting on lower liability schemes acquired by carriers, the shipper and carrier "manipulated" the contractual conditions so as to fall under the volume contract exception, then some intrigue would be incurred; this contract might conceal onerous non-RR standard terms. The latter case should trigger the application of Article 79 of the RR for breach of the limitations by reducing or increasing the liabilities of the parties.[47]

44 See Baatz et al, *The Rotterdam Rules: A Practical Annotation*, para [80-01].

45 See preparatory works at A/CN.9/576, para 55.

46 See Honka, 'Validity of contractual terms', p. 340.

47 For the sensitive borders between Article 79 and 80 see also Honka, 'Validity of contractual terms', p. 340.

Contracting on volume contract terms in this case is convenient for one of the parties, usually the carrier, who limits his liability, and this can lead to inappropriate use of the concept of derogations. This fear is not extreme as service contracts which formed the basis for the provision of volume contracts have been used even for particularly small shipments, such as 10, 20 or 1 TEU.[48] Agreement for carriage of two containers to be transported in three months' time can constitute a volume contract as well as a supply agreement for bulk cargo to be transported for 18 months;[49] the lack of any constraint with regard to quantity or time frame will arguably revolutionise shipping as it is known. This fear is evident in service contracts which have an even more solid and detailed regulation under the US law compared to the RR. The Federal Maritime Commission (FMC) has been given extensive controlling powers especially in relation to service contracts, but the RR do not provide for a similar controlling body.

In the following section, we will delve further into volume contracts, this time looking at its various components, i.e. the individual contracts. The purpose of this is to highlight how volume contracts are constituted, and to go into sensitive details which, depending on the situation, may either recklessly invalidate the ability of the volume contract to deviate from the RR, or worse, signal an oblique intention to juxtapose the compulsory framework of the RR. If the first scenario happens, our findings will contribute to the better awareness and skills of drafting a volume contract. If the second scenario applies, then careful scrutiny of the documents will prevent abusive exclusion of the RR and will guide courts in ascertaining the real intention of the contracting parties. Our focus is on sellers/shippers and receivers/buyers, as they are the protagonists of international trade.

5.2.5 The individual contracts as a precondition for a volume contract that derogates from the Rotterdam Rules

Volume contracts are essentially framework contracts, as they provide a framework for a package deal. Thus, they can be distinguished from the respective carriage contracts included therein, if they are individually negotiated.[50] For the possibility to derogate from the RR, only the contracts where the RR would otherwise apply are eligible. The respective individual voyages in performance of the volume contract also have to meet the applicability of the RR criteria.

There is a serious question to ask in this context is can circumstances around one of the individual voyages prevent a carriage contract from being a volume contract that can derogate from the RR? A suggestion has been made that where part of the package deal falls outside the scope of the RR, then conclusions as to the application of the RR to the whole contract will be made on the basis of the

48 See Asariotis, 'UNCITRAL Draft Convention on Contracts for the International Carriage of Goods Wholly or Partly by Sea: Mandatory rules and freedom of contract', p. 362 and fn 35 therein. TEU means 20-foot equivalent unit, which is used for capacity in container transport.

49 See also the example in Baatz et al, *The Rotterdam Rules: A Practical Annotation*, para [80-01].

50 See Honka, 'Validity of contractual terms', p. 340.

individual contracts.[51] Nevertheless, this cannot always prove adequate if we take into consideration that volume contracts cover series of shipments. An individual contract for the single carriage of goods (as opposed to a contract for a series of shipments) cannot, by definition, be a volume contract. The former suggestion would make sense only if there are at least two consecutive questionable contracts, so that there is at least in principle a case of a "package deal". On the other hand, two "controversial"[52] non-consecutive voyages would be isolated, so they could not easily qualify as part of a volume contract. Instead, we suggest checking not only the individuality of the separate contracts, but also the interaction and relationship between the individual contracts.[53]

The difficulty lies in this: should an intricate, non-volume like voyage be seen as a slight exception, which is not important for the framework contract (so the RR will apply), or should it be regarded as an important link of the volume contract chain, which should also independently meet the requirements of Article 1(2) and 80 of the RR?

The view expressed, that an individual contract should be looked at for confirming whether the RR apply, does not give straightforward answers.[54] In cases where an individual voyage dramatically differs from the other ones in execution of the volume contract, attention shifts to this specific one. Maybe the parties wanted to contract on non-RR terms, and the difference in the execution of these voyages is an important indicator of this. However, even if this is the case, other factors will need to be examined.

The following scenario will be of some help: the volume contract provides for transportation by sea in four shipments. If the majority of the cargo is transported in the third shipment, but the quantity of the first, second and fourth are so minimal as to cast doubts on the nature of the contract as a "volume" one, then indeed, the apportionment of quantity is a factor that needs to be taken into consideration.[55]

Our view is that an individual voyage of a volume contract will be considered to be subject to Article 80 of the RR, and therefore capable of derogating from the RR, if the intention of the parties to ship the cargo on a package deal has been ascertained from the rest of the voyages. However, a paradox is subsequently revealed: how can a framework contract as a whole be subject to Article 80, whereas separate constituents of it are not?

Our opinion is that the individual contracts[56] of the volume contract should mirror the contract itself, meaning that they should allude to a framework contract. If one or several individual contracts, alone or studied together, raise suspicions as to their compatibility with the volume contract provisions of the

51 Ibid.

52 That is, contracts which do not have the characteristics to be classified as volume contracts.

53 For instance whether the voyages are repeated periodically, whether the quantities of cargo shipped are comparable etc.

54 See von Ziegler, Schelin and Zunarelli (eds), *The Rotterdam Rules 2008*, para 16.3.2, p. 342.

55 Article 1(2) of the RR does not impose an obligation that the quantities of the voyages are fairly evenly spread.

56 That is, the contracts which compose the volume contract.

RR, first Articles 1(2) and 80 should be checked to investigate whether the intention of the parties is to ship on a certain frequency of voyages and quantities in a given time scale. This is why we suggest that the test for determining whether there is a valid volume contract which can derogate from the RR is multiple: a test of the intention of the parties, of the facts (i.e. of the respective individual voyages), and, where appropriate, of the previous business dealings of the specific parties. If this test fails, then Article 79 should be checked in case the parties indirectly try to benefit from the privileges of Article 80, which would not originally be applicable.

In the following section particular focus is devoted to the individual preconditions of derogation from the RR.

5.2.6 Preconditions of Article 80 for derogation from the Rotterdam Rules

Article 80 allows for greater or lesser rights, obligations and liabilities between shipper and carrier derogating from those originally prescribed in the RR; only rights and obligations provided in Articles 14(a) and 14(b), 29 and 32 or liability arising from the breach thereof, and any liability arising from an act or omission referred to in Article 61 "cannot be excluded by carrier and shipper".[57]

A valid derogation needs to satisfy four cumulative main prerequisites listed under Articles 80(2)(a) to 80(2)(d). As per Article 3 of the RR, the prerequisites of Articles 80(2) and 80(5) need to be in writing. According to Article 80(2)(a), the volume contract should contain a particularly noticeable statement that it derogates from the RR. According to scholars, this requirement can be satisfied if the contract has a clause stating "This contract is a volume contract and it derogates from the Rotterdam Rules".[58]

Article 80(2)(b) requires that (i) the volume contract is individually negotiated or that (ii) it prominently specifies the sections of the volume contract containing the derogations. The second requirement of section (b) is clear, asking that the sections of the volume contract containing the derogations are obviously listed, at least by numeric reference. In contrast, the first segment of the section, requiring that the volume contract is individually negotiated, is difficult to be evidenced in the contract. In our opinion, this is better shown in Article 80(2)(d), which states: "The derogation is neither (i) incorporated by reference from another document nor (ii) included in a contract of adhesion that is not subject to negotiation."

In that sense, it is submitted that Article 80(2)(b)(i) and Article 80(2)(d) do not differ much.

How parties prove individual negotiations is a serious issue. Conflictingly, Article 80 can be technically satisfied through a phrase on a coversheet attached to the contract: "A and B, the undersigned, have agreed to the following volume contract. See terms attached for details."

57 Article 80(4) of the RR.

58 See Baatz et al, *The Rotterdam Rules: A Practical Annotation*, p. 248, fn 20 therein.

5.2.7 Article 80(2)(c) of the Rotterdam Rules

Article 80(2) contains the formal requirements which validate the derogation from the RR when a volume contract is concluded. One of the most controversial ones is that stated under paragraph 80(2)(c):

> The shipper is given an opportunity and notice of the opportunity to conclude a contract of carriage on terms and conditions that comply with this Convention without any derogation under this article.

In our opinion, the requirements for an opportunity and notice of the opportunity to contract in terms which do not derogate from the RR are impractical and perhaps confusing, especially in terms of evidence. A notice can be in writing, but the same cannot apply separately to the opportunity; the opportunity per se cannot be evidenced through writing if there are no more specific indicators.[59]

Surprisingly, the rationale behind Article 80(2)(b)(i) of the RR, instead of providing for the protection of parties in an unprivileged bargaining position, serves to extend the conclusion of contracts which form a commercial practice;[60] instead, this is the rationale behind Article 80(2)(b)(ii).[61] It has to be clarified that a mere indication that the contract has been individually negotiated does not necessarily mean that the contract is a volume contract, or more importantly that the shipper is fully aware of all or some of the derogations.

The parties may sign a coversheet stating: "On date x, Y and Z have entered into individual negotiations and concluded a volume contract that derogates from the RR. Sections 5, 13 and 8 are agreed outside the stipulations of the RR. See Annex attached."

Evidently, such a contract has the guise of an individually negotiated contract, whereas this may not be the case. Besides, there is only an indication of derogations, without exact knowledge of the aspects of the terms that constitute derogations. This obstacle can be avoided in two ways: either by way of interpretation, if it is inferred that the requirement for the opportunity is satisfied through the tender of a written notice of the opportunity; or by a specific provision in the volume contract with a simpler wording. For clarity, the parties can stipulate in their contract that the shipper was offered an opportunity to contract on standard terms and conditions subject to the RR, and rejected it.

However, even in that case, there does not seem to be a way to prove whether the intention of the carrier to enter into a *non-volume* carriage contract has actually occurred. If the terms of the volume contract are a lot more attractive (low freight rates for instance), there is nothing to prevent the shipper from being

59 See 15th session Report, A/CN.9/576, para 83, where there was an official suggestion for inserting indicators specifying the individuality of the negotiations, e.g., the bargaining power of the parties.

60 See 15th session Report, A/CN.9/576, para 82, where "a need to maintain a measure of commercial pragmatism" was acknowledged.

61 See 15th session Report, A/CN.9/576, para 83.

induced by the carrier because of the commercial pressure exercised or the standardisation of the freight market. The reason why this is said is because Article 80(2) of the RR seems to insert steps showing that there is adequate consideration before the volume contract is concluded.

Individual negotiations needed to be a separate and independent precondition to assure that there is abundant clarification of the sections that will be derogated. The word "sections" used in Article 80(2)(b)(ii) mostly refers to the numbers of the derogations, so it is used figuratively. In our view, the logical order of steps that should have to be proven in writing is as follows: the opportunity to contract on conventional terms; individual negotiations about the content of the intended derogations; and, lastly, a prominent statement of the content of the derogations on the contract itself. If there is issuance of a transport document or record, then the sections may be explicit therein, but, as we shall see later, it is ambiguous whether this affords legal certainty to third parties.

We will now expand on the deficiency of the combined application of Articles 80(2)(b) and 80(2)(c).

5.2.8 Article 80(2)(b) and its relation with Article 80(2)(c) of the Rotterdam Rules

The drafting of the preconditions of Article 80(2)(b) of the RR raises concerns as to the potential protection afforded to the freedom of negotiation. More specifically, the two requirements that are alternatively requested there do not equally protect a "weaker" shipper. Article 80(2)(b)(i) is of particular importance, as it aims to ensure that the derogations are contemplated and examined properly in the context of the negotiation. This is further supported by the preparatory works: it was *inter alia*[62] suggested therein that subsection (ii) should be deleted, so that it is explicitly required that *all* the volume contracts derogating from the RR were individually negotiated.[63] In our view, a court will be more convinced on the negotiations and the shipper will be surer of their content if there is an individual document containing the substance of the derogations and the signature underneath.

Professor Tettenborn also criticises the Convention's permissiveness to volume contracts.[64] The first point of critique is that Article 80(2)(c) of the RR is incomplete in not specifying that the counter-offer of the carrier to contract on non-exceptional terms has to be at a reasonable cost. However, he counter argued that such a contingency would be discouraged by another provision of Article 80 as the contract might qualify as a contract of adhesion.[65] The latter is

62 See A/CN.9/576, para 83.

63 Italicisation added by the author.

64 Tettenborn, 'Freedom of contract and the Rotterdam Rules: framework for negotiation or one-size-fits-all?', para 4.19.

65 Tettenborn, 'Freedom of contract and the Rotterdam Rules: Framework for negotiation or one-size-fits-all?', para 4.20. *The Starsin* [2004] 1 AC 715, para 144. Lord Hobhouse said: "If a party, otherwise liable, is to exclude or limit his liability or to rely on an exemption, he must do so in

defined as a contract where one party imposes its contractual will to the other party, without mutuality of assent.[66] Their distinctive characteristic is that they are not open to negotiation. Other indicators that a contract may be a contract of adhesion[67] are that the terms are standardised or pre-printed, or appearing in fine print. Additionally if the counterparty is presented on a "take it or leave it" basis, this means that he can have no contribution to the agreement on the terms, or if there is grave inequality[68] between the weaker and the stronger party, then, it can be assumed that this contract may qualify as a contract of adhesion.

In the next section, the complexities arising from the application of volume contracts to third parties will be examined.

5.3 Article 80(5): third parties bound by a volume contract

As far as parties other than the shipper and carrier are concerned, Article 80(5)(a) of the RR applies. This holds a party bound by the terms of the volume contract, if that party has received information prominently stating that the volume contract derogates from the RR and has expressed his consent to these derogations. This consent must be in writing or through electronic communication.[69]

The intricacy of this provision derives from its inconsistent wording.[70] On the one hand, there is a general requirement that the third party is notified that the contract merely *derogates* from the RR. On the other, the third party has to expressly consent to be bound by such derogations.

clear words. Unclear words do not suffice [...] the 'Standard Conditions' of bills of lading are not the subject of negotiation or amendment by the shipper; they are printed conditions which the shipper is required to accept (i.e. a contract of adhesion); the wording is chosen by the issuer of the bill of lading." Lord Justice Aikens, Richard Lord QC, Michael Bools, *Bills of lading* (Informa 2006), para 7.41. Courts may strike out terms contained in contracts of adhesion because of the superior bargaining power of one of the parties, or due to the unfairness, unconscionability of a term in the said contract: see www.law.cornell.edu/wex/adhesion_contract_contract_of_adhesion.

66 Pamela Tepper, *The Law of Contracts and the Uniform Commercial Code* (2nd edn, Delmar Cengage Learning 2011), p. 118.

67 A test for identifying whether a standard contract is a contract of adhesion is when the said contract is submitted to the adherent in a "quick-hand" transaction, on a "take it or leave it" dilemma, or when terms have unlikely been negotiated: see A Garro, 'Rule-setting by private organisations, standardisation of contracts and the harmonisation of international sales law' in Fletcher et al (eds) *Foundations and Perspectives of international Trade Law*, para 22-006; Ole Lando, 'Standard contracts. A proposal and a perspective' *Scandinavian Studies in Law* (1966), at www.scandinavianlaw.se/pdf/10-5.pdf.

68 Vladimir Rossman and Morton Moskin (eds), *Commercial Contracts – Strategies for drafting and negotiating* (Wolters Kluwer 2013), para 8-06A, fn 205 therein.

69 Article 3 of the RR.

70 Ioanna Magklasi, 'Volume contracts and third parties: "Red-hand rule" or Red-herring?' (2015) 7(1–2), *European Journal of Commercial Contract Law*, 39.

The article is not clear on whether the third party needs to be notified of the fact that there is a derogation in general, or whether he needs to be aware of every individual derogation either.[71] If the former is the case, then there are fewer complications. The issue of concern is how the third party is supposed to consent to something so specific, if Article 80(5) of the RR explicitly requests that only the fact of the derogation is known.

Furthermore, Article 80(5) may have serious trade law dimensions for various reasons.[72] Frequently in the sale of commodities, the goods are sold afloat several times. The issue here is whether the agreement of the initial shipper and carrier on derogations under a volume contract will be approved of by the third parties/successive buyers of the same goods, in the case of CIF sales down the line. The reasons why a buyer may not like a volume contract concluded outside the scope of the RR are several. This volume contract could be possibly transferring obligations which would normally be for the account of the carrier to the shipper or holder of the transport document. It may also reduce the rights of the third party/holder against the carrier, or contain extensive limitations of liability which can be superimposed against both the shipper and the third party. Especially if a third party buys the goods in order to sell them on, it is in his own interests to check whether these derogations may bring him in breach of his sale contract.

Moreover, this is important in order to know whether a third party can be bound by some of the derogations, if he refuses to consent to others, or lastly whether all the derogations should be accepted or rejected as a whole. The word "information" is not defined in the article either. The vagueness of the article will trigger issues of construction of contracts and incorporation of unusual clauses. In our opinion, it can be inferred from the article that a sufficient type of notification, and not necessarily the volume contract itself, must be provided to the third party, in written or electronic form. This can be a document which will contain the main terms of carriage, an overall derogating statement and the individual derogations in their substance. These individual derogations must be clearly identifiable.

Our opinion is that since the aim of Article 80(5) is to contribute to the better awareness of third parties that the contract of carriage derogates from the norm of the RR, this information should be as full and accurate as possible.

Yet another issue is the time at which a third party receives the information that a volume contract with derogations has been entered into. A more specific scenario is the following: a volume contract is concluded and a CIF buyer receives a transport document from his seller. The goods have arrived with a delay, or in a shortage, or another type of damage. It is important that the CIF buyer learns that the carriage contract derogates from the RR after this volume contract has

71 Ibid, p. 40.
72 Ibid.

been performed. He will realise his rights at the moment he wants to sue the carrier, and he may find out that, for instance, the carrier has an extremely limited liability towards him. What is the true potential of the consignee's contractual freedom to reject this volume contract, according to Article 80(5) of the RR?[73] It is our view that the buyer cannot realistically reject at that stage, as it is too late for him to decide to buy the same goods under different carriage terms.[74] Essentially, he would have to choose a different seller who could procure a contract under normal RR terms, which would now be impossible.

Let us now suppose that the buyer receives both the transport document and the goods at the same time. Although, in theory, the buyer would not otherwise have been willing to accept these derogations from the RR, if he finds himself in a position where the market is rising, he will be inclined to accept both the transport document evidencing a volume contract which derogates from the RR and the non-contractual goods, instead of having to buy at a higher price. Consequently, it can be predicted that, practically, there may be cases where third parties are exposed to unpleasant surprises under Article 80(5). Moreover, Article 80(5) of the RR does not provide an answer to the case of the third party agreeing to be bound by some and not all of the derogations. We believe that the third party will be bound only by the derogations he has approved of. For this reason, his consent has to be as detailed as possible.

All of the above are also burdensome for an FOB seller, who may be the documentary shipper under the volume contract.[75] Documentary shippers are also third parties for the purposes of Article 80(5) of the RR. According to Article 1(9) of the RR, the documentary shipper is the person that accepts to be named as 'shipper' in the transport document or electronic transport record. Under an FOB contract, the buyer enters into the contract of carriage, and hence is the original shipper. If the contract of sale does not specify that the volume contract should not derogate from X, Y or Z obligations, the documentary shipper, as third party to the volume contract may not be willing to accept and be bound by the derogations introduced by the volume contract. This contract, entered into by the buyer *qua* shipper, may for instance specify that the documentary shipper has more obligations and liabilities than the shipper himself. If the documentary shipper knows the liability standards imposed by the RR on the shipper and documentary shipper, he may want to deny consenting to the derogations agreed by the shipper and carrier.

Nevertheless, the will of the documentary shipper cannot be easily imposed against the contrary opinion of the shipper. For example, under Article 35 of the RR, the documentary shipper may request the transport document from the carrier, only if the shipper consents. In light of this remark, the documentary shipper's sole secure method of protecting his interests may be to draft his sale

73 Ibid, p. 41.
74 Ibid.
75 Ibid.

contract in a way that prohibits such deviations. Then, a volume contract that derogates will be a breach of the sale contract.

Thus, because of the nebulous drafting of Article 80(5) of the RR, the piece of contractual advice that can be advanced is the following:[76] a third party to a volume contract needs to pay attention to two elements: a) he should find out all the derogations in detail, and b) if possible, before the contract is executed. Both of these requirements can be safeguarded by explicit terms in the contract of sale, especially if it is concluded prior to the carriage contract.

As for the subsequent third parties (potential buyers down the line), these could be sufficiently informed about derogations through their sale contracts and their counterparties (seller or buyer).[77] The sale contracts should preferably contain the acceptable derogations in the form of conditions, so that in case of any breach, the sale contract can be terminated.

Now it is time for another intricacy of Article 80(5) of the RR to be discussed: it has been commented that for the purposes of Article 80(5), regardless of whether information on derogation(s) appears in a sale contract, the 'actual derogation' should be included in the transport document or record, so that Article 80(2)(d) of the RR is satisfied.[78] This provision states that the derogation should be neither incorporated by reference from another document nor be included in a contract of adhesion which is not subject to negotiation. However, one should not forget that a transport document alone is not a volume contract.[79] It has also been clarified that issuance of a transport document is not necessary for the applicability of Article 80 of the RR.[80] Although it can be understood that the transport document is most probably the only document a third party can see, the volume contract itself will most likely be with the original parties. An important issue arises here.[81] Acceptance of the transport document/bill of lading with the statement as to the derogation does not suffice to bind the third party without express consent.[82] If a transport document/record has not been issued, and the sale contract does not give an indication that the volume contract derogates, then how is the required disclosure/notification of the derogations satisfied in the first place? This means that it should not be taken for granted that the supply contract will necessarily be concluded before the volume contract, or that this contract and the transport document (if issued) will contain a statement that alludes to derogations.[83] These are mere possibilities.

76 Ibid.

77 As we shall see, this is a vexing issue, but we have devised solutions.

78 Comment included in Lorenzon, 'Validity of Contractual terms', in Baatz et al, *The Rotterdam Rules: A Practical Annotation*, para 80-10.

79 Article 80(3) of the RR.

80 See specifically Baatz et al, *The Rotterdam Rules: A Practical Annotation*, para 80-07.

81 Magklasi, 'Volume contracts and third parties: "Red-hand rule" or Red-Herring?', p. 42.

82 Sturley, Fujita and van der Ziel, *The Rotterdam Rules*, para 13.061. See also Lorenzon in Baatz et al, *The Rotterdam Rules: A Practical Annotation*, para 80-10.

83 Magklasi, 'Volume contracts and third parties: "Red-hand rule" or Red-Herring?', p. 42.

5.3.1 The impact of volume contracts on CIF sales down a string: transferability of the transport document and passage of risk

Below we deal with case scenarios that will reveal how the regulation of volume contracts under the RR may discourage consecutive sales of goods, from the viewpoint of third parties, i.e. documentary shipper and consignee, for additional reasons.

If the shipper is also the consignee, then agreeing to a regular volume contract or to a volume contract which derogates does not have any practical differences, except maybe in relation to freight rates. Complications arise when a volume contract entered into contains three shipments, which are destined to three different buyers.

If it is assumed that all the sales are concluded on CIF terms with buyers that have an established business past with the shipper, a volume contract might not necessarily cause concern: the seller will be the shipper and the respective three buyers need to consent to the derogations of the volume contracts, as consignees, as per Article 80(5) of the RR. If however the goods are then sold to another buyer, trading for the first time under volume contract terms might create hesitance or distrust, as seen in the following example: there is a buyer interested in buying goods from a certain country and this is offered by two sellers *qua* shippers, where one ships under the RR and the other under volume contract terms which derogate from the RR.

An inexperienced trader or a trader with business in trades or countries not familiar with volume contracts would prefer buying from the first trader. This is because the possibility that the volume contract embraces lesser liabilities for the carrier is not a welcome situation for the buyer, as this affects his right to bring a claim against the carrier in case of defective delivery of the goods.

The existence of provisions of the RR on liability which do not fall under the volume contract exception provides more safety to the buyer-consignee. It can also be argued that volume contract terms may affect the transferability of title to the goods and increase preference for usual contracts of carriage by the buyer-consignee. This is justified because the volume contract bears for the buyer the extra burden of ascertaining the liability undertaken, in case litigation arises and the contract is silent.

Assuming it is proven that volume contracts increase hesitance, traders might decide to become more competitive by shifting, from volume contracts with derogations to volume contracts governed by the RR. The implications of this change are evident in the following hypothetical scenario:

> Three shipments of cargo are scheduled: one in February, one in June and one in September. After encountering difficulties in selling the first shipment of cargo, the shipper then decides to sell the June cargo on regular RR terms. If the first shipment was on volume contract terms and, difficulties arise, can the "original" trading parties then decide to make the other two shipments on regular RR terms?

There is no specific article for such a scenario in the RR. If the answer inferred is that changing from volume to regular contract terms is prohibited, it is self-evident that the shipper/seller is in a very difficult position, as it seems not so straightforward (or possible) for him to subsequently manage to sell his cargo under volume contract terms. If, on the other hand, the answer to this is positive, this will require explicit agreement by the parties.

Essentially, the potential difference between trading on regular and volume contract terms is that volume contracts increase the risk borne by the buyer until the goods are delivered to him. If the volume contract reserves lesser liability for the carrier, this imposes on the CIF shipper the duty to obtain an all-inclusive and more expensive insurance offer to his buyer. The insurance is fixed before the goods are shipped; if the decision to change from volume to usual contract terms is made while the goods are afloat, it is perhaps late for the insurance offer to be renegotiated, as it has already been crystallised; this is a potential difficulty.

The risk borne and the insurance are inherent characteristics of CIF sales. The above example is used to highlight that trading on volume contracts is not only a decision with unpredictable negative consequences in overseas sale contracts, but even worse, it is also a decision which cannot be easily reconsidered once the volume carriage contract is entered into. It is also evident that burdens and difficult decisions, affect the legal duties of the CIF seller (original party) towards the third party. Some critical reflections on determining the applicable law of volume contracts that derogate will now be discussed forthwith.

5.3.2 Determining the law applicable to volume contracts that derogate from the Rotterdam Rules: some critical reflections

A main concern expressed[84] about Article 80 of the RR was this: due to the fact that it is believed that the vast majority of containerised cargo is transported under service contracts, there is a fear that this in effect may facilitate carriers to "impose" their terms via Article 80 of the RR. This article allows the RR to be displaced by agreement and consequently, it is feared that this will bring "shipping trade" back to the 1930s where no international regime applied.[85] Indeed it cannot be disregarded that the problem is not so much that Article 80 opens the window for the non-application of the RR per se, but the consequential legal uncertainty caused, as it remains to be found which will be the applicable law to the contract. The contract may contain specific clauses in that respect.

84 See Asariotis, 'UNCITRAL (Draft) Convention on Contracts for the International Carriage of Goods Wholly or Partly by Sea: Mandatory rules and freedom of contract', p. 358 stating: "In practice, however, it may well be possible for a small shipper who opted to contract without derogation from the Draft Convention to find itself compelled to accept a significantly higher freight rate."

85 This was a fear expressed by the European Shippers' Council, also by the Canadian International Freight Forwarders Association See 'Questions and answers: Why the MLA needs an open debate concerning the "volume contracts" exception to the proposed Rotterdam Rules', p. 1–2 at www.mcgill.ca/files/maritimelaw/Questions_and_Answers_USMLA.pdf.

However, if the contract is not sufficiently precise, this may be another international treaty, or national law.

This being the case, whether cargo interests will stipulate favourable terms against carriers (or vice versa), is something to be assessed on the basis of who has greater bargaining power. This risk is anticipated to be borne by small shippers. Thus, carriers could impose most of the terms of the volume contracts, and the shippers would merely accept them because of cheaper freight rates. Confidentiality of freight rates is the greatest advantage of service contracts, in the US.[86]

One should also be reminiscent of the fact that different courts will approach the same problems with a different inclination. For instance, French courts seem to be more protective for the weaker party, whereas English courts may not have to question the viability of the negotiation process.[87]

It is feared that the volume contract concept will also push carriers to insert jurisdiction provisions for more favourable forums, especially outside the US, after the judgment in *The Sky Reefer*.[88] It is noteworthy that there have been official opinions by organisations against volume contracts. The Maritime Law Association, for instance, supported the view that the possibility of carriers limiting their liability due to the RR not being applicable will be detrimental for the American economy, as they are of the view that much of the liability will be transferred from foreign interests to US interests.[89]

Moreover, an article which allows derogation from the RR restoring things back to contractual freedom hampers uniformity.[90] This will not promote the ambition for global application of the RR.

Moreover, it seems that section 80(4) of the RR contains a paradox: how are these rules "super-mandatory", when it is already known that this contract is a volume contract and the RR already do not apply? Are we invited to think that on the one hand Rules are set aside and then they become applicable in relation to specific fields? How can we say that the RR will be applicable instead of another treaty or convention? This will be difficult for all states: both for those which are under a formal obligation to denounce the predecessors of the RR they had adhered to, and the ones that applied different laws. Even if this is accepted, there are difficulties in evidencing how thoroughly a contract should be scrutinised in order to determine if it is a volume contract and what constitutes a breach of Article 80(4) of the RR, and this justifiably causes legal uncertainty.

86 See Philippe Bonnevie, 'Evaluation of the new Convention from the perspective of cargo interests', 9-2009 *Transportrecht* 361, p. 363.

87 Ibid, p. 364.

88 *Vimar Seguros y Reaseguros, SA v. M/V Sky Reefer* (94–623), 515 US 528 (1995): see 'Questions and answers: Why the MLA needs an open debate concerning the "volume contracts" exception to the proposed Rotterdam Rules', p. 3.

89 Ibid, p. 4.

90 See Tetley W, '*Responsibility, Fraternity and Sustainability in Law-A symposium in Honour of Charles D. Gonthier*', Conference proceedings, at cisdl.org/gonthier/public/pdfs/papers/Conf%C3%A9rence%20Charles%20D%20Gonthier%20-%20Benoit%20Mayer.pdf, p. 15.

In our opinion, a volume contract may have dimensions that necessitate the understanding of two concepts: not only are there volume carriage contracts of affreightment, but also volume sale contracts. This is not only notional, but also practical. Overseas sales and contracts of affreightment are an entrenched "commercial twin". The RR purport – albeit not very successfully – to initiate, a carriage concept which extends further and outside carriage regimes. Third parties are lightly protected from a drafting perspective, and if only this provision exists without further actions taken or clarification suggested by the courts, Article 80(5) of the RR will result in their exposure and not their protection. This will be more probable in the event of collusion between shipper and carrier, whereby derogations may be agreed but not properly reported to the third parties so that they can agree upon them.[91]

We shall subsequently illustrate more uncertainties stemming from volume contracts, focusing on Article 80(5) of the RR and will suggest ways of rectifying them.

Prior to this, we will assess how existing standard contracts of affreightment are in compliance with the RR provisions on volume contracts.

5.3.3 Standard contracts of affreightment: INTERCOA 80, VOLCOA, GENCOA 2004 and SERVICECON

Regardless of the peculiarities of volume contracts or their frequency in certain ranges of ports or types of trade, the needs that volume contracts satisfy (booking of vessel for a period of time etc.) have led to the creation of standard contract formats; this comes as proof that volume contracts, although intricate and not widely spread, are not unknown. BIMCO has created three types of standard volume contracts of affreightment: INTERCOA 80, VOLCOA and GENCOA 2004.[92] BIMCO has recently adopted a standard service contract, called SERVICECON.[93] It has been said that: "The new agreement is designed to meet the contractual needs of small to medium sized shippers, which, despite the large number and global value of the shipments they transport, often lack the legal resources to develop their own agreements with carriers."[94]

Our aim is to see their level of alignment with the RR in order to suggest areas of additional contractual drafting for a positive trade impact when the RR come into force.

The oldest standard volume contract is INTERCOA 80,[95] headed "tanker contract of affreightment", whereas, as will be discussed below, VOLCOA is

91 See Baatz et al, *The Rotterdam Rules: A Practical Annotation*, para [80-10], p. 252.

92 Issued by BIMCO, November 2004.

93 Issued in 2014. This is essentially a volume contract for containers: see 'BIMCO launches Standard Service Contract – SERVICECON' at www.globalshippersforum.com/media/1240/explanatory_notes_servicecon_bulletin_5-2014.pdf and www.bimco.org/Chartering/Documentary_Projects/New_contracts.aspx.

94 www.bimco.org/news/press-releases/20150428_servicecon.

95 Issued in 1980.

called "volume contract of affreightment". GENCOA 2004 is headed "standard contract of affreightment", and it is for carriage of dry bulk cargo. In the preamble of this contract, it is requested that the maximum and minimum quantity of each shipment is stated, at the owner's option. This requirement is maintained in the other two contracts, but there are more stipulations as to the overall quantity, as will be discussed below. The second most important requirement, which has been altered in the other two standard contracts, is that the shipments need to be fairly evenly spread within each year.[96]

To visualise changes after the RR come into force, let us imagine a scenario where a volume contract is made subject to English law, as with VOLCOA and GENCOA 2004. The mere indication in the *chapeau* of the contract that it is a volume contract will not make INTERCOA 80 capable of derogating from the RR. For this to happen, Article 80 of the RR needs to be complied with.

As far as VOLCOA is concerned, it is stated in its heading that it is a "standard volume contract of affreightment" and applies to transportation of dry bulk cargo. The question now is whether this is enough for the contract to be subject to Article 80 of the RR, which, as discussed above, requires a prominent statement that the contract derogates from the RR. Arguably the words "volume contract of affreightment" leave no doubts as to the type of the contract. However, Article 80(1) specifically requests, at least, a particularly noticeable statement of the derogations. Hence, the heading on its own does not suffice to classify VOLCOA as a volume contract which derogates from the RR; the specific clauses derogating from the RR need to be clearly stated.

A look at the first page of the contract gives hints as to the special characteristics of volume contracts: firstly, BOX 6 and 7 are for loading and discharging ports or ranges and BOX 8 is for the stated fixed period of the contract, as the cargo of volume contracts is transferred over a period of time. In the same vein, BOX 12 indicates the programme of shipments. Box 9 is for the total quantity, asking for the minimum and maximum to be declared. This is an important discrepancy from Article 1(2) of the RR as the specified quantity is part of the definition of volume contracts.

Interestingly, in lines 80 and 81 of VOLCOA, it is stated that "in the event of any conflict between the terms and conditions of a single voyage charterparty issued and this Contract, the latter shall prevail", which shows that the framework contract is the overriding contract in relation to the individual voyages. Moreover, in addition to the specification of INTERCOA 80 for declaring the maximum/minimum quantity per voyage, VOLCOA (as well as GENCOA 2004) gives the parties the option to declare the quantity of the whole contract, as well as the quantity of the final shipment. If all of the above is declared by the appropriate parties, then the clause on final shipment takes over the other two.

It can be concluded that the requirements of the RR can be satisfied by the terms of the VOLCOA contract, as there are specifications about time, ranges of

96 See INTERCOA 80, Section B of the preamble.

ports, programme of voyages etc.; however, these are not sufficient for this contract to be excluded from the mandatory provisions of the RR. There also has to be an apparent statement declaring that it derogates from the RR, as well as similar clauses satisfying the rest of the preconditions of Article 80 of the RR in line with our advice in the previous section.

GENCOA is another standard contract of affreightment and is also used for dry bulk cargo,[97] but this time, the word "volume" is not apparent on the face of the contract, or among the terms and conditions. This contract was more recent than VOLCOA and if the RR apply, the same remarks made above will presumably apply to the conditions for derogation also for that one.

As to its similarities with VOLCOA, BOX 12, which in VOLCOA was headed "Programme of shipments (only to be filled in if specific programme agreed)", appears as "shipment periods/period of shipments/scheduling/nomination" in GENCOA. It is also observed that in GENCOA, BOX 8 merges what appeared in BOX 9 and 12 of VOLCOA, so that the charterer/shipper in GENCOA needs to specify either the minimum or maximum of quantity of each shipment, or just state the number of shipments. In both contracts, however, there is a safeguard which does not appear in the RR, which is that "the number of shipments shall be fairly evenly spread over the period of the contract".[98] Nevertheless, the contracting parties will not be bound by it if they have already agreed on a schedule and stated it in the relevant box of their standard contract.

SERVICECON on the other hand is a standard service contract for liner trade, whereby there is a minimum quantity commitment.[99] It is explicit in Box 8 that there is an obligation for a minimum quantity to be shipped, and if the box is left blank, the contract shall be null and void. Clause 12 states that SERVICECON constitutes the entire agreement and that no promise, undertaking, representation, warranty or statement by either party prior to the date stated in BOX 2 shall affect this contract. Additionally, any modification to this contract shall be of no effect, unless in writing and signed by or on behalf of the parties.

5.3.4 Preliminary conclusions for the repercussions of volume contracts on original parties

Volume contracts have been praised as a positive novelty of the RR for giving space for freedom of contract and for acknowledging the need of traders to enter into flexible contracts which are not hindered by compulsory liability frameworks. The criticism made is due to the fact that the RR are an international convention,

97 It has been submitted that GENCOA, as it is destined for non-liner bulk dry cargo transport will be outside the application of the RR. Kozubovskaya-Pellé, 'Contractual flexibility in volume contracts: Rotterdam Rules and French law perspective', p. 329. However, we examine GENCOA from a perspective of contract structure, as a contract of affreightment is a contractual scheme close to volume contracts.

98 See GENCOA, lines 45–46 and VOLCOA, lines 23–25.

99 Users/em6c14/Downloads/Sample%20copy%20SERVICECON.pdf

and trends or customs of a particular country may be totally unknown to another. Hence, instead of enhancing harmonisation, the RR may bring disharmony and uncertainty in international trade law. One could say that the provision for tailor-made agreements is an element of modern trade. The only positive aspect that can be observed about them is that shippers, i.e. sellers or buyers, will book space on a vessel at probably low tariffs. However, this advantage is one-sided, as the original party will be affected by the derogations only until the transport document gets transferred to the buyers. Therefore, it can be argued that mostly receivers of the goods (who are not the sellers at the same time) will be detrimentally affected. We will deal with them in turn.

One however has to see whether the shippers themselves are in a position to get an essential contractual benefit from volume contracts. In the briefing note for SERVICECON, it is explained that:

"The agreement is being developed by representatives from a number of major liner operators and targets *small to medium sized shippers* who sign the majority of such volume contracts" (emphasis added).[100] It is this target group which is, from a negotiation viewpoint, more vulnerable compared to major liner operators.

Lack of knowledge about these specific commercial trends, such as the volume contracts or the OLSAs, makes it more likely that the "weapons of contractual freedom" will be misused or used to circumvent the stricter provisions of the RR. This was also the thread of argument used behind the analysis of Article 35 in Chapter 3 of this book.

To be accurate, our stance is that volume contracts should unequivocally require that the uniqueness or individuality of specific terms is concretely addressed in the contract. This seems to be inferred overall by Article 80, but not in a certain, homogeneous way. In other words, Article 80(2)(b) initiates a presumption that the derogations have been a product of specific agreement, and that parties are fully aware of the derogations. We disagreed with the way obligations are vaguely drafted. A convention which was spearheaded to crystallise an international liability regime, thus inviting to set the framework on new grounds, as it does in several articles,[101] needed to delineate unequivocal conditions, positive and or negative. If the exception to the rules is more vaguely drafted than the rules themselves, these deficiencies cannot be seen as mere oversights, and this is why the parties need to secure their position through carefully drafted carriage and sale contracts.

Time will prove whether the legal risks lurking behind the veil of vagueness or insufficiency of Article 80 of the RR will prove true, or be eliminated through contract drafting and possibly additional consistent international legislation. For now, the "traps" can be avoided at least through enhanced awareness and cautious drafting of contract terms.[102]

100 See BIMCO 'New Contracts' www.bimco.org/Chartering/Documentary_Projects/New_contracts.aspx.

101 See for instance Articles 4, 79, 83, as well as chapters 5 and 12 of the RR dealing with liability.

102 Magklasi, 'Volume contracts and third parties: "Red-hand rule" or Red-Herring?', p. 49.

National legislations can give more definition to the requirements of Article 1(2) of the RR, setting limits and may also set up supervisory and controlling committees, like the FMC, where contracts will be filed and checked.

The fact that there is no independent obligation that the volume contract is individually negotiated has a strong significance.[103] As cited several times in this chapter, there can always be oblique ways of inducing a party to enter into a non-standard volume contract or of suggesting that it is the only way forward.

The volume contract provisions mostly seem to establish a trend, already convenient for concluding carriage contracts in some parts of the world, such as for shipments from US ports, rather than equitably balance rights and obligations between carriers and shippers.[104] There are no important conventional obstacles in this process; what best suits the parties' financial and commercial interests can be the subject of the agreement.

Nevertheless, in our opinion, the exception should not be more attractive than the norm, as the case seems to be here, otherwise the rule can be completely superseded. The minimum obligations which should be complied with, such as that the ship is seaworthy, are rather self-evident; more super-mandatory provisions along these lines should be inserted to work as a deterrent/caution, making parties carefully consider the possibility of deviating from the mandatory provisions of the RR. A provision about volume contracts should be thoroughly drafted, demanding that such requirements are complied with as to render it unattractive for the parties to enter into them. On the other hand, the contention that it is not a concern that volume contracts might become prevalent, thus constraining the RR to apply to very few carriage contracts, is not a plausible argument. This is due to the fact that the RR are not yet in force, and as commercial practices change, the effect of the RR cannot be predicted. Besides, the use of service contracts is prevalent and, as pointed out, volume contracts are the RR's equivalents.

Therefore, it is submitted that there are drafting insufficiencies that need to be rectified through contractual provisions or even legislation. The aim should be to make the general requirements of Article 1(2) of the RR more specific so that the volume contract concept applies to specific volumes of cargo, preferably to a specific minimum, or to specific types of trade, for example specific commodities, or ports where shipping in "particularised contractual transportation service arrangements"[105] is a custom, usage or practice of the trade.

This suggestion makes practical sense, if it is taken into consideration that, as per section 8(c) of the US Shipping Act 1984, certain details of the contracts had

103 See Asariotis, 'UNCITRAL (DRAFT) Convention on Contracts for the International Carriage of Goods wholly or partly by Sea: Mandatory rules and freedom of contract', p. 363.

104 The argument that we disagree with here was expressed in p. 605, Muckerjee, 'A legal and economic analysis of the volume contract concept under the Rotterdam Rules: Selected issues in perspective'.

105 The expression in quotation marks appears in the preparatory works, Doc A/CN.9/WG.III/WP.34, para 27.

to be submitted to the FMC.[106] Among these were the ports of destination and origin and the intermediate ports, or the general geographical area of dispatch and destination, as well as details of the type of cargo transported, the quantity, the duration of the contract and the line haul rate.[107]

In our view, the requirements of Article 80 can be criticised to portray too much abstraction: "opportunities", "information" and "individual negotiations" are terms referring to concepts that exist in commercial practice, but which are difficult to prove in writing. More pragmatic stipulations are needed, so that compliance can be easily ascertained. Similarly, another method of ensuring that volume contracts are used as a flexible scheme of contracts for more efficient and worldwide trading, and not as a vehicle to circumvent liabilities, is by inserting provisions about publicising these contracts to specific committees, such as is the FMC,[108] or possibly in the future in other similar committees of acknowledged international trust; that way abuse of terms by parties with higher bargaining power can be discouraged. This is again not far from the framework of service liner agreements under the US Shipping Act 1984, where the duration of the service contract, for instance, has to be disclosed to the FMC.[109] Thus, contracts need to be registered with and supervised by these committees, and their terms should be approved before shipment, so that the volume contract derogations are legitimate. If authorisation is denied and the shipment proceeds and unfolds, the contract should be deemed to be in compliance with the RR, thus it should not derogate from the RR. As to the remaining obligations, these should be fulfilled according to the contracts of previous businesses of the parties or according to the custom and usage of the particular trade and ports.

Article 8(c) of the OSRA[110] also maintained the requirement that certain details have to be deposited with the FMC, with the only difference being that

106 For the role of the FMC, see US Shipping Act 1984, section 1710a(6)(b).

107 See Peter Marlow and Nair Rawindaran, 'Service contracts – An instrument of international logistics supply chain: Under United States and European Union regulatory frameworks' (2008) 32 *Marine Policy* 489, pp. 490–491.

108 See US Shipping Act 1984, section 1710a(6)(b):The FMC shall investigate whether any laws, rules, regulations, policies, or practices of foreign governments, or any practices of foreign carriers or other persons providing maritime or maritime-related services in a foreign country result in the existence of conditions that (1) adversely affect the operations of United States carriers in United States ocean borne trade; and (2) do not exist for foreign carriers of that country in the United States under the laws of the United States or as a result of acts of United States carriers or other persons providing maritime or maritime-related services in the United States.

109 See Marlow and Rawindaran, 'Service contracts – An instrument of international logistics supply chain: Under United States and European Union regulatory frameworks', p. 491.

110 As it is stated in its heading, the OSRA came with the purpose "to amend the shipping Act of 1984 to encourage competition in international shipping and growth of United States exports and for other purposes". The US Senate COGSA 1999, defines service contracts in 3(21): "service contract" means a contract between a shipper and an ocean common carrier or conference in which the shipper makes a commitment to provide a certain minimum quantity of cargo over a fixed time period, and the ocean common carrier or conference commits to a certain rate or rate schedule as well as a defined service level—such as, assured space, transit time, port rotation, or similar service features; the contract may also specify provisions in the event of non-performance on the part of either party.

these do not additionally need to be made available to the public. After examining this provision, it is asserted that it is of a positive impact, as there are still details which have to be checked by an authority, namely the FMC. This is a provision which in our opinion safeguards against contracts being "dangerously" negotiated with too much freedom. Had this provision appeared in the RR, it would have prevented small shippers from being forced into contracts with very low rates (and favourable low obligations for the carrier) in a market that surges, and give him broader shipment options.[111] However, this can be the subject of national legislation.

In our opinion, the problem with volume contracts and the constraints around them could have been rectified by a better systematic structure of the RR. For instance, if the volume contract exception of Article 80 came exactly after Article 6 or better Article 7, this would better show that they are prima facie outside the scope of the RR, but exceptionally, as with charterparties, are subject to the RR when a transport document or electronic transport record is issued.

Nevertheless, the above arguments should not be mistakenly interpreted as condemning the scope of application of the RR for liberating the shipping customs through widening the volume contract exception. The RR have been the product of yearly negotiations and are the snapshot of international compromises reached on several aspects, and volume contracts is one of them. The question and the criticism made is not about the existence of the volume contract exception, but about the need to internationally apply the framework in a way that does not bring turmoil in commercial and shipping contracts.

Below, the focus is on third parties, in order to illustrate how buyers may be exposed to receiving volume contracts affording them with ambiguous rights against the carrier. At the end, advice will be given for ensuring timeliness and accuracy in the way the third party becomes privy to and, if he consents, also bound by the derogations.

5.4 Specific issues to be addressed for third parties

It is asserted that the way volume contract derogations are regulated by the RR is particularly ambiguous and thus risky for third parties.[112] There are formalities relating to consent that are worth exploring as the third party will be a key party to the international sale contract for the goods carried under the volume contract.

111 See Asariotis, 'UNCITRAL Draft Convention on Contracts for the International Carriage of Goods Wholly or Partly by Sea: Mandatory rules and freedom of contract', p. 362, illustrating the fear of "abuse of the freedom of contract". Also Baatz et al, *The Rotterdam Rules: A Practical Annotation*, para [80-01] for freedom of contract and para [80-05] therein, for compliant but not viable offers.

112 Francis Reynolds, 'Transport documents under the international conventions' in Thomas (ed) *The Carriage of Goods by Sea Under The Rotterdam Rules*, paras 13.40, 13.41. Reynolds QC considers bill of lading "a trap for third parties".

The following issues will be originally deciphered and addressed in depth for the first time in an international commercial law context:[113] the form of consent to a volume contract which derogates from the RR; the identification of the party who has to request consent (of the party that has to approve of); whether it is the same with the party who has to notify on the derogations; and, last but not least, the time[114] of the request and that of providing consent on the derogations, as well as other characteristics of the notice informing on the derogations. The controversies stemming from the above uncertainties[115] and their commercial implications will be underlined. In the end, optimal ways of securing the position of third parties under international sale contracts will be suggested with the assistance of principles deriving from English common law.[116] These mainly concern the form of acceptance of derogations and the requirements that need to be fulfilled in terms of a notice on derogations/exemptions from liability.

The contextual background for this discussion is deemed to be English common law. As shall be seen the requested consent may be pre-contractual or post contractual,[117] according to the time the sale contract was entered into and its specificity on what the carriage contract should entail. Therefore, our objective is to investigate how judges in English courts would reach the answer to the above questions and facilitate in attaining the drafting ambitions of the draftsmen of the RR.

The case scenarios contemplated will concern CIF sales, where the seller enters into a volume contract. If the goods are sold in transit, then it is indisputable that the original party to the contract of carriage from a trade viewpoint is only the shipper *qua* seller, as the potential buyer(s) may be unknown at that stage.

Evidently, the analyses of renowned academics on the formalities of providing information and requesting consent for volume contract derogations are not perfectly consistent with each other. The objective for the analysis to follow is to see how English courts seized with a dispute involving third parties and volume contracts would dilute the vagueness of Article 80 of the RR.[118] Perhaps it is the mission of the applicable national law to set additional safeguards in the article in order to resolve the confusion arising thereunder.

113 Magklasi, 'Volume contracts and third parties: "Red-hand rule" or Red-Herring?', pp. 39–46.

114 On this point it has been submitted that the time of giving consent is immaterial: Francesco Berlingieri, 'An analysis of two recent commentaries on the Rotterdam Rules', p. 110. Nevertheless, in our opinion the time of notifying on derogations and/or requesting consent has to take place at a time when the consignee/buyer can still accept or reject the contractual evidence containing the derogations.

115 For the endorsement on the vagueness around these issues see Reynolds, 'Transport documents under the international conventions', para 13.41; also Treitel and Reynolds (eds), *Carver on Bills of Lading* (4th edn), para 10-072.

116 Magklasi, 'Volume contracts and third parties: "Red-hand rule" or Red-Herring?', pp. 39–46.

117 As to the possibility of declaring consent after the volume contract is entered into, see Honka, 'Validity of contractual terms', para 16.3.6.

118 Magklasi, 'Volume contracts and third parties: "Red-hand rule" or Red-Herring?', pp. 45–49.

Our objectives are as follows:[119] first, to identify whether each derogation shall be individually communicated or whether the initial notification of a derogated volume contract is sufficient; and second, to ascertain whether the derogations initiating exemption from liability have to be specifically addressed to the third party, or whether the general knowledge of the existence of derogations means that the third party alone should discover them. In other words, what the information received should comprise of, and ultimately what the court is to decide when a derogation which proves onerous, unreasonable or unusual is proven not to have been pointed out to the parties' attention will be deciphered forthwith.

5.5 First reflections on the prerequisites for binding a third party to a volume contract

From the preamble of Article 80(5) RR, it can be assumed that a third party for volume contract purposes is any person other than the shipper and carrier, for example the documentary shipper or the consignee. In this regard, it becomes essential to determine the conditions for making a third party bound by an already concluded volume contract and verify whether the enhanced protection considered by the draftsmen of the RR for third parties ensures adequate notice and consequently knowledge of what they are agreeing to.[120]

Article 80(5) of the RR requires the third party to have received information which prominently states that the volume contract derogates from the RR, and to have given its express consent to be bound by such derogations; such consent shall not be solely set forth in a carrier's public schedule of prices and services, transport document or electronic transport record. There is a notional gap at this stage, as it would be assumed that the information received has to satisfy two requirements: first, that the contract in question is a volume contract that derogates from the RR in general; and second, that the individual derogations in their substance are pointed out to the third party, or as per the logic of the article, at least briefly mentioned by reference to article numbers.

A first issue already identified[121] is whether the source of this information as to the derogation of volume contracts will be the sale contract, or the volume contract or another document. It has been advised that by signing a sale contract which among other clauses states that the carriage contract is a volume contract which derogates from the RR (and presumably specifies the derogations), traders are deemed to have also consented to the derogations.[122] This is not the only advocated opinion, as in another commentary of the RR[123] there is a case scenario illustrating that the handing over and acceptance of a transport document which

119 Ibid, pp. 39–50.

120 For the specific contemplation on the vulnerability of third parties, see A/CN.9/645 paras 237, 241; also UNCTAD/SDTE/TLB/2004/2 para 15.

121 Baatz et al, *The Rotterdam Rules: A Practical Annotation*, para 80-10.

122 Ibid.

123 Sturley, Fujita and van der Ziel, *The Rotterdam Rules*, Illustration 13-13.

the holder browses through to see its terms and conditions, in the knowledge that it derogates from the RR, and non-rejection of the document, are insufficient to validate consent as per Article 80(5); this consent needs to be provided in writing too.

Two remarks may be made at this point.[124] Even the commentators themselves may have different expectations as to what a third party will in most circumstances receive as evidence of a volume contract (a supply contract and a transport document, or a volume contract and a transport document). Furthermore, receipt of the volume contract itself or conclusion of the sale contract in sufficient detail in terms of derogations are both ideal scenarios. Article 80(5) does not seem to impose any such obligations either on traders or on the carrier. "Information" is not defined by the article. This, in our opinion, leaves open the possibility of tender of documents with even fewer prerequisites met.[125] And this, in turn, can lead to litigation or at least loss of time, as the third party may exercise pressure or seek additional details before providing consent. Not knowing what has to be submitted to the third party is of great commercial uncertainty.[126] Questions also remain as to the importance of the actual knowledge of the derogations.[127]

It has been submitted that a term to the sale contract such as "by accepting this document the Merchant is deemed to have given its express consent to be bound by any derogation from the Rotterdam Rules herein contained[128] [...] will make the terms fully binding [...] whether the parties are aware of the derogatory terms or not" does not protect a third party.[129] In an illustration from a commentary on the RR, it is stated that due to the lack of the formal requirement of consent, the third party is not bound even though he has checked the terms and conditions and intends to accept.[130] The illustrations provided in the above commentaries show the importance of formalities (of the reference to derogations and consent) as well as their failure to ensure knowledge of derogations, and consequently protection.[131] Consent may be provided without actual knowledge. One scholarly view seems to assume that the third party will make the effort to localise and understand the derogations.[132] However, it is not clear whether the commentator based this on Article 80 or on what was discussed in the negotiations of the RR. Whether the individual effort of the third party to identify the sections that derogate will depend on how prominent, specific or abstract the information on derogations is appears to be unclear too. This shows the need for

124 Magklasi, 'Volume contracts and third parties: "Red-hand rule" or Red-Herring?', p. 42.
125 Ibid.
126 Ibid.
127 Ibid.
128 See Lorenzon in Baatz et al, *The Rotterdam Rules: A Practical Annotation*, para 80-10.
129 Ibid.
130 Ibid.
131 Magklasi, 'Volume contracts and third parties: "Red-hand rule" or Red-Herring?', p. 43.
132 Sturley, Fujita and van der Ziel, *The Rotterdam Rules*, Illustration 13-13.

interpretational help, as the vague drafting of Article 80(5) of the RR does not seem to explicitly specify this.[133]

In our opinion, actual awareness of the derogations, or at least directions as to where they can be found (in full text, and not just figuratively), does not seem necessary from the articles, whereas it should be. This is the *rationale* of the notification requirement of Article 80(5) of the RR. Therefore a narrow purposive interpretation should be given to Article 80(5)(a). Since this article has been included for the protection of the third party, doubts as to whether a party has knowledge followed by approval of certain derogations should be resolved in favour of the third party, especially if that party is not a sophisticated one.[134] This suggestion aims to reduce the possibility of ignorance of a liberty clause or a limitation of liability provision, which would work in favour of the carrier, due to the lack of proper notification of the third party by the shipper or carrier.

Article 80(5) states that the third party "has received" information on derogation.[135] In our view, this should lead to this interpretation: information as to the derogations has to be furnished by someone else and the derogations need to be specifically pointed out, without requiring search initiated by the third party.[136] Article 80(5) does not specify whether all the information has to be provided by someone else, or whether it is the third party's duty to scrutinise the documents that the shipper will make available to him. It seems that one view has been reluctantly expressed through a practical scenario:[137] "the holder who received the document noticed the statement, checked the terms and conditions of the volume contract, and received the transport document without objection." From the wording of this scenario, it may seem implied that it is the third party's duty to check and therefore identify the derogations. However, this scenario assumes that the volume contract itself will be tendered to the third party, even though this is not a formal obligation explicitly prescribed by the RR. Next, we decipher who has to approach the third party to provide him with information and seek consent.

5.6 Whose responsibility is it to notify the third party of the derogations?

The RR do not explicitly address this obligation.[138] Some analyses move to estimations,[139] and others go a bit further in specifying the commercial consequences of this uncertainty.

133 Magklasi, 'Volume contracts and third parties: "Red-hand rule" or Red-Herring?', p. 43.

134 Ibid, p. 43.

135 For a criticism of the verb "received" used by the draftsmen, see also Treitel and Reynolds (eds), *Carver on Bills of lading* (3rd edn), para 10-072.

136 Magklasi, 'Volume contracts and third parties: "Red-hand rule" or Red-Herring?', p. 43.

137 See Sturley, Fujita and van der Ziel, *The Rotterdam Rules*, pp. 382, 383.

138 See Lorenzon in Baatz et al, *The Rotterdam Rules: A Practical Annotation*, para 80-10. See also Treitel and Reynolds (eds), *Carver on Bills of lading* (3rd edn), para 10-072.

139 See among others Roberto Bergami, 'Rotterdam Rules: Volume contracts, delivery terms, transport documents and letters of credit' (2010) *The Vindobona Journal of International Commercial*

Request for express consent is very difficult for a party who is not in some proximity to the shipper or the carrier.[140] Therefore, it has been argued that the easiest case for getting consent would be that of the shippers' affiliated companies based in other countries. However, it has also been stressed that for the sale of goods already afloat, "there is no realistic procedure for obtaining the consignee's consent to be bound by the derogations [...]".[141] The choice of verbs in the illustration of the commentator discussed above is noteworthy: it is assumed that the document leaves the hands of the shipper and *is received*[142] by a lawful holder who goes through the diverting terms and conditions and *receives* (this verb is used twice) *it without objection.*

In any case, the relevant excerpt of the commentary used phrases such as "it is difficult for *the shipper* to obtain consent" (emphasis added). Only once is there a phrase saying "before *the carrier* can invoke the derogation against any person other than the shipper" (emphasis added). So far, seemingly, the person in charge of informing and thus requesting consent is the shipper.

Professor Berlingieri[143] and Diamond QC[144] have also agreed that Article 80(5) of the RR is ambiguous. A point of conflict concerns whether the information must be received from the carrier, or if it is sufficient that it is received by the buyer of the goods from its supplier.[145] It has been suggested that it may be received from any source, so long as it is "prominent".[146]

It is important to know who gives information on derogations and who notifies the shipper or carrier of the third party's acceptance or rejection of the derogation.[147] If it can be ascertained who has these obligations, it will be possible to identify who is to be blamed if the information on derogations on the one hand and consent on the other are communicated wrongly, insufficiently or with delay.[148] Accuracy and commercial certainty are indispensable in international trade.[149]

With regards to whether express consent must be given to the carrier or whether it may be contained in the supply agreement, Diamond states that it is difficult to predict the courts' approach to that, but he is inclined to believe that the provision in Article 80(5)(b) of the RR may tend to indicate that the consent must be given to the carrier. In that respect, Berlingieri considers it important

Law and Arbitration 14(1), pp. 9–32, who asserts that the consent needs to be communicated to the carrier.

140 See Sturley, Fujita and van der Ziel, *The Rotterdam Rules*, para 13.061.

141 Ibid.

142 This is the exact verb used in the problem question, which is italicised as it has to be examined further for its possible repercussions.

143 Francesco Berlingieri, 'Revisiting the Rotterdam Rules', p. 611.

144 Diamond, 'The Rotterdam Rules', pp. 487–488.

145 In this debate, the opinion of Lorenzon about the shipper having to notify of the derogations in Baatz et al, *The Rotterdam Rules: A Practical Annotation* is also relevant.

146 Diamond, 'The Rotterdam Rules', p. 488.

147 Magklasi, 'Volume contracts and third parties: "Red-hand rule" or Red-Herring?', p. 44.

148 Ibid.

149 Ibid.

to draw a distinction between the contract of carriage and the contract of sale, as usually the purpose for which the contract of carriage is entered into by the shipper is related to the sale of the goods to the consignee. For Berlingieri, the contract to look at is the contract of carriage and the issue is whether the carrier may avail himself of the terms of the contract of carriage agreed with the shipper that derogate from the RR. Therefore, it is emphasised that the consent must become a supplementary term of the contract of carriage and must be received by the carrier. Berlingieri does not reject the possibility that the consent reaches the carrier indirectly, but he highlights that ultimately it must be addressed to the carrier.[150]

However, one cannot be absolute in favour of one opinion or the other, as in most cases the particular factual matrix will signify the party which can give the information on derogations and receive the third party's consent. Of course, the consent directly affects the cargo interest and the carrier, but sometimes due to the specific requirements that a transport document has to fulfil under a sale contract (e.g. reasonableness),[151] it is the seller *qua* shipper's responsibility to provide evidence that the volume contract or transport document is approved of and authorised by his buyer/consignee.[152] Another factor to be taken into consideration is whether the dispute about whether derogations are incorporated is between the parties to the first sale contract if there are sales down a string.

The above diversity of opinions could seem of less problematic effect where the volume contract is entered into by the shipper who is at first also the consignee, and then decides to sell the goods afloat. This means that the buyer (new consignee) has to consent to the derogations. In that case, the transport document will already be concluded; therefore, the consent needs to be somehow registered on this document. As it will be discussed below, the problem in that case is that according to Article 80(5)(b) of the RR, evidence of consent only through the transport document is not sufficient to bind a third party to the contract.

It has also been submitted that Article 80(5) of the RR is there to protect parties who become involved in the volume contracts of others, particularly by taking up transport documents issued under such contracts.[153] The lack of guidance in Article 80 has also been criticised, as the past tense "received" is perceived as unnecessarily imprecise as it does not say how and in what form consent should be manifested or evidenced.[154]

Moreover, it has been highlighted that Article 80(5) of the RR is there to protect parties who become involved in the volume contracts of others, particularly by taking up transport documents issued under such contracts.[155] And this is why the identification of the party who sends the acceptance form and

150 Ibid.

151 Discussed below.

152 See for instance section 32(2) of the SOGA.

153 Treitel and Reynolds (eds), *Carver on Bills of Lading* (4th edn), para 10-072.

154 Ibid.

155 Ibid.

thus communicates the information on derogations in the first place has to be clarified.[156]

One could argue that this will be the original party to the contract of carriage, the shipper or carrier. A narrow purposive interpretation could be that since the only permanent party in this volume contract is the carrier, whereas third parties may be several, then it is his responsibility to notify any party, other than the shipper, of the derogations. However, third parties (CIF buyers, FOB documentary shippers, banks etc.) are mostly connected with the shipper (seller or buyer) and not the carrier, by virtue of the underlying sale contract.[157] The shipper has to ensure that his carriage arrangements are approved by his sale contract counterparty, but the central role of the carrier cannot be disregarded. On the other hand, the carrier is the only person who remains the bill of lading holder's counterparty, regardless of whether he is a first buyer or a subsequent third party.

Generally, it has been suggested that the document which lists the derogations has to be a contractual document.[158] This will vary in practice, depending on whether the volume contract had also been concluded or not. If so, then presumably the transport document will be a source of information as long as it is accompanied by additional evidence of communication between shipper and carrier, such as a recap telex. We have come to this conclusion because of the restriction of Article 80(3), which states that a transport document alone is not a volume contract. Although Article 80(5) states "received information" and not "received the volume contract", for reasons of consistent interpretation of subsections of Article 80, the latter extra requirement has to be implied also in Article 80(5). This other written or electronic document can be the email, fax or telex, or ideally a counter-acceptance slip where the original shipper and carrier confirm the agreed derogations.

A balanced solution, where both carrier and shipper are responsible for the accurate communication of derogations, is the use of a countersigned acceptance form in Article 80(5) of the RR.[159] Such a form, as we shall see, can be used for the conclusion of sale contracts. The appropriateness of this solution, in light of case law, will appear in a later section. For now, the focus is on how relevant parties should cooperate for purposes of information on derogations and consent.

The form will first be signed by the shipper and carrier and address sufficient vigilance to the derogations, and will subsequently be delivered to the third party by the shipper, or even the carrier. However, the opportunity for the carrier to be notified of the acceptance of derogations is preserved, if there is a requirement under the carriage and sale contracts to present the second copy of the form containing the third party's approval or rejection to the carrier.[160] In

156 Magklasi, 'Volume contracts and third parties: "Red-hand rule" or Red-Herring?', p. 44.

157 For an illustration of how the international trade context affected the drafting of the RR, see von Ziegler, 'The Rotterdam Rules and the underlying sale contract'.

158 See *Parker v. South Eastern Railway* (1877) 2 CPD 416.

159 Magklasi, 'Volume contracts and third parties: "Red-hand rule" or Red-Herring?', p. 44.

160 Ibid.

case of an FOB contract where the third party is the documentary shipper *qua* seller, the countersigned acceptance form can be delivered back to the carrier before loading commences, so that the carrier is aware of whether the RR liability regime or the derogations he has negotiated with the shipper will apply. Thus, the derogations can accurately originate from both original parties to the volume contract, without undermining the role of the carrier or transposing all of this responsibility merely on the shipper's shoulders.

By adopting this device of contract formation, which is recognised under common law,[161] English contract law seems to suggest the optimal way for manifesting or evidencing the third party's consent, which was another ambiguity of Article 80(5). However, it needs to be emphasised that it is first and foremost the parties that need to unequivocally stipulate this methodological obligation of exchange of slips in their sale and volume contracts.[162] The clear intention of the parties will clarify whose obligation it is to inform, in which detail, way and at what time.[163] However, we believe that a form/slip which lists the derogations and produces binding results only with the signature of the third party is a balanced commercial solution.[164] This is the platform for providing information and seeking consent, as we shall see in a subsequent section.[165]

5.7 Source of information on derogations: additional issues

Article 3 of the RR states that the notices, confirmation, consent, agreement, declaration and other communications referred to in the prerequisites of entering and extending the scope of a volume contract[166] need to be in writing. In practice, the furnishing of this information and secondly of consent will trigger difficulties. Considering that the RR allow the parties to derogate only from some of the provisions of the RR and abide by the others (the so called "cherry-picking"[167] effect of volume contracts), it seems that it is open to the third party to approve of only one or some derogations. Consequently, if the third party gives a general consent instead of a specific one, then presumably all of the derogations will be valid against him. Even if the third party had specified his approval/rejection to one of the derogations orally, this will not be sufficient to protect him as the consent has to be in writing.

Since consent has to be specific, it can also be assumed that a signature of the consignee or the documentary shipper next to a list of derogations is sufficient.[168] Contrast this with a situation where the consignee/documentary shipper

161 See *SARL v. Parkinson* [1953] 2 Lloyd's Rep 487 (CA).This case will be analysed in depth in a subsequent section, when evidence of consent is discussed.

162 Magklasi, 'Volume contracts and third parties: "Red-hand rule" or Red-Herring?', p. 45.

163 Ibid.

164 Ibid.

165 Ibid.

166 Articles 80(2) and 80(5) of the RR.

167 See Asariotis, 'UNCITRAL Draft Convention on Contracts for the International Carriage of Goods Wholly or Partly by Sea: Mandatory rules and freedom of contract', p. 357.

168 Magklasi, 'Volume contracts and third parties: "Red-hand rule" or Red-Herring?', p. 45.

has signed a large pack of documents with the list of derogations squeezed in the bundle.[169] This is an awkward situation, as the party might have signed without specific attention pointed out to the derogations and thus knowledge of them. Whether this possible lack of awareness would be sufficient to displace the principle that a signature in a document is binding remains to be seen.[170] Otherwise, such a signature could correlate just to the confirmation of notification that this is a volume contract which derogates from the RR.

To ensure that the third party has been notified and consented to all derogations, a phrase saying "I hereby confirm that I am aware and abide by the derogations" before the signature would not give rise to the above ambiguity. This is why, in our opinion, lack of reference or consent to derogation(s) should be construed strictly as non-approval, so that the mandatory provisions of the RR apply between the third party and the carrier, regardless of whether a different regime applies between carrier and shipper.

The second issue which needs to be identified concerns the documents suitable for embracing volume contract derogations through which the consent needs to be expressed. One such means could be the transport document or the volume contract itself, which is the classic example used by the analyses on the RR on the matter.[171] This would mean that the transport document has to be checked to see whether it can incorporate derogations.[172]

In theory, this information or source of information on derogations could be an email, a recap telex, a written charterparty etc. Depending on the circumstances, not all of the above contracts however can be deemed to be incorporated from one of the above to a bill of lading. Support for this argument can be demonstrated by the two conflicting cases of *The Heidberg*[173] and *The Epsilon Rosa*.[174] *The Heidberg* shows that terms in oral agreements cannot be validly incorporated and therefore they cannot bind transferees of bills of lading. What was transferred to the consignee consisted only of the terms which appeared on the face and reverse of the bill of lading; collateral oral terms were not transferred. A bill of lading does not incorporate the terms of a charterparty, which, at the date the bill of lading is issued, has not been reduced to writing. This makes commercial sense, as it is difficult for the transferee of the bill of lading to refer to terms which are not ascertainable in a written contract.[175] In *The Epsilon Rosa*, however, the arbitration clause was held incorporated even though it was included in a recap telex, contrary to the holding in *The Heidberg*. Depending on which case is followed by

169 Ibid.

170 Two lower courts in the UK have considered the applicability of the red-hand rule to signed documents. In *Do-Buy 925 Ltd v. National Westminster* [2010] EWHC 2862 (QB), Andrew Popplewell QC, at para 91, stated that "It remains an undecided question whether the Interfoto principle can ever apply to a signed contract." In 2012, in *One World (GB) Ltd v. Elite Mobile Ltd* [2012] EWHC 3706 (QB), Behrens J was prepared to concede *obiter* that the special notice doctrine might sometimes apply even to signed contracts.

171 Sturley, Fujita and van der Ziel, *The Rotterdam Rules*, Illustration 13-13.

172 Diamond, 'The Rotterdam Rules', pp. 488–489.

173 *The Heidberg* [1994] 2 Lloyd's Rep 287.

174 *Welex AG v. Rosa Maritime Ltd* [2003] 2 Lloyd's Law Rep. 509.

175 [1994] 2 Lloyd's Rep 287, p. 310.

the courts, an analogy can be drawn according to which a recap telex/email can be produced to the third party as information on derogations.[176]

It was also mentioned in *The Heidberg*[177] that where wide words of incorporation have the effect of incorporating terms which would not be generally known to the party against whom they are sought to be enforced, then under English law the party who seeks to enforce the term must normally show that the term has been fairly and reasonably brought to the other party's attention.[178]

5.8 Repercussions of the above conclusions for buyers/receivers of the transport documents

First of all, it has been shown that if *The Heidberg* is followed, the recap telexes of volume contracts which have not been otherwise reduced to writing will not suffice for incorporation, or to be more accurate, they will not qualify as sources of information or notification of derogations.[179]

However, some more questions spring forth from the judgment which preclude saying anything conclusive on the matter, at least not yet. Arguably the recap telex (nowadays email) is usually exchanged at the stage of pre-contractual negotiations, whereas the third party becomes part of the volume contract picture after it is concluded and the transport document is transferred to him. However, it is possible to have a scenario where the seller *qua* shipper negotiates the volume contract and the sale contract at the same time. It has to be remembered at this stage that according to the RR, consent should not only be registered on the transport document, which at that stage will not be issued anyway. This is why we have to investigate what other type of written communication can be used as evidence of consent.[180] Additionally, it is not clear in the RR whether the consent of the third party needs to coexist in the volume contract where the carrier's and the shipper's confirmation of derogations will appear. If the answer is negative, then how can the third party be assured that the derogations are finalised and properly communicated to the carrier who is his counterparty to the transport document?

The Heidberg is relevant because the bill of lading was concluded before the charterparty was written down.[181] This should be of concern where volume contracts are negotiated at the same time, for instance when no formal volume contract has been signed at the date of the issuance of the transport document. Our purpose is to draw ideas from the complex concept of incorporation, as reflected in *The Heidberg* and *The Epsilon Rosa*.[182] These two conflicting cases will make parties particularly vigilant in order to know which document truly reflects a volume contract and is capable of making third parties bound by the derogations.[183]

176 Magklasi, 'Volume contracts and third parties: "Red-hand rule" or Red-Herring?', p. 45.

177 *The Heidberg* [1994] 2 Lloyd's Rep 287, p. 313.

178 *Parker v. South Eastern Railway Co* (1877) 2 CPD 416; *Interfoto Picture Library Ltd v. Stiletto Visual Programmes Ltd* [1989] QB 433, cited in *The Heidberg*, at p. 313.

179 Magklasi, 'Volume contracts and third parties: "Red-hand rule" or Red-Herring?', p. 46.

180 Ibid.

181 See also Gaskell, Baatz and Asariotis, *Bills of Lading: Law and Contracts*, para 21.28.

182 Magklasi, 'Volume contracts and third parties: "Red-hand rule" or Red-Herring?', p. 46.

183 Ibid.

Next, a more certain solution is discussed to ensure parties (carrier and traders) are aware of how and what derogations are.

5.9 Evidence of a third party's consent to be bound by the derogations

The RR do not suggest a formal way of registering consent. This means that in the lack of further specification from the RR, general commercial and contract law principles will determine the steps or the alternatives which validate the binding of the third party to some or all of the derogations. Since the fear of all the commentators is that the RR will serve for the effortless legitimisation of carrier's privileges which were not allowed under the RR, i.e. limitation of liability without the obstacle of Article 79 of the RR, the issue of consent deserves special consideration.

We submit that in line with English law, consent could be safely registered and exchanged through delivery of confirmation slips and completion and dispatch of a countersigned acceptance form.[184] In our opinion, this form should contain the signatures of the original parties to the contract of carriage, namely of carrier and shipper.[185] It is stated by Schmitthoff[186] that "where an offer stipulates that acceptance must be by return of an attached form, it being expressly understood that no other form of acceptance will be valid or binding, then unless acceptance is by the prescribed form there will be no contract". This, in our opinion reflects exactly the wording of Article 80(5) of the RR.

This is an acknowledged way of contracting in international sale contracts.[187] The form can be sent in duplicate: one for the buyer's or third party's records; and one to be sent, initially perhaps to the shipper and then to the carrier, to trigger application of Article 80(5). Importantly Schmitthoff[188] submits that the two acceptance forms which can be drafted (one for the seller and one for the buyer) should tally in their terms, and where appropriate contain a "red hand" clause, which confirms our arguments to be analysed later in this chapter.[189] It is our opinion that volume contracts are a representative example of commercial contracts in international trade that have to embrace these views so as to satisfy visibility of derogations and guarantee the third party's awareness.[190]

There is already commercial case law on obtaining the offeror's written agreement to the terms of a commercial contract. In *Compagnie de Commerce et Commission, SARL v. Parkinson Stove Co*,[191] a dispute arose as to whether there

184 Ibid.
185 Ibid.
186 Murray, Holloway and Timson-Hunt (eds), *Schmitthoff's Export Trade: The Law and Practice of International Trade*, para 3-010.
187 Ibid, para 3-011.
188 Ibid.
189 See earlier our submission with regards to why limitation or exclusion of liability derogations need to be conspicuously addressed in a written form to the third party.
190 Magklasi, 'Volume contracts and third parties: "Red-hand rule" or Red-Herring?', p. 46.
191 [1953] 2 Lloyd's Rep 487.

was a binding sale contract concluded on FOB terms. The order form sent by the sellers to the buyer stated the following:

> Acceptance. This order constitutes an offer on the part of the First Party upon the terms and conditions and at the prices stated herein and to constitute a binding contract upon the First Party, said offer must be accepted by execution of the acknowledgment in the form attached by Second Party, it being expressly understood that no other form of acceptance, verbal or written, will be valid or binding upon First Party. There are no agreements or understandings other than those contained in this order.[192]

This explicitly drafted clause is in our opinion the optimal example of drafting a clause to be communicated to a third party, so that he can validly adhere to a volume contract which derogates from the RR.[193] This judgment is useful for considering what happens in case the parties to an international sale contract have shown communication and conduct of acceptance of contract terms.[194] However, it was the buyer's non-compliance with the formality of acceptance which determined, despite the buyer's opposite view, that the contract had not been concluded. That could save uncertainty when the volume contract is unavailable.[195]

5.10 Providing consent to whom? Other alternatives

Another issue which has to be resolved is the identification of the party to send the acceptance form in the first place. One could argue that this will be the original party to the contract of carriage, the shipper and carrier. A narrow interpretation could be that since the only permanent party in this volume contract is the carrier, whereas third parties may be several, then it is his responsibility to notify any party other than the shipper of the derogations. However, it needs to be understood that the RR cover these parties, such as the documentary shipper or consignee, merely because their duties under the underlying sale contract make them

192 Ibid, at 490.

193 Magklasi, 'Volume contracts and third parties: "Red-hand rule" or Red-Herring?', p. 47.

194 However there is case law showing that long negotiations between the parties make it difficult to ascertain whether a contract has been subsequently effectively varied. See *Port Sudan Cotton v. Govindswamy* [1977] 1 Lloyd's Rep 166. Despite an initial agreement on an FOB sale of cotton, a subsequent cable (containing the additional clause for destination India) dispatched by the sellers was held by Donaldson J to constitute the offer. The acceptance of this offer was expected by the sellers to be the merest formality. There was further a cable sent by the sellers on the 14th of June which was unclear. Ultimately it was held that the negotiations never reached a stage where there was a clear offer to be clearly accepted by the other party, therefore it could not be asserted that a contract was concluded. See also *Pagnan v. Granaria BV* [1986] 2 Lloyds Rep. 547; *Pagnan SpA v. Feed Products Ltd* [1987] 2 Lloyd's Rep 601; *Manatee Touring Co v. Ocean Bulk Maritime SA* [1999] 2 All ER (Comm) 306; *Gordon Russell (UK) v. Warwick* [2006] EWCA Civ 1851.

195 However, here we anticipate that even this form may not be sufficient to hold the parties bound by incorporation if the "red hand" rule principle does not apply.

involved in the carriage context too. These parties are mostly entangled with the shipper rather than the carrier by virtue of the underlying sale contract.[196]

With regards to the question of who is responsible for obtaining consent, it is difficult to express a firm answer. Although this is feasible for the shipper, as he has to ensure his carriage arrangements are approved by his sale contract counterparty, the important role of the carrier cannot be disregarded. The carrier is the only person who remains the bill of lading holder's counterparty, regardless of whether it is a shipper or a subsequent third party. A balanced solution, where both carrier and shipper are responsible for the reasonably sufficient communication of derogations, is the application of formation of the contract through a countersigned acceptance form in Article 80(5) of the RR. The form will first be signed by the shipper and the carrier and address sufficient vigilance to the derogations, and will be delivered to the third party by the shipper, or even the carrier. However, the opportunity for the carrier to be notified of the acceptance of derogations is preserved, if the second copy of the form containing the third party's signature is presented to the carrier. In case of an FOB contract where the third party is the documentary shipper *qua* seller, the countersigned acceptance form can be delivered to the carrier before loading commences, so that the carrier is aware of whether the RR liability regime or the derogations he has negotiated with the shipper will apply. Thus, consent of the derogations can be sufficiently communicated to both original parties of the volume contract, without undermining the role of the carrier or transposing all of this responsibility merely on the shipper's shoulders. By adopting this method of acceptance of contractual terms (derogations), which is recognised under common law,[197] English contract law seems to suggest the optimal way for manifesting or evidencing the third party's consent, which was another ambiguity of Article 80(5) of the RR.

An acceptance form to be exchanged in the case where the carrier has signed works better where the transport document has been transferred to another receiver.[198] In this scenario, the initial shipper will no longer have an interest in the goods, and he is being replaced by the on-buyer/holder of the transport document.[199] That way the role of the carrier is preserved, whereas the initial shipper is logically dismissed without enhancing the danger that the third party may receive altered, less or inaccurate notification of the derogations.[200]

Generally, as far as the identification of the type of document which lists the derogations is concerned, it has been suggested that this has to be a contractual document.[201] This will vary in practice, depending on whether at the time of notification to the third party the volume contract had also been concluded or

196 For an illustration of how the international trade context affected the drafting of the RR see von Ziegler, 'The Rotterdam Rules and the underlying sale contract' .

197 See *SARL v. Parkinson* above.

198 Magklasi, 'Volume contracts and third parties: "Red-hand rule" or Red-Herring?', p. 47.

199 Ibid.

200 Ibid.

201 See *Parker v. South Eastern Railway Co* (1877) 2 CPD 416.

not. If yes, then presumably the transport document will be a source of information as long as it is accompanied by additional evidence of communication between shipper and buyer, such as a recap telex. We have come to this conclusion because of the restriction of Article 80(3) of the RR, which states that a transport document alone is not a volume contract. Although Article 80(5) states "received information" and not "received the volume contract", for reasons of consistent interpretation of subsections of Article 80, this consideration also has to be implied in Article 80(5). Ideally other written or electronic document can be the email, fax or telex, or counter-acceptance slip where the original shipper and carrier confirm the agreed derogations.

5.11 Refining issues stemming from the notification duty

When it comes to notification of terms of volume contracts and third parties, the following should be clarified: that there is not an issue of incorporation as such, as the derogations need to be approved formally. However, case law on incorporation of exemption clauses or onerous terms gives an important indication as to how English courts may (or may have to) assess the exchange of information so that the parties give their consent, in particular as to what should be addressed to the third party in order to constitute a sufficient notification of derogations.[202] Although most cases referred to below are ticket cases between business and consumers, whereas shipping and sales of commodities are business to business transactions, the analogy is justified when volume contracts are concluded by unsophisticated traders.[203]

The cases on the "red hand" rule will be of great help so that the way in which the notification of derogations should take place is further clarified; this will ensure that the party that invokes them has pointed them out properly.[204] Of course, this does not render the need for specific consent redundant, but it is in a way the preamble to guarantee that there is proper consideration of the derogations.

There are two levels of requirements that English law imposes on the transferability of the exemption of liability derogation clauses: one is that specific attention has to be drawn to the "conditions" onerous clauses; and the second is a filter of which individual clauses/terms can be incorporated,[205] first to the transport document, as this will be in the hands of the third party, but also to the sale contract, so that the main obligations between seller and buyer are not

202 Magklasi, 'Volume contracts and third parties: "Red-hand rule" or Red-Herring?', p. 47.

203 Ibid.

204 Ibid.

205 On this point, one could argue that Article 80 of the RR itself is the cap which determines that if all the prerequisites are met, then all the permissible articles of the RR would be validly excluded. However, especially in view of Article 80, it is realised that the article enters qualitative obligations; therefore, it will be up to the court to decide whether the contracting parties have taken sufficient steps, so that the prerequisites are satisfied.

unreasonably varied. For the first level, general contract law will apply, as there are no specific shipping cases on the issue. These ones will be dealt with in turn.

The correlations of English common law on the first question will be discussed forthwith. It has to be remembered that at some points the terms "usual" and "reasonable" are used as different standards of clauses, leading to different considerations. In light of *Interfoto*,[206] it has to be examined whether a volume contract where not all reasonable steps have been taken to inform the third party of exemptions, unusual or onerous terms should lead to the assumption that the third party (ignorant of them) has not consented to them, although it may have blindly consented to the volume contract in general.[207] As it can be assumed, there is a notional gap, stemming from the use of different terms which do not necessarily overlap.

So far, identification of who requests and who receives consent to derogations has been sought. The vexing issue of which document other than the transport record has to contain information of derogations has been analysed in light of English law. A suggestion has also been proposed as an identical way of evidencing consent through counter-acceptance slips in possession of carrier, shipper and third party.

We have advised specific stages so that proper notification is secured. What if a bill of lading merely states "The volume contract evidenced in this transport document (bill of lading) derogates from the RR?". The crucial question at this stage is whether the third party can adhere to all of the derogations by a general consent, or whether acceptance of a contract that derogates (volume contract) embraces every derogation that this volume contract contains. It is for these cases that we believe that the "red hand" rule may be a protective mechanism which can be activated for the protection of third parties.

5.12 The "red hand" rule

Although under common law, incorporation of terms can take place in three ways, namely by signature, notice and conduct, the combined reading of Articles 3 and 80 of the RR make only incorporation via notice workable for volume contracts. The terms should have been contained or referred to in a document which was intended to have contractual effect and reasonable steps must be taken to bring the terms to the attention of the other party.[208]

Before embarking on a review of case law, it has been established by cases that in instances of unsigned documents, the general rule is that the party affected by the clause will be bound if the party tendering the document has done what may be considered sufficient to give notice of the clause to persons of the class where he belongs.[209]

206 [1989] QB 433.

207 Magklasi, 'Volume contracts and third parties: "Red-hand rule" or Red-Herring?', p. 47.

208 Ibid.

209 See MG Bridge (ed), *Benjamin's Sale of Goods* (10th edn, Sweet & Maxwell, 2017), para 2-012, HG Beale (ed), *Chitty on Contracts* (32nd edn, Sweet & Maxwell 2015), paras 13-012 to

In *Parker v. South Eastern Railway*,[210] the cloakroom ticket contained no specific warning as to the "conditions" (in their entirety) being addressed to the attention of the passenger, so the issue was whether the customer was bound by the limitation of liability condition,[211] despite the fact that he had never read them. Mellish LJ held that where an action is brought on a written agreement which is signed by the defendant, the agreement is demonstrated by proving his signature, and, in the absence of fraud, it is wholly immaterial that he has not read the agreement and does not know its contents: "The parties may, however, reduce their agreement into writing, so that the writing constitutes the sole evidence of the agreement, without having any signature; but in that case there must be evidence independently of the agreement itself to prove that the defendant has assented to it".[212] The party receiving the ticket is bound by the condition even if unread, if there is reasonably sufficient notice on it pointing that there are conditions written on the document received.[213]

It was also submitted as *obiter* by the judge[214] that bills of lading are different from tickets or cloakroom vouchers, in that even if not read, any businessman who ships the goods and receives this document should expect that this contains the terms of the contract of carriage. If that *obiter dictum* applied also to the derogations of volume contracts, it would seem to establish a burden both on the shipper and the third party to examine the terms of the volume contract (and therefore also the derogations).[215] Accordingly, a noticeable statement that "this is a transport document deviating from the RR" would suffice to make the third party bound by the derogations. The notice which has to be addressed to the party depends on whether the restriction introduced by the condition "is not shown to be usual in that class of contract".[216]

Unlike with *Parker v. South Railway*, in *J Spurling v. Bradshaw*,[217] the court considered the incorporation of clauses not as a whole, but considered incorporation of a condition which was *particularly onerous* independently.

This case established the "red hand" rule: "Some clauses would need to be printed in red-ink with a red hand pointing to it before the notice could be held

13-014, 13-017; *Parker v. South Eastern Railway Co* (1877) 2 CPD 416; *Richardson, Spence & Co v. Rowntree* [1894] AC 217; *Hood v. Anchor Line (Henderson Bros) Ltd* [1918] AC 837; *McCutcheon v. David Macbrayne Ltd* [1964] 1 WLR 125 HL; *Thornton v. Shoelane Parking Ltd* [1971] 2 QB163; *Shepherd Homes Ltd v. Encia Remediation Ltd* [2007] EWHC 70 (TCC) [2007] Build. LR 135.

210 (1877) 2 CPD 416.

211 The judgment just refers to conditions without further qualifying whether they are exemption of, or limitation of liability clauses.

212 (1877) 2 CPD 416, 421.

213 (1877) 2 CPD 416, p. 423. See also Elizabeth Macdonald, 'The duty to give notice of unusual contract terms' (1988) *JBL* 375, p. 379.

214 (1877) 2 CPD 416, 422.

215 Magklasi, 'Volume contracts and third parties: "Red-hand rule" or Red-Herring?', p. 48.

216 (1877) 2 CPD 416, p. 424. This case was considered in the body of judgment *Interfoto v. Stiletto*.

217 [1956] 1 WLR 461.

to be sufficient".[218] Denning LJ held that the more unreasonable a clause is, the greater the notice which must be given of it. This is reminiscent of the requirement as to the prominent statement needed to show that a given contract of carriage is a volume contract in Article 80 of the RR, which is particularly onerous for the third party clauses.

The case is not very enlightening in providing guidance as to which clause may be "unreasonable", because all the judges agreed that the clause had been incorporated.[219] The "red hand" rule was better clarified in *Thornton v. Shoe Lane Parking*,[220] as being applicable to cases not only of onerous terms, but also of unusual ones. *Thornton* went one step further than *Parker* in examining incorporation of particularly onerous exemption conditions establishing a reasonableness test that the notification should embrace so that it is proportionate to the exemption that the condition accommodates. This judgment could be useful for assessing whether derogations incorporated through a bill of lading or other document satisfy the reasonable notification requirement, so that it is ascertained whether the *Thornton* case could impose restrictions on the impact of unreasonable derogations on third parties.

This case talks about unusual terms rather than unreasonable ones, unlike *Spurling*. In *Thornton*, the entire question was about whether the exemption of liability clause was part of the contract[221] and the dicta of both Lord Denning and Megaw LJ are important. Lord Denning clarified the application of the "red hand" rule in that an exclusion clause such as that of the case was "so wide and destructive of rights that the court should not hold any man bound by it unless it is drawn to his attention in the most explicit way".[222]

Megaw LJ used a different approach:

> Where the particular condition relied on involves a sort of restriction that is not usual in that class of contract, a defendant must show that his intention to attach an unusual condition of that particular nature was fairly brought to the notice of the other party. How much is required depends upon the restrictive condition.[223]

Megaw LJ endorsed Lord Dunedin's test in *Hood v. Anchor Line*.[224]

All of the above cases were considered in *Interfoto Picture Library Ltd v. Stiletto Visual Programmes Ltd*.[225] *Thornton* was approved, especially as to the point that

218 Ibid, p. 466. Contrast this with *Hood v. Anchor Line (Henderson Bros) Ltd* [1918] AC 837.
219 See Macdonald, 'The duty to give notice of unusual contract terms', p. 376.
220 [1971] 2 QB 163
221 As Lord Denning highlighted at [1971] 2 QB 163, p. 170.
222 Ibid, p. 170.
223 Ibid, p. 172.
224 *Hood v. Anchor Line (Henderson Bros) Ltd* [1918] AC 837, 846, 847. "Accordingly it is in each case a question of circumstance whether the sort of restriction that is expressed in any writing (which, of course, includes printed matter) is a thing that is usual, and whether, being usual, it has been fairly brought before the notice of the accepting party."
225 [1989] QB 433.

it applied to exemption clauses which would deprive the party on whom it was imposed of their statutory rights.[226] This is remarkably analogous to the potential derogations from the RR, as they are expected to concern exemption of liability provisions favourable to the carrier, rendering the RR's standard inapplicable.[227]

If these cases apply, a mere reference to derogations on the transport document or to a list attached will not be capable of incorporation unless there is specific attention pointed to them and to the extent that courts do not find them unreasonable.[228]

5.13 Preliminary observations

These cases and especially *Interfoto* would impose further difficulties on the fulfilment of the conditions of Article 80(5) of the RR for binding a third party on derogations of which they are not properly invited to be aware of.[229] More concretely, this would mean that the notifying party should not only warn that this is a volume contract, but also designate the derogations one by one.[230] A scenario where the shipper just tenders a bill of lading (with a coversheet followed by annex of the terms of the volume contract) saying "this is a contract which partly or in whole derogates from the RR, as you can see in the document furnished", would not be sufficient to validate the consent given, if there is no proper presentation of the individual derogations or the third party is not directed to them.[231] The situation would be different and the shipper would be released from the need to act further if he furnished a document which clearly states the provisions which derogate from the RR exactly as modified outside the scope of the RR.[232]

It has been submitted that[233] there would be no issue as to the difference between what is reasonable and usual in the context of an established widely known trade practice. The same author comments that a test of whether a clause is usual would embrace research as to what may be "commonly used in the sort of situation or commonly used by those parties".[234] The question triggered thereafter is what would be the decision of the court in a case with the following specifications: a dispute arises under a volume contract[235] where parties are

226 Ibid, p. 438.

227 Magklasi, 'Volume contracts and third parties: "Red-hand rule" or Red-Herring?', p. 49.

228 For the "red hand" rule test in commercial cases see also Melis Ozdel, 'Incorporation of charterparty clauses into Bills of Lading' in Clarke (ed), *Maritime Law Evolving: Thirty Years at Southampton*, pp. 181, pp. 188–190.

229 Magklasi, 'Volume contracts and third parties: "Red-hand rule" or Red-Herring?', p. 49.

230 Ibid.

231 Ibid.

232 Ibid.

233 McDonald, 'The duty to give notice of unusual contract terms', p. 377.

234 Ibid, p. 378.

235 The governing law of the contract is deemed to be English law on purpose, because our objective is to foreshadow the English law perspective on the issue of consent on derogations from the RR. The link of the case with the US is not random either, as this is a jurisdiction familiar with the concept of OLSAs.

trading within the US, or where there is some additional link with the US where OLSAs are according to the draftsmen of the RR widely known. The link with the US may derive from the destination of the voyage under the volume contract of discussion. Is it not possible that the courts take the approach that excluding or limiting liability beyond the requirements of a given international carriage convention such as the RR is a widely known trade practice?

It is probable that if the RR are enacted with the force of law, English courts may consider or accept the example of OLSAs as "known trade practice" in the context of the specific commercial transaction. In the remote future, nothing precludes the possibility that the first volume contracts which derogate from the RR will formulate the point of reference of what is "usual". For the moment, a notification that "this is a volume contract with derogations" might well suffice for the derogation clauses to be binding on the third party/consignee in the US, without the specific aspects of the derogations having to be individually addressed to and accepted by the third party. Of course, it could be counter argued in this case that Article 80(2)(b)(ii) of the RR requires that the volume contract specifies the derogations, but it has to be remembered that this is an alternative requirement, it applies to the original parties of the volume contract, and that Article 80(5) is more vaguely drafted. Moreover, it has to be recalled that it talks about "information that prominently states that the volume contract derogates from this Convention and gave its express consent to be bound by such derogations"; the tenor of "information" on derogation from the RR does not necessarily contain the individual sections, duties and rights that are derogating, whereas the acceptance of the third party has to concern "such derogations".

Therefore there is no clear guidance as to what the information/notification to the third party has to indicate so as to embrace *any* derogation under the RR. To come back to the above scenario, it is possible that the English courts could take the view that if shipment was from and to US ports[236] (or a country or trade where exemptions of liability are usual) and the contract was on the example of OLSAs, then a general notice such as "this is a transport document in pursuance of a volume contract where the RR do not apply" would be sufficient to incur upon the third party even an absolute exemption of liability, always within the constraints of Article 80(3) of the RR. The outcome may be similar in a volume contract which uses a standard contract of affreightment, such as a standard service contract, or in a volume contract which does not incorporate a standard contract of affreightment, where the court uses as assistance that in previous volume contract shipments the same parties had incorporated a standard volume contract. The unpleasant surprise for the third party would be that although in the previous volume contract there was a detailed notification as to the applicable derogations, therefore they were known and perhaps accepted by the third party in total, in the present dispute, an exclusion clause which was not specifically communicated and therefore was not drawn to the attention of the third party

236 The example of the US is used here, because it is the jurisdiction in which service contracts were first regulated.

might be construed by the courts as "commonly used by those parties". On the other hand, in our opinion, this should be expected if the notification clause was "usual derogations as between A and B parties' volume contracts to apply", as it is explicit which dealings between which parties should be of consideration for the given volume contract. Most importantly, the main difference between this variation and the previous notification clause is that the carrier and the third party themselves pinpoint which derogations are "usual", so that the court does not need to go beyond this and therefore avoids taking occasional and sparse volume contracts[237] into consideration. All the above cases also generate ambiguities as to the classification of a derogation term as "usual" or "reasonable" under a contract of carriage.[238] However, for the moment, the issue is the form and content of the notice whereby the derogations will be communicated to a third party. What the courts' judgment will be if there were no previous dealings between the parties is something that remains to be seen, as is the case about volume contract derogations in general.[239]

The author now deals with the much anticipated relation between volume contract derogations and section 32(2) of the SOGA.

5.14 Repercussions of volume contracts: derogations triggering the application of section 32(2) of the SOGA

The SOGA, to which several references have been made so far, is a codification of pre-existing case law and principles.[240] Section 32(2)[241] will be subject to scrutiny, insofar as it may be breached via derogation(s) of a volume contract entered into by a CIF seller. Section 32(2) reads:

> Unless otherwise authorised by the buyer, the seller must make such contract with the carrier on behalf of the buyer as may be reasonable having regard to the nature of the goods and the other circumstances of the case; and if the seller omits to do so, and the goods are lost or damaged in the course of transit, the buyer may decline to treat the delivery as a delivery to himself or may hold the seller responsible in damages.

The question to be deciphered is whether the concept of reasonableness can be breached by the exclusion of certain articles of the RR through a volume

237 For instance, consider a scenario where volume contracts containing three specific derogations have been entered into twice in the past, whereas the remaining ones only exclude one provision of the RR.

238 If derogating from the RR becomes the norm, since it is more appealing to traders and carriers to contract on absolute freedom of contract, the conclusions discussed now may be outweighed, as what is today unusual, could potentially become the usual form of carriage contracting.

239 Further repercussions of derogations which are unreasonable or unusual in a volume contract issued in execution of a sale contract, are discussed below.

240 Bennion, *Statutory Interpretation* (4th edn, Butterworths London 2002) at [214].

241 For an in-depth analysis of the section see Lorenzon, *Sassoon on CIF and FOB Contracts*, para 2-028 onwards.

contract which derogates from the RR. The starting point being this section, it has been proven that the meaning of reasonable contract of carriage is threefold:[242] the contract of carriage tendered must be on usual terms;[243] it must give proper rights against the carrier;[244] and, lastly, it must grant sufficient protection to the goods while in transit. The most important aspects of unreasonableness in relation to the volume contract exceptions are the last two aspects of reasonableness. In *Hansson v. Hamel & Horley*,[245] it was held that the contract of carriage in question, in which the goods were transhipped, had to cover the buyer in documents from shipment to destination.[246] In the *Holland Colombo Trading Society Ltd v. Segu Mohammed Khaja Alawadeen and Others*,[247] it was held that the buyer is entitled to a document which provides him with "continuous documentary cover",[248] and that this was not fulfilled if in the bill of lading the shipowner disclaimed all liability in respect of the goods in the event and as from the time of transhipment.[249]

However, the exact content of "continuous documentary cover", and thus the rights that the document has to confer to the buyer, cannot be predicted or defined without reference to possible facts. Moreover, in the case *Buckman v. Levi*,[250] Lord Eldborough held that the buyer must be put in a position to return to the carrier for his indemnity.[251] Such clauses limiting liability of the carrier and the rights of the endorsees/assignees of the bill of lading to be indemnified are the ones to be abandoned via a volume contract. Therefore cases concerning the reasonable contract of carriage (before and after section 32(2) of the SOGA) will become more and more of reference. In our opinion, the important aspect to be covered is that the third party/consignee/bill of lading holder has to have a proper defendant, the carrier, for claims under the transport document.[252]

It has been suggested[253] that although the section does not cast upon the seller the duty to ensure the success of litigation against the carrier, the contract of carriage and the transport document tendered must not be actually depriving

242 See Lorenzon, 'When is a CIF seller's carriage contract unreasonable? Section 32(2) of the Sale of Goods Act 1979', p. 244.

243 Ibid, p. 244 fn 20 therein. *Ceval Alimentos SA v. Agrimpex Trading Co Ltd (The Northern Progress)* [1996] 2 Lloyd's Rep 319 per Rix J at 328; *Tsakiroglou & Co v. Noblee Thorl GmbH* [1962] AC 93 PER Lord Radcliffe at pp. 121–22, and Lord Guest at pp. 132–333; *Finska Cellulosaforeningen (Finnish Cellulose Union) v. Westfield Paper Co Ltd* (1940) 68 Ll Rep 75.

244 Bridge (ed), *Benjamin's Sale of Goods*, paras 19-025 to 19-026.

245 [1922] 2 AC 36.

246 Bridge (ed), *Benjamin's Sale of Goods*, para 19-027.

247 [1954] 2 Lloyd's Rep 45.

248 Bridge (ed), *Benjamin's Sale of Goods*, para 19-027.

249 Ibid.

250 (1813) 3 Camp 414.

251 Ibid, 415.

252 This protection is not granted when, for instance, the goods are shipped at the owner's risk, as was the case in *Thomas Young & Sons Ltd v. Hobson & Partners* (1949) 65 TLR 365.

253 See Lorenzon, 'When is a CIF seller's carriage contract unreasonable? Section 32(2) of the Sale of Goods Act 1979', p. 246.

the buyer of substantive legal rights against the carrier. The above deterrent is mirroring exactly what Article 80 of the RR does: "a volume contract to which this Convention applies may provide for greater *or lesser rights, obligations and liabilities than those imposed by this Convention*" (emphasis added). This draws support from the case law supporting the third aspect of reasonableness, namely that the contract tendered must grant sufficient protection to the goods while in transit.

A particular obligation of the carrier which may be contracted out is the cargoworthiness duty in Article 14(c) of the RR:

> Make and keep the holds and all other parts of the ship in which the goods are carried, and any containers supplied by the carrier in or upon which the goods are carried, fit and safe for their reception, carriage and preservation [during and at the beginning of the voyage].

One of the criticisms to be advocated with regards to volume contracts, is that since the third party is in a position to reject the derogations, he is having the chance to contract on normal RR terms and thus to have recourse against the carrier. However, since the exclusions of liability may be so exquisitely drafted as to pass unnoticed or simply be summarised and not properly addressed, and since the available market opportunities may shrink for other normal terms, the possibility of rejection may be forfeited.[254] Therefore, a third party/buyer/consignee may accept without realising how important the rights that he has surrendered against the carrier are. Or, he may accept because he may have no choice, but to tolerate these agreements.

That aside, the practice of volume contracts, if the RR are enacted with the force of law, could trigger a reform of the UCP 600, as we shall discuss forthwith.

5.15 Repercussions of volume contracts with derogations on sales involving letters of credit

Letters of credit represent the foremost method of payment of international commercial sales. Volume contracts with derogations from the RR will seemingly introduce a new category of documents and ignite risks which have to be accommodated through the UCP 600. The transport document issued under a volume contract will perhaps convey the derogations, at least by numeric reference to the sections displaced by agreement. The confirming bank before which the documents will be presented for payment by the seller will raise grounds for rejection, for the first time, if the buyer is not already notified of the derogations. Rejection will be conditional upon extra requirements inserted in the letter of credit so that the documents' checker is aware of what constitutes a

254 It has to be understood that the prominent statement concerns that this is a volume contract which derogates from the RR and not the specific content of the individual derogations, according to Articles 80(2)(a) and 80(5)(a).

non-compliant presentation as far as volume transport documents and the UCP 600 are concerned. Such an extra requirement would be to get informed of the articles of the RR whose contractual exclusion is undesirable by the buyer.

This step however has to fall under the scope of the UCP 600 and therefore may be refrained by some of its articles. According to Article 4(a) of the UCP 600, a credit by its nature is a separate transaction from the sale or other contract on which it may be based. In addition, according to Article 14(a), a confirming bank must examine a presentation to determine, on the basis of the documents alone, whether or not the documents appear on their face to constitute a complying presentation. This means that the bank's clerk will only check the front page of the transport document. Therefore, if the derogations are listed on the back of the bill of lading, where the conditions of carriage are usually clustered, the checker is dismissed from the possibility to check and assess them. According to Article 80(2) of the RR, there shall be a prominent statement of the derogations on the transport document.[255]

Two suggestions are noteworthy. It has already been proposed that additional documents may be required under the letter of credit to provide conclusive and straightforward evidence of unacceptable derogations.[256] The same author has recommended that a statement made by the carrier on the face of the transport document or in other written form that no derogation from the RR has been agreed, could sufficiently protect the buyer.[257] Extra insurance cover for the risk discharged might be necessary, even if this sounds quite exceptional.[258] In his view, insurance for the liability stemming from the exclusion of the RR might therefore be an additional documentary requirement of the credit.[259] Nevertheless, a bank may still have no interest in receiving a transport document with derogations.

Whether the transport document is made to the order of the bank or to the order of the buyer/receiver of the goods may or may not have any implication here. A waiver of the derogations/discrepancies is harmless for the bank if the bill of lading is to the order of the buyer. If the bill of lading however is consigned to the bank as security, the letter of credit will have to be complied with and seemingly the confirming bank may or may not exercise its discretion to approach the issuing bank for a waiver (should the buyer be willing to accept the derogations). In the latter case, it is in the bank's interest to reject tenders confirming the existence of derogations, because its position as a claimant against the carrier will be weak.

Evidently, the volume contract documentation in the hands of a buyer on the one hand and under a letter of credit on the other have substantial differences

255 Article 80(2)(a).

256 Bergami, 'The Rotterdam Rules and bills of lading: Challenges for letter of credit transactions', p. 18.

257 Ibid.

258 Ibid.

259 Ibid.

because of the separation of the letter of credit from the underlying transactions and the possibility of acceptance by the buyer of the derogations.[260] Generally, in our view, acceptance or rejection of the derogations makes the purchase of the particular cargo entirely different from purchase of goods under a contract where the carrier has undertaken extra liabilities. Therefore the carrier will prefer to conduct voyages where he knows that the consignee has accepted the derogations, so that he can predict his litigation position in a certain way. The former may use as a "threat" that he will not discharge or delay discharge to a consignee who rejected derogations, simply because he wants to avoid accruing claims which will worsen his position, if the RR applied. It has been supported that to prevent this, the seller *qua* shipper will not want to run the risk of his goods being undelivered to a consignee who has rejected derogations, and he will therefore buy additional cargo or liability insurance for these goods.[261]

5.16 Conclusion

Ostensibly the concept of contracting out of the mandatory scope of the RR is not *ipso facto* wrong or dangerous when trade practice has shown evidence of the parties standing on an equal foot. Of course, it is an innovative concept of the RR, which however had to be drafted in a way that attributes this freedom to the parties and circumstances that would justify this choice. With major shipping associations having drafted standard service/volume contracts (e.g. SERVICECON),[262] it is indispensable that any ambiguities deriving from the (de)regulation of volume contracts are addressed before it is too late.

The primary observation one would make on the freedom framework that the RR allow to volume contracts, is the lack of specification that they should only apply between parties of equal bargaining power. The *chapeau* of Article 80 recites "validity of contractual terms" and not "validity of contractual terms between parties of equal bargaining power", confirming that the safeguard contemplated in the delegations on the RR has not been reflected in the text.

This is where every possible uncertainty towards volume contracts emanates from. With the rationale of freedom of contract, as contemplated in the deliberations missing from the Convention, nothing precludes the "extension" of the freedom of contract triggered by the definition of volume contracts, to more contracts of carriage, as easily, even the majority of carriage contracts could fall under the scope of the RR if a transport document is issued. Therefore, we embarked on the first holistic and thorough analysis to investigate these concerns, but also proceeded to solutions.

260 Or intention to waive them due to the position of the market.

261 This, in the opinion of Bergami, 'The Rotterdam Rules and bills of lading: Challenges for letter of credit transactions', is a significant security for banks that are consignees under the bill of lading.

262 BIMCO is undertaking work to launch its Standard Service Agreement for the liner sector, under the suggested name SERVICECON, see www.bimco.org/en/chartering/documentary_projects/new_contracts.aspx.

If abuse of the derogations from the RR is possible for the original parties to volume contracts, this prepares us for the vulnerability that lurks for third parties, who are outside the negotiation context. A third party/buyer waiting for his goods overseas will have to check not only the transport document, but also the volume contract information indicating the derogations. This is an even weightier issue, if one considers that the RR apply irrespective of whether a transport document is issued.[263]

Under the RR, there is no obligation that the information has to be furnished in writing, but it can be argued that this should be the proper form, as the consent to derogations also has to be provided in a written text.

Under English law, the two conflicting cases of *The Heidberg* and *The Epsilon Rosa* were used as examples of cases, which, by analogy, could show how derogations of a volume carriage contract which has not been reduced in writing may be of relevance in case a (transport) document is issued under such a volume contract. Secondly, questions as to what may constitute information on derogations and how prominent these derogations should be in order to be considered as properly communicated to a third party have been discussed.[264]

Identification of the party to the carriage contract in charge of communicating the derogations and drawing consent was another vexing issue. We have theorised that *the form* of the case *SARL v. Parkinson* can be utilised to suggest that a volume contract has to be followed by a slip listing the derogations by substance and section, signed by shipper and carrier initially, and then transferred with responsibility of the controlling party, carrier or shipper (depending on the view followed) to any subsequent third party, with a record of this acceptance still with the carrier.

Moreover, the reference to English judgments, such as *J Spurling v. Bradshaw*, has shown that English law very much supports the position that onerous or unreasonable terms and conditions have to be addressed in a particularly noticeable way, and in writing. Exclusions of the carrier's liability could fall under this description of terms, but Article 80(5) of the RR fails to explicitly introduce a similar comprehensive set of requirements to ensure acceptance of derogations by the third party.

Essentially, no one can guarantee that a volume contract which derogates from the RR cannot ultimately be rejected by a third party/buyer as contravening section 32(2) of the SOGA, which dictates that the seller prepares a carriage contract which affords protecting rights to the buyer vis-à-vis the carrier.

The occurrence of the fears illustrated in this chapter would be diminished if the safeguards discussed are either imposed by courts when such disputes arise, or, at least, if an overseeing international authority, like the FMC in terms of service contracts in the US,[265] was established to ensure whether volume contracts

263 Article 35 of the RR.

264 Magklasi, 'Volume contracts and third parties: "Red-hand rule" or Red-Herring?', pp. 39–50.

265 Asariotis, 'Reflections on the Rotterdam Rules', pp. 154–155, highlighting the stricter regulation of service contracts in the USA.

are actually individually and independently negotiated and agreed upon. Nevertheless, one should not underestimate the power of careful and thorough contract drafting; therefore, the eradication of the undesirable contingencies discussed could ideally be promoted by commercial men themselves. It is in the interest of legal certainty that the provisions of the RR on volume contracts do not work as mechanisms for exercising commercial pressure to less sophisticated parties, thus destabilising instead of reinforcing modern overseas trade.[266]

Overall, in order to preserve the legal and also commercial viability of derogating from the RR without unpleasant surprises, transparency and noticeability of information on derogations will become of immense value as far as third parties to volume contracts are concerned.[267]

266 Diamond, 'The Rotterdam Rules' stated that Article 80 "is a set-back to the cause of standardisation of carriage terms".

267 Magklasi, 'Volume contracts and third parties: "Red-hand rule" or Red-Herring?', p. 50.

6 The way forward

Reconciling the Rotterdam Rules with international trade law

6.1 Introduction

We have now concluded the topics which best illustrate the challenges that await international trade law, if the RR apply.

So far, our aim has been to critically consider the controversial issues surrounding the application of the RR, assessing them from the trade law perspective, and to ultimately propose possible alternatives, by revisiting self-regulatory terms,[1] and suggesting additional contractual drafting provisions or legislative reforms.[2]

This is the chapter that will show how the individual chapters interrelate in terms of concepts and principles. Carriage of goods laws, of which the RR will form part once the minimum ratifications are collected, and international trade laws interrelate in terms of concepts and principles. There is a different priority of principles behind trade, English law and self-regulatory terms on the one hand, and in the harmonising conventions, such as the RR, on the other. This will be explained where appropriate and be shown through cross-reference among the chapters. A certain scenario of string sales has often been devised to visualise the trade "knock-on" effect caused by the application of the RR to a carriage contract. This contract scenario will be used as a common platform to evaluate the complexities that traders will encounter, and as an illustration of our suggestions.

In this chapter, we conclude that the shortcomings of the application of the RR in international trade derive from the uneven interfaces of the following principles: freedom of contract; harmonisation, as standardisation of terms on the one hand, and codification on the other; and trade facilitation. Freedom of contract is at stake as a fundamental characteristic of English law[3] and EU law.[4]

Harmonisation of laws has been the big goal justifying the rule-setting work in the area of international commerce. CMI, UNCITRAL and the International Institute for the Unification of Private Law (UNIDROIT) are international

1 Such as Incoterms® and the UCP 600.

2 Namely reforms of the COGSA 1992, COGSA 1971, the SOGA, Factors Act 1889.

3 HG Beale (ed), *Chitty on Contracts* (32nd edn), Vol I, General Principles, paras 1-026 to 1-027.

4 Ibid, 1-028 to 1-029.

organisations which have undertaken the codification of rules in this field, through the drafting of international conventions. There are also rules originating from business self-regulation, such as those by the ICC, GAFTA and FOSFA. Trade facilitation is another principle at stake, as it has specifically underpinned the formation of the RR and is a common objective of all the above organisations. Trade facilitation essentially permeates any legislative procedure and uniformity effort, as it is of the essence that the rules produced are clear, simple, consistent and, above all, commercially operative. These four principles form the ideals of international sales regulation, but one has to look beneath the problems of modern trade to see that its context is an amalgam of all of the above, and the implementation of all these principles has its obstacles. These obstacles will be analysed in the following paragraphs to give the *raison d'être* of the possible repercussions that the RR cause to international trade law. Understanding which principle is sacrificed with the effect of creating a trade law problem, will justify our solutions.

A diligent study will reveal the following underpinnings of modern international trade law: first there is a plethora of sources of obligations in an international sale contract. Because most contracts are governed by English law, one will find that the classic components of English commercial and contract law are applicable, and often, not in line with the Rotterdam Rules. Among them one can find international conventions on carriage of goods, and in this book's context, this Convention is the RR. This means that freedom of contract is intertwined with mandatory national/international legislation, as seen also from the RR case scenarios. When examining an international sale contract more in particular, one will also observe that parties often incorporate terms of self-regulation drafted by international formulating agencies, such as Incoterms® of the ICC, and standard/model contracts of big trading associations like GAFTA and FOSFA. While international conventions are negotiated by governmental representations, model contracts and standard terms are drafted by recognised professional, and thus, business organisations. This automatically connotes that in rules of trade, harmonisation is achieved by states on the one hand and by professional organisations on the other, which respectively have a different approach in drafting their texts and different objectives to achieve.

Private rule-setting organisations/committees on the one hand have a contractual approach. They are mostly interested in narrowing down and recognising the main practices and usages in a certain area of trade. The delegations participating in international harmonising conventions, such as the RR, on the other hand, aim at producing more updated and doctrinally optimal regulations. Schmitthoff has lucidly concluded that self-regulatory schemes pursue a "consolidating method", whereas international unification conventions are underpinned by a "codifying method". This means that conventions come to implement the trait of fairness in the texts produced. This is obvious in Article 9.2 of the CISG, which makes the binding effect of a trade usage dependent upon the true consent of the contracting parties. Next to the element of fairness, one can see the importance of having a true and broad participation of delegations from various backgrounds, which, as remarked by the circles of business private rule-setting committees themselves, has to become wider in order to ensure the participation of developing countries.

Therefore, it seems that standard texts have an indirect factor in the harmonisation of international trade laws, being contractual-oriented, from users for users on the other hand, international conventions come specifically to unify and harmonise international trade law, being open to different nations and preserving important doctrines, such as that of fairness. A main perspective from which we have been examining the impact of the RR on international trade law, however, is that of efficacy of performance of a sale contract by the trade protagonists through problems in the operation a carriage contract which is governed by the RR and English law, as shown by the title of this book.[5] It is therefore important to have a set of rules which is specific and unambiguous, as with most self-regulatory terms. At the same time, the RR are laudably a more universal and updated international convention. However, this does not mean that their text is pellucid and unambiguous all the way through.[6]

The repercussions identified and the scenarios shown are there to illustrate that, at times, the RR may be more universal or mindful of customs and practices in their scope, but they fail to work effectively in international trade, if the contracts of sale and carriage are not sufficiently comprehensive. The suggestions that we have advocated have come from a proper identification of the problems and a hierarchy between the principles at stake. These principles may be: business efficacy, legal certainty, fairness, flexibility or freedom of contract. Although seemingly the above principles coincide, this is not the case, as the RR may, in certain articles, highlight one of these principles, while unintentionally discrediting the others. Our suggestions are offered in order to prevent international trade repercussions of any kind, when the above principles are in danger. That way, the RR can have a positive effect on international trade law.

Next, we focus more on the most intense conflict of concepts that pervades the trade law repercussions illustrated in this book. This is the contrast between freedom of contract underpinning international trade law, and the spirit of harmonisation and codification that characterises the RR. The initial four principles are still relevant, but as we will show, they are contained in different proportions in trade on the one hand and the RR on the other, which corroborates why the RR occasionally create ambiguities that can undermine the compliant performance of a sale contract instead of facilitating it. In the next section, we shed some more light on the evolution of the principle of freedom of contract under English law and in maritime trade law in particular.

6.2 Freedom of contract versus codification: the eternal battle

Freedom of contract is a fundamental principle of English contract law. It can be traced back to the 19th century, deriving from the "will theory of contract" and the "laissez-faire" approach underpinning liberalism.[7] In modern times, the

5 The book is studying the *impact* of the RR.

6 As seen with Articles 9, 35 and 80 of the RR.

7 Beale, *Chitty on Contracts* (32nd edn), para 1-028. See also Dicey, *Law and Opinion in England* (2nd edn, 1914) pp. 150–158; *Printing & Numerical Registering Co v. Sampson* (1875) LR 19 Eq. 462 at [465], per Jessel MR; *Manchester, Sheffield and Lincolnshire Ry v. Brown* (1883) 8 App. Cas. 703 at [716]–[720], per Lord Bramwell; *Salt v. Marquis of Northampton* [1892] AC 1 at

principle is still strongly upheld.[8] In *Photo Production Ltd v. Securicor Transport Ltd*,[9] Lord Diplock stated that "A basic principle of the common law of contract [...] is that parties to a contract are free to determine for themselves what primary obligations they will accept."[10] The importance of freedom of contract is particularly emphasised in the commercial realm through English case law, namely *The Starsin*[11] and *The Achilleas*.[12]

The importance of freedom of contract is also administered by the ECJ.[13] This is lucidly apparent in the following statement of AG Kokott:

> Contractual freedom is one of the general principles of Community law. It stems from the freedom to act for persons. It is inseparably linked to the freedom to conduct a business [protected by article 16 of the EU Charter of Fundamental Rights]. In a Community which must observe the principle of an open market economy with free competition, contractual freedom must be guaranteed.[14]

Moreover, freedom of contract has been considered sacrosanct for the development of European contract law[15] and has been referred to as a "general principle" in the Proposal for a Regulation on a Common European Sales Law.[16]

Freedom of contract has gone through various stages in the specific context of maritime law. In the 1800s, there was uncontrollable use of exclusion clauses in bills of lading. This gave rise to the Harter Act and then to the Hague Rules. Since carriage conventions have come to preserve a standard of allocation of risks associated with carriage, they contain an inherent element of compromise. This is an international compromise, which pervades not only the Hague Rules but also all of its successors. Until the RR, when it came to maritime liability, because of the successors of the Hague Rules, freedom of contract was limited. On the other

[18]–[19], per Lord Bramwell. For a considerable analysis see also Patrick Atiyah, *The Rise and Fall of Freedom of Contract* (Clarendon Press 1979), pp. 214–217; also FH Buckley (ed), *The Fall and Rise of Freedom of Contract* (Duke University Press 1979).

8 Beale, *Chitty on Contracts* (32nd edn), para 1-029.

9 [1980] AC 827.

10 Ibid, at 848.

11 *Homburg Houtimport BV v. Agrosin Private Ltd (The Starsin)* [2003] UKHL 12, [2003] WLR 711 at [57].

12 *Transfield Shipping Inc v. Mercator Shipping Inc (The Achilleas)* [2008] UKHL 48 at [12], [2009] 1 AC 61 at [12].

13 Beale, *Chitty on Contracts* (32nd edn), para 1-028 citing C-240/97 *Spain v. European Commission* [1999] ECR I-6571 at [99], on the common agricultural policy; C-277/05 *Société Thermale d'Eugenie-les-Bains v. Ministere de l'Economie, des Finances et de l'Industrie* [2007] ECR I-6415 at [21], [24], [28] and [29] (on VAT).

14 C-441/07 *European Commission v. Alrosa Co Ltd* [2010] 5 CMLR 11 at AG para 225.

15 EU Commission, *First Annual Progress Report on European Contract Law and the Acquis Review* COM (2005) 456 final, para 2.6.3, as cited in Beale, *Chitty on Contracts* (32nd edn), para 1-028.

16 Proposal for a Regulation of the European Parliament and of the Council on a Common European Sales Law Com (2011) 635 final, Annex I, article 1 CESL, cited in Beale, *Chitty on Contracts* (32nd edn), para 1.028.

hand, trade risks and obligations are traditionally subject to contract. This freedom of contract is subject to limitations, such as public policy and other mandatory rules. The RR, also put a limit to the freedom of contract, since they regulate rights and obligations under the contract of carriage, only with the exception of volume contracts. However, they also manipulate the concept of contractual freedom by allowing it under certain circumstances when it comes to volume contracts. In that respect, we will see that trade problems arise, if freedom of contract is granted to parties with uneven bargaining power; thus the risk of traders being subject to undesirable contracts becomes greater. Secondly, under the RR, the contractual freedom allowed in the context of volume contracts with derogations may undermine party autonomy and the performance of the respective sale contracts. A volume contract that derogates from the RR could also sometimes trigger the breach of section 32(2) of the SOGA. Enhancement of contractual freedom by the RR in areas where there is a gap in the bargaining power between the parties, arguably, conflicts with the other important principles of harmonisation and legal certainty.

Our point is that, generally freedom of contract, which characterises international trade law, is often confined under the RR, as the latter convey a tendency of consolidation; this consolidation can in turn refrain the contractual freedom on which string sales rely. Quite conflictingly, when it comes to volume contracts, freedom of contract is enshrined through the respective provisions of the RR with such ambiguity, that it may surprisingly trap traders into undesirable derogations.

Next comes the analysis of the factual underpinnings of international trade law on the one hand, and of the RR on the other.

6.3 In defence of the link between carriage of goods law and international trade law

> The transport regime significantly affects the risks and the contract practices of the exporters and importers of goods and the banks financing such transactions.[17]

This statement in the foreword of one of the major commentaries on the RR, proves that the original scope of the study presented in this book, has been worthwhile. Concerns that commercial parties will be affected by the RR have been voiced since the launch of the Convention, through articles, papers and positions of important trading associations and UNCTAD.[18] The RR's success in bringing the desirable uniformity is ambiguous, which means that there is leeway

17 Jernej Sekolec, 'Foreword', in von Ziegler, Schelin and Zunarelli (eds), *The Rotterdam Rules 2008*.

18 Review of Maritime Transport 2009, p. 130 "costly litigation may be required before a desirable degree of legal certainty may be achieved [...] it may also be of concern to commercial parties whose rights and liabilities may in future be regulated by the Rotterdam Rules". UNCTAD has participated as an an observer and has, over the years, prepared a number of documents to provide technical legal analysis of the draft text for consideration by the Working Group; See also (UNCTAD/SDTE/TLB/4) and (UNCTAD/SDTE/TLB/2004/2).

for complexities. The aim of the book has been to unearth these complexities and offer knowledge on how to address them in the international trade law realm.

We have provided an overview of the characteristic principles underpinning international trade law on the one hand and the RR on the other with a focus on international sale contracts concluded on shipment terms.[19] Overseas sales on shipment terms attribute particular significance to documentary performance.[20] Accordingly, among the leading underpinnings of international trade, one would cluster the high importance of documents. The foremost documents are *transport documents*: the RR define them as documents issued by the carrier under a contract of carriage that evidence the receipt of goods under a contract of carriage, and evidence or contain a contract of carriage.[21] This immediately signifies that, to the extent that the RR recognise these documents, providing definition and divisions of form, negotiability and entitlement to them, they are affecting a core concept of international trade law.

The particular significance of transport documents in terms of performance of a sale contract empowers another characteristic of international sale contracts. This is the characteristic of string sales, which separates export trade from domestic commerce. It is frequent in the sale of commodities to see more than one buyer while only the first seller will be responsible for arranging shipment of the goods. All buyers, and especially the intermediate ones that do not actually see the cargo when buying and selling, are making their decisions on the basis of documents. Therefore, there is a particular interest for a document of title when sales down a string are involved.[22] Payment in string sales usually takes place via a letter of credit. Therefore compliance of the RR with the UCP 600 justifiably had to be assessed too.

At the same time, because the RR is a carriage (wholly or partly) by sea convention, they accord the consignor and shipper on the one hand, and (more indirectly) the receiver of the goods on the other, with rights and liabilities. These parties, from the international trade law viewpoint, are the seller and buyer, regardless of whether the RR attribute different names to these parties, as prescribed by their scope and terminology.

Goods, transport documents, the contract for their transport and the parties involved in the sea transit constitute the context and the area that the RR regulate. However, the foregoing aspects are not of least concern for international trade. In fact, they altogether make up the frame of reference of international trade. Quite justifiably, every book dedicated to carriage law analyses international

19 Bridge, *The International Sale of Goods*, para 10.63.

20 Ibid, p. 58; Takahashi, 'Right to terminate (avoid) international sales of commodities', p. 126. See also Odeke, 'The nature of a CIF contract – Is it a sale of documents or a sale of goods?'.

21 Article 1(14) of the RR.

22 Additionally, even if only one sale contract has been initially concluded, but the buyer considers re-selling before the goods arrive, a certain degree of flexibility and rights of negotiation with the carrier should be given both to the holder and consignee. Moreover, sales down a string usually show preference for payment via letters of credit.

trade law aspects, and, equally, every book on international trade law explains the fundamentals of carriage, especially by sea.

Thus, international trade and carriage is "a couple", perhaps "not married", as their individual evolution or deterioration is influenced by the different dynamics of each other. The General Assembly has confirmed the link between the regulation of carriage and international trade, by saying that the hope is that the RR will reduce or remove legal obstacles to the flow of international trade, and consequently will enhance the progressive harmonisation and unification of international trade law.[23]

The choice of questions to be addressed, and thus, the sequence of the individual chapters has been designated by the identification of aspects of the RR that have a trade law significance. The common purpose of the questions addressed and researched in this book has been to evaluate whether the new provisions of the RR in terms of documents, parties, etc. do promote trade and eliminate legal obstacles. Where possible, this has been shown by comparing these provisions with the predecessors of the RR. Where the said provisions of the RR are brand new, we have tried to visualise their potential impact on international trade law through case scenarios.

6.4 An overview of the issues discussed

A sale contract concluded on shipment terms is a multitier agreement engaging several sources of terms and legislation. One will usually observe the incorporation of standard terms[24] launched by the ICC, such as Incoterms®[25] and the UCP 600, and English law being chosen as the applicable law. This will automatically trigger the application of national statutes such as the SOGA, COGSA 1992 and COGSA 1971 to the sale and carriage contracts respectively. It is the national statutes which constitute the threshold for embedding international carriage conventions. To date, the UK has enacted the HVR. If the RR gain the necessary number of ratifications and the UK also ratifies them, the RR will take the force of law; this will happen respectively with other states that ratify them.[26] This is further evidence of the interconnection of carriage and trade laws: the RR will not only be relevant to the contract for the carriage of goods to which they will apply. As we have seen, they could also affect the performance of the obligations arising under the contract of sale of those goods.

Another objective of this book has been to present the novelties of the RR, and especially, their classification of the trade entities and divisions of documents.

23 See the resolution adopted by the General Assembly 63/122. United Nations Convention on Contracts for the International Carriage of Goods Wholly or Partly by Sea, at www.uncitral.org/pdf/english/texts/transport/rotterdam_rules/09-85608_Ebook.pdf.

24 For the contribution of ICC voluntary texts in harmonisation of international commercial law see Alejandro Garro, 'Rule setting by private organisations, standardisation and the harmonisation of international sales law' in Fletcher et al (eds), *Foundations and Perspectives of International Trade Law*, paras 22.015 to 22.022.

25 Bridge, *The International Sale of Goods*, para 10.62. Incoterms® are frequently incorporated in the bulk oil trade.

26 Article 89(1) of the RR.

Subsequently, the purpose has been to illustrate who can take a transport document depending on the type of sale contract entered into (CIF or FOB) and, if so, what type.

Next, to offer the complete picture, we will illustrate the trade law complexities posed by the RR through a sale scenario, which at specific points may be varied: the seller (S) and buyer (B) are located in different countries and enter into a sale contract. S asks B to tender the usual transport documents. The goods are resold by B to F and by F to Z, either before or after shipment of the goods. The first sale contract may be on FOB or CIF terms, but the remaining ones will be on CIF terms.

6.4.1 FOB sellers not in possession of a transport document

The documentary shipper has been introduced in the RR to give more legal status to the FOB seller in terms of his legal relationship to the carrier until the shipment of the goods.

The RR are mindful of the difficulties that the FOB seller has in obtaining the transport document under FOB contracts, where the buyer organises the contract of carriage.[27] They therefore devised the entity of the documentary shipper,[28] mainly in order to bring the FOB seller in the nexus of entities where the RR apply. However, in getting a transport document or record that contains and evidences a contract of carriage, the documentary shipper *qua* seller has to ensure that the shipper/FOB buyer consents that he obtains the document from the carrier.[29]

In the case scenario, it is assumed that S, the FOB seller, ships the goods in good order and condition, but is not the documentary shipper. The negotiable transport document is directly issued to the buyer/shipper, B, who fails to pay the seller, S, for the goods.[30]

Three possibilities had to be investigated, as suggested by Zwitser:[31] firstly, whether S can claim the goods from the carrier; secondly, whether or not he can ask for the transport document so that he exercises control over the goods until payment is obtained; and lastly, whether he can at least instruct the carrier not to deliver the goods to B until payment is received.[32]

If the transport document names the seller as documentary shipper, then the seller is perfectly entitled to request that it is issued to him, meaning that he has the control and title to the goods as a protection and as an offset until he receives payment. However, as there is no obligation for the seller to be named as the documentary shipper in a transport document, the FOB seller can secure his position by inserting a relevant provision in the contract of sale. As the sale agreement is usually concluded prior to the shipment of the goods, it may provide

27 The buyer is the shipper according to Article 1(8) of the RR

28 Article 1(9) of the RR

29 Article 35 of the RR.

30 The same steps need to be followed when it is impossible to request a transport document and instead only a mate's receipt is issued.

31 Zwitser, 'Cash against mate's receipt under the Rotterdam Rules'.

32 These concerns were expressed and discussed in depth in the article of Zwitser, 'Cash against mate's receipt under the Rotterdam Rules'.

for all the obligations of the parties. This being the case, it is permissible that the sale agreement illustrates how the carriage contract should be drafted. The role of the documentary shipper introduced by Articles 1(9) and 35 of the RR, would arguably allow an exception to the doctrine of privity of contract,[33] as indeed the seller becomes, with the consent of the buyer/shipper, an original party to the contract of carriage from the perspective of the RR.

Next, assuming that the seller is not mentioned as a documentary shipper, the ensuing question of interest for international trade, as per Zwitser, is this:[34] in a case where a buyer (B) has further sold the goods, but the first seller (S) remains unpaid, can S ask for the delivery of the goods at the port of destination, bypassing the last buyer (F or Z)? Article 47(1) of the RR is critical.

With regards to who is to claim delivery of the goods, the wording of the RR is sufficiently clear. No party other than the holder of the transport document, i.e. the buyer, has the right to claim delivery. Therefore the real owner of the cargo, S, (the FOB seller) remains unprotected.

To conclude, it seems that the RR do not provide a solution to this complexity; it is apparent that the mate's receipt does not qualify as a transport document, as it is merely a receipt for shipment and does not evidence the contract of carriage.[35] When it comes to the mate's receipt, again the RR show a consolidating rather than a codifying approach. Although the increase in the use of documents other than the bill of lading has been acknowledged by the RR, the Convention covers non-negotiable documents, such as sea waybills, but does not go further to also cover mate's receipts. The root of the problem in the bove case scenario of Zwitser is, that the RR do not automatically consider the consignor as a documentary shipper.

Coming back to the principles analysed at the beginning of this chapter, the RR acknowledge only the main shipping documents, going just one step further than their predecessors. They are in this context more restrictive than Incoterms®, which also cover mate's receipts. The RR therefore consolidate rather than codify in this respect, but this restriction can create problems, since they do not make reference to a possible custom crediting a mate's receipt with all the characteristics of a bill of lading. This, as shown by the case *Kum v. Wah Tat Bank*,[36] can be somewhat controversial in jurisdictions or practices of trade where such a document is customarily issued as a document of title. The reason is that the document cannot be considered a transport document under the RR.

33 See The Law commission, 'Privity of contract: contracts for the benefit of third parties'. The doctrine is explained to mean "a contract does not confer rights on someone who is not a party to the contract".

34 This is the scenario aptly devised by Zwitser, 'Cash against mate's receipt under the Rotterdam Rules'.

35 *Brown AR, McFarlane & Co v. C Shaw, Lovell & Sons* (1921) 7 Ll LR 36. Exceptionally, in the case *Kum v. Wah Tat Bank* [1971] 1 Lloyd's Rep 439, the Privy Council, on appeal from the Malaysian Court of Appeal, recognised that instead of a bill of lading, a mate's receipt was customarily issued by the carrier in the trade between certain geographical ports, and it could qualify as a document of title. However, in that specific case, the mate's receipt had the annotation non-negotiable and therefore it did not qualify as a document of title.

36 [1971] 1 Lloyd's Rep 439.

The situation thus remains as it was under the HVR. This is because the document of title function is left to national law. However, we propose that when the goods have been sold on, the legal position of the FOB seller (S) and mate's receipt holder against the non-contractual buyer's actions should be secured otherwise. One solution would be to request for the tender of a transport document, and to insert a provision into the contract of sale requiring that the seller is mentioned as the documentary shipper on the transport document. Alternatively the parties could agree to trade over the mate's receipt instead of a negotiable transport document.[37] Nevertheless, it is doubted whether this would be well-received by the trade community, as it is risky to trade over a document which does not give title to sue.[38]

The principles responsible for the controversies identified in this section focus on codification and consolidation of trade practices, with a narrow scope. In that respect, the RR do not particularly allow much flexibility, as the documents that trigger rights under a contract of carriage cannot go beyond the ones provided for by the RR.

The unfairness noted for the unpaid documentary shipper/mate's receipt holder stems from the importance attached by the RR to transport documents, divided into negotiable and non-negotiable, thus embracing the current trade division of bills of lading, straight bills of lading and sea waybills. The importance of transport documents will be more visible in the next section. What if S is left unpaid, because B becomes insolvent?

6.4.2 Control of the goods under the SOGA and the Rotterdam Rules

Now, we will by way of revision deal with the compatibility of the right of control initiated by the RR with the SOGA right to stop the goods in transit.[39] The scenario being recalled here will re-emphasise that the carrier may find himself in the middle of conflicting instructions from traders. The repercussions illustrated, in our view, will call for a case of possible redrafting of the UK carriage and trade legislation to avoid possible conflicts.

37 See Zwitser, 'Cash against mate's receipt under the Rotterdam Rules', p. 381.

38 Under English law, the mate's receipt is not mentioned by section 1(4) of the Factors Act 1889, which lists examples of documents of title; Debattista, 'Legislative methods in International trade: Madness or method?', p. 629. It is our opinion that if no step is taken to that direction by the parties, it will then be up to the decision of the courts to resolve the inequitableness that arises in the above situation. This means that the unpaid FOB mate's receipt holder should be considered as a party to the contract of carriage. This could be achieved if the courts adopt a reasoning similar to the one taken in *Pyrene v. Scindia*. It should be implied that since the contract of carriage affects the seller, the intention of the original parties to the contract should have been that the seller is also a party to it.

39 For a considerable analysis on this issue, see Treitel and Reynolds (eds), *Carver on Bills of Lading* (4th edn), para 1.038.

The scenario to help our study is that of Carver, also used at the beginning of Chapter 2:[40]

The seller (S) ships the goods and gets a transport document to be transferred to the buyer (B). S is not the controlling party, either because the transport document was transferred to B, or because the contract of carriage initially designated another person, in this case B, as the controlling party. B then sells the goods to F and instructs the carrier to deliver to F.

Supposing that B is the controlling party and while goods are in transit, B becomes insolvent. S, as the seller to B, wants the goods redirected to himself (S), as entitled under section 46(4) of the SOGA.[41] If both the RR and the SOGA apply, shall the carrier follow the instructions of S for delivery to himself, or of B for delivery to F? Evidently, it seems that a conflict arises between section 46(4) of the SOGA and Article 51(2) of the RR.[42]

Section 44 of SOGA provides that when the buyer of the goods becomes insolvent, the unpaid seller who has parted with the possession of the goods has the right of stopping them in transit; that is to say, he may resume possession of the goods as long as they are in course of transit, and may retain them until payment or tender of the price.[43] Evidently, the right of stoppage is a property right, the transfer of which is subject to national laws.[44] However, the RR prescribe rights and liabilities stemming from the contract of carriage.

From the perspective of Article 50(1)(a) of the RR, the carrier is in no breach if he abides by the instructions of B, as this is the controlling party. On the other hand, the property rights of the unpaid seller remain unprotected. However, this manifest conflict of the SOGA and the RR is justified[45] by the different relationships that the two instruments protect. This could lead to litigation, and therefore needs to be resolved.

In our view, this issue is so serious that it should be up to the English legislation to be updated in order to either harmonise or put a hierarchy between the sections,

40 This case scenario is from Treitel and Reynolds (eds), *Carver on Bills of Lading* (4th edn), para 1-038. This consideration also arose, rather as *obiter*, in *AP Moller Maersk A/S v. Sonaec Villas Sen Sad Fadoul* [2010] EWHC 355 Comm. where a straight bill of lading had been issued with the buyer being the named consignee under an FOB sale contract.

41 Article 46(4) of the SOGA recites: "When notice of stoppage in transit is given by the seller to the carrier or other bailee or custodier in possession of the goods, he must re-deliver the goods to, or according to the directions of, the seller; and the expenses of the re-delivery must be borne by the seller."

42 Article 51(2)(a) of the RR reads: "When a non-negotiable transport document has been issued that indicates that it shall be surrendered in order to obtain delivery of the goods: (a) The shipper is the controlling party and may transfer the right of control to the consignee named in the transport document by transferring the 35 document to that person without endorsement. If more than one original of the document was issued, all originals shall be transferred in order to effect a transfer of the right of control".

43 Debattista, *Bills of Lading in Export Trade*, para 2.55. These requirements need to run concurrently.

44 The SOGA applies to domestic sales, but also to international ones when the contract specifically requires that it be governed by English law.

45 Treitel and Reynolds (eds), *Carver on Bills of Lading* (4th edn), paras 1-038 to 1-042.

or up to English courts, to shed light on these sensitive interfaces of these rights. Otherwise, one right could work to the detriment of the other.

Alternatively, it can be argued that the sale contract being concluded before the carriage contract can prevent such a contingency. The sale contract may designate that a negotiable bill of lading requiring surrender is issued,[46] made out to the order of the seller. In this case, the seller may, by withholding the bill of lading, pass title to the goods only after payment is made.[47]

From the carriage perspective, the carrier in that case has to give precedence to the RR, as this is the regime applicable to carriage relations and also because he is not privy to the underlying sale contract.[48] However, if such a case goes to litigation, it would be interesting to see how the courts will protect the unpaid seller's property rights. Therefore, it is well apparent that the right of control may cause confusion in the trade.

The problem of conflicting instructions shows that again the RR have gone far in codifying rights of the controlling party, without being able to prevent possibilities of confusing operation in international trade. Especially, when thinking in terms of stoppage in transit, a concurrent trigger of rights under the SOGA or other remedies associated with property rights, which are usually regulated by national laws is highly possible, meaning that the trade protagonist needs to be aware of both the applicable carriage and sale/property frameworks. Extensive codification again will create disharmony and undermine the business efficacy of the RR. This problem is aggravated by the fact that the RR in this aspect show that they work in a narrow carriage law scope, and miss the wider trade law picture, although clearly they do not want to deal with property rights. Litigation will increase, possibly with different outcomes in different jurisdictions. Incoterms®, wisely again are more flexible and leave property issues and instructions, in general, to the agreement of the parties or national laws.

We will now go through the loose identification checks under Articles 45 and 46 of the RR, advising on ways of providing security through the sale contract.[49]

6.4.3 *Article 45 of the Rotterdam Rules*

It has been established that Article 45(a) of the RR is particularly significant for international trade law, because it prescribes the steps that the carrier *may* or *should* take before releasing the goods to the alleged consignee. The use of "may" in the text of the article plays an important role[50] and entails two considerable stipulations: first, the consignee needs to identify himself only *if the carrier asks him to*;[51] and secondly, (even) if the carrier does ask him to identify himself

46 As contemplated by Articles 35 and 45 of the RR.

47 *(Ross) T Smyth & Co Ltd v. TD Bailey, Son & Co* [1940] 3 All ER 60; Debattista, *Bills of Lading in Export Trade*, para 5.18.

48 See Treitel and Reynolds (eds), *Carver on Bills of Lading* (4th edn), para 1.038.

49 See Chapter 2 for more detail.

50 "The carrier shall deliver the goods to the consignee at the time and location referred to in article 43. The carrier may refuse delivery if the person claiming to be the consignee does not properly identify themself as the consignee on the request of the carrier".

51 Emphasis added by the author.

and the consignee fails to do so, the carrier *may*, but does not need to, refuse to deliver the goods to him.

It follows that in practice, Article 45(a) of the RR entitles the carrier to deliver the goods to a person who asks for the goods and simply *says* he is the consignee. It does not impose on the carrier an obligation to ask for identification, neither does it oblige him to deny delivery to someone who refuses or fails to identify himself as the consignee.

Hence, Article 45(a) is crucial for the players of international trade: the position of the seller is affected as the article contains very few check requirements, thus making the risk of him not being paid more likely, as the goods may reach the wrong hands.[52] Instead, had there been a duty to ask for identification, as opposed to a *discretion* to do so, the seller would not have been put in such a vulnerable position.

Our opinion is that this article offers great liberty to the carrier in terms of delivery and it is very surprising that the prerequisites for identification checks seem to leave the carrier not liable, irrespective of whether the carrier delivers to the right person or not. It is advisable that sellers avoid requesting sea waybills or straight bills when they doubt the ability or certainty of the buyer to pay.

This could be avoided via a condition to that effect in the sale contract. This may either take the form of a duty to tender a negotiable bill of lading that requires surrender, or through the prohibition that the seller tenders a non-negotiable document to the buyer.

Now, in terms of documentary sales, banks should also consider Article 45 of the RR with much caution and take their own measures against possible risks of non-entitlement to payment.[53] They should ensure that it is themselves and not the buyers who are mentioned as the consignees on a sea waybill.

The lenience awarded to the carrier by Article 45(a) can prove detrimental to both the consignee and the seller *qua* shipper. This provision might cause controversies. The word "may" refutes the previous reliance (and practice) that in the case of sea waybills and straight bills the carrier will ensure that he delivers to the actual consignee. He has the discretion to ask for identification and is also *entitled* to deliver even if this identification is deliberately withheld or without fault given.

On the one hand, this provision constitutes an innovation of the RR since it was missing from all their predecessors. It purports to address a problem of commercial reality which was left unresolved.[54] On the other hand, the fact that the carrier is left non-liable, even if he delivers without asking or delivers to who he thinks is the right person, manifests the inadequacy of this provision. We understand that the carrier is not an expert and that he does not possess investigative skills that pertain to the police. It is also acknowledged that time is precious and that delay under one contract of carriage might trigger his liability for breach of

52 See Debattista, 'The Rotterdam Rules appraised', p. 4.

53 Ibid.

54 See Debattista, *Bills of Lading in Export Trade*, pp. 38–39: such a case would arise when the ship arrives before documents.

the subsequent ones. Had the verb "may" been replaced by "must", no additional requirements for identification would have been necessary in the sale contract. Timely delivery to the right consignee can be secured through the following term in the sale and carriage contracts:

> The carrier *shall* deliver the goods to the consignee at the time and location referred to in Article 43. The carrier *must* refuse delivery if the person claiming to be the consignee does not properly identify itself as the consignee on the request of the carrier. (emphasis added)

Nevertheless, there are also counterarguments which do not see any particular risk behind Article 45(a).The article as it currently is might not be used frequently, in the sense that, in practice, the majority of sale contracts (especially if a letter of credit is involved) have the issuance of a negotiable transport record among their documentary requirements. Especially in CIF sales, article A8 of the Incoterms® asks the seller to provide the buyer, at his own expense and without delay, with the usual transport document for the agreed port of destination.[55]

This requirement remains the same under Incoterms® 2010. Similarly, in FOB (Incoterms® 2010 sales), article A8 requires that "the seller must provide the buyer, at the seller's expense, with the usual proof that the goods have been delivered in accordance with A4."[56]

Interestingly, this provision of Incoterms® also entails that unless such proof is a transport document, the seller must provide assistance in obtaining a transport document at the buyer's request, risk and expense.

Taking into consideration the frequency of international sale contracts concluded on CIF and FOB terms, it can be argued that although Article 45 seems problematic, most frequently a bill of lading (negotiable transport document) is requested. Therefore, we hope that the above paradox is unlikely.

6.4.4 Article 46 of the Rotterdam Rules

Article 46 of the RR keeps the wording of Article 45(a) that the carrier may refuse delivery if the person claiming to be the consignee fails to properly identify himself on the former's request. Article 46(a) differs in stating that the carrier shall refuse delivery if the non-negotiable document is not surrendered.

Again, the carrier may ask for identification and may or may not act upon it. It has been advocated that the type of identification needed for these documents is merely the surrender of the document.[57]

55 See Incoterms® 2000, ICC Official Rules for the interpretation of trade terms, ICC, p. 70.

56 ICC Guide to Incoterms® 2010, p. 175.

57 See Debattista, 'The Rotterdam Rules appraised', p. 5. Also at www.rotterdamrules2009.com/cms/uploads/Def%20%20tekst%20Charles%20Debattista%2031%20OKT29.pdf.

6.4.5 Delivery without surrender of the bill of lading: the role of the bill of lading under the Rotterdam Rules

The draftsmen of the RR thought of loosening the obligation to present the bill of lading. It has been observed from practice, particularly in a series of voyages when a string of sales is involved, that the bill of lading may not have arrived when the goods arrive at the port of destination.[58] This was especially frequent in the oil trade.[59]

However, in the opinion of several commentators,[60] the problematic practice of the bill arriving late has received too much drafting attention, with the trade repercussions being worse than the practical problems so far. Let us recall the sale scenario used throughout this chapter: There is a CIF sale contract between S and B; goods are then resold to F, and ultimately to Z.

Z has paid for the goods and is awaiting the documents, but because of negotiations with F as to some defects of the said goods, what is he to do if Article 47(2)(b) of the RR applies, namely if (a) he is notified of the arrival of the goods at destination but shows up late to request delivery,[61] or (b) does not identify himself properly or (c) cannot be located? The carrier may deliver the goods without receiving the bill of lading, seeking alternative delivery instructions from the shipper, or documentary shipper.[62]

Two remarks can be made. First, S, the shipper in the above scenario, who has paid and has no legitimate or other property interest in the goods, and will be contacted by the carrier[63] may be entirely ignorant as to who B may have sold the goods to. The same applies to B, who may be approached as the documentary shipper. One should not underestimate the risk of fraud lurking in such a situation, if B for instance designates delivery to F, despite knowing that F has bought the goods to resell them.[64]

Moreover, supposing that Z obtains the transport document after the carrier delivered to F, unfortunately by virtue of Article 47(2)(e) of the RR, Z cannot sue the carrier for misdelivery.[65]

58 A/CN.9/642, para 52. See also A/CN.9/591, paras 232–233.

59 A/CN.9/642, para 52. Additional statistics have shown that in liner trade, in 15% of the occasions where a bill of lading should have been presented, it was eventually unavailable. In the bulk trade on the other hand, the percentage of unavailability reaches 50%, whereas in the oil trade, which was of particular concern to the draftsmen the bill of lading is almost always not in the possession of the buyer when delivery is claimed (van der Ziel, 'Delivery of the Goods').

60 Ramberg, 'UN Convention on Contracts for the International Carriage of Goods Wholly or Partly by Sea', p. 280.

61 Article 47(2)(b) of the RR.

62 Asariotis, 'Reflections on the Rotterdam Rules', pp. 151–152.

63 Article 47(2)(b) of the RR.

64 See Ramberg, 'UN Convention on Contracts for the International Carriage of Goods Wholly or Partly by Sea', p. 280.

65 Asariotis, 'Reflections on the Rotterdam Rules', p. 152.

Possibly traders who are not familiar with the peculiarities of the RR noted above, should carefully consider what the term "negotiable document" would mean. First of all, requesting a negotiable document does not mean that the words "the goods may be delivered without the surrender of the transport document or the electronic transport record" are not going to appear on it. Therefore commercial parties should prohibit this contingency by stating that the negotiable transport document must be presented for delivery. Otherwise, even banks involved in a letter of credit may encounter serious repercussions from the application of Article 47(2)(b) of the RR. If they have not shown care to be named on the bill of lading as parties to be contacted by the carrier, they will face serious risks. After the RR come into force, the above category of documents may officially operate. It is our suggestion that the only protection for the buyer would be to explicitly prohibit the tender of a negotiable document which does not require surrender, in the sale contract and the letter of credit.

Consequently, taking into consideration the foregoing concerns gleaned from Article 47(2) of the RR, one could say that there is a case for reform of the UCP 600;[66] in the revised version of the UCP, such documents could either be clustered as a "risky" tender, or otherwise be accepted, perhaps with some additional security required.

The main underpinning of trading over documents of title in sales down a string is under attack here, once again because of extensive proactive codification. This is particularly so, because such a document is for the first time recognised by the RR as a type of transport document, which may be issued unbeknown to the buyers. Therefore, careful contract drafting and prohibiting its issuance, if undesirable, may protect against this surprise.

6.5 Types and forms of documents, Incoterms® and the UCP 600

We have also studied the requirements for obtaining a transport document, in paper or electronic form, negotiable or non-negotiable. A grey area in Article 35 of the RR has been whether an agreement can supersede a contrary custom. Considering a view of a commentator,[67] we have advised that since the RR do not put a hierarchy between custom and agreement on the final issuance of a document, a thoroughly drafted sale contract shall not only be explicit on what transport document it requires, but it must also convey that the existing contrary custom is within the parties' knowledge and they want to exclude it.[68] The carriage contract should also be equally thoroughly drafted.

66 Ibid.

67 Filippo Lorenzon, 'Transport Documents and Electronic Transport Records' in Baatz et al, *The Rotterdam Rules: A Practical Annotation*, paras 35-02, 35-03.

68 The ability of the agreement to prevail over a custom is established under English law.

If the sale contract is governed by English law without the incorporation of any Incoterms®, then case law[69]demands the issuance of a negotiable transport document. If there is a custom or usage not to issue a transport document of any type in particular, and no relevant agreement, a transport document does not have to be issued.[70]

The above concerns are very significant for international trade law, as the seller *qua* shipper *may* be in breach under the sale contract if it is governed by English law. The problem remains if the purchase contract incorporates CIF Incoterms®, as under article A8 of the CIF Incoterms® the seller is obliged to provide the buyer with the usual transport document.[71]

For this reason, we recommend that before the sale and the carriage contracts are entered into, the seller or the buyer, depending on who is going to be the shipper, will have to find out whether they can arrange an appropriate contract of carriage and transport document. If they discover that there is custom or usage not requiring the issuance of a transport document at a specific port/trade, the party who is responsible for carriage might have to ship elsewhere, or otherwise draft a specific and detailed relevant clause requesting a certain transport document.

If sales are concluded on FOB terms, things become even more difficult with regard to documentary credits, as the transport document needs to be presented to the bank so that the beneficiary-seller can receive payment. Let us suppose that the seller, S, was expecting to receive the customary documents. Thus, it may be that the only document the FOB seller is entitled to is the mate's receipt, for instance, and not a transport document, or, in some cases, no document at all. The letter of credit will be opened; according to Article 19 of the International Standard Banking Practice (ISBP), a mate's receipt is not a transport document, unlike the documents in Articles 19–25 of the UCP 600. As such, Article 14.C of the UCP 600 would not apply to the mate's receipt.[72] Therefore, although theoretically it is a great freedom and factor of flexibility that no particular document is required unless requested, trading without the bill of lading attacks the flow of international trade, and of the payment mechanism. If a particular FOB buyer wants to sell the goods on CIF terms, a mate's receipt will be of very little value. As discussed in Chapter 2, the mate's receipt is not a transport document under the RR, and therefore it does not give the right of control to its holder.

We suggest this solution: the contract of sale will have to provide for cash against documents. However, this is impractical due to current anti-money laundering regulations. In such a case, however, it is difficult to see how the goods in question might be sold down a string (most likely in CIF terms).

69 *Soproma SpA v. Marine and Animal By-Products Corp* [1966] 1 Lloyd's Rep 367.

70 See von Ziegler, Schelin and Zunarelli (eds), *The Rotterdam Rules 2008*, p. 163.

71 Article A8 of the CIF Incoterms® 2000, ICC, p. 70 and Incoterms® 2010, ICC, p. 238 (of the Dutch–English edition), respectively.

72 According to the same article of the ISBP, a mate's receipt will be examined in the same manner as other documents for which there are no specific provisions in UCP 600, i.e. under sub-article 14.F.

Especially if traders are based in several countries, and they need the bank's assistance to finance the sale contract, the letter of credit is their optimal solution. This complexity is remarkably detrimental for international trade, hindering its very essence; thus sales down a string cannot be performed smoothly or at all.

Another significant question which we have posed is whether the CIF seller/shipper needs to be aware of customs that juxtapose the stipulations of the sale contract. And can he be held liable if he has not informed the other parties so that they can make different arrangements? It could be argued that if the carrier is aware of the contrary custom, he will never agree to issue a transport document that is not customarily issued. However, although the above scenario is prima facie extreme, it is likely to occur, especially after the sale contract has been concluded and the goods are on board. If the buyer, in a CIF case, is waiting for the transport document to be issued, but receives notification by his shipper that one cannot be issued, he will be faced with difficult decisions that have to be made promptly.

The lack of information with respect to the unexpected practice might trigger a delay in the performance of the contract of sale. This delay will then cost money, time and commercial efficiency.

Buyer F expects a specific transport document; his seller, B, will face substantial commercial pressure. The seller may eventually fail to ship within the shipment period, giving the buyer the right to terminate the sale contract.[73] Consequently, there are two possibilities. Either the seller will have to find another carrier and ship elsewhere; or it might be in the buyer's interest to enter into a sale contract with another trader at another port. This in turn might lead to a loss of profit and time or to the marginalisation of traders from specific countries where the trade customs are strict.

Alternatively, transhipment of the goods could be a solution, so that the transport document is issued at a subsequent port.[74] Thus, the sale contract will be performed in the first place by a shipment evidenced in another shipping document, perhaps falling outside the definition of the transport document, as is the case with the mate's receipt. However, as the desired transport document will then be issued by a subsequent carrier, the sale contract requirement can be ultimately satisfied. For this solution to be practical, the shipper has to act promptly, so as not to ship outside the shipment period.

Therefore, here again we recognised the need for express stipulation in the sale contract. More specifically, the parties have to clarify whether and what type of document is needed first, and whether there is an existing custom or usage to the contrary. Evidently, buyers in the middle of the trade chain have to be

73 Time is of the essence in a sale contract. See *Bowes v. Shand* (1877) 2 App Cas 455 (HL); Takahashi, 'Right to Terminate (avoid) international sales of commodities'.

74 This is not without risks as the buyer will want protective rights against the carrier for the first leg of the voyage. This solution can work if the seller consigns the goods to himself in the first place and then tranships.

more cautious. They have to always make sure that the first and the subsequent sale contracts are back to back, so that they can coordinate their sellers/shippers accordingly. In the terminology of Incoterms®, the document will be "procured".[75]

If the ambiguity of Article 35 of the RR can be rectified only through far-fetched and impractical solutions, arguably the RR seem to fail to bring the desirable trade facilitation they were heralding.

Under A8 of FCA Incoterms® 2010:

> The seller must provide the buyer, at the seller's expense, with the usual proof that the goods have been delivered in accordance with A4. The seller must provide assistance to the buyer, at the buyer's request, risk and expense, in obtaining a transport document.

This means that, if the document the seller gets is a mate's receipt, but the sale contract still requires a transport document, whether this will be ultimately issued depends on Article 35 of the RR.

Incoterms® are particularly relevant in this discussion, as nothing guarantees that the terms usage and practice coincide with what is usual in the RR. A mate's receipt could be recognised as a delivery document under Incoterms®, and the case *Kum v. Wah Tat Bank*[76] would be relevant, but it does not qualify as a transport document under the RR. If a non-negotiable document is usual, it can validly be requested under the RR, but when a letter of credit is involved, it would minimise the banks' security when financing a letter of credit.

Then attention shifted to the UCP 600. This study has been necessary, as the modern method of payment of international sales are letters of credit.[77]

Article 36(2)(b) of the RR specifies that the contract particulars of the transport document should contain the name and address of the carrier. However, the UCP 600 only request that the name of the carrier is specified. This discrepancy among the two texts is due to the fact that the draftsmen were using the UCP 500 as an example and they wanted to align the RR to them. The UCP 600 on the other hand, have more comprehensive signature requirements compared to the RR. Therefore a trader may find himself complying with the RR, but not with the UCP 600, which might ruin his payment expectation under letters of credit.

The UCP 600 are stricter in their requirements, as they ask concretely for a shipped on board bill of lading which names the carrying vessel. This means that traders have to be able to comply with the stricter provisions of the UCP 600 to secure payment. Accordingly, this further means that sellers *qua* shippers/documentary shippers should be afforded the possibility, by the sale contract, to exercise pressure on the carrier to comply with the more stringent provisions of the RR. FOSFA and GAFTA contracts have also been studied and they have proven to be much in the same vein as the RR.

75 Article A8 of the CIF Incoterms®.

76 *Wah Tat Bank Ltd and Overseas Chinese Banking Corp Ltd v. Chan Cheng Kum and Hua Siang Steamship Co (Singapore) Ltd (Third Parties)* [1967] 2 Lloyd's Rep 437; affirmed by the Privy Council, *Kum v. Wah Tat Bank Ltd* [1971] 1 Lloyd's Rep 439 PC.

77 Also to prevent money laundering through transfers from one bank account to the other.

6.6 Electronic commerce

The need for speed in obtaining the bill of lading and the need to accommodate the different usages, practices and customs of the trade in this regard were the great incentives for freedom behind Article 47(2) and Article 35 of the RR.[78] The realisation of the need for paperless transactions in modern trade could only signify that a commercial critical analysis of the RR and a focus on the new provisions on electronic communication and records was imperative. This shows how Chapters 2, 3 and 4 of the book are inter-connected in international trade law terms.

The big challenge of the RR when it comes to e-commerce has been to show neutrality,[79] so that they do not block future technological advancement. The trade issues engendered by the provisions on electronic records stem from the dipole of carrier-shipper. These are the only parties that decide on issuance, transfer and times of transfer of the record.

Firstly, the wording of Article 8(a) of the RR does not clarify whether consent given for the first use is also valid for any subsequent use of the electronic transport record or whether every individual usage needs a new specific consent from the shipper and carrier. The holder and the documentary shipper are left outside. We have used case scenarios to highlight the deficiencies of Article 8 of the RR, which are particularly obvious in string sales.[80] The omission of the holder and consignee also has repercussions shown in another scenario. Especially, as far as the latter parties are concerned, there are further letter of credit complexities.

The practical significance of this recommendation is even more apparent when payment is agreed to be effected via a letter of credit under an FOB sale contract; the letter of credit is made before the carriage contract, and it is explicitly made subject to the UCP 600. The buyer *qua* shipper, knowing that trading in electronic sea waybills is the new commercial trend and knowing that the carrier has an established registry for issuing electronic sea waybills, agrees to the issuance of one. However, the seller is uncertain of whether the paper equivalent of the non-negotiable record is necessary. This is a typical situation, when the parties want to conform to the letter of credit. As shown by the terminology of the UCP

78 von Ziegler, Schelin and Zunarelli (eds), *The Rotterdam Rules 2008*, para 9.6.2. The delay and unavailability of the transport document at the moment of claiming delivery has been noted particularly in the oil trade.

79 Report of the Working Group III on the work on its 15th session (New York, 18–28 April 2005), UN Doc. A/CN.9/576, para 203; Jose Angelo Estrella Faria, 'Electronic Transport Records', in von Ziegler, Schelin and Zunarelli (eds), *The Rotterdam Rules 2008*, para 3.1.

80 An overseas sale concluded on FOB terms and the goods are to be carried by sea. The RR apply. The sale contract is silent with regards to whether the transport document is going to be in paper or electronic form, and for the moment it is needless to say whether it will be negotiable or non-negotiable. If the carrier and shipper decide that the transport document will be in an electronic format and freely transferrable, but the seller/documentary shipper disagrees, the latter cannot object to the issuance of an electronic record under the RR. The only way through which the seller could have protected his position would be by having a relevant provision in the contract of sale exactly prescribing what the document should be like and how it would be issued, or requiring that his consent should also be requested where an electronic transport record is under negotiation between shipper and carrier.

600, banks deal with documents. Although there is no definition of the document in the UCP, it can *a contrario* be concluded that by the existence of the "Supplement for Electronic Presentation eUCP Version 1.1"[81], when the word "document" is used in the general UCP context, only a document in a traditional paper form is denoted.

It is our view that Article 8(a) should not have left the consignee's/holder's consent out of its scope. This is justified by the practicalities of the trade; normally, thinking in trade terms, the consensus of both traders is needed over the type (electronic or paper) of the transport document or record, as it is the cornerstone of the shipping documents in their transaction. Accordingly, if the consignee-buyer requests an electronic transport record under article A8 of the CIF Incoterms® 2000/2010, the seller has to accept this fundamental requirement of the sale, and the contract of carriage will be drafted accordingly. In pursuance of the former, the shipper and carrier will have to agree that an electronic record will be issued, particularly a negotiable one.

However, in sales down a string, traders do not always have the luxury of the sale contract being concluded before the carriage contract. It is also possible that in a string of consecutive sales, the same traders want to (or have to) trade with their potential buyers on different terms. Things could potentially prove problematic when our model sale scenario arises.

The shipper *qua* seller (S) and a buyer (B) enter into a CIF sale contract. As per the sale and carriage contract, it is expressly written or implied that the transport document will be issued in paper. The transport document is issued to the order of the consignee (B) or his assigns. After the goods have been shipped, and while they are still afloat, the consignee (B) wants to sell the cargo to (F). (F) is a big trading company which conducts business globally only on the basis of electronic transport records, to correspond to the need for speed and its customary preference. Thus, it is against its practice and interests to accept a paper transport document. Neither (B) nor (F) are shippers under the contract of carriage. Can they enforce their wish to issue an electronic transport record, either against the shipper or the carrier?

As the shipper is not a party to the second contract of sale, he is not obliged to agree to the procurement of an electronic record. The contract of carriage is still operative as the goods have not been delivered and only the carrier and the consignee (B) are the common parties to this contract of carriage. Hence, the question posed above will be answered negatively. Article 8(a) does not give the holder the power to ask for an electronic record.

However, the above deadlock is resolved through Article 10 of the RR, which refers to replacement[82] of a transport document by a record and *vice versa*.

81 Hereafter, any article of the eUCP cited without any other reference is considered to be an article of eUCP V1.1 Supplement to UCP 600.

82 Generally on replacement see Hakan Karan, 'Transport Documents in the light of the Rotterdam Rules'.

We have also justifiably criticised the one-sided focus of the electronic provisions of the RR only on negotiable records. Replacement (and reissuance) could have been an option also for non-negotiable records, and something similar is afforded by the UCC.

In letters of credit, electronic documents are left to be covered by the eUCP supplement in specific eUCP articles.[83] Technically, replacement would not be necessary if eUCP could automatically apply. Although, according to article e2(a) of the eUCP "a credit subject to eUCP is also subject to the UCP without express incorporation of the UCP", the opposite is not allowed. In our case, article e1(b) of eUCP V1.1 Supplement to UCP 600 is relevant: "The eUCP shall apply as a supplement to the UCP *where the credit indicates that it is subject to eUCP*" (emphasis added).

Returning to the FOB example under discussion, where only the UCP 600 and not eUCP apply, the bank will want to examine the paper version of the electronic transport record. Since the example is about a non-negotiable electronic transport record, its paper equivalent is a sea waybill.[84] Accordingly, the bank will request the paper version of the sea waybill, and will examine compliance of the document with the credit as per Article 21 of the UCP 600. This article is applicable by definition as it is entitled "Non-negotiable sea waybill".[85]

The only solution available to the FOB seller/documentary shipper would be to request his buyer, the applicant of the documentary credit, to amend the letter of credit, stating that "this letter of credit is made subject to the eUCP by an amendment".[86]

As to whether the answer would be different if the buyer wanted a negotiable transport record instead, the answer is likely to be the same as above, as there is no direct article on this in the RR. In theory, both requests of the consignee can be satisfied insofar as the carrier agrees. The latter is the person that issues

83 These are the following articles: 1) Article e-1(a): The supplement to the Uniform Customs and Practice for Documentary Credits for Electronic Presentation ("*e*UCP") supplements for Uniform Customs and Practice for Documentary Credits (2007 Revision, ICC Publication No. 600) ("UCP") in order to accommodate presentation of electronic records alone or in combination with paper documents. 2) Article e2(c): If an *e*UCP credit allows the beneficiary to choose between presentation of paper documents or electronic records and it chooses to present only paper documents, the UCP alone shall apply to that presentation. If only paper documents are permitted under an *e*UCP credit, the UCP alone shall apply. 3) Article e3(a)(ii): document shall include an electronic record. 4) Article e3(iv): paper document means a document in a traditional paper form.

84 See Baatz et al, *The Rotterdam Rules: A Practical Annotation*, para [45-01], comments under Article 45 (Delivery when no negotiable transport document or negotiable electronic transport record is issued), where it is submitted that the article applies to straight bills of lading or sea waybills.

85 This is the reverse example of the one in Sturley, Fujita and van der Ziel, *The Rotterdam Rules*, p. 57, fn 69 therein.

86 This is by virtue article e1(c) of eUCP V1.1 Supplement to UCP 600, which recites: "This version is Version 1.1. A credit must indicate the applicable version of the eUCP. If it does not do so, it is subject to the version in effect on the date the credit is issued or, if made subject to eUCP by an amendment accepted by the beneficiary, on the date of that amendment."

the document, but it seems that there is no legal obligation in this respect under the RR.

This is practically relevant in the context of market prices rising; the buyer under the first sale of the cargo may be interested in selling it further. Therefore, he wants to replace his non-negotiable transport record with a negotiable electronic transport record. As discussed, this is not a possibility offered by the RR, as replacement refers to forms of the same documents, and it only applies to negotiable documents/records. This is a missed opportunity that would have allowed consecutive sales to multiply with flexibility and speed. However, there may be contractual options to achieve this flexibility. This possibility may be offered through a private agreement with an electronic registry system, or included in national legislations, which should step in and encourage electronic commerce.

However, from an *a contrario* interpretation of Article 8(a), it looks as though the alternative side of the phenomenon, i.e. the possibility to turn a negotiable record to a non-negotiable one, is permitted by the RR.[87] Since the article does not distinguish between negotiable and non-negotiable records, the mere disagreement of carrier or shipper on the subsequent use of a negotiable transport record seems to suffice to render it technically and *practically* non-negotiable.[88]

However, in the context of this example, we only deal with the position of a consignee who is in good faith and has indeed lost possession of the transport document. We have limited the scope of the case scenario because otherwise the provision suggested would permit itself to be abused. The provision should only stand for the protection of the real consignee who, due to unforeseen circumstances, cannot for instance identify himself, or any other reason within the limits allowed by the RR. Otherwise, the provision would juxtapose legal certainty, whereas our aim is to enhance it. Consequently, this is why occurrence of loss should be further qualified; it is suggested that only exceptional circumstances pertaining to *force majeure* and theft should permit replacement of the original.[89] Subsequently how contract drafting can complement Article 10 of the RR if the situations like the above arise has been investigated.

Article 10 of the RR states that the document or record needs to be submitted in exchange or substitution of the record for replacement to occur;

87 Although it looks like this omission by the drafters is more accidental than intentional.

88 For additional certainty, if the words "to order" or "negotiable" appear on the document, they should be deleted from an *a contrario* interpretation of Article 1(19) this time. This additional step is justified by the reading of the definitions for negotiable documents/records, the usage of the document is not a criterion on its own to classify it as such. The only criteria for understanding the type of the document are the words: "to order" or "negotiable" and/or the applicable law to the record.

89 A similar clause, as far as documents of title are concerned, appears in the UCC, applying in the US, section 7-502(b)(2) stating: "Subject to Section 7-503, title and rights acquired by negotiation are not defeated by any stoppage of the goods represented by the document of title or by surrender of the goods by the bailee and are not impaired even if: [...] (2) any person has been deprived of possession of a negotiable tangible document by misrepresentation, fraud, accident, mistake, duress, loss, theft, or conversion". In our opinion, the same protection, if available, under the RR, or the UK COGSA, when amended, can be afforded to sea waybills.

something which is impossible here. Unfortunately, there is no other article in the RR suggesting a solution, so ultimately the right to a second chance has to be stipulated elsewhere to protect a bona fide receiver who loses the transport document.

We have taken the view that to address a situation like the above, a contract between the carrier and shipper should have an additional provision heading titled "exceptional cases", with two subsections: one for replacement without use of the original, the other for reissuing. However, these provisions should be thoroughly drafted, and, if possible, mention the exceptional circumstances for their application.[90]

The need for this precise wording and guidance as to the restrictive interpretation of the provision is for the protection of the buyer's interests. The provision should be explicit and exhaustive in order to discourage the carelessness of holders; only exceptional circumstances would be covered. If the carrier (or the court) is convinced by the evidence, the carrier could *reissue* a transport document or *replace* the lost document with an electronic transport record. Of course, if reissuance or replacement occurs, it should have the effect that the previously issued document or record stands void. The clause should be explicit in this regard, and also specify that reissuance or replacement due to loss is only allowed once in order to prevent abuse of the provision.[91]

This solution has been devised because, by virtue of Article 45(c) of the RR, if the goods are undelivered to the consignee, the carrier may seek instructions for delivery by the shipper or documentary shipper. If the seller is any of these two parties, depending on whether this is a CIF or FOB contract and assuming he has been paid, he may exercise fraud to have the goods delivered to a person other than the consignee. If seller and buyer are the shipper and documentary shipper, and they give conflicting instructions, unusual delay may also arise. Therefore, our suggestion for a contractual provision inserted in the sale and carriage contract, will secure the consignee who cannot present the non-negotiable transport record/document at the port of discharge. If this provision is inserted in the sale contract, it will ensure which person has to be approached for instructions, and thus the seller and buyer will have to unanimously designate the buyer in that case.

Reissuance will provide the legal basis for preventing the goods from falling in the wrong hands, thus attacking misdeliveries. In other words, it would, in actuality, suggest a way of attacking fraud, which was among the objectives of the RR for e-commerce. It would also explicitly give guidance as to what a carrier should do when the holder cannot identify himself as the party entitled to the goods. So far, where the holder is unable to present the document, it is the decision of the carrier to seek other evidence or request instructions from the shipper as to whether to deliver without presentation of the document. The parties might even have to wait for a court order providing guidance so

90 An *ejusdem generis* construction to be applied.

91 This however does not seem to apply in replacement under Article 10, as it now stands.

as to know whether to deliver or not. This legislative lacuna can be effectively superseded by the adoption of our suggestion. Ultimately, the benefit of this insertion will be threefold.

Firstly, replacement will not be a privilege of negotiable documents/records, thus the use of non-negotiable documents/records will not be discouraged. Secondly, replacement as promulgated will allow for the parties to accommodate their commercial needs, as electronic or paper versions of the contract may be equally necessary under different contracts (e.g. the electronic *record* may be necessary for the carriage contract, whereas the *straight bill of lading* is suitable for compliance with the letter of credit). Thirdly, the consignee who is unable to identify himself will not have to depend on the honesty of his own seller, especially since the latter will have received payment.

To the extent that carriers are willing to reissue transport documents in specific circumstances, the insertion of this contractual provision in the sale and carriage contracts will ensure that the practice is enveloped within a legal framework which may potentially be an exemplary way for setting letters of indemnity aside.

A concept of reissuance much in line with what we have suggested is inserted in the UCC.

These deficiencies have made us conceive the way that the national frameworks have to change or individual agreements have to be secured by tradesmen to prevent certain repercussions.

The RR are also one-sided towards procedures for the integrity of issuance for negotiable records, which might motivate use of non-negotiable records through ambiguous frameworks. The focus of the RR only on negotiable records may be due to the market preference at the moment.

Should the reluctance of the market towards electronic sea waybills change, however, the RR will have failed to pave the way for their promotion, and this can also be seen as a cap for future modernisation.

The common thread of this problem with all of the above is that the RR show firm codification in the e-commerce realm, which is narrow when it comes to sea waybills. Should customs and preferences of the trade change, the RR would become outdated, and by leaving the issues identified out of their cover, they have failed to promote business efficacy.

Having dealt with the problematic aspects of documentary sales and paperless transactions under the application of the RR, we have also identified the deeper clash of principles lurking underneath. As established, the balance of freedom of contract in the trade realm has to be of particular attention after the instantaneous consolidation or codification of rights of parties with regards to documents and records, and the simultaneous ambiguous interpretation of articles of the RR. However, the research would not be complete without an analysis of the type of carriage contracts under which allegedly 90% of trade is performed.[92] However,

92 Marlow and Nair, 'Service contracts – An instrument of international logistics supply chain: Under United States and European Union Regulatory frameworks'.

there is also a more abstract teleological reason for this search: the RR are a piece of codification that comes as the pinnacle of a series of conventions that aimed to strike a fair allocation of risks in maritime carriage, so, arguably, they are an exception that puts a limit to freedom of contract. Quite interestingly, the RR are at the same time the first convention that encapsulates freedom of contract in the international carriage of goods wholly or partly by sea. Such a direct conflict of freedom of contract and codification has never existed in this field of law, and it is of imperative, practical and doctrinal interest to study its legal dimensions.

6.7 Volume contracts

The idea of freedom of contract underpins not only the RR but also their predecessors (although this is very indirect in the latter).[93] However, freedom of contract to date was only allowed for charterparties, where traders and carriers stood on an equal footing, to the extent that a bill of lading was not issued. Thus, the delegations drafting conventions allocating risks in maritime carriage decided on the non-interference in these contracts as there was no obvious need for protection – all parties were considered. To date the Hague Rules and HVR allowed contracts in the tramp trade outside their scope, as cargo interests could conveniently protect their interests, and therefore did not need additional protection.[94]

What is negative, however, is that liner trade is not globally uniform, and thus is characterised by a gap of negotiating power between carriers and medium and small shippers. The prerequisites that the RR impose for derogation from their mandatory scope are only superficial.

The requirements for an opportunity and notice of the opportunity to contract in terms that do not derogate from the RR are impractical and perhaps confusing, especially in terms of evidence. A notice can be in writing, but the same cannot apply separately to the opportunity; the opportunity per se cannot be evidenced through writing if there are no more specific indicators.[95] Our view has been that these indicators should be written statement(s) confirming that the contract has been individually negotiated with respect to the provisions of the volume contract that derogate from the RR. Surprisingly, the rationale behind Article 80(2)(b)(i) of the RR, instead of providing for the protection of parties in an unprivileged bargaining position, serves to extend the conclusion of contracts which form a commercial practice;[96] this is the rationale behind subsection (b)(ii).[97] It has to be clarified that a mere indication that the contract has been individually negotiated

93 Francesco Berlingieri, 'Freedom of contract under the Rotterdam Rules' (2009) 14(4) *Unif L Rev* 831.

94 Ibid.

95 See preparatory works, A/CN.9/576, para 83, where there was an official suggestion for inserting indicators specifying the individuality of the negotiations, for example the bargaining power of the parties.

96 See 15th session Report, A/CN.9/576, para 82, where "a need to maintain a measure of commercial pragmatism" was acknowledged.

97 See 15th session Report, A/CN.9/576, para 83.

does not necessarily mean that the contract is a volume contract, or more importantly that the shipper is fully aware of all or some of the derogative provisions.

The parties may sign a coversheet at the beginning of their contract stating: "On date x, Y and Z have entered into individual negotiations and entered into a volume contract that derogates from the RR. Clauses 5, 13 and 8 are agreed outside the stipulations of the RR. See Annex attached."

Evidently, this contract has the guise of an individually negotiated contract, whereas this may not be the case. Besides, there is only an indication of derogations, without exactly knowing the different content of the provisions. This obstacle could be avoided in two ways: either by way of interpretation, if it was inferred that the requirement for the opportunity is satisfied through the tender of a written notice of the opportunity, which is the second sentence of Article 80(2)(b); or if the provision was drafted more simply. Assuming that the Article of the RR is as drafted and will not change, the parties can have a clearly worded provision in their individually negotiated volume contract. The first way would be by omitting the first use of the word "opportunity" from the article, so that it reads:

> (c) The shipper is given an opportunity and a notice of the opportunity to conclude a contract of carriage on terms and conditions that comply with this Convention without any derogation under this article (and has confirmed that the opportunity to contract on usual terms has been rejected).

Nevertheless, we have suggested an alternative phrasing which would render the obligation even more straightforward; it would be more comprehensive if *the notice of rejection of the opportunity to contract on regular Rotterdam Rules' terms* was stated in the contract. This is an advice that buyers can request from their sellers, if the former have to enter into a volume contract. This would also make commercial sense: as the opportunity of contracting in usual terms is the rule, it means that it does not need to be included in the contract particulars; conversely, it is the exception that needs to be explicit in the contract. This leads to the need of comprehensive contract drafting, so that the parties specify that the notice of the opportunity to contract on regular terms has been offered but rejected before concluding their volume contract. Such a wording could be:

> 1) The shipper is given a notice of the opportunity to conclude a contract of carriage on terms and conditions that comply with this Convention without any derogation under this article.
>
> The carrier is given a notice of the rejection of this opportunity.

Besides, there does not seem to be a way to prove whether the intention of the carrier to enter into a *non-volume* carriage contract has actually occurred. If the terms of the volume contract are a lot more attractive (providing for low freight rates for instance), there is no way to prevent the shipper from being induced by the carrier. The reason why this is said is, because Article 80(2) of the RR seems to insert steps showing that there is adequate consideration before the volume contract is concluded.

Let us now re-examine our common case scenario more closely: B, the CIF buyer, receives a transport document from his seller under a volume contract. The goods have arrived with delay, or a shortage, or another type of damage. It is important for the conclusions made, to remember that the CIF buyer will learn that the carriage contract derogates from the RR after this volume contract has been performed. He will realise his rights when he will want to sue the carrier, and he will find out, for instance, that the carrier has an extremely limited liability. Is there effectively any contractual freedom left to that third party, as Article 80(5) in principle, administers?

In a variation of our scenario, we have theorised that the buyer receives the transport document and the goods at the same time. Although the buyer would not otherwise accept these discrepancies from the RR, if he finds himself in a position where the market is rising, he will not have any other choice but to accept both the transport document evidencing a derogative volume contract and the non-contractual goods. Consequently, it is proven that, practically, there are cases where third parties are exposed to unpleasant surprises under Article 80. Moreover, Article 80(5) does not provide an answer to the case where the third party agrees to be bound by some but not all the derogations. Will it then be said that he will be bound by some of them, or that the volume contract will generally not be binding upon him? We support that the third party will be bound only by the derogations he has approved of.

All of the above are also burdensome for an FOB seller, who is the documentary shipper under the contract of carriage. If the contract of sale does not specify that the volume contract should not derogate from X, Y or Z obligations, the documentary shipper may find himself in a dilemma: at first, he may be willing to accept and be bound by the derogations. This contract entered into by the buyer may, for instance, specify that the documentary shipper has more obligations than the shipper himself. Since the will of the documentary shipper cannot be superimposed against the contrary opinion of the shipper, the documentary shipper's only secure method of protecting his interests is to exhaustively draft the sale contract against such deviations, so that a volume contract derogating from the RR is a breach of the sale contract.

It is submitted that the ability to consent to an undesirable volume contract (with derogations) is substantial, only to the extent that a consignee or documentary shipper can do something to prevent this contract or avoid it at a later stage. Thus, the third party needs to pay attention to two elements: firstly, he needs to find out all the derogations in detail; and secondly, if possible, he needs to be aware of them before the contract is executed. Both of these requirements can be safeguarded by explicit terms in the contract of sale.

As for the subsequent third parties (F and Z in our scenario), these may only be sufficiently informed through their sale contracts. These should preferably contain the derogations which are agreed between seller and buyer, so that in any breach relating to the volume contract, the sale contract can be terminated.

If the sale is on CIF terms, the same considerations apply as between carrier and the consignee/holder of the transport document who will also be the buyer without the above complexities. The consignee or holder is bound by the derogations only if he specifically approves of them.

One however has to see whether the shippers themselves are in a position to get an essential contractual benefit from volume contracts. In the briefing note for SERVICECON, it is explained that "The agreement is being developed by representatives from a number of major liner operators and targets small to medium sized shippers who sign the majority of such volume contracts."[98] It is this target group which is, form a negotiation viewpoint more vulnerable compared to major liner operators.

Lack of knowledge about these specific commercial trends, such as volume contracts or OLSAs, makes it more likely that the "weapons of contractual freedom" will be misused or used to circumvent the stricter RR provisions. This was also the thread of argument used behind the analysis of Article 35 in Chapter 3.

Supplementary national or international legislation can give more definition to the requirements of Article 1(2) of the RR, setting limits and potentially setting up supervisory and controlling committees like the FMC, where contracts will be filed and checked for compliance with the RR.

The SOGA is a codification of pre-existing case law and principles, and it becomes sacrosanct in our analysis of the trade repercussions of volume contracts with derogations.[99] Section 32(2)[100] was subject to scrutiny, insofar as it may be breached via derogation(s) of a volume contract entered into by our CIF seller, S, or a seller on a variation of an FOB contract.[101]

The question which was deciphered was whether the concept of reasonableness can be breached by the exclusion of certain articles of the RR through a volume contract which derogates from the RR. The starting point being this section, it has been proven that the meaning of a reasonable contract of carriage is threefold:[102] firstly, the contract of carriage tendered must be on usual terms;[103] secondly, it must give proper rights against the carrier; and lastly, and it must

98 BIMCO, 'New Contracts'.

99 See Lorenzon, 'When is a CIF seller's carriage contract unreasonable? Section 32(2) of the Sale of Goods Act 1979', p. 243. Bennion, *Statutory Interpretation*, at [214].

100 For an in-depth analysis of the section see Lorenzon, 'When is a CIF seller's carriage contract unreasonable? Section 32(2) of the Sale of Goods Act 1979' and Lorenzon, *Sassoon on CIF and FOB contracts*, para 2-028 onwards.

101 The scenario examined only applies to CIF sale contracts, and not to contracts on F terms, as clearly section 32(2) refers to a carriage contract that the seller must procure. However, if one pays attention to the phrase "on behalf of the buyer", nothing precludes the application of the article also to the variation of FOB contracts where the seller enters into the contract of carriage.

102 See Lorenzon, 'When is a CIF seller's carriage contract unreasonable? Section 32(2) of the Sale of Goods Act 1979', pp. 243, 244.

103 Ibid, p. 244 fn 20 therein. *Ceval Alimentos SA v. Agrimpex Trading Co Ltd (The Northern Progress)* [1996] 2 Lloyd's Rep 319 per Rix J at 328; *Tsakiroglou & Co v. Noblee Thorl GmbH* [1962] AC 93 per Lord Radcliffe at pp. 121–22, and Lord Guest at pp. 132–333; *Finska Cellulosaforeningen (Finnish Cellulose Union) v. Westfield Paper Co Ltd* (1940) 68 Ll Rep 75; *TW Ranson Ltd v. Manufacture d'Engrais et de Produits Industriels Antwerp* (1922).

grant sufficient protection to the goods while in transit. The most important ones, in relation to the volume contract derogations, are the last two aspects of reasonableness. In *Hansson v. Hamel & Horley*,[104] it was held that the contract of carriage in question, in which the goods were transhipped, had to cover the buyer in documents from shipment to destination. In *Holland Colombo Trading Society Ltd v. Segu Mohammed Khaja Alawadeen and Others*,[105] it was held that the buyer is entitled to a document which provides him with "continuous documentary cover"; this was not fulfilled if the shipowner disclaimed all liability in respect of the goods in the event and as from the time of transhipment in the bill of lading.[106]

However, the exact content of "continuous documentary cover", and thus the rights that the document has to confer to the buyer, cannot be predicted or defined without reference to possible facts. Moreover, in *Buckman v. Levi*,[107] Lord Eldborough held that the buyer must be put in a position to return to the carrier for his indemnity.[108] Such rights of the shipper and his endorsees/assignees to be indemnified are the ones to be abandoned via a volume contract; therefore, cases concerning the reasonable contract of carriage (before and after section 32(2) of the SOGA) will become more and more of reference.

In our opinion, the important aspect to be covered is that the third party/consignee/bill of lading holder must have a proper defendant, the carrier, for claims under the transport document. This protection is not granted when, for instance the goods are shipped at the owner's risk.[109] It has been suggested[110] that although the section does not cast upon the seller the duty to ensure the success of litigation against the carrier, the contract of carriage and the transport document tendered must not be actually depriving the buyer of substantive legal rights against the carrier. The above deterrent is mirroring exactly what Article 80 of the RR does: a volume contract to which the RR apply may provide for greater *or lesser rights, obligations and liabilities than those imposed by this Convention* (emphasis added). This draws support from the case law on the third aspect of reasonableness, namely that the contract tendered must grant sufficient protection to the goods while in transit.

A particular obligation of the carrier which may be contracted out through a volume contract is the cargoworthiness duty outlined in Article 14(c) of the RR. The same exclusion will be an issue under the Incoterms® as well, as under article A3 the contract of carriage that the seller concludes has to be reasonable. Volume contracts may constitute an unusual and unreasonable contract of carriage by reference to both the SOGA and the Incoterms®.

104 [1922] 2 AC 36.
105 [1954] 2 Lloyd's Rep 45.
106 Ibid, at p. 53; Bridge (ed), *Benjamin's Sale of Goods*, para 19-027 to 19-028.
107 (1813) 3 Camp 414.
108 Ibid, p. 415.
109 *Thomas Young & Sons Ltd v. Hobson & Partners* (1949) 65 TLR 365.
110 See Lorenzon, 'When is a CIF seller's carriage contract unreasonable? Section 32(2) of the Sale of Goods Act 1979', p. 246.

Arguably, one of the criticisms to be advocated with regards to volume contracts is that since the third party is in a position to reject the derogations, he is having the chance to contract on normal RR terms and thus to have recourse against the carrier. However, since the exclusions of liability may be so exquisitely drafted as to pass unnoticed or simply be summarised and not properly addressed, the possibility of rejection may be forfeited.[111] Therefore, a third party/buyer/consignee (B, F or Z) may accept without realising how important the rights that he has surrendered against the carrier are. If one adds to the above, the vagueness floating around the time, the way and the form of gaining the consent of the third party, it becomes obvious that the position of the latter is at particular risk. These are impliedly left to be resolved in the trade sphere by the respective parties. The RR do not show a robust way of assessing or providing a remedy for the failure to properly notify of derogations. We have therefore advised on how traders can draft their contracts in order to have their sale contract interests secured.

6.8 Repercussions of volume contracts that derogate on letters of credit transactions

The trade implications of the provisions of the RR on volume contracts do not stop there. We believe that volume contracts with derogations from the RR will seemingly introduce a new category of documents and ignite a different allocation of risks which have to be accommodated through the UCP 600. The transport document issued under a volume contract will perhaps convey the derogations, at least by numeric reference to the sections displaced by agreement. The confirming bank, before which the documents will be presented by the seller for payment, will raise grounds for rejection, for the first time, if the buyer is not already notified of the derogations. Rejection will be conditional upon extra requirements being inserted in the letter of credit, so that the documents' checker is aware of what constitutes a non-compliant presentation, as far as volume transport documents are concerned. Such an extra requirement would be to get informed on the articles of the RR whose contractual exclusion is undesirable by the buyer.

This step also has to comply with the UCP 600 and it could be refrained by some of its articles. According to Article 4(a) of the UCP 600, a credit by its nature is a separate transaction from the sale or other contract on which it may be based. In addition, according to Article 14(a) of the UCP, a confirming bank must examine a presentation to determine, on the basis of the documents alone, whether or not the documents appear on their face to constitute a complying presentation. Therefore, if the derogations are listed on the back of the bill of lading, where the conditions of carriage are usually clustered, the checker is dismissed from the responsibility to

111 One has to understand that the prominent statement concerns that the volume contract derogates from the RR, and not the specific content of the individual derogations, according to Articles 80(2)(a) and 80(5)(a).

check and assess them. If Article 80(2) of the RR is recalled, it is important that there shall be a prominent statement of the derogations on the transport document.[112]

Two suggestions are noteworthy. Bergami has already proposed that additional documents may be required under the letter of credit to provide conclusive and straightforward evidence of unacceptable derogations.[113] Bergami also argued that a statement made by the carrier on the face of the transport document or in another written form that no derogation from the RR has been agreed, could sufficiently protect the buyer.[114] According to Bergami, extra insurance cover for the risk discharged might be necessary for a bank to issue a letter of credit, even if this sounds quite exceptional.[115] In Bergami's view, specific insurance cover for the liability stemming from the exclusion of the RR might therefore be an additional documentary requirement of the credit.[116] Nevertheless, a bank may still have no interest in receiving a transport document with derogations.

Whether the transport document is made to the order of the bank or to the order of the buyer/receiver of the goods may or may not have any implication here. A waiver of the derogations/discrepancies is harmless for the bank, if the bill of lading is to the order of the buyer. If the bill of lading, however, is consigned to the bank as security, the letter of credit will have to be complied with and seemingly the confirming bank may or may not exercise its discretion to approach the issuing bank for a waiver (should the buyer be willing to accept the derogations). In the latter case, it is in the bank's interest to reject tenders confirming the existence of derogations, because its position as a claimant against the carrier can be weak.

Evidently, the volume contract documentation in the hands of a buyer on the one hand, and under a letter of credit on the other, have substantial differences because of the separation of the letter of credit from the underlying transactions and the possibility of acceptance by the buyer of the derogations.[117] Generally, acceptance or rejection of the derogations makes the purchase of the particular cargo entirely different from purchase of goods under a contract where the carrier has undertaken standard RR (or extra) liabilities. Therefore, the carrier will prefer to conduct voyages where he knows that the consignee has accepted, so that he can predict his litigation position in a certain way. The former may use as a threat that he will not discharge or delay discharge to a consignee who rejected derogations simply because he wants to avoid accruing claims which will worsen his position, if the RR apply. To prevent this, the seller *qua* shipper will not want to run the risk of his goods being undelivered because a consignee wishes to reject the derogations, and he will therefore buy additional cargo or liability insurance for these goods.[118]

112 Article 80(2)(a) of the RR.

113 Bergami, 'The Rotterdam Rules and bills of lading: Challenges for letter of credit transactions', p. 18.

114 Ibid.

115 Ibid.

116 Ibid.

117 Or intention to waive them due to the position of the market.

118 This, in the opinion of Bergami, 'The Rotterdam Rules and bills of lading: Challenges for letter of credit transactions', is a significant security for banks that are consignees under the bill of lading.

The rationale of the uncertainties lurking beneath freedom of contract granted to volume contracts is that they are not restrictively described in the RR. Therefore, the RR become inconsistent as to their main approach, which is extensive codification; it can even be argued that they open the back door to great universal disharmony should small and medium sized carriers and cargo interests have to trade with canny counterparts without the market giving them a better alternative.

6.9 Conclusion

The RR may be a carriage convention, but they will undoubtedly have an international trade law impact. Although, by scope, they are restricted to the relationship between the original parties to the contract of carriage, they attempt to show an overall consideration for trade parties, as we saw with the case of the documentary shipper. It has also been observed that they try to become more aligned with current practices of maritime trade. Sometimes, however, their impact on the trade legal territory may show complexities. This is what is feared for Article 47(2) of the RR.

Moreover, on the understanding that different trades or ports have particular customs and trades, and in an attempt to be broader than the HVR and the Hamburg Rules, the RR have adopted the contractual approach. This means that they will apply to a contract of carriage, under specific circumstances, regardless of whether specific documents are issued. However, a deeper analysis of the articles of the RR on e-commerce has revealed that the RR have administered integrity obligations and the possibility of replacement only for negotiable documents. This is in contrast with the wider contractual approach[119] that the RR take, which is beyond documents and trades, and therefore rebuts the heralded abstraction of e-commerce provisions, for the sake of neutrality and adaptability to emerging technologies. Otherwise definition of non-negotiable records would be obsolete.

The RR have been administered to bring modernisation and uniformity in modern trade. However, they are not as "courageous" in defining what custom or usage or practice is, leaving it to national law. Perhaps this is also purposefully left vague, so that commercial reality and different customs can fit in along with the desired widespread application of the RR. Unfortunately, the perception of custom in one country may be totally different from another. The definition of custom has been a vexing issue internationally and, perhaps some clarification could have been provided by the RR. A definition could provide uniformity across civil and common law jurisdictions, putting an end to the international fragmentation. Therefore, the drafting burden that remains for the clarification of such issues in the context of a sale contract should not be overlooked.

By virtue of their definition and designated area of application, the role that the RR give to the shipper (who may be the seller or buyer in the sale contract) automatically makes this party more powerful than his trade counterparty.

119 Sturley, 'Scope of application', in von Ziegler, Schelin and Zunarelli (eds), *The Rotterdam Rules 2008*, para 2.1.

When examining the RR from an international trade law perspective, one will understand that occasionally they do more than expected (entitlement to documents, recognition of types of documents, volume contracts) and on other occasions they are more hesitant than expected (in the area of electronic commerce).

Overall, from the trade law viewpoint, the RR have proven to be an instrument that promotes flexibility for carriers to the detriment of legal certainty for traders. This is obvious, through Articles 35 and 47(2), and through the provisions on e-commerce and volume contracts. A liability regime like that of the RR should weigh certainty more. Therefore, since the RR are not always systematic with what their draftsmen administered, it is expected that they will trigger complexities. There is a permeating inconsistency of approach, which, as repeatedly conveyed in this book, unfortunately could cause complexities in the international trade law realm; this is where de facto the commercial parties need to think outside the narrow context of their sale contract.

If one wants to link the above conclusions with the principles analysed at the beginning of the chapter, the following becomes evident: the RR seem to consolidate and not only codify existing trade practices. This is not without its risks, as the RR regulate limited rights in an extensive way, only for certain documents. Sometimes, forgetting that they come to codify, the RR generalise practices, which may not be global. This means that enhanced codification comes to the detriment of harmonisation, which is the common objective of all international and private international rule-setting processes. The consequences in terms of commercial certainty would be less detrimental if the RR were a Model Law convention, but they are not.

Moreover, the balance of codification and freedom of contract enshrined in the RR is perpetually fluctuating throughout their text. More concretely, because of volume contracts, it is the very first time that we see a piece of international codification giving extensive contractual freedom to certain contracts. However, as we have seen, the relevant provisions can cause interpretational difficulties. Because of its abstract and sometimes ambiguous drafting, Article 80 of the RR may serve as a loose set of guidelines on how to bring any carriage contract within that contractual freedom. The way of *codification* of contractual freedom in the context of volume contracts (may sound paradoxical, but it is not) therefore restricts legal certainty and protection of the weaker parties, which has been a traditional principle of all conventions of this type. It also undermines global harmony as not all trades and countries (including national legislations) may be prepared for the widespread use of such contracts. More dangerously, the convention through the above, can be legitimately where it should not, any time. When it comes to third parties and volume contracts, the codification is unjustifiably loose. Special care is usually dedicated to third parties, so, in that respect, the RR show an internal inconsistency of approach, as this protection, as discussed in Chapter 5, is not robust.

The clash of principles of codification and freedom of contract explains the commercial law background but also foreshadows the future impact of this convention. Freedom of contract, as a virtue of commercial law, is theoretically enhanced through volume contracts, but if one looks deeper, it will be concluded that freedom of contract under the RR is essentially channelled; therefore, it will have to be used cautiously and in a preventative fashion in order to prevent the hindrances noted above in the drafting of sale contracts. Party autonomy probably never had to be so driven in specific directions for the sake of achieving legal certainty. So far, legal certainty has been safeguarded through codification rather than party autonomy. After the RR, this will be reversed, to the cost of trading parties and to the benefit of legal counsels and practitioners. It is diligent contract drafting for rescuing from the drawbacks of ambiguous codification that will set the platform of future international sale contracts.

The above analysis in our opinion best explains how the individual issues researched in the separate chapters are of international trade law relevance, and provides a deeper and solid corroboration of our conclusions.

The final conclusion comes next.

Conclusion

The overriding aim of this book has been to foreshadow and assess the impact of the Rotterdam Rules on international trade law. In order to reach an answer, we have examined the different underpinnings of carriage and trade laws. In Chapter 1, the different principles and sources of the law of carriage and international trade law were discerned. We have shown that there are varied legal sources which compose these laws. In international trade law, there is a tendency for self-regulation, and the terms are purposefully drafted to solve commercial needs, usually by the ICC, with the approach "from business to business". In international commerce, we tend to see more model contracts and standard terms, to allow the parties to tailor-make their agreement. Freedom of contract underpins commercial transactions, therefore English law is most often incorporated justifiably in commercial contracts.

In carriage laws on the other hand, the international conventions in place have higher policy missions. The predecessors to the RR have been deployed to regulate uncontrollable use of freedom of contract exercised by carriers through exclusion of liability clauses. The primary principle has been to protect the party that has not participated in the negotiation of the carriage contract. However, in the recent years, it has been observed that the market has changed, and the bargaining position of cargo interests has improved; therefore, the RR have come to provide flexible solutions to modern trade, and thus aspire to promote its facilitation. However, this flexibility can be seen differently in the carriage and international trade law realms. The RR are more comprehensive and more in line with modern maritime trade, in containing provisions on right of control, e-commerce and choice of formats as well as forms of documents to be issued. However, their scope focuses on the original parties to the carriage contract and not on the trade protagonists as such. Therefore, the priority as to choices is given to the carrier and the trader/original party to the contract of carriage.

As examined in Chapter 2, when dealing with string sales, the new provisions of the RR on the right of control and delivery instructions may seem to conflict with stoppage in transit provisions. Essentially the RR's concept of the right of control does not relate to possessory rights *stricto sensu*. This, however, can give rise to conflicting instructions. Unless these similar RR and SOGA concepts are properly understood and possibly judicially refined, these controversial instructions can lead to disputes. Moreover, national reform (or contractual designation that a negotiable document is issued at the seller's order) would be necessary to allow stoppage in transit under the SOGA and right of control under the RR to operate in a reconciled way, with clearly divided lines.

The flexibility given to the buyer to seek instructions in cases of problems with delivery is not rigorously drafted, and occasionally it gives stronger powers to the shipper than to the holder of the negotiable transport document. In Chapter 2, the investigation of Article 47(2) of the RR revealed that, if negotiable documents not requiring surrender make their appearance, the security of negotiable documents as documents of title will be substantially altered. If a negotiable transport document that does not require surrender has been issued, the surrender of the negotiable transport document will no longer be mandatory for the goods to be delivered. This means that, before agreeing to the sale contract, the parties should carefully consider the implications that the issuance of this transport document has. Otherwise, if contrary to the agreement of the parties, the negotiable document issued does not require surrender. If this were paramount, this may trigger litigation, in cash, against documents transactions and cases involving letters of credit.

Article 47(2) of the RR and its weaknesses, as criticised in Chapter 2, show that the contract of carriage may dramatically denude the negotiability of the document of title; therefore, the contract of carriage appears to be stronger than its document/evidence under the RR. What is sacrosanct in international trade is to get the transport document contracted for, and Article 47(2) shows how much a non-conforming contract of carriage (or transport document) can forfeit the expectations of the traders in sales down a string. The RR are in that respect too forward in standardising the law, as negotiable documents of title, in the minds of traders, have to be presented. This confirms once more how carriage laws have an impact on trade laws, and why carriage regulations cannot be disregarded by trade players, who may be faced with such a document without realising the possible repercussions. This again may lead to legal uncertainty in international commercial transactions.

A positive facet of the overall trade facilitation objective of the RR is seen through the broad entitlement to documents and records. The RR also welcome e-commerce. They do not shape it, restrict it or have an actual effect upon it, but rather give the green light to party autonomy and national legislations to step in with more thorough provisions. English law can assist in the promotion of e-commerce by adopting the RR, or in any case, by adopting the new terminology and concepts of the RR in its national legislation.

The RR are flexible in not requiring issuance of transport documents to provide for different trade customs. This flexibility, and at the same time the ambiguity of Article 35, may affect traditional principles of trade, such as the importance of documents (especially of the bill of lading in string sales). We have discussed the ways in which an agreement has to be drafted to address this uncertainty in Chapter 3. When compared with Incoterms® and the UCP 600, the RR have shown themselves much in the same line, but in some areas, such as through Article 35, they are inclusive of more options, which necessitate clearer agreements, as well as awareness on how to displace adverse customs, usages and practices of the trade. It is not certain whether the meaning of custom and usage will differentiate the relevant perceptions under English law or civil law. However, when English law applies, as long as thoroughly drafted sale contracts are entered into and (ideally) with provisions evidencing knowledge but exclusion of the custom, no unpleasant surprises should be encountered, as we have suggested.

Again, the RR seem to credit international trade with flexibility and options, but they fail to provide a set of standards for the systems of paperless trade. This is another factor that may trigger uncertainty, and an extra burden in the exercise of contractual freedom, which again is at odds with the underpinnings of trade. The reluctance of the market towards paperless shipping contracts is due to the lack of a robust framework that would ensure safety of the transactions and enforceability of rights, and the RR do not seem to provide a better solution for that. When it comes to their provisions for electronic trading, the RR seem to stand as an encouragement for legislation, rather than bring forward an effective change in the law. However, guidance on what the parties will voluntarily need to regulate in their e-commerce agreements, and advice on the way in which legislation in the UK can be updated in this regard have been provided.

Lastly, the RR take into consideration peculiarities of liner trade, such as volume contracts to which they allow a greater extent of freedom of contract, on the assumption that shippers and carriers are of equal bargaining power. The definition of volume contracts and the prerequisites of derogation from the RR seem too vague. Small and medium sized shippers may be induced into entering into such contracts due to low freight rates, and thus be enticed into acceptance of a contract prescribing a lower liability undertaking by the carrier. These contracts of carriage may suggest a breach of the seller's duty under section 32(2) of the SOGA, especially if the cargoworthiness obligation of the carrier, as imposed by the RR, can be contracted out. Nations can adopt specific legislation, perhaps by defining the distinctive characteristics of volume contracts more clearly than the RR. Alternatively, a supervisory committee can be set up to overlook the evidence of fairness of the negotiations, the transparency and the legitimacy of the derogations from the RR in the volume contracts that would otherwise fall under their scope.

The unwelcome uncertainty caused for third parties to volume contracts with derogations is multiplied by the fact that the traders have to make themselves privy to the contractual details of carriage, without always succeeding in getting that information, or accessing everything that would constitute their claim status against the carrier. Derogations from the RR may conceal exemptions from liability which traders cannot disregard, and which may have to be struck down by the courts. We believe that the "red hand" rule will have to come of assistance, to set up criteria for arguing whether there is a binding effect of the derogations through transport documents or other documents on third parties.

Traders, as third parties, are directly affected if they do not specifically understand the risks associated with volume contracts with derogations. The duty of cargoworthiness may be easily removed from the mandatory scope of the RR if a volume contract with derogations is entered into; therefore, the parties will have to insist that this duty is not contractually displaced. The only remedy available for buyers would be the revival of the long-unused section 32(2) of the SOGA. Indeed, the tremendous trade significance of volume contracts is that they increase the risks for international traders/third parties, and especially for unsophisticated ones. The reason is that the commercial pressure and need for speed in practice rather undermine a real possibility for open, let alone lengthy or specific, negotiations between carriers and traders. It has to be clarified, here, that the criticism has nothing to do with the principle of freedom of contract – the disagreement focuses on the particular drafting insufficiencies of Article 80. The example of OLSAs can teach us that an overriding supervisory entity is crucial for supporting contractual freedom, while preventing legal uncertainty.

In Chapter 6, the legal-teleological thread of the implications that the RR produce for trade has been revealed. Up until then, the trade synergies were shown in the individual chapters through case scenarios. In essence, all the scenarios, when added and discussed again in a holistic trade context, show the common problem. This can be attributed to the inconsistent way of standardisation that the RR convey, and this produces legal uncertainty. Trade on the other hand can be abstract and specific, in different self-regulation texts. The inconsistency in the extent and exhaustion of codification within the RR proves risky when the sale contract is specific and the RR are ambiguous, particularly where the party that exercises a right under the RR, usually the first shipper, is completely isolated from the string sales that follow. The effect of the RR is strong yet unpredictable, by making the decisions of the trader/original party to the contract of carriage have a direct or indirect reflective effect on the position of buyers/third parties.

As underlined throughout the book, insofar as there is thoroughly diligent drafting of a sale contract, and sufficient awareness of the surprises in terms of getting the transport document, or the desired type of it, traders will be able to reduce legal uncertainty to the minimum. This is the contribution that we aspire to offer to the development of international trade law: the aim has been to identify the practical implications a carriage convention can have on trade as a seismograph to show the interfaces of international carriage and trade standardisation of terms. This can only lead to a better understanding of international carriage and trade laws. This, in turn, shows us the need (or way) for future legal reform and contract drafting, for more advanced, yet secure and harmonious, international trade.

This book's suggestions will be relevant regardless of the ratification of the RR, as arguably despite the possible complications stemming from some articles, this Convention has taken on board problems of modern trade and introduced concepts or ways of looking at carriage contracts, which are beneficial for carriage and trade parties, regulators, courts and policy makers. Therefore, any legal framework which might replace or envelop the RR would ideally keep the main concepts of the Convention, as they address needs of modern trade, but would advisably secure against the shortcomings of the RR through clearer and more explicit provisions in the respects that we have illustrated.

Freedom of contract can prevent against the risks of inconsistent or ambiguous codification (as is the case with the RR), at least to a significant extent. The rest is up to individual national legislations.

We are confident that the diligent sale and carriage contract drafting, and where necessary additional national, regional and international legislation, will make the RR, or their possible successor, not only a workable Convention for both carriage and international trade laws, but also an effective one.

If the RR do not come into force, the ways in which the shipping world can utilise the positive innovations they embrace in order to avoid commercial pitfalls will be the subject of further national and international legislation and of private self-regulation respectively, and we sincerely hope that this book makes a step in this direction.

Bibliography

Books/Chapters in books

Aikens R, Lord R and Bools M (eds), *Bills of Lading* (Informa 2006)

Antapassis, Athanasiou and Røsæg (eds), *Competition and Regulation in Shipping and Shipping Related Industries* (Martinus Nijhoff 2009)

Asariotis R, 'Loss due to a combination of causes: burden of proof and commercial risk allocation' in DR Thomas (ed), *A New Convention for the Carriage of Goods by Sea – The Rotterdam Rules: An Analysis of the UN Convention on Contracts for the International Carriage of Goods Wholly or Partly by Sea* (Lawtext Publishing Ltd 2009)

Asariotis R, 'Reflections on the Rotterdam Rules' in MA Clarke (ed), *Maritime Law Evolving: Thirty Years at Southampton* (Hart Publishing 2013)

Atiyah P, *The Rise and Fall of Freedom of Contract* (Clarendon Press 1979)

Baatz Y et al, *Maritime Law* (2nd edn, Sweet & Maxwell 2011)

Baatz, Debattista, Lorenzon, Serdy, Staniland and Tsimplis, *The Rotterdam Rules – A Practical Annotation* (Informa 2009)

Baskind E, Osborne G and Roach L, *Commercial Law* (OUP 2013)

Baskind E, Osborne G and Roach L, *Commercial Law* (2nd edn, OUP 2016)

Baughen S, 'Obligations Owed by the Shipper to the Carrier', in DR Thomas (ed), *A New Convention for the Carriage of Goods by Sea: The Rotterdam Rules: An Analysis of the UN Convention on Contracts for the International Carriage of Goods Wholly or Partly by Sea* (Lawtext Publishing 2009)

Beale HG (ed), *Chitty on Contracts* (30th edn, Sweet & Maxwell 2008)

Beale HG (ed), *Chitty on Contracts* (31st edn, Sweet & Maxwell 2012)

Beale HG (ed), *Chitty on Contracts* (32nd edn, Sweet & Maxwell 2015)

Bennion F, *Statutory Interpretation* (4th edn, Butterworths 2002)

Berger KP, *The Creeping Codification of the Lex Mercatoria* (Kluwer Law International 1999)

Blancard L (ed), *Documents Inédits sur le Commerce de Marseille au Moyen Age* (Barlatier-Feissat, Pere et Fils 1884), II, p. 109; reprinted in Roy C Cave and Herbert H Coulson (eds), *A Source Book for Medieval Economic History* (The Bruce Publishing Co, 1936; reprinted Biblo & Tannen, 1965)

Bridge MG (ed), *Benjamin's Sale of Goods* (10th edn, Sweet & Maxwell 2017)

Bridge MG, *The International Sale of Goods* (3rd edn, OUP 2013)

Bridge MG, *The Sale of Goods* (OUP 2003)

Bridge MG, *The Sale of Goods* (OUP 1997)

Buckley FH (ed), *The Fall and Rise of Freedom of Contract* (Duke University Press 1979)

Burnett R, *Law of International Business Transactions* (3rd edn, The Federation Press 2014)

Burrows A (ed), *English Private Law* (3rd edn, OUP 2013)

Campbell D (ed), *E-Commerce and the Law of Digital Signatures* (OUP 2005)

Carr I, *International Trade Law* (4th edn, Routledge-Cavendish 2010)
Chuah J, *Law of International Trade: Cross-border Commercial Transactions* (5th edn, Sweet & Maxwell 2013)
Clarke MA, *Aspects of the Hague Rules* (Martinus Nijhoff 1976)
Clarke MA (ed), *Maritime Law Evolving: Thirty Years at Southampton* (Hart Publishing 2013)
Davidson A, *The Law of Electronic Commerce* (Cambridge University Press 2009)
Debattista C, *Bills of Lading in Export Trade* (3rd edn, Tottel Publishing 2009)
Dicey, *Law and Opinion in England* (2nd edn, 1914)
Emparanza A, *Las reglas de Rotterdam: la regulación del contrato de transporte internacional de mercancías por mar* (Marcial Pons 2010)
Fletcher I, Mistelis L and Cremona M (eds), *Foundations and Perspectives of International Trade Law* (Sweet & Maxwell 2001)
Gaskell N, Baatz Y and Asariotis R (eds), *Bills of Lading: Law and Contracts* (LLP 2000)
Gilmore and Black, *The Law of Admiralty* (2nd edn, Foundation Press 1975)
Girvin S, *Carriage of Goods by Sea* (2nd edn, OUP 2011)
Goldby M, *Electronic Documents in Maritime Trade: Law and Practice* (OUP 2013)
Goode R (ed by Ewan McKendrick), *Goode on Commercial Law*, (4th edn, Penguin Books 2010)
Goode R (ed by Ewan McKendrick), *Goode on Commercial Law*, (5th edn, Penguin Books 2016)
Goode R, *Commercial Law* (2nd edn, Penguin Books 1995)
Gorton L et al (eds), *Shipbroking and Chartering Practice* (7th edn, Informa 2004)
Gorton L, *A Practical Guide to Contracts of Affreightment and Hybrid Contracts* (2nd edn, Lloyd's of London 1990)
Güner-Özbek MD (ed), *The United Nations Convention on Contracts for the International Carriage of Goods Wholly or Partly by Sea: An Appraisal of the Rotterdam Rules* (Springer 2011)
Heard S, 'E-bills: Will they deliver?' (2000) Oct LEGAmedia, as cited in M Goldby, *Electronic Documents in Maritime Trade: Law and Practice* (OUP 2013)
Herrmann G, 'The role of UNCITRAL', in I Fletcher, L Mistelis and M Cremona (eds), *Foundations and Perspectives of International Trade Law* (Sweet & Maxwell 2001)
Honka H, 'Validity of contractual terms' in A von Ziegler, J Schelin and S Zunarelli (eds), *The Rotterdam Rules 2008: Commentary to the United Nations Convention on Contracts for the International Carriage of Goods Wholly or Partly by Sea* (Kluwer Law International 2010)
Korotzis I, *Carriage of Goods by Sea According to the International Rotterdam Rules 2009* (AN Sakkoulas 2010)
Laryea E, *Paperless Trade, Opportunities, Challenges and Solutions* (The Global Trade and Finance Series Kluwer Law International 2002)
Lista A, *International Commercial Sales: The Sale of Goods on Shipment Terms* (Informa 2017)
Lorenzon F, *Sassoon on CIF and FOB Contracts* (6th edn, Sweet & Maxwell 2017)
Lorenzon F, *CIF and FOB Contracts* (5th edn, Sweet & Maxwell 2012)
Murray C, Holloway D and Timson-Hunt D, *Schmitthoff's Export Trade: The Law and Practice of International Trade* (12th edn, Sweet & Maxwell 2012)
Ramberg J, *Guide to Incoterms®* (1980 edn)
Ramberg J, *ICC Guide to Incoterms®* ICC
Ramberg J, 'Synchronisation of contracts of sale, carriage, insurance, and financing in international trade' in P Šarčević (ed), *International Contracts and Conflicts of Laws: A Collection of Essays* (1990)

Reed C, Walden I and Edgar L (eds), *Cross-Border Electronic Banking: Challenges and Opportunities* (Informa 2000)

Rossman V and Moskin M (eds), *Commercial Contracts – Strategies for Drafting and Negotiating* (Wolters Kluwer 2013)

Šarčević P (ed), *International Contracts and Conflicts of Laws: A Collection of Essays* (1990).

Schmitthoff, *Commercial Law in a Changing Economic Climate* (2nd edn, Sweet & Maxwell 1981)

Schoefield J, *Laytime and Demurrage* (6th edn, Informa 2011)

Sealy LS and Hooley RJA, *Commercial Law, Text, Cases and Materials* (5th edn, Oxford University Press, 2017)

Sturley MF, Fujita T and van der Ziel G, *The Rotterdam Rules* (Sweet & Maxwell 2010)

Tepper P, *The Law of Contracts and the Uniform Commercial Code* (2nd edn, Delmar Cengage Learning 2011)

Thomas DR (ed), *The Carriage of Goods by Sea Under The Rotterdam Rules* (Lloyd's List 2010)

Thomas DR (ed), *A New Convention for the Carriage of Goods by Sea – The Rotterdam Rules: An Analysis of the UN Convention on Contracts for the International Carriage of Goods Wholly or Partly by Sea* (Lawtext Publishing Ltd 2009)

Thomas DR (ed), *The Evolving Law and Practice of Charterparties* (Informa 2009)

Todd P, *Bills of Lading and Bankers' Documentary Credits* (4th edn, Informa 2007)

Todd P, 'Dematerialisation of shipping documents' in C Reed, I Walden and L Edgar (eds), *Cross-Border Electronic Banking: Challenges and Opportunities* (Informa 2000)

Treitel G and Reynolds FMB (eds), *Carver on Bills of Lading* (4th edn, Sweet & Maxwell 2017)

Treitel G and Reynolds FMB (eds), *Carver on Bills of Lading* (3rd edn, Sweet & Maxwell 2011)

van Hoecke M (ed), *Methodologies of Legal Research: Which Kind of Method for What Kind of Discipline?* (Hart Publishing 2011)

von Ziegler A, Schelin J and Zunarelli S (eds), *The Rotterdam Rules 2008: Commentary to the United Nations Convention on Contracts for the International Carriage of Goods Wholly or Partly by Sea* (Kluwer Law International 2010)

Walter M (ed), *Social Research Methods* (2nd edn, Oxford University Press 2010)

Wang F, *Law of Electronic Commercial Transactions: Contemporary Issues in the EU, US and China* (Routledge 2010)

Wilson J, *Carriage of Goods by Sea* (7th edn, Longman 2010)

Yiannopoulos AN (ed), *Electronic Bills of Lading: Traditional Forms, Substitutes, and EDI Systems* (Kluwer 1995)

Hard copy journal articles/newsletters/looseleafs

Alba M, 'Electronic commerce provisions in the UNCITRAL Convention on Contracts for the International Carriage of Goods Wholly or Partly by Sea' (2009) 44 *Texas International Law Journal* 387

Alba M, 'The use of electronic records as collateral in the Rotterdam Rules: Future solutions for present needs' (2009) Vol. XIV *Uniform Law Review* 801

Alcántara G JM, 'The Rotterdam Rules: Prelude or premonition?' (2010) 2(1) *Cuadernos de Derecho Transnacional* 25 at e-revistas.uc3m.es/index.php/CDT/article/viewFile/95/93

Asariotis R, 'Burden of proof and allocation of liability for loss due to a combination of causes under the new Rotterdam Rules' (2008) 14(6) *JIML* 537

Asariotis R, 'Main obligations and liabilities of the shipper under the UNCITRAL Draft Instrument' (2004) *Transportrecht* 284

Asariotis R, 'The Rotterdam Rules: A brief overview of some of their key features' (2009) 3 *EJCCL* 111

Asariotis R, 'What future for the bill of lading as a document of title?' (2008) 14(2) *JIML* 75

Bal B, 'A legal and economic analysis of the volume contract concept under the Rotterdam Rules: Selected issues in perspective', *Journal of Transportation Law Logistics and Policy*, 27

Bal B, 'The impact of the volume contract concept on the global community of shippers: The Rotterdam Rules in perspective' (2010) 16 *JIML* 352

Barnett M and Isaacs M, 'International trade finance – Letters of credit, UCP 600 and examination of documents' (2007) 22 (12) *Journal of International Banking Law and Regulation* 660

Bergami R, 'Rotterdam Rules: Volume contracts, delivery terms, transport documents and letters of credit' (2010) *The Vindobona Journal of International Commercial Law and Arbitration* 14(1)

Berlingieri F, 'A review of some recent analyses of the Rotterdam Rules' (2009) Il *Diritto Marittimo* 955

Berlingieri F, 'An analysis of two recent commentaries on the Rotterdam Rules' (2012) *Il Diritto Marittimo* 3

Berlingieri F, 'Freedom of contract under the Rotterdam Rules' [2009] 14 *Unif L Rev* 831

Berlingieri F, 'Revisiting the Rotterdam Rules' [2010] *LMCLQ* 583

Bonnevie P, 'Evaluation of the new Convention from the perspective of cargo interests' 9 2009 *Transportrecht* 361

Bradney A, 'Law as a parasitic discipline' (1998) 25(1) *Journal of Law and Society* 71

Bridge M, 'Uniformity and diversity in international sale contracts' (2003) 15(1) *Pace International Law Review* 55

Carlson MH, 'US participation in private international law negotiations: Why the new UNCITRAL carriage of goods convention is important to the US' (2009) 44 *Texas Int'l Law Journal* 269

Chan F, 'In search of a global theory of maritime electronic commerce: China's position on the Rotterdam Rules' *JMLC* 40 (2009) 185

Chuah J, 'The Bolero Project – The International Chamber of Commerce's electronic Bill of Lading project' (2000) *SL Rev* 30(Sum) 56

Chuah J, 'The FOB seller as shipper' (2007) *SL Rev.* 50(Spr), 54

Chuah J, 'The new German Act on the reform of Maritime Trade Law' (2013) 19(1) *JIML* 5

Chuah J, 'UCP 600 new challenges and issues' (2007) 13(2) *JIML* 73

Clarke M, 'Transport documents: Their transferability as documents of title; electronic documents' [2002] *LMCLQ* 356

Davies JM, 'What is a reasonable contract of carriage', Shipping and Trade Law (2003) 3 STL 4 1

de Haan J, 'A test case for the Rotterdam Rules' (2011) *Maritime Risk International* 25(7) 20

Debattista C, 'Carriage conventions and their interpretation in English courts' [1997] *JBL* 130

Debattista C, 'Laytime and demurrage clauses in contracts of sale – Links and connections' [2003] *LMCLQ* 508

Debattista C, 'Legislative techniques in international trade: Madness or method?' [2002] *JBL* 626

Delebecque P, 'L'évolution du transport maritime' (2009) *DMF* 16

Diamond A, 'The next sea carriage convention?' [2008] *LMCLQ* 135

Diamond A, 'The Rotterdam Rules' [2009] *LMCLQ* 445

Djakhongir S, 'English sale of goods law', [2013] *IMCLY* 83.

Dubovec M, 'The problems and possibilities for using electronic bills of lading as a collateral' (2006) 23 *AJICL* 437.

Eftestöl-Wilhelmsson E, 'The Rotterdam Rules in a European multimodal context' (2010) 16 *JIML* 274

Foglar V, 'Volume contracts after the Rotterdam Rules' (2010) 49(164) *Comparative Maritime Law* 221

Gaskell N, 'Bills of lading in an electronic age' [2010] *LMCLQ* 233

Gaskell N, 'Book Review, Sturley M, Fujita, van der Ziel, The Rotterdam Rules, The UN Convention on Contracts for the International Carriage of Goods Wholly or Partly by Sea' (2013) 27 *A&NZ Mar LJ* 42

Goldby M, 'A re-assessment of the CMI rules for electronic bills of lading in the light of current practices' [2008] *LMCLQ* 56

Goldby M, 'Electronic alternatives to transport documents and the new convention: A framework for future development?' (2008) 14 *JIML* 586

Goldby M, 'Electronic bills of lading and central registries: What is holding back progress?' (2008) 17 *Information and Communications Technology Law* 125

Goldby M, 'The performance of the bill of lading's functions under UNCITRAL's draft convention on the carriage of goods: Unequivocal legal recognition of electronic equivalents' (2007) 13 *JIML* 160

Goode RM, 'Usage and its reception in transnational commercial law' (1997) 46(1) *ICLQ* 1

Goulandris A, 'Electronic bills of lading have come of age' (2011) 25(3) *MRI*

Harrington R, 'News from the United Nations Commission on International Trade Law (UNCITRAL): The work of the fiftieth commission session' (2017) 22(4) *Uniform Law Review* 996

Higgs A and Humphreys G, 'Waybills: A case of common law laissez-faire in European commerce' [1992] *JBL* 453

Hoskins H, 'Contractual obligations to negotiate in good faith: Faithfulness to the agreed common purpose' (2014) *LQR* 131

Hwaidi M, 'The story of the English strict compliance principle in letters of credit and its consistency with the UCP' (2014) *JIBLR* 71

Illescas R, 'Project of UN Convention over the contract of international carriage of goods wholly or partly by sea' (2008) 210 *El Derecho de los Negocios*, Madrid (translation)

Jones P, 'A new transport convention: A framework for e-commerce?' (2002) 9 *Electronic Communication Law Review* 145

Kelly RB, 'The CMI charts a course on the sea of electronic data interchange: Rules for electronic bills of lading' [1991–1992] *Tulane Maritime Law Journal* 349

Kian Sing T, 'Of straight and switch bills of lading' [1996] *LMCLQ* 416

Kozubosbskaya- Pellé A, 'Contractual flexibility in volume contracts: Rotterdam Rules and French law perspective' (2013) 115 *Il Diritto Marittimo* 326

Levie JH, 'Trade usage and custom under the common law and the Uniform Commercial Code' (1965) 40 *NYU LRev* 1101

Liu E, 'Whether a term as to satisfactory quality is to be implied into Norwegian Saleform 1993 (NSF 1993) by way of section 14 of the Sale of Goods Act 1979' *Shipping & Trade Law* (2013) 13 STL 2 3

Lloyd, 'The bill of lading – Do we really need it?' [1989] *LMCLQ* 47
Lorenzon F, 'When is a CIF seller's carriage contract unreasonable? Section 32(2) of the Sale of Goods Act 1979' (2007) 13(4) *JIML* 241.
Macdonald E, 'The duty to give notice of unusual contract terms' (1988) *JBL* 375
Magklasi I, 'Documents' complexities under the Rotterdam Rules' (2011) *International Journal of Public Law and Policy* 1(4)
Magklasi I, 'Electronic transport records: Assessing the contribution of the Rotterdam Rules to e-commerce' (2013) 29(2) *Computer Law and Security Review* 120
Magklasi I, 'Volume contracts and third parties: "Red-hand rule" or Red-herring?' (2015) 7(1–2), *European Journal of Commercial Contract Law* 39
Mallon P, 'The legal implications of electronic commerce in international trade' (1997) 8 *Computers and Law* 24
Mankowski, 'The Rotterdam Rules – Scope of application and freedom of contract' (2010/12) *EJCCL* 9
Marlow P and Rawindaran N, 'Service contracts – An instrument of international logistics supply chain: Under United States and European Union regulatory frameworks' (2008) 32 *Marine Policy* 489
Mbiah K, 'Updating the rules on international carriage of goods by sea: The Rotterdam Rules', *CMI Yearbook* 2013, 310 at www.comitemaritime.org/Uploads/Rotterdam%20Rules/Paper%20of%20Kofi%20Mbiah.pdf
Merges R and Reynolds G, 'Towards a computerized system for negotiating ocean bills of lading' (1986) 6 *Journal of Law and Commerce* 36
Møllmann A, 'From bills of lading to transport documents: The role of transport documents under the Rotterdam Rules'(2011) 17 *JIML* 50
Mukherjee PK and Bal AB, 'A legal and economic analysis of the volume contract concept under the Rotterdam Rules: Selected issues in perspective' (2009) 40(4) *Journal of Maritime Law and Commerce* 579 at www.rotterdamrules2009.com/cms/uploads/Def.%20tekst%20Abhinayan%20Basu%20Bal%20-%20Volume%20Contract%20Final.pdf
Munday, 'The uniform interpretation of international conventions' [1978] *ICLQ* 450
Murray D, 'History and development of the bill of lading' (May-Sep 1983) 37 *U Miami L Rev* 689
Myburgh P, 'Uniformity or unilateralism in the law of carriage of goods by sea?' (2000) 31 *VUWLR* 355
Nikaki T, 'Conflicting laws in "wet" multimodal carriage of goods: The UNCITRAL Draft Convention on the Carriage of Goods [Wholly or Partly] [by Sea]' (2006) 37 *Journal of Maritime Law & Commerce* 521
Nikaki T and Soyer B, 'A new international regime for carriage of goods by sea: Contemporary, certain, inclusive, and efficient, or just another one for the shelves?' [2012] 30(2) *J Berkeley Int'l Law* 303
Nikaki T, 'Himalaya clauses and the Rotterdam Rules' (2011) 17 *JIML* 20
Nikaki T, 'The carrier's duties under the Rotterdam Rules: Better the devil you know?' (2010) 55 *Tulane Maritime Law Journal* 1
Nikaki T, 'The fundamental duties of the carrier under the Rotterdam Rules' (2008) 14 *JIML* 521
Nikaki T, 'The statutory Himalaya-type protection under the Rotterdam Rules – Capable of filling the gaps?' [2009] *JBL* 403
Odeke A, 'The nature of a CIF contract – Is it a sale of documents or a sale of goods?' [1993] *Journal of Contract Law* 158
Ozdel M, 'Multimodal transport documents in international sale of goods' (2012) 23(7) *International Company and Commercial Law Review* 238

Pejović C, 'Article 47(2) of the Rotterdam Rules: Solution of old problems or a new confusion?' (2012) 18 *JIML* 348

Pejović C, 'Main legal issues in the implementation of EDI to bills of lading' [1999] *European Transport Law* 163

Posner R, 'Legal scholarship today' (2001) 115 *Harvard Law Review* 1314

Ramberg J, 'INCOTERMS® 2000 – The necessary link between contracts of sale and contracts of carriage' (2008) 58(1–2) *Zbornik PFZ* 35

Ramberg J, 'UN Convention on Contracts for the International Carriage of Goods Wholly or Partly by Sea' (2009) *CMI Yearbook* 2009, 277

Ravillon L, 'Chronicle of informal sources on Business Law' [2012] 5 *IBLJ* 519

Reynolds F, 'The Hague Rules, the Hague-Visby Rules and the Hamburg Rules' (1990) 7 *MLAANZ Journal* 16

Røsæg E, 'New procedures for bills of lading in the Rotterdam Rules' (2011) 17 *JIML* 181

Saidov D, 'English Sale of Goods Law' [2013] *IMCLY* 83

Sassoon DM, 'Application of FOB and CIF sales in common law countries' (1981) 1 *European Transport Law* 50

Sassoon DM, 'The origin of FOB and CIF terms and the factors influencing their choice' (1967) *JBL* 32

Schelin J, 'Documents' (2004) *Transportrecht* 294

Schmitthoff C, 'International trade usages' (1987) *Institute of International Business Law and Practice*, ICC

Schmitthoff C, 'The unification or harmonisation of law by means of standard contracts and general conditions' (1968) 17 *Int'l & Comp L Q* 551

Schrama W, 'How to carry out interdisciplinary legal research: Some experiences with an interdisciplinary research method' (2011) 7 (1) *Utrecht Law Review* 147

Sturley MF, 'What has become of the Rotterdam Rules' (2016) 83(4) *Journal of Transportation Law, Logistics and Policy* 275

Sturley MF, 'Modernising and reforming US maritime law: The impact of the Rotterdam Rules in the United States' (2009) 44 *Texas International Law Journal* 427

Sturley MF, 'The UNCITRAL carriage of goods: Changes to existing Law', *CMI Yearbook* 2007–2008, 254

Sturley MF, 'Solving the scope-of-application puzzle: Contracts, trades and documents in the UNCITRAL transport law project' (2005) 11 *J INT'L MAR L* 22, 39

Sturley MF, 'The history of COGSA and the Hague Rules' (1991) 22(1) *Journal of Maritime Law and Commerce* 1

Sturley MF, 'International uniform laws in national courts: The influence of domestic law in conflicts of interpretation' (1987) 27 *Va J Int'l L* 729

Takahashi K, 'Right to terminate (avoid) international sales of commodities' [2003] *JBL* 102

Tetley W, 'Waybills: Modern contract of carriage of goods by sea' (1983) 14(4) *JMLC* 465

Thomas DR, 'Publication review of "The sale of goods carried by sea" of Charles Debattista' (2000) *LQR* 326

Thomas R, 'A comparative analysis of the transfer of contractual rights under the English Carriage of Goods by Sea Act 1992 and the Rotterdam Rules'(2011) 17(6) *JIML* 437

Tiller E and Cross F, 'What is legal doctrine?' (2006) 100(1) *Northwestern University Law Review* 517

Todd P, 'Dematerialisation of shipping documents' (1994) 10 *JIBL* 410

Todd P, 'Excluding and limiting liability for misdelivery' (2010) *JBL* 243

Ulfbeck V, 'Contracts of logistics under the Rotterdam Rules' (2011) 17(3) *JIML* 219

van der Ziel GJ, 'Delivery of the goods, rights of the controlling party and transfer of rights' (2008) 14 *JIML* 597 van der Ziel G, 'The legal underpinning of e-commerce in maritime transport by the UNCITRAL Draft Instrument on the Carriage of Goods by Sea' (2003) 9 *JIML* 461

van der Ziel G, 'The right of control and the controlling party' (2009) 44 *Texas Int'l Law Journal* 377

van Hoecke M and Warrington M, 'Legal cultures, legal paradigms and legal doctrine: Towards a new model for comparative law' (1998) 47(3) *International and Comparative Law Quarterly* 495

von Ziegler A, 'The Rotterdam Rules and the underlying sales contract', *CMI Yearbook* 2013, 273 at www.comitemaritime.org/Uploads/Rotterdam%20Rules/Paper%20of%20Tomotaka%20Fujita.pdf

Walden I and Savage N, 'The legal problems of paperless transactions' [1989] *JBL* 102

Whittaker S, 'A framework of principle for European contract law?' (2009) *LQR* 616

Williams R, 'The Rotterdam Rules: Winners and losers' (2010) 16 *JIML* 191

Williams R, 'Transport documentation under the new convention' (2008) 14 *JIML* 566

Wood D, 'National Report: An Australian perspective on the Rotterdam Rules' (2001) 17 *JIML* 147

Yongjan Z, 'On the international transport laws' uniformity which the Rotterdam Rules aim for' *CMI Yearbook* 2013, 287

Zwitser R, 'Cash against mate's receipt under the Rotterdam Rules' (2010) 16(5) *JIML* 380

Thesis

Nikaki T, '*The scope of application of the UNCITRAL Draft Instrument on the Carriage of Goods [wholly or partly] by sea*' (PhD Thesis, University of Southampton 2005)

Dictionary

Mann T (ed), *Australian Law Dictionary* (Oxford University Press 2010)

Online articles/materials

'A response to attempt to clarify certain concerns over the Rotterdam Rules' at www.mcgill.ca/files/maritimelaw/Summationpdf.pdf

'A single transport document and uniform liability regime for intermodal transport in Europe' at www.shortsea.fr/Extrait-magazine_BIC-CONTAINERS-1-2-2012.html

'Adoption of a new United Nations Convention on Contracts for the International Carriage of Goods Wholly or Partly by Sea: The Rotterdam Rules', Review of Maritime Transport 2009

'Australian comments on the UNCITRAL draft convention on contracts for the international carriage of goods wholly or partly by sea' (2008) 22 *A&NZ Mar LJ* at maritimejournal.murdoch.edu.au/index.php/maritimejournal/article/viewFile/63/106

'BIMCO: Documentary Committee meets in Dubai' at www.bimco.org/News/2014/05/09_Documentary_Committee_meets_in_Dubai.aspx?RenderSearch=true'BIMCO launches Standard Service Contract – SERVICECON' at www.globalshippersforum.com/media/1240/explanatory_notes_servicecon_bulletin_5-2014.pdf and www.bimco.org/Chartering/Documentary_Projects/New_contracts.aspx

BIMCO 'New Contracts' www.bimco.org/Chartering/Documentary_Projects/New_contracts.aspx

'Comments of the National Industrial Transportation League in support of the Petition P1-08' (before the Federal Maritime Commission) at www.google.co.uk/search?q=Comments++of+the+National+Industrial++Transportation+League+in+support+of+the+Petition+P1-08+(before+the+Federal+Maritime+Commission&sourceid=ie7&rls=com.microsoft:en-gb:IE-SearchBox&ie=&oe=

'Custom and trade usage: Its application to commercial dealings and the common law' (Dec 1955) *Columbia Law Review*, 555(8) 1192 at www.jstor.org/discover/10.2307/1119639?uid=3739256&uid=2&uid=4&sid=21103581046271

'FIATA Position on the UN Convention on Contracts for the International Carriage of Goods Wholly or Partly by Sea (the "Rotterdam Rules")', at www.comitemaritime.org/Uploads/Rotterdam%20Rules/3FIATA.pdf

'Supply of goods in a distance selling contract: the Judicial competence and the role of the Incoterms' at www.picozzimorigi.cn/main/reports.php?id=82

'The Rotterdam Rules: An attempt to clarify certain concerns that have emerged' at www.comitemaritime.org/Uploads/Rotterdam%20Rules/5RRULES.pdf

'The Rotterdam Rules seen by the ESC' at www.europeanshippers.eu/wp-content/uploads/2013/07/pr%C3%A9sentation-RR-pour-MTC-juin-2013.pdf

'Today's number: Trading crude oil electronically' at openmarkets.cmegroup.com/6799

'Declaration of Montevideo' at asadip.files.wordpress.com/2010/10/rr-answer-to-montevideo-declaration-eng.pdf

'Questions and answers: Why the MLA needs an open debate concerning the "volume contracts" exception to the proposed Rotterdam Rules' at www.mcgill.ca/files/maritimelaw/Questions_and_Answers_USMLA.pdf

'Response to the National Industrial Transportation League to the European Shippers' Council Position Paper on the Rotterdam Rules' at www.uncitral.org/pdf/english/texts/transport/rotterdam_rules/NITL_ResponsePaper.pdf

'UNCITRAL Colloquium on Rotterdam Rules: The Goods Carried – Who gets them and who controls them?' at www.rotterdamrules2009.com/cms/uploads/Def%20%20tekst%20Charles%20Debattista%2031%20OKT29.pdf

www.comitemaritime.org/Uploads/Rotterdam%20Rules/Paper%20of%20Prof.%20Si%20Yuzhuo%20and%20Dr.%20Zhang%20Jinlei.pdf

Brooks M, 'Will the Rotterdam Rules be accepted? A liner cargo interest perspective', (2012) 35(2) *Dalhousie Law Journal* 267 at maryrbrooks.ca/wp-content/uploads/2013/06/Brooks_Mackey-Vol-35-No-2.pdf

Alcántara, Hunt, Johansson, Oland, Psyden, Ramberg, Schmitt, Tetley and Vidal, '*Particular concerns with regard to the Rotterdam Rules*' at www.amya.es, www.forwarderlaw.com/library/view.php?article_id=602 and www.comitemaritime.org/Uploads/Rotterdam%20Rules/Particular%20concerns%20-%20Rotterdam%20Rules.pdf

Beare S, '*Rotterdam Rules: Some controversies*' at www.comitemaritime.org

Bergami R, '*The Rotterdam Rules and negotiable electronic transport documents in letter of credit business*' 297 at www.kmice.cms.net.my/ProcKMICe/KMICe2010/Paper/PG296_301.pdf

Bergami R, '*The Rotterdam Rules: The issues-Part 2*' at www.ibt-articles.com/absnet/templates/trade_article.aspx?articleid=362&zoneid=2

Berlingieri F, 'A comparative analysis of the Hague-Visby Rules, the Hamburg Rules and the Rotterdam Rules', paper delivered at the General Assembly of the International Association of Average Adjusters-AMD, Marrakesh, 5–6 November 2009, at www.uncitral.org/pdf/english/workinggroups/wg_3/Berlingieri_paper_comparing_RR_Hamb_HVR.pdf

Berlingieri F, Delebecque P, Fujita T, Illescas R, Sturley MF, van der Ziel G, von Ziegler A and Zunarelli S '*The Rotterdam Rules, an attempt to clarify certain concerns that have emerged*', on CMI and UNCITRAL websites

Berlingieri F, '*Multimodal aspects of the Rotterdam Rules*' at www.rotterdamrules2009.com/cms/uploads/Def.%20tekst%20F.%20Berlingieri%2013%20OKT29.pdf

Chami D, '*The obligations of the carrier*' at www.rotterdamrules2009.com/cms/uploads/Def.%20tekst%20Diego%20Chami%20-%20Obligations%20of%20the%20Carrier.pdf

CLECAT, Position Paper on the Rotterdam Rules at www.comitemaritime.org/Uploads/Rotterdam%20Rules/4CLECAT.pdf

Dicker D, '*How electronic trading changed (ruined) crude oil prices*' at www.futuresmag.com/2013/10/01/dan-dicker-how-electronic-trading-changed-ruined-c

Frisch D and Gabriel H D, 'Much Ado about Nothing: Achieving essential negotiability in an electronic environment'(1995) 31 *IDAHO LREV* 747

ESC '*View of the European Shippers' Council on the Convention on Contracts for the International Carrying of Goods Wholly or Partly by Sea also known as the "Rotterdam Rules"*' at www.uncitral.org/pdf/english/texts/transport/rotterdam_rules/ESC_PositionPaper_March2009.pdf

FIATA, Position Paper on the Rotterdam Rules at www.comitemaritime.org/Uploads/Rotterdam%20Rules/3FIATA.pdf

Fujita T, '*Shipper's obligations and liabilities under the Rotterdam Rules*' at www.gcoe.j.u-tokyo.ac.jp/pdf/GCOESOFTLAW-2010–3.pdf

Gauthier J, '*The Rotterdam Rules and the facilitation of e-commerce*', at www.comitemaritime.org/Uploads/Rotterdam%20Rules/Summary%20Johanne%20Gauthier%20-%20Annex%201%20-%20english.pdf

Gorton L, '*Volume contracts of affreightment: some features and principles*', at www.scandinavianlaw.se/pdf/46-3.pdf

Heydon JD, '*How the courts develop commercial law by looking outside the trial record into the external world; usage of trade: impact on agreement*' at learntheucc.wordpress.com/2011/11/06/usage-of-trade-impact-on-agreement/

Honka H, '*Scope of application, freedom of contract*' at www.rotterdamrules2009.com/cms/uploads/Def.%20tekst%20Hannu%20Honka.pdf

www.immta.org/uploads/ImmtaNews_2009_2.pdf

www.rotterdamrules.com/sites/default/files/pdf/Rotterdam-Rules-rebels-intent-on-rocking-the-boat-Lloyd's-List-28-08-2009.pdf

www.google.co.uk/url?sa=t&rct=j&q=&esrc=s&source=web&cd=17&cad=rja&ved=0CGkQFjAGOAo&url=http%3A%2F%2Fwww.dpps-mlas.si%2Fwp-content%2Fuploads%2F2011%2F03%2FRotterdam-Rules_Between-Old-problems-and-New-Sollutions-Jana-Rodica-2009_PUBLIKACIJE-PUBLICATIONS.ppt&ei=Vm04Uu7UFcON7Abz6YGgCg&usg=AFQjCNFUQbmzoN-PoZT2QKCjywBmf8NIDw

Kuusniemi I, '*European Transport Policy: challenges for Finnish shipping Industry*' www.helsinki.fi/katti/ITPRESENTATIONS/IlkkaKuusniemi-Europeantransportpolicy-ChallengesfforFinnishshippingIndustry.pdf

IM Technologies Ltd, *Executive summary and final report of the economic impact of carrier liability on intermodal freight transport*, London 10.1.2001, for use and information of the European Commission at ec.europa.eu/transport/strategies/studies/doc/2009_05_19_multimodal_transport_report.pdf

Jones P, '*The UNCITRAL Convention on Carriage of Goods by Sea: Harmonization or De-harmonization*', at www.forwarderlaw.com/library/view.php?article_id=602

Lando O, 'Standard contracts. A proposal and a perspective' *Scandinavian Studies in Law* (1966), at www.scandinavianlaw.se/pdf/10-5.pdf

Lannan K, '*Navigating the UN Convention on Contracts for the International Carriage of Goods Wholly or Partly by Sea*' at www.unece.org/fileadmin/DAM/trans/wp24/wp24-presentations/documents/pres10-05.pdf

Maloof M, '*Concerns about volume contracts*', at mlaus.org/archives/library/1904.pdf

Møllmann A, '*Right of control and transfer of rights*' at curis.ku.dk/ws/files/22386264/Right_of_control_and_transfer_of_rights.doc

'Professor Debattista on Incoterms® 2010 in the Lloyd's List', on 2nd February 2011 at www.southampton.ac.uk/iml/news/incotersm_ll_article.shtml

Ramberg J, '*Incoterms® 2010 – Why and how*' (presentation 22 July 2010) under the heading "The interrelation between Incoterms® and other contracts" at www.law.utoronto.ca/documents/conferences2/IACCL10-Ramberg.pdf

Schmitt DG, '*Will Rotterdam succeed? Testing the waters at CMI Buenos Aires*' at www.ahbl.ca/wp-content/uploads/2012/05/Will_Rotterdam_Succeed-Testing_the_Waters_at_CMI_Buenos_Aires-Douglas_Schmitt-May2011.pdf

Shipping Australia Limited, '*SAL comments on the proposed Australian delegation position and country position paper regarding a draft Convention on Contracts for the International Carriage of Goods Wholly or Partly by Sea*' at shippingaustralia.com.au/wp-content/uploads/2012/10/Sub-UNCITRAL-Draft-Convention1.pdf

Steamship Mutual '*Bills of lading – Liability for incorrect clausing*' (April 2004) at www.simsl.com/Publications/Articles/Articles/BoL_DavidAg0404.asp

Tetley W, '*Responsibility, Fraternity and Sustainability in Law – A symposium in Honour of Charles D. Gonthier,*' Conference proceedings, at cisdl.org/gonthier/public/pdfs/papers/Conf%C3%A9rence%20Charles%20D%20Gonthier%20-%20Benoit%20Mayer.pdf

Tetley W, '*Transports de cargaison par mer, les Règles de Rotterdam, leur adoption par les États-Unis, le Canada, l'Union Européenne et les pays transporteurs du monde?*' (Conference Proceedings of the Responsibility, Fraternity, and Sustainability in Law, A Symposium in honour of Charles D Gouthier delivered at the Faculty of Law, McGill University, 20–21 May 2011), online: Center for International Sustainable Development Law at cisdl.org/gonthier/public/pdfs/papers/Conf%C3%A9rence%20Charles%20D%20Gonthier%20-%20William%20Tetley.pdf

van der Ziel G, '*The issue of transport documents and the documentary shipper under the Rotterdam Rules*' available online

Vicary I, '*New Incoterms® set sail*' at www.lloydslistintelligence.com/llint/print-article.htm;jsessionid=C615CE19402D23B6F2814D08608AAF9F?documentId=262122&docType=

Yonge M, US Dept of Transport, Maritime Admin, 'European Union short sea shipping' 9 (2004) at advancedmaritimetechnology.aticorp.org/short-sea-shipping/create3s-european-commission-initiative-/EUSSS_04-2004.pdf

Yuzhuo S and Zhang J, '*An analysis and assessment on the Rotterdam Rules in China's marine industry*' at www.comitemaritime.org/Uploads/Rotterdam%20Rules/Paper%20of%20Prof.%20Si%20Yuzhuo%20and%20Dr.%20Zhang%20Jinlei.pdf

Zekos, '*The use of electronic technology in maritime transport: The economic necessity and the legal framework in European Union law*' webjcli.ncl.ac.uk/1998/issue3/zekos3.html#Heading16

Conference papers

Lorenzon F, '*Transport documents through the bankers' sieve: Rotterdam Rules v. UCP 600*', Conference paper at the 3rd Arab Conference for Commercial and Maritime Law (ACCCML 09), Alexandria, Egypt, 18–19 April 2009

Debattista C, '*The Rotterdam Rules appraised*', Rotterdam, 24–25 September 2009.
London Shipping Law Centre, '*Electronic transport records – How secure are they in shipping transactions?*', February 2011
Bergami R, '*The Rotterdam Rules and bills of lading: Challenges for letters of credit transactions*', Paper from Conference Proceedings, CITEM, Tabor, 7–9 December 2011, 14, at www.academia.edu/2542584/BERGAMI_Rotterdam_Rules

Papers

www.gpo.gov/fdsys/pkg/PLAW-105publ258/pdf/PLAW-105publ258.pdf
www.comitemaritime.org/Uploads/Yearbooks/YBK_2009.pdf
Goldby M, 'Legislating to facilitate the use of electronic transferable records: A case study. Reforming the law to facilitate the use of electronic bills of lading in the United Kingdom', Paper prepared for the UNCITRAL Colloquium on Electronic Commerce, New York 14th to 16th February 2011 at www.uncitral.org/pdf/english/colloquia/EC/Legislating_to_facilitate_the_use_of_electronic_transferable_records_-_a_case_study_.pdf

Law Commission Papers

Electronic Commerce, '*Formal requirements in commercial transactions, advice from the Law Commission*', August 2001 lawcommission.justice.gov.uk/docs/Electronic_Commerce_Advice_Paper.pdf
The Law Commission, '*Privity of contract: Contracts for the benefit of third parties*', Item 1 of the Sixth Programme of Law Reform: The Law of Contract, at lawcommission.justice.gov.uk/docs/lc242_privity_of_contract_for_the_benefit_of_third_parties.pdf

Negotiation Documents

UNCTAD

UNCTAD Secretariat, '*Multimodal transport: The feasibility of an international instrument*', UNCTAD/SDTE/TLB/2003/1 (2003)
UNCTAD Secretariat, '*The use of transport documents in international trade*' at unctad.org/en/docs/sdtetlb20033_en.pdf
UNCTAD Document, '*Carrier liability and freedom of contract under the UNCITRAL draft instrument on the carriage of goods [wholly or partly] [by sea]*', UNCTAD/SDTE/TLB/2004/2 at unctad.org/en/Docs/sdtetlb20042_en.pdf

UNCITRAL Working Group III (Documents and Reports)

A/CN.9/645
A/63/17
A/CN.9/WG.III/WP.88
A/CN.9/612
A/CN.9/658/Add.2
A/CN.9/658/Add.11
A/CN.9/658/Add.11

UNCITRAL Doc A/CN.9/526, para 32 Report of Working Group III (Transport Law) on the work of its eleventh session (New York, 24 March to 4 April 2003)

United Nations Commission on International Trade Law, Working Group III (Transport Law) Twelfth session, Vienna, 6–17 October 2003, Transport Law: Preparation of a draft instrument on the carriage of goods [by sea], Proposal by the United States of America, A/CN.9/WG.III/WP.34

Report of Working Group III (Transport Law) on the work of its fifteenth session (New York, 18–28 April 2005), A/CN.9/576

Report of Working Group III (Transport Law) on the work of its nineteenth session (New York, 16–27 April 2007)

Report of Working Group III (Transport Law) on the work of its twenty-first session (Vienna, 14–25 January 2008), A/CN.9/645

A/CN.9/SR.871, Summary Record of the 871st meeting, Finalization and approval of a draft convention on contracts for the international carriage of goods wholly or partly by sea (continued) (A/CN.9/642, A/CN.9/645 and A/CN.9/658 and Add.1–13)

UNECE

'*Reconciliation and harmonization of civil liability regimes in intermodal transport*', Informal document WP.24 No. 2 (2009) at www.unece.org/fileadmin/DAM/trans/wp24/wp24-inf-docs/documents/id09-02e.pdf

EC Commission Reports and Proposals

EC Commission, *First Annual Progress Report on European Contract Law and the Acquis Review COM* (2005)

Proposal for a Regulation of the European Parliament and of the Council on a Common European Sales Law Com (2011)

Websites

www.uncitral.org/uncitral/uncitral_texts/transport_goods/2008rotterdam_rules.html

www.uncitral.org/uncitral/uncitral_texts/transport_goods/2008rotterdam_rules.html a

www.iccwbo.org/products-and-services/trade-facilitation/Incoterms®-2010/

'History of the Incoterms®: From 1936 to today: the Incoterms® rules' at www.iccwbo.org/products-and-services/trade-facilitation/Incoterms®-2010/history-of-the-Incoterms®-rules/

'What do we do?: Commission on Commercial Law and Practice' at www.iccwbo.org/about-icc/policy-commissions/commercial-law-and-practice/what-do-we-do-/

www.rotterdamrules2009.com/cms/uploads/Def%20%20tekst%20Charles%20Debattista%2031%20OKT29.pdf

www.shortsea.be/html_nl/publicaties/documents/Rapportv5E.pdf

www.law.cornell.edu/wex/adhesion_contract_contract_of_adhesion,

www.bimco.org/Chartering/Documentary_Projects/New_contracts.aspx

www.gpo.gov/fdsys/pkg/PLAW-105publ258/pdf/PLAW-105publ258.pdf

www.bimco.org/Chartering/Documentary_Projects/New_clauses.aspx

www.bimco.org/News/2014/05/09_Documentary_Committee_meets_in_Dubai.aspx?RenderSearch=true

www.ukpandi.com/fileadmin/uploads/uk-pi/Documents/2017/Legal_Briefing_e_bill_of_Lading_WEB.pdf|

Index

For Product Safety Concerns and Information please contact our EU
representative GPSR@taylorandfrancis.com
Taylor & Francis Verlag GmbH, Kaufingerstraße 24, 80331 München, Germany

www.ingramcontent.com/pod-product-compliance
Ingram Content Group UK Ltd.
Pitfield, Milton Keynes, MK11 3LW, UK
UKHW010959180926
475701UK00004B/456
* 9 7 8 0 3 6 7 5 8 7 2 9 1 *